Presented to

_____

By

_____

On the Occasion of

_____

Date

_____

TOMORROW STARTS TODAY

365 Devotional Guidelines for Daily Living

Harold J. Sala

BARBOUR
PUBLISHING, INC.
Uhrichsville, Ohio

TOMORROW
STARTS
TODAY

Published by Barbour Publishing, Inc., P.O. Box 719, Uhrichsville, Ohio 44683, http://www.barbourbooks.com

Member of the
Evangelical Christian
Publishers Association

Printed in the United States of America.

Dedication

To my friend Dr. Andrew Liuson,
a source of constant encouragement,
a role model, and encourager—
not only to me—but,
over the years, to thousands of men
and women throughout Asia.

PREFACE

Daily renewal is what *Tomorrow Starts Today* is all about!

"Though outwardly we are wasting away," wrote Paul to the Corinthians, "yet inwardly we are being renewed day by day" (2 Corinthians 4:16). So many forces in our lives today seem to pull us down, drive us into the asphalt, and cause us to want to give up.

Rather than focus on what tears us down, I've tried to concentrate on those things that build us up, that encourage us to take the upward look, that help us to get up when we've been knocked down by life. In the process, I hope to show you how to draw strength from the reservoir that never runs dry.

As a resource to encourage you, I've included a short Scripture passage for each day of the year, which parallels what I've talked about in the daily selection. Devotional books are never a substitute for your personal reading of Scripture, but are windows that let in light and help you to stay focused on God.

As with every book I have done, I am deeply indebted to a wide array of individuals who have helped me edit materials originally written for my radio program, *Guidelines—A Five-Minute Commentary on Living*. In this regard, I am grateful to Luisa Ampil, Joe de la Pena, Dr. Maynard Eyestone, Nancy Deushane, and my wife, Darlene, for helping me with editing and proofreading. I am also grateful to Susan Schlabach, of Barbour Publishing, for her encouragement and helpful comments.

Undesignated Scripture references are from the New International Version of the Bible; however, the following keys represent other versions accordingly:

KJV – King James Version
NKJV – New King James Version

NASB – New American Standard Bible
TLB – The Living Bible
GW – God's Word
TM – The Message

May God's strength and encouragement be yours as you find His strength and guidance day by day.

Harold J. Sala
Laguna Hills, CA

EMBRACING THE NEW YEAR

Before you lies a new year untainted by the failures and troubles of the past. Like an emerging tender shoot through the barren ground of spring, the new year gives hope of something better to come. Have you ever walked on the beach after a wave has swept away the footprints and imperfections in the sand? The renewed sand is clean, fresh, virgin—like a fresh snowfall.

Though man may pollute the environment and leave behind waste and destruction, God's gentle touch brings restoration in nature as well as in our lives. Renewal is a fundamental part of nature. In His creation, God made rest and recovery essential. The Sabbath is *our* day of rest, and God decreed that even farmland must be rested periodically, a truth that modern agriculture often neglects.

Renewal is also a spiritual matter. The work of God's Holy Spirit can never be accomplished on your own. Spiritual renewal occurs only as you allow God to work in your life, bringing renewal day by day. Some people's lives are broken pieces glued together with bitterness. Renewal means change, and they don't want change. Rather than risk the adventure of God's renewal, they live in a world of bitterness, excuses, failures, shattered dreams, broken marriages, and crushed hearts.

I'm reminded of the Peanuts cartoon where Charlie Brown says to Lucy, "You're going to be proud of me, Lucy. . . . I've decided that this year is going to be my year of decision! This is a list of the things in my life that I'm going to correct. I'm going to be a better person!"

Lucy responds, "Not me. . . . I'm going to spend the whole year regretting the past. It's the only way, Charlie Brown. I'm going to cry over spilt milk, and sigh over lost loves. . . . It's a lot easier. It's too hard to improve. I tried it once. It drove me crazy!"

Friend, are you holding on to the past instead of letting go to grasp the new? Reread the apostle Paul's words from Philippians 3:13–14, and thank God for the renewal of His Spirit and presence. You're on the threshold of a new year. Make the best of it with His help.

RESOURCE READING: Philippians 3:1–15

January 2

IF YOU MAKE 'EM, CAN YOU KEEP 'EM?

A re you like the fellow whose annual list of New Year's resolutions is a carbon copy of the previous year's? Every January, he gets out his paper and pencil, and every year his list includes the same bad habits and shortcomings. Nevertheless, with resolute determination, he's certain that this year will be different.

The record reads like this: January 1—"Everything fine, kept all my resolutions." January 2—"Quite busy at the office. During a phone conversation, a few swear words slipped out—accidentally." January 3—"Oops. Had a drink at lunch and ordered a second before I remembered my resolutions." January 4—"Too busy to think about resolutions today. Put a big deal together." January 10—"New Year's resolutions are impossible. Maybe next year."

When you make a definite commitment to let Jesus Christ control your life, things change. Life is not the same. As the apostle Paul says, "Therefore, if anyone is in Christ, he is a new creation; the old has gone, the new has come!" (2 Corinthians 5:17). When you take the step of faith to allow Christ to control your life, there are seven resolutions you can make and *keep:*

Resolution #1: I will keep my relationship with Christ warm and vibrant day by day.

Resolution #2: When I stumble or fall spiritually, I will immediately confess my failures before God and ask His help in overcoming wrong. He has promised to help us if we'll come to Him: "If we confess our sins, he is faithful and just and will forgive us our sins. . ." (1 John 1:9).

Resolution #3: I will extend forgiveness to others, just as God forgives my failures.

Resolution #4: I resolve to rely completely on God's strength in moments of temptation and weakness.

Resolution #5: I will avoid situations that I know will bring temptation.

Resolution #6: I will make time every day to read God's Word and talk with Him.

Resolution #7: I will live for others rather than for myself.

When you get to the point that you can say with the apostle Paul, "For me, to live is Christ," you'll discover that life takes on a new dimension. The chains of habit are strong, but by faith they can be broken and replaced. It's an exchange well worth making.

RESOURCE READING: 1 John 1

January 3

DNA AND EVOLUTION

When the results of scientific research fly in the face of the accepted evolutionary dogma, many scientists either ignore the data, try to explain it away, or suggest that the research is "inconclusive" and reject it entirely. That's much the way it was when the results of a study by a group of evolutionary biologists was announced.

In an effort to trace the evolution of males in different parts of the world, biologists Robert Dorit of Yale, Hiroshi Akashi of the University of Chicago, and Walter Gilbert of Harvard studied the Y chromosome—which is carried only by men—to determine how it had mutated or changed. By documenting the changes, they expected to prove that evolutionary changes could be observed over time.

Thirty-eight men with different ethnic backgrounds from different parts of the world were selected for the study. Despite the diverse physical characteristics of the men in the research sample, the study revealed not even slight differences at the chromosomal level.

"To their great surprise," says Dr. Hugh Ross, commenting on the research, "Dorit and his associates found no nucleotide differences at all in the nonrecombinant part of the Y chromosomes of the thirty-eight men [tested]. This non-variation suggests [that] *no* evolution has occurred in male ancestry. . . . Based on this analysis, they concluded that man's forefather—a single individual, not a group— lived no more than 270,000 years ago."[1]

DNA studies have given evolutionary biologists a difficult time, because the facts contradict the theory. Far from producing evidence of a vast spectrum of evolutionary development, genetic research consistently demonstrates that we descended from a single pair of parents—the same thing that Moses wrote some thirty-four hundred years ago.

If you wonder whether the Bible holds up to scientific scrutiny, start by learning what the Word says. Dig it out for yourself. As the apostle Paul put it, "Do your best to present yourself to God as one approved, a workman who does not need to be ashamed and who correctly handles the word of truth" (2 Timothy 2:15). It's the only way to go.

RESOURCE READING: Genesis 2:1–14

January 4

KEEPING YOURSELF PURE

T he Christian in a non-Christian world has always been a misfit—and our culture doesn't make it any easier. In your office at work, you may be the only one who doesn't laugh at off-color stories or use street language. The people who work alongside you know who you are and what you stand for. Like it or not, you bear the imprint of the Lord in your life.

The Bible makes it clear that God expects His children to be different. To the Corinthians, who lived in a morally polluted culture, Paul wrote the following advice: " 'Therefore come out from them and be separate,' says the Lord. 'Touch no unclean thing, and I will receive you. I will be a Father to you, and you will be my sons and daughters,' says the Lord Almighty" (2 Corinthians 6:17–18).

Another thought: The world expects more of us as well. Have you noticed how the smallest moral failure by a Christian leader makes headlines? An incident that wouldn't even merit a mention on an inside page were it someone else gets full-photo coverage when it involves a Christian.

How do we survive without either selling out or feeling that we are a constant target of those who would splatter us with mud? Three guidelines offer some insight:

Guideline #1: Protect your space. You can't escape the world, but you don't have to lower your standards to make others comfortable. Be yourself. Life is a spiritual battle, but we have the spiritual resources to win.

Guideline #2: Renew your commitment to decency and purity. Pray for God's strength, then rise from your knees with renewed determination to walk in the light of what you know is right.

Guideline #3: Refresh yourself periodically. Part of the
  secret of renewal is the washing of the Word and
  the cleansing of the Holy Spirit. When sunshine
  follows rain, its brilliance is refreshing.

In Paul's letters to the Ephesians and to Titus, he talks
about the washing with water by the Word and the washing
of rebirth and renewal by the Holy Spirit. These elements
combine to keep you pure.

A final thought: When you commit yourself to moral
purity, others who lack the courage to lead will follow in
your footsteps.

RESOURCE READING: 2 Corinthians 6

January 5

THE HAND OF
THE POTTER WITHIN

When I was a boy, I visited the old Van Briggle pottery
plant near my home. To this day, I can recall watching with amazement as the potter took a lump of clay, put it
on the wheel, and began to work. Almost as if by magic, a
vessel began to emerge. As the clay took shape, the potter
put one hand inside the pot to keep it from collapsing while
he applied pressure from the outside to mold it and shape it.

I'm reminded of how difficult it is for some people to
cope with outside pressure in their lives. When they collapse, they blame God—the Potter—for allowing too much
pressure, but I'm convinced that God gets blamed for a lot
of things that are not His doing. You see, the problem is
not that there is too much outside pressure, but not
enough of the hand of the Potter within. The more there

is of the hand of the Potter within, the less you will feel of the pressure without.

I'm convinced that if people had more of Christ in their inner lives, we would see fewer casualties today. Jesus Christ doesn't want to be a mere part of your life—an occasional Helper you call upon when you are afraid of collapse or defeat. He wants to be the Lord of your life. Surrendering to the lordship of Jesus means that He is in control—not simply of those issues you can't handle—but of every part of your life, including your work life, your social life, your thought life, your spiritual life, and your inner, personal life.

Examine your relationship with God and honestly assess how much you are willing to let Him invade the inner recesses of your heart and life. Keep up your strength by studying the Word of God, memorizing Scripture, reflecting on the words of old hymns and songs, and maintaining fellowship with other believers.

The hand of the Master Potter within us is what keeps our lives from collapsing. The outside pressures of the world will always be there, but as Jesus said, "Be of good cheer; I have overcome the world" (John 16:33 KJV). With His help, you can overcome as well.

RESOURCE READING: Jeremiah 18:1–4

January 6

THE CHAMULAS

When Bible translators Ken and Elaine Jacobs finished translating the New Testament into the Chamula language in Mexico, they ordered five hundred copies for their initial distribution. To their surprise, more than three thousand people showed up, and they all wanted a copy.

As the Chamulas read the Word of God in their own language and began to grasp the meaning of the gospel, their lives began to change. They stopped drinking *posh,* an intoxicating sugar cane rum; telling the truth began to prevail over dishonesty; and husbands stopped beating their wives and began treating them with kindness and affection—which was viewed by other Chamula men as a sign of weakness.

As the Chamula believers came to understand how God wanted them to live, their transformed lives impressed their friends and neighbors. In spite of persecution and hardship, their new lifestyles, integrity, and family relationships stood out.

Of course, these new believers did not become plastic saints who never made mistakes. Some failed morally, falling back into old habits, and a few reverted to pagan ways, but most of the new believers committed themselves to follow the Lord regardless of the cost.

One of the things that disturbs me deeply about many of the churchgoers who call themselves Christians in our country is not that they have problems, but that their lifestyles are often no different from the nonbelievers around them. Not that we must become perfect, but how we live ought to be noticeably different from the ways of the world. Throughout the history of the Church, the lives of those who have truly been touched by the Almighty become transformed.

The Chamulas took to heart Paul's words to the Thessalonians: "Make it your ambition to lead a quiet life, to mind your own business and to work with your hands, just as we told you, so that your daily life may win the respect of outsiders and so that you will not be dependent on anybody" (1 Thessalonians 4:11–12). Who can find fault with a changed life?

RESOURCE READING: 2 Corinthians 5:11–21

BELIEFS:
CONVICTIONS OR PREFERENCES?

D o you prefer your coffee strong or mild? With sugar and cream, or black? Do you like to sleep with the window open or tightly closed? How strongly would you insist that your way is the better choice? Would you be willing to die for your belief?

There is a great deal of difference between a preference and a conviction. "A belief," says David Gibbs, "is merely a person's *preference* when certain circumstances will motivate him to change it. A *conviction* is a belief that does not change, regardless of circumstances."

Are your beliefs about God convictions or merely preferences? Are you a believer because Christianity seems preferable to other options, or do you believe based on the conviction that God has spoken?

According to Gibbs, convictions are distinguished by four characteristics: They are predetermined, nonnegotiable, confidently held, and lived out in a lifestyle. How do your beliefs measure up?

When Daniel faced the decision to either bow down to Darius or face the consequences, he didn't have to consider his options. He had already made up his mind to serve God, no matter what:

"Now when Daniel learned that the decree had been published, he went home to his upstairs room where the windows opened toward Jerusalem. Three times a day he got down on his knees and prayed, giving thanks to his God, just as he had done before" (Daniel 6:10). For Daniel, the issue was decided by conviction, not choice. Convictions are born when we decide that our beliefs are nonnegotiable.

Christianity becomes anemic when we allow our beliefs to become preferences instead of convictions. Convictions are born out of a knowledge of God's Word. When we encounter absolute truth about right and wrong in the pages of the Bible, it puts steel in our backbones. A wishy-washy, "don't offend anyone" belief system is a poor alternative.

Convictions are not always easy to live with. They become our masters, but they also make life worth living. Mere preferences never stand up when the going gets tough, because preferences can change. Sugar in your coffee is a preference; standing for truth is a conviction. There's a difference.

RESOURCE READING: Daniel 6

January 8

THE HIDDEN CODES OF THE BIBLE

You'll find them on the newsstands and in bookstores—an array of books claiming to reveal hidden, secret codes contained in the Bible. You might be tempted to think, "Wow! This is great. It's amazing what computers can do!"

Although it's true that computers have become a powerful tool for students of the Bible—analyzing word patterns and synthesizing missing portions of the text—they don't necessarily unlock new revelations. Depending on how the control factors are handled, statistical analysis can be used to prove almost anything.

This fad of trying to make the Bible reveal its hidden secrets isn't new at all. In Paul's day, a group called the Gnostics claimed distinctive insights into God's revelation—and Paul condemned them. At the beginning of the twentieth century, someone measured the Egyptian pyramids and converted the numbers into "precise, allegedly scientific findings," which in turn led to supposedly prophetic utterances. In reality, these "discoveries" were based on myth, not truth. The New Testament condemns this kind of speculation about "hidden secrets."

Don't waste your time or money on hidden revelations; instead, focus on clear biblical truth. Make it a practice to read God's Word every day. But don't just pick up your Bible and read wherever it happens to fall open. Read systematically. Study it and make it yours.

The Bible is an anthology of history, letters to churches and individuals, and prophecy. As you read and study this awesome book, ask yourself three questions:

1) What does it say? Take a notebook and summarize what you have read. Writing a few sentences or a paragraph or two will help you retain the core of what you have studied.

2) What does it mean? If you wonder whether you're qualified to answer this question, remember that God's Word was given to common men and women, not to intellectuals or clerics who alone understand the "inner secrets" of truth. Usually, the obvious interpretation is exactly what God intends for you to understand. Forget the mysteries. Stick with the obvious.

3) How do I apply it to my life? When you understand the Word of God and apply it to reality, God's truth makes the difference. Go with it. You'll be glad you did.

RESOURCE READING: 1 Timothy 4; 2 Timothy 3

CAN MEN LIVE WITHOUT GOD?

S hortly before his death, historian Will Durant wrote,
"The greatest question of our time is not Communism
versus individualism, not Europe versus America, not even
the East versus the West; it is whether men can live without God."

During the 1930s, Joseph Stalin ordered the destruction of the Cathedral of Christ the Savior to make way for a
colossal monument to Communism. When hard times fell,
however, the building was never constructed. After the Iron
Curtain fell, the mayor of Moscow, Yuri Luzhkov, teamed
up with Aleksi II, the patriarch of the Russian Orthodox
Church, to rebuild the landmark cathedral. Working from
the original nineteenth-century drawings, architect Kon-
stantin Ton engineered the new building to duplicate the
original as nearly as possible. A church now stands where
Stalin's palace was to have been built.

Throughout the former Soviet empire, churches have
been rebuilt as a testimony that God has outlived another
system of government that had intended to set Him aside.

Elsewhere in the former USSR, however, former Communists, whose ideologies haven't changed, are regaining
power. In Belarus, recent elections returned former
Communists to power and put the hammer and sickle back
on the flag. Similar "post-Communist" movements are under
way in Hungary, Czechoslovakia, Bulgaria, Romania, and
East Germany.

How is all this possible when only a few, short years ago,
democracy was achieved with massive popular acclaim? The
issue is not a matter of ideology—Communism versus
democracy. It is economic—bread and butter, meat and
potatoes. "Life was so much better for us under
Communism," a Ukrainian Christian meatpacker told me.

He has no desire to return to the wholesale fear and suspicion that sent seventeen members of his church's congregation to Siberia, but he wants to be able to work a full shift at the plant and earn enough to provide for his wife and their two teenage girls.

Some would say that political labels have lost their meaning, that post-Communist governments are different. If man can live without God, perhaps that line of reasoning would be appealing. But one thing is certain: Governments are ultimately not the ones rebuilding the churches and cathedrals. Of that, there is no doubt.

RESOURCE READING: Psalm 1

January 10

CAN TIME BE REVERSED?

"In a U-turn that will send shock waves through the universe," reported the London *Sunday Times* on October 1, 1995, "professor Stephen Hawking, Britain's leading cosmic physicist, has accepted the possibility of time travel. Having ridiculed the concept for years, Hawking now says that it is not just a possibility, but one on which the government should spend money."

This respected Cambridge University professor, known for his brilliant deductions on time, had reversed a position held for many years. At one time he had said, "The best evidence that time travel will never be possible is that we have not been invaded by hordes of tourists from the future." His new hypothesis, based on Einstein's theory of relativity and quantum physics, says, in effect, that we can turn back the clock in a strange time warp that would let us relive our lives.

Intriguing, isn't it, even to think about the possibility? Take, for example, this past year. How long and hard would you have to think to come up with one mistake that you would like to change? Something you said, something you did, or something you failed to do?

What I am about to say may come as a shock, but it's true: Time can be reversed. Put another way, the effects of the past can be reversed.

There is One who is more powerful than space or time, One who has the power to reverse the past. Have you ever considered the fact that when God forgives you, He goes back in time and changes the effect of what took place in your life, erasing it as though it had never happened?

Standing at zero meridian in Greenwich, England, you can measure precise distances east or west—but, technically, east and west never meet. Now consider what the psalmist wrote: When God forgives, He removes your sin as far as the east is from the west (Psalm 103:12).

Good news, my friend. When you bow your knee in repentance and humility and ask God's forgiveness, it changes your past—permanently. Changing the past is possible. This is good news, whether you are beginning a new year or a new life.

RESOURCE READING: Psalm 103

January 11

WHEN YOU BECOME A VICTIM OF EVIL

After an arsonist burned down his church, Pastor Ted Cole picked his way through the charred rubble and sat down at the piano. Defiantly he began playing an old hymn written more than four centuries ago by Martin Luther—who himself experienced trouble—that bears testimony to God's provision for every person who is assaulted by hostile forces: "A mighty fortress is our God, a bulwark never failing. Our helper He amidst the flood of mortal ills prevailing."

When life torches your dreams and ambitions, you have two choices: Either turn to the Lord for strength and comfort, or blame Him and lapse into bitterness.

Seeing the whole picture from God's perspective makes all the difference in the world. Proverbs 21:30 says, "There is no wisdom, no insight, no plan that can succeed against the LORD."

You are not without defense when Satan's evil darts come your way. Speaking of believers who were suffering assault, the apostle John writes, "They overcame him by the blood of the Lamb and by the word of their testimony. . ." (Revelation 12:11).

The blood of the Lamb is not some mystical Christian magic that we use to protect ourselves. It speaks of what Jesus did in leaving the presence of His Father in heaven to come to our world, give His life, and rise again. It speaks of God's plan of redemption.

The second way to overcome attack is through the word of your testimony. When a young woman was brutally murdered and the accused killer was acquitted, the mother of the victim refused to let bitterness and hatred overwhelm her life. Instead, she affirmed the eternal love and purpose of God, based on Scripture, and undertook the responsibility of raising her two grandchildren.

Until Christ returns, some warped souls will burn churches, assault innocent people, and mistreat others with no provocation. Driven by the hatred of Satan himself, they will slander and lie, but they can be overcome through the blood of Jesus and the power of our testimony.

RESOURCE READING: Revelation 12:7–12

January 12

CHARACTER ASSASSINATION IS
A CHEAP SHOT

Character assassination is like a drive-by shooting, when bullets are sprayed at random in the dark. Our words can be almost as devastating as bullets.

A certain pastor was doing his best to preach the Word, but someone in the congregation didn't like him. The anonymous critic would drop unsigned notes in the offering plate. As the rhetoric became more intense, the pastor grew increasingly frustrated. The final straw came when he received a note with a single word—STUPID—scrawled in large letters across the entire page.

The next week, the pastor announced from the pulpit, "Recently, I have received several unsigned letters from people criticizing my sermons, but this past week I received one from someone who signed his name but forgot to write the letter." The pastor held up the page with the word STUPID written on it, and everyone had a good laugh.

Never give credence to charges that are so weak that the instigator refuses to attach his name to them. John Hancock, one of the signers of the Declaration of Independence, signed his name in very large letters. Historians tell us that when Hancock was asked why he had written so large, he replied, "So the king, with his failing eyesight, could see my name."

I have news for you, friend. The King of Kings has perfect eyesight, and He beholds everything we do, say, or write—whether we put our name on it or not. "Nothing in all creation is hidden from God's sight. Everything is uncovered and laid bare before the eyes of him to whom we must give account" (Hebrews 4:13).

The Bible gives us a framework for dealing with genuine issues of wrongdoing. In Matthew 18:15, Jesus tells us to confront the individual directly. If this doesn't resolve the issue, take someone else with you as a witness to your testimony. If even that doesn't work, Jesus said to confront the wrongdoer openly before the church.

Solomon said, "Do not rebuke a mocker or he will hate you; rebuke a wise man and he will love you" (Proverbs 9:8). But never are we given license to assassinate a person's character through inference, gossip, or innuendo. Avoid taking cheap shots.

RESOURCE READING: Proverbs 6

January 13

A MILLION

Jan Nichols, the chairman of a high school science department, devised a project to demonstrate how small things are that can only be seen with intense magnification, and how large some things are in space. When he introduced the concepts of light-years and millions of miles, he discovered that his students didn't have the foggiest notion what he was talking about. To help them begin to understand the enormous dimensions of space, Nichols assigned the students the task of counting to one million. It took nine hundred participants three hundred hours (the equivalent of twelve-and-a-half days) to finish counting. When they got down to the last ten thousand, they started placing kernels of popcorn into large bottles. Before they were done, they had filled seventy-five five-gallon water cooler jugs with popcorn. Tara Schafer, a thirteen-year-old participant in the project, later said, "If we hadn't counted it ourselves, I wouldn't believe it was one million. I would probably think it was about ten million, because I could never imagine exactly how much that really was."

Numbers are almost meaningless unless we have something by which to measure them. When it comes to space, however, fixed standards are hard to find. That's why in 1888 scientists devised the term "light-years" to express intergalactic distances. Technically, a light-year is equal to the distance that light travels in one year in a vacuum, or about 5.878 trillion miles.

The nearest star is Alpha Centauri. It takes 4.5 years for its light to reach us. Compare that with the 1.5 seconds it takes for light to reach us from the moon.

Fortunately for us, God is not bound by space or time. He's beyond that. With God, numbers never represent separation or a challenge—whether they represent numbers of people or the distance between objects in space. As Isaiah writes, "Behold, the LORD's hand is not so short that it cannot save; neither is His ear so dull that it cannot hear" (Isaiah 59:1 NASB). Be thankful that God is as close as the faintest cry of your heart.

RESOURCE READING: Isaiah 59

January 14

TIRED OF HOW BAD THINGS ARE?

D o you sometimes get tired of hearing how bad things have become? Marriages are in trouble. Teenagers are going to the devil. Governments are corrupt. The world is on a bobsled run toward Armageddon. We already know that things are pretty bad, but it helps to realize that the filth and garbage occupying so much of the evening news are symptoms of the sickness in our world called sin.

Still, our hearts cry out, "Lord, we're tired of looking at the dirt. We're tired of hearing about the problems. We want a new glimpse of You. We'd like to see through the clouds and behold Your face."

Things were pretty tough in Isaiah's day as well. The king had died. Israel's ten northern tribes had fallen into captivity to the Assyrians. The economy was in a shambles. Nevertheless, Isaiah wrote, "I saw the Lord seated on a throne, high and exalted, and the train of his robe filled the temple" (Isaiah 6:1).

If you walk with your head down, you may find a few coins on the ground, but you won't see the stars reflected in the mud. It takes an upward look, a renewed focus on God, to find hope and help. It's the upward look that gives us perspective. When we focus on the majesty of God, we're able to navigate the stormy seas of life. We must consciously let the light of God's glory penetrate the gloom and the darkness. We must join with the apostle Paul in "wait[ing] for the blessed hope—the glorious appearing of our great God and Savior, Jesus Christ" (Titus 2:13).

Shut off the television, throw away your newspaper, and get away from the noise and clutter of life. Take the upward look. God is far more willing to let you see His face than you might think. The upward look gives perspective, and as Fanny Crosby wrote, "One glimpse of His dear face, all sorrow will erase; so bravely run the race, till we see Christ."

RESOURCE READING: Isaiah 6

January 15

YOUR NUMBER ONE PROBLEM

How would you describe your number one problem? Is it relational—your husband or wife, or your boyfriend or girlfriend? Your in-laws or parents, who criticize everything you do? Maybe it's your irrational boss, or the neighbor down the street who complains about your kids.

Or is it financial—not enough money at the end of the month? A mountain of debt or a series of bad investments? Maybe you think that a better-paying job, or any job, would be the answer.

Some would say that their number one problem is social—feeling rejected by society. Perhaps you think you were born in the wrong place, to the wrong family or race.

What's your number one problem? It may surprise you to discover that your number one problem is YOU. Your biggest problem is between your ears—how you think, how you look at yourself, how you reason.

Challenges, on the other hand, are what make the taste of victory seem sweet. Apart from challenges, our accomplishments would mean nothing. Facing a challenge is the difference between shooting a white-water rapids and splashing in the bathtub. When you recognize that your biggest problem is YOU, you're ready to face the challenge head-on—with the help of God—and refuse to accept defeat.

When you begin to see the challenges in your life as temporary obstacles instead of insurmountable, final, or permanent blockages, you can then figure out how to move to the left or the right to get around them, tunnel under them, or climb over them.

Excuses are a shallow rationalization for doing nothing, but with God's help you can overcome. It's amazing how many people are willing to give you a hand up the ladder when you get your feet moving, when you begin reaching out for a hand instead of a handout, when you put a smile on your face and refuse to quit.

The real test of success is not what you accomplish, but what you overcome in the process. Refuse to accept defeat. Never forget that you are your own worst enemy, but with God's help you can tackle any challenge, because He makes the difference.

RESOURCE READING: John 7:1–19

January 16

GOING ON WHEN YOU DON'T FEEL LIKE IT

The most difficult part of the Christian experience is when the sky seems to fall and your world comes apart. No, you don't deserve it. No, you're not being punished. God hasn't closed the door on you and shut off the phone service, and He hasn't selected you to see whether you can withstand the same testing that Job endured. Nevertheless, when you are hurting—from the loss of a baby, the loss of a job, a serious illness, or some other cause of pain and sorrow—it's easy to feel alone and estranged from God.

At times like these, regardless of how you feel, regardless of your emotions or what your body tells you, refuse to believe what you know is untrue and hold on to the assurance that God is still in control.

It's okay to tell Him that you don't understand, but don't measure God's goodness or faithfulness by the bad things that happen to you or the good things that happen to others. Instead, focus on the promises of God, which cannot change. Did God ever promise that you would always understand? Would you really want to worship a God who was so small that you understood His every thought and action?

Peter tells us to cast all our anxiety on Him because He cares for us (1 Peter 5:7). David says if we throw our burdens on the Lord, He will sustain us (Psalm 55:22).

Sometimes, just getting up in the morning, pointing your feet in the right direction and giving yourself a "kick start" isn't very glamorous, but it's what God requires. Getting the kids off to school, downloading the E-mail, dealing with the customer who is standing there tapping his credit card on the counter to get your attention, taking one day at a time—sometimes one hour or one task at a time—is what God wants you to do.

Trusting God for *today* is what He asks. And when we get to the dawn of a new day, God will again be there to meet us and lead us, even though circumstances may obscure the warmth of His presence or make us forget He's still in charge. Some things have to be taken by faith. It's the only way.

RESOURCE READING: Psalm 46

January 17

WHY IS LIFE VALUABLE?

I 'll never forget the day Jessica McClure was rescued. I was in Dallas the weekend of October 17, 1987, when the eighteen-month-old girl was pulled from an abandoned well after a fifty-seven-hour ordeal that captured the hearts of people around the world. I still have the front page of the next day's *Dallas Morning News,* with the headline emblazoned across the top in bold letters: "Baby Jessica Freed From Well."

What makes human life valuable? Why would weary paramedics labor for two-and-a-half days to save a little girl's life? What motivates people to risk their lives to save someone else's? Why bother to screen thousands of potential donors just to find one bone marrow match? Concern for human life reflects a person's spiritual views. When you believe that every person is created in the image of God and that every person has a human soul, then saving a life— whether an unborn child or a gray-haired grandmother—is worth the risk and effort.

Not every society shares this perspective, however. Most Buddhists, for example, believe that when you save a life, you interfere with the person's karma, which would have resulted in death. Therefore, if you pull someone out of the water and save his life, you are responsible for that person for the rest of his life. The prevailing attitude of "why bother?" allows people to step over the dead and dying in the streets and ignore their plight.

The Bible tells us that God views every person as an individual with value and worth. Some of the most important conversations Jesus had were with individuals who were considered unimportant by society—prostitutes, social outcasts, blind beggars, lepers, and corrupt tax collectors.

Jesus said, "For the Son of Man came to seek and to save what was lost" (Luke 19:10). God says that you are a person of value and worth, and it's that view which motivates people to face great hazard to save another person's life. When one of the men who had rescued Baby Jessica was asked whether he would risk his life to do it again, he replied, "In a heartbeat." Thank God for those who care.

RESOURCE READING: Luke 19

January 18

THE IMPORTANCE OF MOM AND DAD

M any people would say that the most important influence in the life of a teenager is peer pressure. *What do my friends think of me?* But a comprehensive new study now indicates that parents—not other teenagers—are the most significant force in the lives of teens today.

Preliminary results from the National Longitudinal Study on Adolescent Health (NLSAH), published in the *Journal of the American Medical Association,* suggest three factors that help combat risky behaviors and attitudes in teens:

1) *Family cohesiveness,* which includes a sense of belonging and being a valued member of the family. Family cohesiveness results in a realization by the child that she is wanted, loved, and cared for.

2) *Parental expectations.* When a child knows that his parents believe in him and expect him to avoid drugs, alcohol, and promiscuity, he is far more apt to avoid what his parents condemn—especially when the parents model their expectations.

3) *Parental involvement* in the life of the child. According to the NLSAH report, "having a parent home at important times of the day, such as after school, at dinner, and at bedtime, also were associated with less risky behavior." The myth of "quality time" compensating for a lack of real time spent together just doesn't pan out. As parents, we must be there for our kids.

Of course, the Bible summarized the results of the study almost three thousand years before the report was written. In one sentence, Proverbs declares what was true then, is true today, and will be true in the next generation: Parents are the most important force in the life of a child. "Train a child in the way he should go, and when he is old he will not turn from it" (Proverbs 22:6).

When parents live out the expectations they have for their children, the kids have a benchmark to shoot for. It doesn't mean they'll always fly right, but when we teach our children right from wrong, what is moral and immoral, what is acceptable and what will not be tolerated, we pass the baton of decency and a sense of values to those who will someday take our places in the world. And may our own conduct measure up to what we say.

RESOURCE READING: Proverbs 22

FROM REACTION TO RECOVERY

How long does it take you to recover when you have been wronged? A few minutes, a few days or months, even years? The elapsed time between the pain of reaction and the healing of recovery is a pretty good measure of your emotional and spiritual maturity. In his book, *Under His Wing*, author Bernie May describes it as the R & R response, or the time it takes to go from response to recovery. Some people never recover. They spend the rest of their lives in angry, bitter, unforgiving reaction.

I'll never forget the man who sat in my office shortly after we moved to Manila in 1974. He presented me with a legal file about two inches thick. He was angry. His eyes narrowed and his voice tensed as he told me of being fired without cause.

"And when did this happen?" I asked.

"Twelve years ago," he responded.

Okay, you've been wronged. Maybe you got fired without real cause, or your husband walked out on you and broke up your marriage—and you reacted, of course. Whenever a nail gets driven into your heart or your hand, you react, but how long does it take for you to cry out, "Father, forgive them, for they know not what they do"? That's the measure of your maturity as a Christian. Those who hold on to anger, living for revenge or restitution, are the real losers. They're incarcerated in a prison of hate. But those who say, "Okay, this happened, but I'm going to get on with my life," are the ones who find the grace of God to put matters behind them—which is what forgiveness is all about. They are the real winners.

An old gentleman, nearly ninety, seemed to be happy all the time. A friend said to him, "You don't seem to have an enemy in the world. What's your secret?" The old man replied, "You're right. I don't have any enemies. I outlived 'em all."

If you want to outlive your enemies, get on with your life, forget that they're enemies, ask God to help you forgive them, and release the bitterness of the past. That's how you move from reaction to recovery.

RESOURCE READING: 2 Timothy 2:1–13

January 20

AURORA SERAPIO

As early as she could remember, church was important to Aurora Serapio. She had been christened as a Catholic, and she was convinced she would die a Catholic. She believed in God, Jesus Christ, the Holy Spirit, and the Virgin Mary. What more was necessary?

When Aurora was diagnosed with cancer, she and her husband commuted between Manila and the United States for treatment. At family gatherings, when Aurora's cousin Eddie, who had become a "born-again" Christian, talked about the Bible and his faith, Aurora either got uptight or walked out.

During her hospitalization, Eddie kept visiting, not to talk "religion," but simply to comfort her. He prayed silently that God would let him talk to her before she died. When Aurora's doctor gave up on treating her, she decided to go back to Manila to die.

About this time, Pope John Paul II visited Manila and addressed thousands of youths in Rizal Park. During his address, he said, "You need a personal relationship with Jesus Christ." Some were surprised by his rhetoric, which sounded more like evangelical Christianity than Roman Catholicism, but when Eddie heard the pope's words, he thought, *That's it. That's what I'm talking about.*

Finally, Eddie had his opportunity to speak to Aurora. Based on what the pope had said, he told Aurora that she needed a personal relationship with Jesus Christ. Eddie's words made sense to Aurora, and she agreed to pray with him. In communion, every Roman Catholic accepts the body of Christ in the wafer. *But this is different,* she thought. This was a personal relationship with Jesus, not just intellectual knowledge.

Aurora returned to Manila and was hospitalized. She slipped into a coma, but on the fourth day, she regained consciousness. She amazed her family when she said, "You should believe Eddie when he speaks of heaven, because there really is a heaven and the only way to go there is by accepting Jesus Christ as your own Lord and Savior." Aurora had caught a glimpse of heaven, and soon she was there.

The Bible says, "He who has the Son has life; he who does not have the Son of God does not have life" (1 John 5:12). It's the personal relationship that counts.

RESOURCE READING: 1 John 5:1–12

January 21

THE GREATEST SERMON IN THE WORLD

The world has seen great orators—from Demosthenes, Cicero, and Plato in ancient Greece, to Abraham Lincoln and Winston Churchill in modern times. But no one will ever match the powerful message from the lips of Jesus Christ that we know as the Sermon on the Mount.

Matthew 5–7 records Jesus' famous words, which contain the heart of His teaching, and a condensed version, from a different viewpoint, appears in Luke 6. As a medical doctor, Luke was sensitive to people's needs and attuned to people-related problems that others might miss. He describes the needs of the people who had come to hear Jesus, people with physical and emotional pain and suffering. He makes it clear that what Jesus said was a response, a pointed, straight-on answer to their deepest needs.

These guidelines are not simply words spoken to a large group assembled in the spring of A.D. 26, but timeless remedies for the sicknesses that tear our lives apart today. Human needs are the same in every generation. In the Sermon on the Mount, we find fundamental principles to guide our conduct, our attitudes, and our spirits.

God loves you so much that He sent His Son to your planet, to your neighborhood, to confront you with His care. The writers of Scripture tell us that when Jesus saw the crowds of people, His heart was moved with compassion. He felt what they were feeling, He hurt where they hurt, He related emotionally to the pain they were experiencing.

Jesus begins His message by pronouncing a series of blessings, known as *beatitudes*, from the Latin for *blessing*. Matthew records nine of these blessings, which we will explore over the next several days.

I'm convinced that hearing the voice of Jesus and feeling His touch on our lives will bring healing to our hearts and lives.

Do yourself a favor. Take time to read Matthew 5–7 and listen for your name as God calls out to those who need a blessing.

RESOURCE READING: Luke 6:17–26

BLESSINGS OR LAST RITUALS

When a large crowd of men and women—troubled, hurting folks—came to see Jesus, believing that to touch Him physically would be the answer to their needs, He seated them on the grassy slopes of a mountain and taught them. This teaching, which we call the Sermon on the Mount, was an open-air discourse on the resources of God. When Jesus was done, the people walked away blessed and happy.

They came wanting a quick fix, but Jesus instead fixed the emptiness within their hearts, filling the void that can only be filled by a relationship with God.

According to Luke, Jesus had gone to a mountain and spent the entire night in prayer. In the morning, He chose twelve of His disciples to be apostles and began ministering to the needs of the people who had gathered, healing physical sicknesses for which there was no cure.

Finally, He found a level place and sat down to teach the crowds who had come—some from many miles away. Jesus talked to them—not as sinners who had to walk an aisle and join a church—but as citizens of the kingdom of God. Christ addresses them as brothers and sisters whose value system had become warped by the thinking of the world, whose focus had been dimmed because they had no North Star by which to guide their lives.

Much of what Jesus taught was a sharp break with conventional wisdom. He talked about things like poverty of spirit, meekness, and making peace—subjects that are not given much serious consideration today.

Question: Have we got it all wrong? Have we been misled by thinking that the one with the biggest pile of toys is the winner, that the most powerful, most beautiful, or strongest is really the one on top? Is it possible that the way up is down, and what we thought was so important in life, is not really that important after all?

Jesus was right, and real happiness lies in learning those lessons He taught long ago. We still haven't learned what Proverbs recorded: "There is a way that seems right to a man, but in the end it leads to death" (Proverbs 14:12). It is still true today.

RESOURCE READING: Matthew 5:1–11

January 23

BLESSED ARE YOU

In the Sermon on the Mount, Jesus begins by pronouncing nine "blessings." He describes conditions of the heart that result in real blessing and bring wholeness and healing to our relationships.

A quick count of the blessings would seem to indicate that Jesus is identifying eight categories of people—those usually considered not very important by the world—who are blessed, but in reality each of these groups represents the family of God and different attitudes of the heart, or aspects of behavior, that result in blessing.

Some of today's modern Bible translations use the word *happy* instead of *blessed*. Our word *happy* comes from the Middle English *hap*, which means good luck, chance, or good fortune. When you hear the word *happy*, it conveys something quite different from what Jesus was talking about. The Greek word used by the New Testament writers refers primarily to a good mood that results from one's circumstances, or to be fortunate or well off.

Jesus wasn't trying to be a motivational speaker, making the crowd feel good so they could go home "pumped up" with a positive mental attitude. Regardless of its popularity, Jesus confronted people with the truth. He was bringing their lives—both their attitudes and actions—into direct confrontation with the resources of God. The result was they walked away with changed attitudes and a resolve to do things differently. No matter how unpopular it may have been, an encounter with real truth could only be described as a blessing.

Let's review these beatitudes, these guidelines for living: "Blessed are the poor in spirit, for theirs is the kingdom of heaven. Blessed are those who mourn, for they will be comforted. Blessed are the meek, for they will inherit the earth. Blessed are those who hunger and thirst for righteousness, for they will be filled. Blessed are the merciful, for they will be shown mercy. Blessed are the pure in heart, for they will see God. Blessed are the peacemakers, for they will be called sons of God. Blessed are those who are persecuted because of righteousness, for theirs is the kingdom of heaven" (Matthew 5:3–10).

Real happiness, the kind that doesn't go out when the party's over, or when your beauty fades, or your resources fail, is found in doing what Jesus says. It's the kind that lasts for a lifetime.

RESOURCE READING: Matthew 5:13–30

January 24

BLESSED ARE THE POOR IN SPIRIT

Captain Scott O'Grady's world came crashing down on June 2, 1995, when a missile struck the F-16 he was flying over Bosnia. As he hit the ground and ran for cover, he knew his world would never be the same. After his dramatic rescue, he confessed in his book, *Return With Honor,* that "as I huddled in the Bosnian woods, I didn't feel like Captain O'Grady, fighter pilot. I was just a scared guy named Scott, getting by on his wits. . . . My priorities were slapped into line during that week in June."

Jesus said, "Blessed are the poor in spirit, for theirs is the kingdom of heaven" (Matthew 5:3). Scott O'Grady understands poverty of spirit, because he's been there. In all his life, he'd never had so little but discovered so much as he did while hiding in Bosnia. He learned that man's extremity is God's opportunity.

I hope you will never face a trauma like Scott's, but in order to inherit the kingdom of God, you must experience the same poverty of spirit that confronted this fortunate young pilot.

What did Jesus mean by the expression "poor in spirit"? Poverty of spirit and poverty-stricken are not the same thing. Jesus is not saying that being financially poor is a great asset—not at all. But He is saying that those who are destitute of resources and strength, and who cannot help themselves, are candidates for God to bring His kingdom to their hearts and blessing to their lives.

Most of us find it difficult to bring ourselves to realize that we are spiritually destitute, that we have exhausted our resources, and that God is our only hope. No wonder we try to fix things ourselves instead of saying, "God, this is absolutely beyond me. I am completely incapable of handling this. I throw myself on Your mercy and want Your help."

Poverty of spirit is the profound realization that your resources are depleted, that you no longer have a quick fix or a simple solution, that there is no hope apart from God.

And then what happens? You will be met by the Prince of Peace Himself, who will not turn you away but will open the door and bless you. Jesus said it Himself, "Blessed are the poor in spirit, for theirs is the kingdom of heaven."

RESOURCE READING: Matthew 5:31–48

THERE CAN BE NO COMFORT
WHERE THERE IS NO GRIEF

Mourning and being blessed at the same time seem contradictory, but they're not. Those who cannot give vent to their emotions and mourn never find emotional healing. Simply put, there can be no comfort where there is no grief.

As I prepared today's devotional, I was sitting at the old kitchen table in my father's home where I grew up. Dad was almost eighty-nine at the time and was fighting a losing battle with melanoma. I was experiencing the grief that Jesus described. Everywhere I looked, my heart was touched with memories; there were pictures of children, grandchildren, and friends. In the basement was the old train track for the Lionel 027 that Dad had put together. Of course, I grieved. Only a heart of stone would not.

Grieving is God's way of purging our hearts of the deep emotions that need to find expression. He promises to be "the God of all comfort" (2 Corinthians 1:3). We also find comfort in the promises of God's Word. Paul says that "we through patience and comfort of the scriptures might have hope" (Romans 15:4 KJV). And, of course, we are comforted by friends and loved ones (see 1 Thessalonians 4:13–18).

Let me share three simple guidelines, which have helped me face grief:

Guideline #1: Externalize your grief. Talk, cry, communicate. In our last few hours together, Dad and I talked about fishing trips, outdoor experiences, and vacations we had enjoyed together. We laughed and cried and thanked God for His goodness. Getting grief out of your heart is part of the secret to getting on with your life.

Guideline #2: Internalize your faith. Some things that your mind knows are true your emotions challenge. We take it by faith that someday the dead in Christ will rise from the grave and we will be together again. When Mabel Clark's husband died and people said, "I'm sorry you lost your husband," she replied, "I didn't lose him; I know exactly where he is."

Guideline #3: Eternalize your hope. Paul reminds the Thessalonians, who had lost loved ones, that Christ will return and our bodies will again rise from the grave. Then he says, "Comfort one another with these words" (1 Thessalonians 4:18 KJV).

Jesus was right. Strange as it may seem, those who mourn are blessed with a comfort that only comes by releasing our grief.

RESOURCE READING: Matthew 5:1–12

January 26

IS MEEKNESS WEAKNESS?

Is meekness weakness? Most people consider meekness something to be disdained. Yet as Jesus taught the people on the mountainside, He candidly said, "Blessed are the meek, for they will inherit the earth" (Matthew 5:5).

What did He mean? Is He saying that those who inherit the earth will have a lot of dust on them from lying down to let others walk over them? Not at all. The word that Jesus used was also used in the first century to describe a horse under the control of a rider—powerful but disciplined. Jesus lifted the word from its cultural context and gave it new strength and meaning.

Modern translations usually render the word *meek* as "humble" or "gentle," but there is no trace of effeminacy or weakness in the word; meekness speaks of gentleness of strength.

It is interesting to note that the only two people described in the Bible as "meek" are Moses and Jesus. Moses was the greatest of all Old Testament leaders, a shepherd by profession, weathered and bronzed by the desert sun and wind—hardly a wimp. Jesus, of course, is the greatest figure in the entire Bible. Taking a whip and driving the money changers out of the temple is hardly an act undertaken by a weakling. Jesus was a man's man, yet—and this is where we turn the corner—He was of such a nature and disposition that children were at ease in His arms and played at His feet.

Jesus made it clear that He had no agenda of His own. He had come only to do the will of His Father in heaven. When we consider ourselves "His to command," our strength comes under His control. In this position of weakness—or humbleness, if you prefer—we become candidates to inherit the earth.

What does it mean to inherit the earth? Some thought it was the Land of Promise, but surely Jesus meant that there will always—anywhere and everywhere—be a place for the person who has humility and gentleness, the meekness of Christ Himself.

This quality of meekness may not be popular today, but it is exactly what we need in our homes, our relationships, and our lives. It's the answer to the sickness of our world.

RESOURCE READING: Matthew 6:19–34

HUNGERING AND THIRSTING
FOR RIGHTEOUSNESS

E very person has certain drives that are fundamental to existence. Among the strongest are the physical yearnings for food and water. In the Sermon on the Mount, Jesus speaks of those two basic drives, but He applies them to a spiritual hunger and thirst for God: "Blessed are those who hunger and thirst for righteousness, for they will be filled" (Matthew 5:6).

Notice what He does not say. He doesn't say that those who hunger and thirst for a promotion, a raise, better benefits, or a shapelier body would find satisfaction, but those who hunger and thirst for righteousness would be filled.

The word that Jesus uses to describe the fulfillment that comes when you make God the focus of your life is the same word used of cattle that are fed or fattened with choice pasture. Picture a cow grazing in a rich, green field, contentedly chewing its cud.

One of my favorite psalms is one that David wrote while he was hiding from Saul in a desolate area, En Gedi. In fear for his life, with everything going against him, David takes refuge in God. He cries out, "O God, you are my God, earnestly I seek you; my soul thirsts for you, my body longs for you, in a dry and weary land where there is no water" (Psalm 63:1).

As he sat in the hot, dry, desolate desert, David experienced physical thirst. But he says that his thirst for God was even greater. He speaks of the long hours of the night when he would meditate on God and the promises of His Word.

Jesus says that your hunger and thirst for God will not go unheeded—and He puts no conditions on this promise. He doesn't say, "Clean up your act, get spiritual, and then get in line for a blessing." He simply promises the blessing of fulfillment for those who hunger and thirst for righteousness.

Jesus says, "Come to me, all you who are weary and burdened, and I will give you rest. Take my yoke upon you and learn from me, for I am gentle and humble in heart, and you will find rest for your souls. For my yoke is easy and my burden is light" (Matthew 11:28–30).

It's still true. Those who hunger and thirst for God will find Him.

RESOURCE READING: Matthew 7:1–12

January 28

BLESSED ARE THE MERCIFUL

A certain woman, whose vanity exceeded her looks, had her picture taken by a local photographer. When she went to view the prints, which had not been touched up to cover her flaws, she was noticeably disturbed. "These pictures don't do me justice," she said angrily. "Lady," the photographer replied, "it isn't justice you need; it's mercy!" The fact is, we all need mercy—and, like the woman, we think we're in better condition than we really are.

The Bible mentions the word *mercy* more than 370 times. Our great and awesome God is a God of mercy. "Rich in mercy" is the phrase Paul uses to describe God in Ephesians 2:4—in stark contrast to pagan gods, whose wrath had to be satisfied, often with human blood. Anthropologists would agree that mercy was not an attribute of pagan deities.

The Romans spoke of four great virtues: wisdom, justice, temperance, and courage. Mercy was not a virtue that governed their lives. In fact, the hallmark of a Roman legion was its ability to inflict cruel punishment or "justice." Only with great reluctance would a Roman emperor give the "thumbs-up" sign to spare the life of a vanquished warrior in the arena.

I hardly expect mercy to be an attribute of a person in rebellion against God, but among the children of God, "like Father, like son" should be the norm.

Here's the way Paul puts it: "Since you have been chosen by God who has given you this new kind of life, and because of his deep love and concern for you, you should practice tenderhearted mercy and kindness to others" (Colossians 3:12 TLB).

A final thought: Although God's mercy has been shown from generation to generation, there is an end to it. Remember before the Flood, God said, "My spirit shall not always strive with man" (Genesis 6:3 KJV). Likewise, you will not find the word *mercy* in the book of Revelation—not even once. Instead, you'll find a generous outpouring of God's wrath and justice. But the door is still open. As Peter put it, "Anyone who asks for mercy from the Lord shall have it and shall be saved" (Acts 2:21 TLB). Wisdom says, "Ask for it, but practice it as well." Jesus was right: "Blessed are the merciful, for they will be shown mercy" (Matthew 5:7).

RESOURCE READING: Matthew 7:13–23

January 29

BLESSED ARE THE PURE IN HEART

The brain may be the center of the intellect, the control center of the human body, but it is the heart that captures the interest of lovers and poets, because the emotions of life come from the heart. Jesus puts this truth in focus when He says, "Out of the overflow of the heart the mouth speaks" (Matthew 12:34). It is your heart, not your head, that reveals the kind of person you are. When Jesus taught the multitudes on the mountainside, He pronounced a special blessing on those whose hearts are pure. "Blessed are the pure in heart," He said, "for they will see God" (Matthew 5:8).

Okay, then, if you want to see God, learn how to purify your heart. The very thought of a pure heart in a world of moral corruption leaves us feeling inadequate, short of the mark, and frustrated, because we know we will never be good enough to qualify—at least that's how I feel. We know that "the heart is deceitful above all things and beyond cure" (Jeremiah 17:9).

The problem is obvious, but what's the solution? God says, "I will give you a new heart—I will give you new and right desires—and put a new spirit within you. I will take out your stony hearts of sin and give you new hearts of love" (Ezekiel 36:26 TLB). That's good news! A transplant! Well, not exactly. You don't receive someone else's partly worn-out model, which they can no longer use. Instead you receive a re-creation, a touch of the Creator that changes the way you think, act, and relate to other people.

Becoming pure in heart isn't a quick fix; it's a lifestyle and a choice that sets your feet on a path that leads to God. Forgive me for stating the obvious, but life at its longest is short, very short, and sooner or later we all face eternity. When Jesus says that the pure in heart shall see God, He affirms the reality of heaven and affirms that the crown of life lies within the grasp of the smallest, the least significant, and the poorest among us. It belongs to any person whose heart is pure and upright before God. That is good news, friend, very good news!

RESOURCE READING: Matthew 7:24–28

BLESSED ARE THE PEACEMAKERS

Have you ever noticed how much easier it is to wage war than to make peace? Strange, isn't it? There's something about human nature that makes us want to assert our authority, to stand up for our rights and what we think should be ours. "What causes fights and quarrels among you?" asks James in his epistle. "Don't they come from your desires that battle within you?" (James 4:1).

Not only is it hard to *keep* the peace, but it's even more difficult to make peace where there is none, to bring angry and hostile individuals to the conference table. However, some rare individuals have the ability to bring others together, whether ministers of defense, employees who can't work together, or husbands and wives who share the same bed but no longer love each other. Thank God for the peacemakers!

You might be surprised to hear that conflict does not destroy relationships. Instead, it is our refusal to resolve conflict that sends hostile armies against each other, or breaks up families or businesses.

The secret to conflict resolution lies in two rather simple ingredients: negotiation and compromise. But the really difficult part is getting people to understand the tremendous cost of stubbornly refusing to resolve issues. Is it really worth it? Ask the husband whose stupid refusal to harness his wandering lust results in losing his wife of twenty years, his reputation, and the respect of his children. In unresolved conflict, there are no winners, only losers.

"Sons of God" is the title that Jesus gives to the peacemakers of the world. If a son reflects the image of his father, surely we can see the nature and character of our heavenly Father in those who broker peace. Not only is God described as "the God of peace" five times in the New Testament, but

He desires that His children be peacemakers as well.

The writer of Hebrews says it well when he writes, "May the God of peace, who through the blood of the eternal covenant brought back from the dead our Lord Jesus, that great Shepherd of the sheep, equip you with everything good for doing his will, and may he work in us what is pleasing to him, through Jesus Christ, to whom be glory for ever and ever. Amen" (Hebrews 13:20–21).

RESOURCE READING: Luke 6:1–26

January 31

YES, REJOICE AND BE GLAD

The person who stands for nothing will fall for anything, so goes conventional wisdom. But even the person who does stand for something—who has the conviction to abide by what she believes is right—will soon discover that not everyone appreciates her commitment to decency. It makes others squirm to have a righteous one in their midst. It's true that people love darkness rather than light, because their deeds are evil.

When Jesus taught the multitude in the Sermon on the Mount, He addressed the issue of righteousnes, which is as old as the sons of Adam and Eve and as contemporary as the morning news. He said, "Blessed are those who are persecuted because of righteousness, for theirs is the kingdom of heaven. Blessed are you when people insult you, persecute you and falsely say all kinds of evil against you because of me. Rejoice and be glad, because great is your reward in heaven, for in the same way they persecuted the prophets who were before you" (Matthew 5:10–12).

How should we respond when we become targets of

hostility or persecution for doing right? The following guidelines will help:

Guideline #1: Pray for your enemies. That's what Jesus told His disciples. Remember, Saul of Tarsus, the archenemy of the early church, became the apostle Paul.

Guideline #2: Realize that Satan is using those who oppose you. Be on your guard. Don't let the enemy get to you. Put on the full armor of God and stand strong and true.

Guideline #3: Remember that nothing is forever. Once, when my brother asked to place Gideon Bibles in a school, the principal sternly said, "Over my dead body." Two years later, the man died of a heart attack. The Gideons quietly went back and were able to place the Bibles with the new principal's blessing.

Guideline #4: Rejoice and be glad. Thank God that His grace is sufficient for your need and that He will sustain you and strengthen you during difficult times.

No one welcomes hostility or persecution for doing right, but when we endure, we are blessed and counted worthy of the kingdom of heaven. God will have His day. Far better to lose the skirmish but win the war than to be on the other side. Blessed are those who persevere!

RESOURCE READING: Luke 6:27–49

INTERPRETING HISTORY

When movie producer Oliver Stone was criticized for bending the truth in his movie on the life of Richard Nixon, he responded by saying that he was simply "interpreting" the truth, and that every production deserved new insights. Since when does truth require interpretation? If something is historical, shouldn't the facts be the truth, rather than how someone would like things to have been? Can truth really be interpreted?

Interpreting the truth is what historians do when they ignore certain events and emphasize others. Interpreting the truth is what a husband does when he lies to his wife by glossing over the details of his lunch with his secretary. Interpreting the truth is what a politician does when he looks the camera in the eye and denies any knowledge of a situation that he's up to his neck in. Interpreting the truth isn't new—Adam did it in the Garden of Eden—but it certainly has become fashionable.

A recent poll indicated that seven out of ten individuals are dissatisfied with current standards of honesty. No wonder there's a growing cynicism today. When "everything is relative," you can't be sure you have the unvarnished facts about a situation, no matter who reports it.

How does God view the practice of interpreting the truth? The same way He responded to Adam's comments in the garden—with disdain! Either something is true or it's a lie. The problem today is that people so commonly distort the truth that it becomes habitual. Then we coin pleasant words such as "misinformation" to obscure the fact that there was deceit and purposeful misrepresentation.

Honesty is the fabric of trust. When we no longer think we can trust each other, we draw back, build walls, and live in doubt and cynicism. A person who is straightforward and honest may at times be upsetting, but he or she is refreshing. When what you see is what you get, you never have to wonder where the person really stands. And when I take my car into the garage for repairs and hear, "You need major repairs," I'd feel somewhat better knowing he would tell his mother exactly the same thing.

RESOURCE READING: Ephesians 4:1–16

February 2

LIKE FATHER, LIKE SON

Have you ever seen a baby and commented, "He looks exactly like his daddy!"? A chip off the old block, the spit and image of his father, right? "There's more to it than that," says psychologist Dr. Nicholas Christenfeld. His theory holds that the father confers "face genes" that make the baby's face resemble his. "While a mother can be quite sure that the baby is hers no matter what it looks like, the father cannot," says Dr. Christenfeld. "It should then be to a baby's advantage to look like the father, to encourage paternal investment."

As reported in *Nature* magazine, Christenfeld asked 122 people to match photos of children ages one, ten, and twenty to photos of their fathers. Matching the photos at ages ten and twenty was rare, but the test subjects consistently matched the photos of the one-year-olds—both sons and daughters—to their fathers.

Physical resemblance is not uncommon, but other similarities in life depend more on habits and learning than heredity. "Like father, like son," we often say when a child duplicates the behavior or lifestyle of the father. Dads who are often separated from their offspring because of work miss a large part of the teaching-learning process. No wonder children who grow up on farms, learning to work alongside their parents, have far fewer problems than kids whose dads disappear on a commuter train before dawn and get home late at night, or are simply not there because of divorce.

A father's influence in the life of his kids is profound. Try these guidelines for starters to maximize your influence in the lives of your children:

Guideline #1: Be there when you can. If you have a choice between working late at the office or taking it home, take it home. Being there makes a difference.

Guideline #2: Think through your priorities. A wise father considers the impact of his priorities on his kids. There are no second chances for some things, such as watching your son catch his first fish.

Guideline #3: Decide what is important. Putting your family first means your job comes second. If Jesus were here today I believe He would say, "What shall it profit a man if he should gain the company presidency and lose his family? Or what shall a man give in exchange for his family?"

RESOURCE READING: Ephesians 6:1–19

February 3

IS YOURS A PAGAN SOCIETY?

Is our culture Christian or pagan? Before you respond, stop and think for a minute. The question cannot be answered without defining what makes a culture Christian or pagan. Merriam-Webster's Collegiate Dictionary, Tenth Edition, defines a pagan as "a follower of a polytheistic religion (as in ancient Rome)," or "one who has little or no religion and delights in sensual pleasures and material goods; an irreligious or hedonistic person." You may be wondering, "Is Webster defining the word or describing our generation?"

In his book *The New Paganism,* historian Harold Lindsell contends that raw paganism has replaced humanism as the dominant philosophy of life today. He says, "Clearly, paganism stands in opposition to the Judeo-Christian tradition and the Christian faith."

Has our culture become pagan? Compare the impact of the church on society with that of a generation or two ago. Look at what has happened to the family. To what degree are Christians impacting our society and our world, or has Christianity simply become a reflection of our culture?

One of the greatest indictments against the church today is that it has become so accommodating that the line of demarcation between the church and the world has been all but rubbed out. In our attempts to make our churches "user friendly," we have lost our distinctiveness. Worship has become a celebration of the attendee's self-esteem. Then, after making people feel good about themselves, churches send them back into the battles of life.

Here's the point: If we genuinely mirror the gospel of Jesus Christ in our lives, our churches, businesses, homes, and marriages will be out of step with the surrounding culture. We will be thought of as radical religious fanatics just as certainly as the sun rises in the east and sets in the west. Remember what Jesus said to His disciples: "Woe to you when all men speak well of you, for that is how their fathers treated the false prophets" (Luke 6:26). A pagan culture will never be a friend to grace. That's just the way it is.

RESOURCE READING: Hebrews 11

LOOKING BACK

A s long as the present is at war with the past," said Winston Churchill, "there is no hope for the future!"

Trying to drive by looking in the rearview mirror is risky business. You may be focused, but your field of vision is limited. You're apt to back over curbs or plow into objects you had no idea were there.

"One of the reasons God doesn't like rearview mirrors," writes Mike Fabarez, "is because He knows that we are good at beating ourselves up with past failures. It's not that we really didn't fail. It's not that there wasn't damage done. It's not even that there is no debt incurred. We did, and there was. The problem is that when we dwell on our past sin and when we beat ourselves up with our failures, we usually believe that in some way we are making amends for them. Basking in our guilt, we think, is our 'payment' for our mistake."[1]

Get rid of the rearview mirror in your life once and for all. How? That's where the grace of God's forgiveness comes into the picture. The apostle Paul bore a load of guilt so great that he would have been a candidate for an institution had he not learned that when God forgives, He forgets. We need to learn the same lesson. God made Christ to be sin on our behalf that we might be made righteous in the sight of God.

What does it take for you to understand that God has forgiven you? Some people are never convinced, in spite of the fact that they have God's word for it. They continue to insist that they're not good enough, or that the promises don't extend to them. The good news is that God is no respecter of persons. His promises wipe the slate clean, allowing you to forget the past and focus on the future and the wonderful things that God has provided.

Would God lie? Never! Then why not accept what He

says about your life and get on with it? Forget the rearview mirror and focus on the road that lies ahead.

RESOURCE READING: Philippians 3:1–14

February 5

DADS WHO ARE THERE

As a father, how much time do you spend with your kids? I know you're busy, but your presence or absence is a powerful factor in their development.

I'm reminded of a breakfast conversation I had with a businessman who talked about the dad he never knew. Until his mother died when he was eleven, he seldom saw his dad other than on weekends. "He worked two jobs," he said, "and when he was home, he was so tired and irritable that we always avoided him."

He added wistfully, "I always wanted to take a trip with my dad, but he never had time." After my friend became an adult, he and his dad were separated by their work and never saw each other. "One day, the phone rang," he said, "and I received a call that Dad had died. I had to fly to where he lived, take care of the arrangements, and escort the body home. The casket was on the same flight as mine." Shaking his head sadly, he added, "I guess that was the trip I had always wanted to take with him."

In the final week of my own dad's life, I sat with him almost day and night. Thinking back over our conversations, as we laughed and reminisced, what sustained us was talking about the family times we had shared together—the fishing trips, vacations, and building projects. Our other accomplishments in life were unimportant.

If your kids are grown, today's thoughts may irritate you.

You can't turn back the calendar to the days when your six-year-old begged you to take him fishing or to the ball game. For others, it isn't too late to become a dad who is there.

Take a look at your values. Negatively or positively, you are shaping the values of your children. Whether you're at home or working two jobs, whether you attend church with your family or sleep in on Sunday, whether you ignore your wife or treat her with respect, your kids are watching and learning.

Dads who are there have a positive impact. Don't forget. Your son or daughter won't. Someday, you'll be glad you remembered.

RESOURCE READING: Genesis 18

February 6

COMFORTING A FRIEND

Someday death, divorce, termination, disaster, or disease will strike your family or a close friend. What do you do when someone close to you sustains a loss? You might send a card, call on the telephone, ignore the situation because it's painful, or stop by for a visit. Trying to ignore the issue only adds to the pain, confusion, and layers of grief, but what do you say when you call? How do you help someone else through a crisis? Start with the following guidelines:

Guideline #1: Just be there. You don't have to talk, send flowers, or write messages. Sometimes the warmth of a hug or a handshake, along with your physical presence, is more of an encouragement.

James Kennedy was playing tennis with a friend one

day when the game was interrupted by the devastating news that the friend's infant son had died of Sudden Infant Death Syndrome.

At first, Kennedy didn't know what to do. As an attorney, he earned his living by logic and persuasion, but there was nothing logical about a baby's death, and nothing that could be said to assuage the parent's grief. He accompanied his friend to the hospital and sat with the family as they absorbed the tragic news. He simply was there, and looking back over his career, he describes it as "the most important thing I have ever done."

Guideline #2: Listen. You don't need to make a
      speech, especially when you aren't sure what to
      say. Just be there and listen. When Job suffered
      the loss of his children, his resources, and his rep-
      utation, the friends who helped him the most
      were the ones who came and sat with him for
      seven days and nights without saying a word.

After sustaining a loss, your friend may want to talk or she may want some space to come to grips with what has happened. Eventually, she'll want to talk about it, but let her do it on her own schedule—not yours.

Guideline #3: Care. The friends who helped us the
      most after my dad's death were the ones who
      showed up in jeans and work clothes and said,
      "What needs doing?" and then didn't mind soil-
      ing their hands doing some pretty unglamorous
      tasks. Compassion in coveralls, demonstrating
      that you care, brings comfort that counts.

RESOURCE READING: 1 Thessalonians 5

February 7

MY GRACE IS SUFFICIENT

I s God's grace sufficient?
Is God really there when we're hurting?

Let me tell you about a man who struggled with this very issue. Trained as a rabbi, a teacher of the Jews, he knew a lot about God. After his conversion to Christianity, he embarked on three missionary journeys, covering thousands of miles, and he spread the good news about Jesus Christ across central Asia. I'm talking about the apostle Paul, of course, the man who wrote thirteen of the twenty-seven books of the New Testament. If "head knowledge" or intellectual understanding about God were all that mattered, Paul would have had no problems. But, like the rest of us, he suffered from physical and emotional challenges that tested his faith.

In Paul's case, he seemed to handle overt persecution better than he did some of the nagging problems that pestered him daily. For example, he wrestled for years with an affliction that apparently bothered his eyes, probably making them run and blurring his vision (see Galatians 4:15). Not too pleasant, right? Paul had seen God do some remarkable healings, even raising people from the dead, so it would have seemed simple for God to have fixed his eyes. Right?

On three recorded occasions, Paul asked God specifically to deal with this "thorn in the flesh." And three times, God said no.

Actually, the answer didn't come quite like that. Instead, God said, "My grace is sufficient for you." What is grace? Grace is God's help, His favor, His strength, His touch that allows us to function without being driven into the asphalt.

Another question must be asked: Was God's promise to Paul for him alone, or can we—each of us today—find the same answer? The good news, friend, is that when God chooses not to deliver us from a problem, He whispers, "Hey, I'm here right by your side, and My grace, My help, My strength is sufficient to meet you where you are. Just be patient and trust Me."

God's awesome, marvelous grace is sufficient to meet your needs, no matter where you are in relationship to Him, no matter how far you may have wandered. That's why grace is grace.

RESOURCE READING: 2 Corinthians 12:1–10

February 8

MY STRENGTH IS
PERFECTED IN WEAKNESS

Three men were discussing their greatest weaknesses. The first said he was unable to resist the temptation of alcohol. The second said, "I can't control the videos I watch." The third man only nodded. Finally, with a sheepish smile, he said, "My problem is, I can't resist gossiping, and right now I can't wait to get out of here."

A chain is only as strong as its weakest link, and spiritually, you are only as strong as the weakest area of your life. Where are you most vulnerable? What is your greatest area of weakness?

Weaknesses come in all sizes and descriptions. Internal, external, habits and thoughts. Some are secret; others are obvious to everyone.

What does God say about your flaws? Sometimes we wish He'd just ignore them, but that isn't what the Bible says. God knows your weaknesses, and the Bible says we're responsible for our failures. God doesn't just say, "Poor fellow, he can't help it; he's only human," but He does say, "My strength is made perfect in weakness."

Paul records God's promise as part of his second letter to the Corinthians, where he's doing some heart searching of his own. God says, "My grace is enough; it's all you need. It is sufficient to meet you at the point of your deepest need, no matter what it may be." And then He adds, "My strength comes into its own in your weakness."

When you admit your weakness and allow God to touch your life, His strength begins to reinforce your resolve to do right. Instead of being defeated time and again, you'll see God's Holy Spirit add the strength you need to do the right thing.

Okay, in all honesty, what's your weakness? Are you involved in an affair? Struggling with your thought life? Addicted to porn, alcohol, or overcome by doubt and fear? God's grace is sufficient; His strength can fill the void of your personal weakness.

God never forces Himself on you. But when you say, "Lord, fill and heal my weakness," He goes to work and meets your need.

RESOURCE READING: 2 Corinthians 12:11–21

February 9

HOLD EVERYTHING, IT'S BIGGER YET

Infinity has multiplied! Hold everything! Based on new calculations, astronomers recently upped their estimate of the number of galaxies from ten billion to fifty billion. This news is so stunning that it defies human comprehension.

Until recently, scientists said there were two galaxies for

every person on planet Earth. Now they are telling us that there are ten galaxies for every man, woman, and child alive today. And keep in mind that a single galaxy contains millions, even billions of stars.

Here's a quick history lesson to put this new discovery in perspective. About 150 B.C., the Greek astronomer Hipparchus determined there were 1026 stars. He was wrong. A century and a half later, Ptolemy, the Roman scientist who lived at the time of Christ, did a recount. He came up with thirty more, to raise the total to 1056.

Things didn't change much until 1610 when Galileo pointed his first primitive telescope up into the heavens and lost his breath trying to see how many stars there were. In modern times, the 200-inch Mount Palomar telescope expanded our view of the heavens—and, today, the $1.5 billion Hubble telescope in outer space can peer at astral bodies fourteen billion light-years away.

Understanding the scope of the universe makes me ponder the power of the Almighty God. The Bible says simply that "By the word of the LORD were the heavens made, their starry host by the breath of his mouth" (Psalm 33:6). God is greater than anything He has made, and the number of the stars is greater than man will ever fathom.

The prophet Jeremiah said, "As the host of heaven cannot be numbered, neither the sand of the sea measured: so will I multiply the seed of David my servant." (Jeremiah 33:22 KJV). Psalm 147:4 says that God calls the stars by name and numbers them. The way things look now, our scientists are so far behind, they will be a long, long time in catching up. Think of it—for every person alive today, there are not just ten stars out there, but ten galaxies, each of which contains millions and millions of stars.

RESOURCE READING: Psalm 8

KNOWING THE DIFFERENCE
BETWEEN TRUTH AND ERROR

Jesus said, "You will know the truth, and the truth will set you free" (John 8:32). A lot of people don't know truth when they see it, and they settle for a deadly mixture of truth and falsehood.

In the Old Testament, a prophet named Balaam earned his living telling fortunes and putting hexes on people's enemies. Balaam enticed Balak, the king of Moab, to send women to tempt the men of Israel sexually and introduce them to foreign gods—all in the name of religion. His name has become synonymous with "false teacher," and the error of Balaam is still alive today.

If the most dangerous false teaching is a mixture of truth and falsehood, how can we tell the difference? Here are some telltale signs:

1. Beware of teachers with strong, forceful personalities and a charismatic manner, who claim new spiritual insights. Balaam's reputation as a spiritual guru was what first led Balak's men to seek him out.
2. False teaching always appeals to the good side of human nature. Who wants to believe that a loving God would actually send people to hell? We would prefer to believe that God wouldn't possibly reprove us for what we are doing.
3. Balaam's error often allows the devotee a great deal of sexual latitude, which traditional churches will not tolerate.
4. Claiming that we need "new truth for a new era," the teaching of Balaam rejects tradition and the teaching of the Bible, in favor of a new creed or "new insights."

5. Balaam's teaching is a strange mixture of truth and error. One of the remarkable things about New Age literature and the writings of cult leaders is that they often quote long passages from the Bible, but taken out of context.

6. Teachers in the spirit of Balaam often become wealthy. No wonder the Bible strongly reproves teachers who follow the error of Balaam's way and warns God's people against being snowed by their smooth talking and charming ways. Jesus said the truth will set you free. Use the Bible as your standard for truth, and when anything contradicts its clear teaching, beware. The spirit of Balaam is alive and well today.

RESOURCE READING: 2 John

February 11

FROM A COCKROACH TO AN EAGLE

A cockroach, a sparrow, and an eagle have three things in common: They're alive, they move, and they reproduce, but that's about it for similarities. I've been thinking, however, that these three creatures correspond to three levels of existence: survival, success, and significance.

The cockroach represents the survival level. Cockroaches are everywhere. They live in bakeries, kitchens, restaurants, hotels, and palaces. But a cockroach has no goal in life. He eats to live and lives to eat. His vision is limited to what lies immediately in front of him. You might not like the analogy, but a lot of people fall into the same category of survival. For them, life is a miserable grind. They never see the light of a new day, because their noses are forever to the grindstone. They exist, but they never get off the ground in life.

Sparrows are way ahead of the cockroaches, but they have their own limitations. They fly. They get off the ground, but they're always close to it. They must always be on the alert, because they have plenty of enemies: big birds, unfriendly cats, and homeowners who don't like nests under the eaves of their houses.

A lot of folks are like the sparrows. Compared to cockroaches, they're miles ahead. They don't crawl; they fly. They don't have to worry about where their next meal is coming from, but they stick pretty close to the ground. Sparrows are successful, but they never really soar in life.

Then there are those who live lives of significance: the eagles, who soar high overhead on the currents of the wind, seemingly unperturbed. They live among the crags of the mountain peaks. I'm convinced that God wants us to mount up with wings like eagles, to trust Him for our daily bread, and to let Him deal with our enemies.

Would you describe your existence as that of a cockroach, a sparrow, or an eagle? Is yours a life of survival, of relative success, or significance? Don't stop short of what God intends. You can soar with the eagles, even when you live with turkeys.

RESOURCE READING: Isaiah 40

February 12

SOAR LIKE AN EAGLE

When eagles take to the air—with their wings stretched out up to seven feet across—their feathers spread out in a curtain, catching the wind currents high above the ground. Eagles don't fly; they soar.

If you were offered the choice of being a sparrow or an eagle, you probably wouldn't hesitate. After all, who wouldn't want to soar with the eagles rather than live in the barnyard with chickens? An eagle with a broken wing, earth-bound, is a sight to be pitied.

I'm convinced that God intends for his children to soar like eagles above the mundane, meaningless existence known as survival. Isaiah says that "those who hope in the LORD will renew their strength. They will soar on wings like eagles; they will run and not grow weary, they will walk and not be faint" (Isaiah 40:31). Isaiah uses three levels of movement to illustrate his point: walking, running, and soaring like an eagle. If we are to rise above the gravitational pull of everyday life, and soar like an eagle, we must place our hope and our lives in the Lord.

"Okay, sounds great," you may be thinking, "but how do I soar like an eagle spiritually?" When you became God's child, the Holy Spirit came to indwell your body and your life. The Bible clearly tells us this, but there is still an ongoing struggle between the flesh—your old nature—and the heavenly pull of the Spirit. You are the one who determines what will dominate your life: your flesh or God's Spirit. And when you make the decision to let God's Spirit guide, motivate, and direct you, you begin to soar in a dimension of life akin to the flight of an eagle.

Though they never get far above the ground, because of the gravitational pull of wrongdoing and wrong thinking, a lot of sparrows—these people who constantly struggle with the issue of sin—will make it to heaven. But I feel for the sparrow who doesn't realize that he could soar like an eagle.

Don't be content to live a sparrow's existence when you could soar with the eagles where the air is pure and fresh, uncluttered by the smog and pollution of your old world. Mount up with wings as eagles. There's plenty of open sky where eagles soar.

RESOURCE READING: Galatians 5:22–26

HOW MEN GET IN THE DOGHOUSE

S ome call it "Le Chateau Bowwow," which is French for "the doghouse." And strangely enough, it's almost always men who end up there. Avoid the following seven mistakes, which are guaranteed to land you in the doghouse:

Mistake #1: Forget birthdays, anniversaries, and other special events. (Psst! Don't forget that tomorrow is Valentine's Day.) These special days mean a lot to women, so if you love someone special, men, don't forget.

Mistake #2: Admit that another woman is prettier than your wife or girlfriend. When you're walking down the street and a pretty woman comes along, naturally you will notice. But keep your mouth shut and don't look lingeringly. Your wife will be watching to see if you're watching.

Mistake #3: Buy your wife or girlfriend a dress two sizes too big. Better to err on the small side than to buy a size fourteen when she wears a ten. If you buy a two-by-four that's a foot too long, it's no big deal. You take a saw and whack off what you don't need. But buy your wife a dress that's way too big, and you might be the one getting whacked.

Mistake #4: Hesitate slightly before answering the question, "Do you think I'm fat?" You don't have to actually say yes. Simply hesitate and you're in the doghouse. Love your wife the way she is. Life has a way of rearranging the corpuscles, and to expect her at age forty to look like she did at twenty-five is unrealistic. Besides, you don't measure up to that standard either.

Mistake #5: Give your wife or girlfriend a small appliance, such as a clock radio or an iron. Gifts like that just don't cut it. I learned that lesson the time I gave my wife a clock radio for Mother's Day. It went over like a ham sandwich in a synagogue. Take it from me, never again.

Mistake #6: After dinner, compliment her by saying, "That was a nice little dinner!" What you meant as a compliment she will take as a backhanded insult.

Mistake #7: Ask "How much did that thing cost?" No matter what she paid for it, the implication is it wasn't worth it.

Men, love your wives, and avoid the doghouse.

RESOURCE READING: Ephesians 5:25–33

February 14

HOW TO GET OUT OF THE DOGHOUSE

A young wife was pouring out her heart to her mother, describing how her husband had forgotten her birthday. Annoyed, she said, "Men are only good for one thing!" "Yes," her mother agreed, adding, "And thank goodness we don't have to parallel park very often."

Yesterday we learned how to end up in the doghouse. Today's advice can get you out.

Key #1: Make it a habit to remember. Write birthdays, anniversaries, and important days on your calendar. It may not be important to you, but it is to the woman in your life.

Key #2: Demonstrate your love. Talk is cheap. Diamonds are not. But flowers are affordable. They show that you remembered and went out of your way to say "I love you." Please don't be like the young man who said, "Why buy flowers? They just die!"

In his book, *The Five Love Languages,* Dr. Gary Chapman describes five basic ways that people express their love: words, gifts, physical touch and closeness, acts of service, and quality time together.

Love is a decision, a commitment to care. Demonstrating your love goes far beyond a Valentine's Day card or a box of candy.

Key #3: Do something special. Try taking your wife breakfast in bed. Baby-sit while she goes shopping. Ask her what she would like to watch on TV, even if it means you'll miss the game.

Key #4: Admit your mistakes and failures. "Before we married, my husband was Mr. Right," said one young woman. "After we married, he became Mr. Always Right!" Let's face it, men. We might know more about some things than our wives. But balance that against what they know that we don't. Saying, "I was wrong. Please forgive me!" with sincerity and genuineness will open the doghouse door.

Key #5: Try to understand, listen, and communicate. Never close your lips to the one to whom you have opened your heart. Openness and vulnerability melts the ice and helps resolve misunderstandings.

Key #6: Lead the way spiritually. Praying together, going to church together, and being together— just having fun—builds strong relationships.

There may be a lot more ways of getting into the doghouse than getting out, but nothing succeeds like sincerity, honesty, openness, and vulnerability. And remember, today is Valentine's Day.

RESOURCE READING: 1 Corinthians 13

February 15

SUBMITTING TO EACH OTHER

Dear Dr. Sala," writes a friend of *Guidelines*, "As a university graduate from a middle-class family, I find it difficult to submit to my husband as the Bible commands. Does that stuff apply to us today? Or was that only for people in Paul's day?"

First, we must settle the issue of whether the Bible contains timeless counsel from a loving God, who knows how couples can best be happy, or is simply the ideas of insecure men. Next, we must ask whether the counsel of Scripture establishes a universal principle for all generations, or applies only to a specific cultural situation.

Some advice that Paul gave was directed to particular situations that were out of hand. For example, his admonition that women should keep silent in church resulted from the commotion that ensued when women, who by custom sat on one side of the synagogue, would talk to their husbands on the opposite side when they didn't understand something.

What the Bible says about our roles in marriage, however, goes to the core of our human nature and isn't based on culture at all. Of course, what the Bible actually says and what some people say it says aren't always the same thing.

Some men have taken the concept of submission to unwarranted and unbiblical extremes, reducing women to a level of servitude that God never intended.

The Bible never says that women are inferior to men. In many respects, women possess talents and strengths that men don't have. God intended men and women to complement each other, not compete with each other.

The New Testament word translated "submit" literally means "to stand under." It was used in the military to describe submission to authority. The Bible says that men and women are to submit to each other out of reverence for Christ (see Ephesians 5:22). Did you notice that last phrase, "out of reverence for Christ"?

A proper understanding of how God designed marriage makes a tremendous difference in our relationships. God never intended for women to surrender their individuality or uniqueness in marriage any more than He intended men to be dictators. God's plan is better. He's the Creator who gave us the blueprint for happiness.

RESOURCE READING: Ephesians 5:22–32

February 16

MARRYING YOUR OPPOSITE

Do opposites attract? You bet they do. Which explains how an individual who never plans anything beyond his next meal can marry a superorganized woman. You know, the kind who is so organized that when her kid gets up to go to the bathroom at night, she has his bed made before he gets back. Some folks like rock music; others prefer classical. Some sleep with the window open; others can't sleep unless it's shut. And do you squeeze the toothpaste in the middle of the tube, or roll it from the bottom? Opposites may attract, but too many differences repel each other, and that's when the fire flies.

One explanation for why opposites marry each other was offered by Dr. Laura Schlessinger. She says we marry to complete ourselves. Thus, the organized person, who wishes he or she were more spontaneous, is attracted to the free-spirited type that seeks adventure. And sometimes a sweet, moral girl ends up marrying a guy who can't hold a job and won't darken the door of a church.

Can two individuals who are as different as day and night make sunshine together? They can, provided they observe and practice the following guidelines:

Guideline #1: Respect your differences. There can be no real love apart from respect. When you really love someone, you're willing to accept that different people operate differently. All differences aside, in a relationship there must be a core of respect, which can't be violated.

Guideline #2: Talk about it. Free and open communication is a must for a successful marriage. Differences can be handled without attacking the other person. Of course, somewhere in between there has to be a solution that keeps you both happy.

Guideline #3: Compromise. Marriage is not a win-lose situation; it's an ongoing dialogue. Someone has said that marriage consists of one "I do" and a lot of little "uh-huhs."

Guideline #4: Submit your differences to a higher court of appeals. Making Christ the head of your home brings an atmosphere that allows you to pray together and openly ask the Lord for His help in reconciling your differences.

Yes, two people can be very different and yet very happy. That's a fact.

RESOURCE READING: Colossians 3:1–17

February 17

IS THERE LIFE OUT THERE?

Why did God create so many stars and galaxies in our universe? Based on our understanding of His nature and character, we know that He never wastes energy or time—even though He is infinitely powerful. We can see by observing the world around us that God does things for a purpose.

Is there a purpose for the vastness of space? Is it possible that, in eternity, mortals will rule some of these areas? But rule over what or whom? It has become almost certain that life as we know it on planet Earth cannot exist on other planets. The conditions are too harsh to sustain human life. But what about other forms of intelligence?

At a symposium on the subject, Professor Richard Berendzen, an astronomer at American University said, "The question has become not so much one of *if*, as of *where*." It is conceivable that life may be considered intelligent that is spiritual in nature but lacking physical bodies such as human beings have. Scientists using the Hubble telescope haven't yet focused on God's heaven, but I am as certain of its existence as I am of anything on planet Earth.

Others—myself included—believe that the vastness of space is of little value in relationship to the value of life itself. Consider the story of a childless couple who had traveled all over the world. To decorate their large mansion, they collected tapestries and marble from Italy, paintings from France, luxurious rugs from Asia, and the finest furnishings money can buy. No one would deny that their home was beautiful, but the couple was childless, and their lives were empty. After many years, God blessed them with a baby boy who looked exactly like his daddy.

They converted one of the upstairs bedrooms into a nursery, and the little fellow was the joy of their lives. One night, however, the couple awakened to the strong odor of smoke. There was no thought of tapestries or diamonds or priceless oil paintings. They thought only of their son. Could this be a picture of the value of human life? Your life? "For God so loved the world that he gave his one and only Son, that whoever believes in him shall not perish but have eternal life" (John 3:16).

RESOURCE READING: Psalm 19

February 18

GOD IS BIGGER THAN WHAT HE HAS MADE

Would it be fair to say that the true measure of a person is his accomplishment? At least in a broad sort of way? For example, James Michener was considered great because of the great books that came from his typewriter. The architecture of St. Paul's Cathedral and dozens of other beautiful buildings made the name of Sir Christopher Wren famous in the sixteenth century. The Sistine Chapel and sculptures such as David and the Pietà are synonymous with the excellence of Michelangelo.

We tend to judge individuals by their accomplishments, but in the scope of eternity, we know that everyone is greater than his or her accomplishments. By the same token, God is far greater than what He has created—and we keep learning more about the greatness of the work of His hand.

For example, astronomers using the Hubble telescope photographed and analyzed a tiny slice of the heavens no wider than one-twenty-fifth of one degree. That's about the size of a grain of sand held at arm's length. The scientists counted 1500 to 2000 galaxies in that tiny sliver of space. When they multiplied this number by 360 degrees, they concluded that the universe contains as many as 50 billion galaxies.

God can no more be separated from what He has done than you can separate the Sistine Chapel from Michelangelo. Those who attempt to remove God from His creative acts fail to see that the Creator and His creation are inseparable. And, if God is bigger than His creation, how big is He? One thing I know for sure is that God is infinitely larger than any challenge or any problem I will ever confront.

I am part of His creation. I am not an accident of chance. Because God created me, I am here, and I must reach out by faith and say, "Thank You, God, for being bigger than my need."

Read Psalm 8. When you consider that the God who created the heaven is also the God who walks with us through the valleys, it's no wonder David cried out, "O LORD our Lord, how excellent is thy name in all the earth!" (Psalm 8:9 KJV).

RESOURCE READING: Isaiah 40:15–31

KARMA

Dear Dr. Sala," writes a friend of *Guidelines,* "Please discuss the subject of karma. I know several people—all highly intelligent—who believe in karma and reincarnation. They say these concepts provide answers to what would otherwise be unanswerable. For example, when they see good people beset by misfortune totally beyond their control, they say, 'They probably did selfish or cruel acts in a past life; therefore, they must pay in this life.'"

First of all, whether or not someone is intelligent is not the issue. The real issue is whether or not what they believe is true. A wrong answer might bring some satisfaction in trying to understand the incomprehensible, but it's not really an answer at all.

Karma and reincarnation are Hindu concepts. Karma means that every action of a person, no matter how small it may be, influences how his soul will be born in his next reincarnation. But if the Bible is true, karma cannot be true.

The Bible makes it clear that we are responsible only for what we do in the here and now, not in some previous existence (see Ezekiel 18). Furthermore, the Bible says that man dies once and then he is judged for his life, whether it is good or evil (see Hebrews 9:27). In parts of the world where there is a great deal of human suffering, the doctrine of karma allows people to do nothing to alleviate the suffering of humanity. "Tough luck!" they say, "They must be paying for previous wrongs." Nonsense!

The judgment of karma also counters the nature of God. Remember, Jesus said that God sent His Son into the world not to "condemn the world; but that the world through him might be saved" (John 3:17 KJV). The whole purpose of Christ's coming was to bring healing and forgiveness, not judgment or retribution for past sins. Hinduism, of course, doesn't recognize a Savior who lived, died, and rose again.

The teaching of reincarnation also contradicts logic. A rose doesn't die in the winter to become a weed the next season. But man, created in the image of God, will come forth a living soul for all eternity. Karma is man's creation, not God's. Remember, a wrong answer is no answer at all.

RESOURCE READING: Ezekiel 18

February 20

YOU CAN ONLY LIVE SO LONG

In a performance at the prestigious Metropolitan Opera in New York City, there was a beautiful and mysterious woman who wanted to live forever. Her father, a chemist-magician, concocted a powerful elixir, which allowed her to live for more than three hundred years.

In the opera, Richard Versalle, portraying a law clerk named Vitek, sang a line that went, "You can only live so long." Little did anyone realize that those would be the last words to come from his lips.

No sooner had Versalle sung the line this particular night than his heart failed. He fell ten feet to the stage, landing motionless on his back with his arms outstretched. Realizing that something was wrong, the stage manager immediately dropped the curtain and the performance was canceled. Versalle was sixty-three and had suffered no previous health problems.

"Man is destined to die once, and after that to face judgment," it says in Hebrews 9:27. We may fantasize about living for three hundred years, but the fact remains that, after a span of years, every person faces death. In life there are many inequities. Some have the money to afford the finest seats in the opera. Others have only enough to sit in the balcony, far away from the action. And some can't even afford to stand in the back. But when the time comes to enter or exit the stage of life, everyone is equal.

Facing death is neither scary nor foreboding, however, when you have the assurance of eternal life. That's the difference that Jesus Christ made in our world. He stood before an open grave and said, "I am the resurrection and the life. He who believes in me will live, even though he dies" (John 11:25).

Jesus Christ faced death and came back to talk about it. The fact that death could not hold Him makes what He said credible and important. He told His disciples that He was going to prepare a place for them and that He would return and receive them to Himself so that they could be where He was. An eternal home in the heavens—as real as anything on Earth—is what Jesus was talking about (see John 14:1–6). "You can only live so long," sang Richard Versalle. He was right.

RESOURCE READING: Revelation 20

February 21

WHEN YOU ARE TEMPTED TO BELIEVE

Former French president Francois Mitterand was an intellectual and an atheist. Yet, in the latter years of his life, he had a fascination with death and a desire to know what lies beyond the grave. He visited the graves of many of France's leading citizens, pondering how they lived and how they died.

When Mitterand was diagnosed with cancer of the prostate and the reality of his own death began to stare him in the face, his atheism was challenged by the reality of life itself. In the autumn, the flowers wither, blighted by the frost of the coming winter. Eventually, they die and the bulbs remain dormant, but in the spring new life comes forth. That fact wasn't lost on Mitterand, who saw the unbroken cycle of nature.

As an intellectual, Mitterand had confronted the possibilities of eternal life but never seemed to embrace it. Toward the end of his life, when asked if he believed in God, he replied, "I don't know if I believe in God, but I am tempted to believe."

When he realized that his time was running out, Mitterand stopped taking his medicine. The next day, he delivered handwritten instructions for his funeral to his doctor and a friend and finished final editing on an 800-page book—the only one he ever wrote. On the third day, he died.

"I don't know if I believe in God," he said, "but I am tempted to believe." What a sad epitaph to a brilliant life.

In the final analysis, God cannot be proved or even discovered intellectually. We must connect with the Almighty at the level of the spirit. The New Testament says that whoever comes to God must believe that He exists and that He rewards those who seek Him (see Hebrews 11:6).

Can God be known with certainty? Paul wrote, "I know whom I have believed, and am convinced that he is able to guard what I have entrusted to him for that day" (2 Timothy 1:12). Millions of searching men and women have found the same answer and have died with the certainty that God through His Son brings us into peace with Himself.

What lies on the other side of death? This question will never be answered by rationalism, philosophy, or mysticism. The answer is found in the Bible. Don't merely be tempted to believe. As the song goes, "Only believe. All things are possible. Only believe."

RESOURCE READING: Revelation 21:1–8

WHAT DOES JESUS HAVE TO DO
WITH CHRISTIANITY?

D o I have to believe in Jesus to be a Christian?" asked a young man whose Russian Jewish background had never exposed him to the gospel. Having been raised in a home in the former Soviet Union where God was seldom if ever discussed, he had heard about Jesus, but didn't know how He fit into Christianity.

For millions of people around the world, the term "Christian" broadly defines certain ethnic or religious roots. We might even think of countries as "Christian" nations. But such broad, sweeping generalizations leave a lot of space between the brush marks.

Rather than asking "What does Jesus Christ have to do with Christianity?" it might be more valid to turn the question around and ask, "What does Christianity have to do with Jesus Christ?"

In Jesus' day, those who followed Him were never identified as Christians. Peter, Andrew, James, and John would have embraced their identity as disciples of Jesus, but ethnically, they were Jews and proud of their heritage.

It wasn't until about fifteen years after the church was established that disciples of Jesus were called Christians—and even then, the term was one of derision and scorn.

The term "Christianity" should never be used to define a religion, because Christianity involves a relationship, not simply a lifestyle or a system of beliefs. The creed of the early church stressed who Jesus was and what He did—not what people must say or believe to belong to a church.

"Do I have to believe in Jesus to be a Christian?" The answer is "Yes. That's what it's all about." By reading the New Testament, anyone can be introduced to the person of Jesus Christ. But only by confessing Christ as your personal

Savior can you come into a saving relationship with Him. And that relationship is then strengthened by fellowship with other Christians.

The acid test for a disciple does not involve your belief system—though what you believe determines what you do. It first involves your relationship with Jesus Christ, then with others. "By this all men will know that you are my disciples," said, Jesus, "if you love one another" (John 13:35).

RESOURCE READING: John 15

February 23

WHEN YOU LOSE AN ENGINE

United Airlines captain Ed Palacio took off from Chicago in an Airbus A-320 for another routine flight. Ed had been flying for a long time and he knew that the Airbus was so computerized that it could practically fly itself.

When the plane had climbed to about 6,000 feet, an explosion in one of the massive Pratt and Whitney jet engines caused the control panel to light up like a Christmas tree—flashing red all over the place. That meant big trouble, because the Airbus is a two-engine aircraft.

Flying a simulator on the ground is one thing, but having the lives of nearly eighty people in your hands when an engine blows up shortly after takeoff is quite another matter. Ed's training and experience immediately kicked into high gear as he brought the plane back to Chicago and landed it safely.

"What did you think about when that engine blew up?" I asked Ed later.

"I didn't have time to think," he said. "I just reacted instinctively."

"Was it an emotional experience?"

He shook his head. "Emotions will mislead you." Then he added, "As Christians, we need to operate that way as well. You don't find your faith in a crisis; you already have it." As a committed Christian, Ed had something going for him that gave him an inside edge, a confidence that made the difference in this difficult situation.

Our conversation reminded me of the way many people relate to God. They ignore Him most of the time, thinking that at the last minute they will get things squared away spiritually. Some call it a "deathbed conversion," like the thief on the cross who cried out at the last minute.

The mistake lies in thinking that we will always have plenty of time later. The Bible stresses the importance of *now*, of living for God today. If we're on good terms with Him today, when the emergency comes, we'll act instinctively, knowing He is with us.

When Ed safely landed the plane, his passengers applauded. I applaud him as well.

RESOURCE READING: 2 Corinthians 6

February 24

GROWING A KID SO STRONG HE WON'T NEED YOU

There comes a time in the life of every teenager when he can do whatever he wants, because he's beyond the reach of Mom or Dad. How do you grow a kid so strong that he won't need you when you aren't there? That should be the goal of every parent, and there aren't many years in which to lay a proper foundation. I call it giving your child the gift of self-reliance.

It's tough to be a successful parent. The media, the peer pressure among teens, and the number of ways there are to go wrong makes it tough on teens as well. The pressure to go along, to be like everybody else, to push aside what Mom and Dad say— to just "do it"—is very powerful.

What can parent do to help their kids grow up strong? Three key factors can help to produce personal strength in the life of your teenagers.

Factor #1: Family identity. This factor is probably the most important of all. The presence of a father in the home, along with family cohesiveness, is a foundation for personal strength. God designed conception in such a way that two people—a mother and a father—are necessary to bring a child into the world. He also intends for both parents to teach and raise the child.

When the family identity is weak, children seek significance through outside relationships. Their values and worth come from their peers, not their parents.

Factor #2: Independence from the culture and the surrounding world. I'm not talking about raising teens who are reclusive and disconnected from the world. But we must instill in them a self-image strong enough that their self-worth is not derived from the world. Secure kids are okay, and they know it. They don't have to "go along to get along."

Factor #3: A sense of value and self-worth that helps them understand their true importance. Faith in God, and an understanding of their true worth in God's sight and in the minds of their parents is a positive force for good in the life of a teenager. With God's help, you can grow a youngster so strong that when you aren't there, he doesn't need you. And, believe me, you will sleep more soundly as a parent.

RESOURCE READING: Colossians 3:12–21

February 25

GROWING KIDS GOD'S WAY

Here are six gifts that you should give to your child. These gifts cost nothing in terms of money, but are very costly in the currency of time, energy, and emotion. All six are important when it comes to successful parenting, or growing kids God's way.

Gift #1 is time spent together. It's strange how some parents will give their kids almost everything but time. These kids have the latest clothes, electronic games, computers, CDs, and stereos, but they lack time spent with Mom and Dad. The true gift of love is the gift of time and attention.

Gift #2 is self-esteem. Very early in life, we learn either self-esteem or self-depreciation. Every child matures at a different rate. Build self-esteem in your child by avoiding comparisons with other kids, by telling your youngster how proud you are when he or she does well, by accepting her the same in success or failure, by being patient and having realistic expectations.

Gift #3 is self-reliance. Your goal as a parent should be to grow a kid so strong that when you aren't there, he won't need you. Your child will have the same emotional strength as your family. When the parents are strong emotionally, they pass that strength on to their kids.

Gift #4 is a sense of value vs. worth. If you offer a four-year-old boy a bright red toy car or a crisp, new $100 bill, he'll take the shiny toy every time. But as he grows older, he needs to learn the difference between satisfying his biological urges and counting the cost of his decisions in life.

Gift #5 is self-discipline. Psychologists have discovered that children who learn to defer gratification become stronger and more productive as adults. Kids who have the strength to wait develop self-discipline, which makes a significant difference in life.

Gift #6 is faith in God. You cannot give this gift unless you possess it yourself. Faith in God isn't passed on through genetics. The baton of faith is passed from hand to hand when parents live what they talk, and practice what they believe.

How many of these gifts have you given to your child?

RESOURCE READING: Colossians 3:12–21

February 26

GROWING FAMILIES GOD'S WAY

Several years ago, I heard about a building superintendent in Hong Kong who was constructing a wall between his house and his neighbor's. To avoid spending money for bricks, he took a hammer and chisel and began to knock out a few bricks at a time from the basement wall of the building where he worked. Each evening, he carried a few bricks home in a satchel.

He carefully concealed what he was doing by covering the missing bricks with cardboard or pieces of plywood, but after several years, the building began to tilt ever so slightly as the weight of the upper stories began to press down where the bricks had been. Structural engineers were called in to find out why the building had begun to tilt, and that's when they discovered the holes in the basement walls.

Any architect will tell you that the most important part of a building is the foundation. Families are a lot like buildings. Lately, someone has been messing with the foundation, and the family has been weakened as a result. A generation ago, couples married "for better or for worse." When the winds of adversity began to blow, they rode out the storm and kept their marriage together. Not so anymore.

Who swiped the bricks from the family's foundation? Should we blame the attitude of personal fulfillment that says, "If you aren't happy or fulfilled in your marriage, then get out"? Blame the economy that took moms out of the home and into the workforce? Blame the men who father children but don't stick around to raise them? Blame the devil—he did it!

Placing blame doesn't solve the problem, but making the foundation of our homes so strong that no force can cause our lives to sway or bend is tremendously important.

Paul tells the Corinthians that "no one can lay any foundation other than the one already laid, which is Jesus Christ" (1 Corinthians 3:11). Simply put, when God is the foundation upon which your life is built, no one can steal bricks from the foundation of your home and family.

Families today are under stress, and the problems aren't going away. You must strengthen the foundation of your family and raise your voice and your hands against those who would weaken the foundation or the walls of your home. If you don't, who will?

RESOURCE READING: Colossians 3:12–21

GOD'S BLUEPRINT FOR THE FAMILY

In the fourth century, Simeon Stylitis lived atop a pillar to escape the hassles of family living. Many years later, Anatole of France decided to do the same thing. Lacking a suitable pillar, he sat down at the kitchen table, fully intending to spend the rest of his of life in righteous meditation. But when the cook, the housekeeper, and his wife objected, he gave up on the experiment and wrote these words in his diary: "I soon perceived it is a very difficult thing to be a saint while living with your own family."

Anatole's problem still confronts us today! It's hard to be much of a saint if you can't get along at home. Fortunately, God has given us a blueprint for the family. It's simple but strong: Make the foundation faith in God. When you have no spiritual foundation for your life, marriage, and family, the house can collapse when the winds of adversity blow. Build your home on a spiritual foundation, by erecting these four walls:

The wall of commitment. No matter what happens
   in your marriage, trust God for a solution.
   Though divorce is common today, it should
   never be considered as an option. Divorce only
   compounds trouble.
The wall of communication. I put commitment
   before communication, because if your commitment to your spouse is not strong, you won't
   bother trying to communicate, to share your
   heart at a deep and intimate level.
The wall of love. Love is like a fire that must be
   rekindled every morning through acts of kindness, expressions of caring, and mutual support.
The wall of forgiveness. You never stand so tall as

when you bow your heart to say, "I'm sorry; forgive me."

What shall we use for a roof? Nothing could be better than the grace of God, freely given and completely undeserved. Grace is when our awesome, loving God reaches down and puts His strong hand of protection and care on our families to guide, protect, and sustain us.

Escaping the family like Simeon Stylitis isn't the solution. Getting along by the grace of God is the blueprint that still works.

RESOURCE READING: 1 Corinthians 3:10–23

February 28

SECOND-GUESSING GOD

Learning to know God is not like taking a college philosophy course, where you grab a textbook and survey centuries of philosophical thought. You don't size up God the way you would a fellow card player, analyzing the expression on his face and trying to guess what he holds in his hand. God is not a man. He is greater than anything we can anticipate or fathom. When Moses had a direct encounter with God, his face glowed with the imprint of the Almighty.

God is free from the failures that plague mankind. With other people, we are never sure they mean what they say, or that they will do what they tell us. But God is always dependable, even when we don't understand His ways.

God often operates on a different wavelength, and attempting to understand Him using our human rationale doesn't work any better than trying to receive an FM radio station on a shortwave receiver. " 'For my thoughts are not your thoughts, neither are your ways my ways,' declares the LORD. 'As the heavens are higher than the earth, so are my ways higher than your ways and my thoughts than your thoughts'" (Isaiah 55:8–9).

Am I saying that it's impossible to know God? Not for a moment. It's just that we have to learn to trust what we cannot understand and realize that there are some things we have to hold on to by faith until we cross the threshold into His presence. That's what the life of faith and trust is about. Here's Paul's summary of the whole issue: "Oh, what a wonderful God we have! How great are his wisdom and knowledge and riches! How impossible it is for us to understand his decisions and his methods! For who among us can know the mind of the Lord? Who knows enough to be his counselor and guide? And who could ever offer to the Lord enough to induce him to act? For everything comes from God alone. Everything lives by his power, and everything is for his glory. To him be glory evermore" (Romans 11:33–36 TLB).

RESOURCE READING: Romans 11:25–36

February 29

THE CALL TO PURPOSE

S trange, isn't it, that our generation, with its digital technology, Pentium-powered computers, miracle drugs, cosmetic surgery, E-mail, faxes and cellular phones, is plagued with an indefinable restlessness and dissatisfaction—more so than any previous generation.

At one point in his life, Steve Rutenbar was somewhat like that—all six feet, seven inches, 350-plus pounds of him. Here's his story:

After he finished college, Steve married Connie, his college sweetheart, and went into business. Their lives, however, turned a different direction one day when Connie saw an advertisement in a newspaper for a TV game show that was looking for contestants. She mailed in an application. Through a strange set of circumstances, the producer of the show had met Steve before and remembered him as "that big guy" who had a warm, infectious smile. Out of the thousands of applicants, Steve and Connie were chosen as contestants, and they won in a big way. They walked away from the show with $1 million in prize money.

Unlike some who win the lottery and then blow it, Steve made good investments and started his own business when the economy was booming. It soon became apparent that money would never be a problem. But gradually, Steve and Connie came to the realization that there had to be more to life than just living the California dream. The notoriety (just ask him how many newly discovered "friends" wanted to let him in on a great new investment idea), the success, and the affluence still left a feeling of dissatisfaction.

That's when Steve and Connie came to acknowledge that everything they had belonged to the Lord. Soon, Steve walked away from his business. Then, using his knowledge and experience, he began to serve as a pastor, and eventually as a missionary statesman at large. By his life, Steve has demonstrated that the term "Christian businessman" is not an oxymoron. Contrary to what some people believe, it is possible to succeed in business without dishonesty.

He learned the truth of what Jesus taught long ago: "Take heed and beware of covetousness, for one's life does not consist in the abundance of the things he possesses" (Luke 12:15 NKJV). Have you learned that lesson?

RESOURCE READING: Matthew 5

THE LOSS OF THE HOLY

Howard Stern is a talk show host whose trademark is vulgarity and profanity. When Stern appeared on the *Tonight Show,* he held up a Gideon Bible and said, "The Gideon Company is now putting my book in the place of Bibles in hotels."

Annoyed by Stern's comments, Jay Leno replied, "Howard, something horrible is going to happen to you. . . . This book [the Bible] will strike you down as you go down the road. It will go through the windshield and pierce your heart." He continued, "I'm sounding like an evangelist now, but I predict that's what will happen. Suddenly, all that's in this Book is making perfect sense to me."

Touché!

Are you surprised by what Leno said? There is a point at which public outrage demands that we draw a line and say, "Enough is enough!" Why make light of the Bible? Why not pick on the writings of Karl Marx, or something from the pen of Plato? The Bible is a convenient target because not only is it the world's best-selling Book, but it has changed more lives than any other book ever printed.

For centuries, men and women have attacked the Bible, predicting its demise; yet like the old blacksmith who wears out his hammer while the anvil remains, these individuals pass from the scene and this grand old Book remains. Generation after generation have discovered how this Book can give them an understanding of God, themselves, and other people that they could never get any other way.

Now, be honest. If you had been where Jay Leno was when Stern spouted off about the Gideon Bible, would you have raised your voice?

If you answered, "Yes!" to the first question, then tell me this: How long has it been since you last read the Bible?

Are you defending a book that you don't read and take advantage of?

Fifteen minutes a day will take you through the Bible in a year. And those fifteen minutes can bring strength, calmness, and direction for living. It is well worth your time.

RESOURCE READING: 2 Timothy 3

March 2

YEP—THERE IS A DIFFERENCE!

D o you know the difference between boys and girls?" a three year-old girl asked her daddy. Her father was taken aback by the question. He had thought he wouldn't have to talk about such issues until his daughter was much older. Swallowing hard, he answered, "No, what's the difference?"

"Girls wear shower caps," she said, "and boys don't!" Right.

Everybody knows there's a difference, but apart from the obvious physical traits, exactly how we're different and how those differences create misunderstandings between the sexes seems to be a dark secret.

Genetic differences between men and women and how those differences affect our behavior have been the subject of serious scientific study only since the early 1980s. Prior to that, men and women joked about misunderstandings between the sexes but simply wrote them off as cultural or behavioral traits.

At the moment of conception, twenty-three chromosomes from your mother combined with twenty-three from your father to give you your unique genetic code. For the next six weeks, the cells within the ovum multiply rapidly, and between the sixth and eighth weeks following conception, the hypothalamus—the part of your brain that controls respiration, your heart, and a lot of your vital functions—kicked in and began a domino-kind of signal to your body.

From that point on, your body, including your brain, began to take on specific gender characteristics in a marvelous development that ultimately controls the way you think, act, and relate to other people.

What I find interesting is that, for the past two decades, feminists and liberals have been trying to debunk the sexual differences between men and women, while at the same time scientific research has been documenting the fact that men and women are different.

One record has stood down through the ages: "Male and female he created them." Our English word *sex* comes from the Latin word *secare,* which means "to divide." God produced the first prototypes, who were distinctly male and female. As science continues to unlock the secrets of the brain and how it develops, we're bound to discover many more differences, besides the fact that girls wear shower caps and boys don't. The facts of life have never been more apparent.

RESOURCE READING: Genesis 1:27–31

March 3

IT'S ALL IN YOUR HEAD

For centuries, men and women have engaged in the battle of the sexes. The battle lines have been clearly drawn: nature vs. nurture, or genetics vs. environmental development. Lately, it seems that the weight of scientific research has come down on the side of genetics. In simple terms, you were born with sexual characteristics, and though they are influenced by your environment, your behavior is driven by the engine of genetics.

In a very real sense, the differences are all in your head. At least, that's how they begin. "Men and women do not think the same way," says Dr. Joyce Brothers. "Their brains are almost as different as their sex organs. The very idea of male and female brains is startling. Until very recently a brain was a brain was a brain. Now we discover that there is *his* brain and *her* brain."[1]

Here's what scientists have discovered: Among prenatal females, the left side of the brain begins to develop first. Among prenatal males, the right side of the brain begins to develop first. The shape of the two brains is not quite the same and their rate of development differs as well. There are also differences in their ability to withstand stress and how they process information. Male brains are specialized in that they can use both sides separately, even at the same time—while females use both sides of their brains as a unit, which gives them intuitive advantages over men. Because male and female brains are different, the two sexes think differently and act differently. Simply put, men and women are different!

Out of the research comes an observation: Though some may still deny it, men and women came from the drawing board of heaven with sexual differences, and these differences are intended to complement each other's weaknesses. Each side has strengths that the other lacks. By coming together, we complete each other and form a whole—which was God's design for marriage. It is His plan that we *complete* each other, not compete with each other. God's plan makes a complete difference!

RESOURCE READING: Genesis 2:1–18

GIVE ME YOUR CHILD
UNTIL HE IS SIX

The controversial psychologist John Watson once wrote, "Give me a dozen healthy infants, well formed, and my own specified world to bring them up in, and I'll guarantee to take any one at random and train him to become any type of specialist I might select—regardless of his talents, penchants, tendencies, abilities, vocations, and race of his ancestors."

In the old battle between nature and nurture, Watson came down on the side of nurture. He believed that environment, not heredity, shaped a person's destiny. In recent years, however, we have come to realize that heredity is a powerful factor, no matter what the environment.

Nonetheless, Watson points out a powerful truth. Your infant's experiences during the early years profoundly influence what happens later in life. As the sapling is bent, so goes the tree, or as Proverbs 22:6 says, "Train a child in the way he should go, and when he is old he will not turn from it."

If you have a child under age six, stop and ask yourself some tough questions: Are you training, or simply letting your child grow up? Are you taking the path of least resistance because you're too tired or too busy, or are you doing the right thing regardless of fatigue?

Discipline, instruction, taking your child to church, reading to him or her, doing the same thing over and over, day after day, time after time is not easy. It's time consuming and physically taxing. But it's worth it. You win or lose a lot of territory before age six.

Psychologists tell us that a child learns half of everything he knows by age three; three-fourths by age seven. They're not talking about cognitive recall, like algebra or computer science. They're talking about the limits of acceptable behavior, right and wrong, what is rewarded and what is punished.

It's easy to be a parent, tough to be a good one; but one thing is for certain: Once you've made a human being in your image, you bear the responsibility of that child. God honors our commitment of time, effort, prayer, and care. Though it seems your preschool youngster will never grow up, you'll look back and be amazed how quickly these years went.

RESOURCE READING: Proverbs 12

March 5

WE THINK DIFFERENTLY

Your brain is divided into two hemispheres connected by nerve fibers. The right side of your brain controls the left side of your body, and vice versa. If you are female, the left side of your brain began to develop earlier than the right side. In addition to motor ability on the ride side of your body, the left side of your brain controls your ability to talk, read, and verbalize thoughts. "We use the left side of the brain," says one authority on human development, "when we read a newspaper, sing a sing, play bridge, or write a letter."[1]

This early left brain development results in a woman's ability to talk circles around the men in her life. Talking is a woman's natural expression of her nature, and she wishes that listening was a man's dominant trait.

The right side of the brain, which develops first in male brains, allows us to see the big picture. We use the right side of the brain "when we consult a road map, thread our way through a maze, work a jigsaw puzzle, design a house, plan a garden, recognize a face, paint a picture, possibly when we listen to music, definitely when we solve a problem in geometry," says Dr. Joyce Brothers.[2]

The right side of the brain is also used to do math, which explains why males tend to be better at math and science than women, though there are exceptions to every generalization.

Neither way is "better" than the other. The simple reality is that we are different. Each sex is unique, and our uniqueness translates into skills that appear stronger in one sex than the other. Understanding the differences helps to bring harmony and eliminate competition.

Function is the result of design. Instead of trying to force men and women into the same mold, it is high time we recognized what Moses knew 3,000 years ago. God made both men and women in His image and equipped them to do tasks that complement each other. Understanding our differences, and respecting them, is the key to harmony and happiness.

RESOURCE READING: Genesis 3:17–24

March 6

RESPECTING THOSE DIFFERENCES

Nearly two hundred years ago, Matthew Henry wrote that when God made woman, he did not take a bone from Adam's foot so he could trample a woman under his feet. Nor did he take a bone from Adam's head so he could dominate her. Instead he took a rib from under his arm so he could protect her, and close to his heart so he could love her.

Although God gave men the instinct to lead, He never gave them license to dominate or abuse. Peter tells husbands to "be considerate as you live with your wives, and treat them with respect as the weaker partner and as heirs with you of the gracious gift of life, so that nothing will hinder your prayers" (1 Peter 3:7).

When sexual differences are respected, individual needs can be met in marriage. Ambrose Bierce writes that "marriage consists of a master, a mistress, and two slaves, making in all just two." God never intended for sexual differences to pit men and women against each other in an unending battle of the sexes. It was His intention to let those differences meet each other's needs—for each one's strength to play the other's weaknesses, to allow each to complement the other. When a couple forms a bond in marriage, it allows each partner to meet the needs of his or her mate in such a way that each derives a level of satisfaction and happiness that can come no other way.

Interdependence in marriage produces harmony and happiness. The concept of absolute independence just doesn't work. A plus and a minus produce a whole, but two minuses only produce negative feelings and emotions. When each person learns what part he or she plays in a marriage, a team spirit develops.

The third result of understanding our differences is an intimacy that touches every part of a person's life. Far more than merely sexual, intimacy is a union that includes the spiritual, emotional, and physical parts of our beings.

Following God's orders in relation to our differences is not only good for a marriage, it is good for the individuals involved. You just can't improve on God's way.

RESOURCE READING: Ephesians 5:22–32

KNOWING WHO YOU ARE
WHEN THE WINDS BLOW

In a day and age when self-esteem has been raised almost to the level of a religion, many of us struggle to keep a sense of balance. During the past decade, we've heard that knowing who you are—having a healthy sense of self-esteem—is the key to preventing juvenile delinquency, getting a handle on job advancement, and generally feeling good about life. Others would say that the importance of self-esteem has been grossly exaggerated.

Meanwhile, you're caught in the middle, not knowing what to think. Some days you feel on top of the world; but other days you feel like a worm. Maybe most days you feel pretty worthless and unable to break out of the depression that has taken you captive. Instead of waking up in the morning with a "go get 'em" attitude, you want to pull the covers up over your head or crawl into the nearest hole.

To get a handle on your true self-worth, you must understand how God views your life. Go back to the events on the original Good Friday—the infamous day when Jesus was crucified at the hands of Roman soldiers outside the city of Jerusalem. Why was He there? And what does His death have to do with your worth as a person?

The only reason that God allowed Jesus to come to Earth and die was because He considered you to be a person worth saving. He created you in His own image, but sin took you far away from the kind of a relationship that God intended. The cross of Jesus Christ is the balance between the overly inflated opinion that some have of themselves and the "worm mentality" that says you are less than nothing.

My old sinful nature destroyed the image of God in my life, but I also recognize that being spiritually reborn makes me a child of the Father. I know I'm not an orphan in the world.

All of God's children go through trials, times of testing, and dark valleys. Because I am a son of God, I can trust the promises of the Father to walk with me and sustain me.

There are times when you've got to tell your emotions where to get off, and refuse to believe your feelings. That's how you move from uncertainty to faith.

RESOURCE READING: Romans 7:21–8:4

March 8

WHEN YOU FEEL BEATEN UP BY CIRCUMSTANCES

When Jim lost his job at age forty-five, he struggled with feelings of self-worth. With a master's degree in physics, he had worked for an aerospace company for almost twenty years. Another year and he would have earned a healthy pay increase and retirement benefits. In fact, that's why his company replaced him with a woman half his age at half the salary.

What do you do when you feel beaten up by the circumstances of life? Sit at home and feel sorry for yourself? Kick the dog? If you have a relationship with the Father through His Son—remind yourself of the following truths:

Guideline #1: You are God's child. When you feel beaten up by circumstances, remind yourself that feelings of worthlessness don't come from God. They are driven by your circumstances, but when you go back to the Word you remember that God is your Father.

Guideline #2: God never promised to exempt you from trouble, but to be with you in trouble. In Isaiah 43, God promises when you go through the waters, He will be with you; when you face the fire, you will not be burned; when you go through the flood, you will not be overwhelmed. We live in an imperfect, broken world. On occasion, we will suffer circumstances that beat us up, but this isn't the last chapter.

Guideline #3: Nothing is forever. That's hard to believe when you are a physicist and the only job opening is for a cook at a local greasy spoon restaurant. You begin wondering if you are worth more than an entry-level salary. Instead of thinking of your situation as fatal, think of it as an opportunity to explore new areas of possibility and regroup.

Guideline #4: Do your part while God does His. God does for us what we can't do ourselves, but He probably won't motivate someone to call you out of the blue with a job offer. Get out there and knock on doors, follow up with friends in the business or industry, place applications and put your best foot forward. Then trust God to open the door and await His timing with patience.

It is the connection with your Father in heaven that keeps you from getting beat up by the circumstances of life.

RESOURCE READING: Romans 8:18–28

TOO MUCH OF A GOOD THING
SPELLS TROUBLE

For the past couple of decades, self-esteem has been touted as the answer to many of society's problems. "There is this idea," says psychology professor Roy Baumeister of Case Western Reserve University, "that raising self-esteem will help prevent crime, drug abuse, and teen pregnancy. But the links are weak, tenuous, and inconsistent."

Professor Baumeister and two others published data from various studies on aggression, crime, and violence spanning more than seventy years—the most definitive research ever done on the subject of self-esteem. They concluded that self-esteem isn't the answer to our societal woes. To the contrary, they proved quite conclusively that "people with violent impulses suffer from excessive self-esteem," whether it's the schoolyard bully, the husband who abuses his wife, or the driver who makes obscene gestures and tries to run others off the road.

If low self-esteem were an underlying cause of violence, contends Baumeister, then shy, self-deprecating, insecure, and depressed individuals would be the ones causing trouble. Instead, it's individuals who have an inflated opinion of themselves who feel challenged by other drivers, or become angry when their spouses point out flaws in their logic. In Baumeister's view, what some people think of as self-esteem is actually unvarnished ego and pride, which spells trouble when it comes to relating to other people.

I am convinced that knowing who you are in the sight of God, and understanding His viewpoint, is the key to this whole issue. The cross of Jesus Christ tells me that the God who first created Adam in His image also considered us to be worth the price of His dear Son. The record is clear: "God made him [that is, Christ] who had no sin to be sin for us, so that in him we might become the righteousness of God" (2 Corinthians 5:21).

When we leave God out of the equation of life, we are bound to come up with skewed, off-balance images of ourselves. To understand the building, we must consult with the architect, get his viewpoint, and see things according to his blueprint. Our understanding of human nature will never be balanced until we view life from God's perspective. That's where the Bible comes in.

An inflated opinion of ourselves is just as deadly as not knowing who we really are.

RESOURCE READING: Jeremiah 1:1–10

March 10

LESSONS FROM OUR FEATHERED FRIENDS

A friend of *Guidelines* sent me the following information under the heading "Lessons from Geese." These facts about geese—and the lessons we can learn—are too good to overlook.

Fact #1: As each goose flaps its wings, it creates an updraft for the geese flying behind. By flying together in a V formation, the flock increases its range by 71 percent. What's the obvious lesson? By working together, we can fly higher and travel farther than going it alone.

Fact #2: When a goose falls out of formation, it suddenly feels the drag and resistance of flying alone. By recognizing our dependence on others and respecting our relationships, we'll all go further, faster, and easier, and accomplish far more than trying to go the distance alone.

Fact #3: When the lead goose tires, it rotates back in the formation and another goose flies to the point position. In a sense, geese are much smarter than their human counterparts whose egos are often so huge that they refuse to let others provide leadership.

Fact #4: Geese flying in formation honk to encourage those up front to keep up their speed. Encouraging each other is so important when it comes to increasing production and a sense of well-being. Whether it is your child, an employee, or a friend, encouragement can make the difference between success and failure.

Fact #5: When a goose gets sick, wounded, or shot down, two geese drop out of formation and follow it down to help and protect it. They stay with it until it dies or is able to fly again. Writing to the Galatians, Paul said, "Brothers, if someone is caught in a sin, you who are spiritual should restore him gently. But watch yourself, or you also may be tempted. Carry each other's burdens, and in this way you will fulfill the law of Christ" (Galatians 6:1–2). Humans tend to shoot their wounded instead of nurturing them and helping them work through their problems.

Fact #6: Geese mate for life. Who said that animals and birds are dumb? In many cases their instincts far exceed those who stand on the ground and watch them fly overhead.

RESOURCE READING: Ecclesiastes 4

THE RIGHT TO BE HAPPY

How would you complete this statement: "If I just had
_____, I would be happy!" Someone
might say, "If I just got married, I'd be happy," or "If I
could get these creditors off my back, I'd be happy," or "If
my health improved, I'd be happy." Whatever your
response, I think you'd agree that most people want to be
happy. As Robert Louis Stevenson once said, "The world is
so full of a number of things, I'm sure we should all be as
happy as kings."

But the fact is, we're not always happy. Happiness in life
is conditional. It usually depends on our circumstances,
environment, achievements, and pleasure. Like a beautiful
sunset that gradually fades to dusk, happiness is usually
momentary and fleeting.

Has our culture placed far too much emphasis on
happiness?

One of C. S. Lewis's last articles was titled, "We Have
No Right to Happiness." Said Lewis, "A right to happiness
doesn't make much more sense than a right to be six feet tall,
or to have a millionaire for a father, or to get good weather
whenever you want to have a picnic." Even though "our
technological skill may help us to survive a little longer," he
continued, "our civilization will have died at heart and will
be swept away" when happiness becomes our driving quest
and goal in life.

There is something far more important than happiness:
Joy. Happiness is the world's substitute for true joy. What's
the difference?

Happiness depends on circumstances; joy transcends our
circumstances. (You can be joyful even when you aren't
happy.)

Happiness involves your environment—your home, money,

friends, health; but joy is internal; it comes from within.

Happiness is temporary; joy abides and remains when beauty fades.

Happiness has little to do with God; joy has everything to do with Him.

Happiness is material; joy is spiritual.

Happiness involves your life here and now; joy encompasses time and eternity.

When you find God, you discover joy; and when you joyfully do God's will, you'll stumble over happiness. No one is ever happier than being where God wants him—no matter where it is.

RESOURCE READING: Hebrews 13:1–10

March 12

WHAT YOU BELIEVE MAKES A DIFFERENCE

What is faith?" asks the writer of the book of Hebrews. He answers his own question by saying, "It is the confident assurance that something we want is going to happen. It is the certainty that what we hope for is waiting for us, even though we cannot see it up ahead" (Hebrews 11:1 TLB).

Biblical faith has two aspects, without which it is defective. The first ingredient is belief, which relates to our knowledge, and the second is trust, which demands commitment and action. Believing is important, but by itself it isn't enough.

Suppose you wanted to hire a person for a position in your company. After an interview, you make an offer and look expectantly at the candidate for a reply. After a long moment of silence, the job seeker says hesitantly, "Well, I believe you can make good on your offer, but frankly, I just don't trust you!"

How would you respond? There is no way you would bring that person into your firm, right? At times, we treat God the same way. We believe He exists, and we even believe His word is true, but we don't trust Him enough to commit ourselves to Him and walk with Him.

Unlike employers who make promises and don't keep them, or friends who forget what they tell you, God is never remiss on coming through with what He says He will do. The foundation of our faith in God is His character. Because people fail us, we often bring God down to their level, wondering if He really can be trusted as well. We forget the times when He has met us in the past.

Your earthly father may not be trustworthy, but your heavenly Father is. The Bible puts it pointedly: "God is not a man, that he should lie, nor a son of man, that he should change his mind. Does he speak and then not act? Does he promise and not fulfill?" (Numbers 23:19). And the obvious answer is, "No!"

The Quaker scholar David Elton Trueblood put it well as he said, "Faith is not belief without proof, but trust without reservation." Believing is important, but trusting is what brings the promises into our lives and our families. Real faith includes both.

RESOURCE READING: Hebrews 11:1–7

March 13

FAITH'S FOUNDATION

At the end of World War II, in one of the Nazi concentration camps, some Allied soldiers found a Star of David carved into a wall with these words beneath it: "I believe in the sun—even when it does not shine. I believe in love—even when it is not shown. I believe in God—even when He does not speak." These poignant words were a statement of faith by someone who had chosen to hold on despite the dark circumstances.

What you believe determines what you are. Faith in God gives people dignity and lets them live with purpose, even in the darkness. How can we have that kind of faith?

First, we must realize that faith is necessary no matter how dark the hour. The Bible says that "anyone who comes to him must believe that he exists and that he rewards those who earnestly seek him" (Hebrews 11:6).

Second, our faith must be simple. Jesus used the analogy of a little child to help His disciples understand faith. There will always be a tension between our circumstances and our faith. But a little child doesn't know enough to worry. He simply places his trust in the one who has promised to care for him.

Third, we must believe in the power of God. Our faith is only as valid as its object, and the object of our faith is God and His power. "All things are possible to him who believes," says Jesus in Mark 9:23 (NKJV). On two occasions, He used the analogy of a faith so strong it could move mountains. Impossible, right? Of course. But the point that Jesus was making was this: "What is impossible with men is possible with God."

Fourth, we must wait for the reward of faith. "According to your faith will it be done to you," Jesus told a blind man who recovered his sight (Matthew 9:29). Augustine put it this way: "Faith is believing what we do not see, and the result of faith is seeing what we believe." Some say that God no longer does the miraculous, and for them, nothing much miraculous ever happens. But for those who simply trust God, it is amazing what happens. Faith does make a difference.

RESOURCE READING: Hebrews 11:24–31

March 14

TRUST AND OBEY

Men and women who have made a mark for God share three common traits: 1) They respond without hesitation to the call of God in their lives; 2) Their simple faith is marked by complete obedience; and 3) They give what they have to the Lord completely and without reservation.

Abraham fit the profile of someone God could use. When called by God, he took his family and his possessions and set out on a long trek through the wilderness. The book of Hebrews says, "By faith Abraham, when called to go to a place he would later receive as his inheritance, obeyed and went, even though he did not know where he was going" (Hebrews 11:8). Did you notice that last phrase? He did not know where he was going.

Stepping out in faith to trust God often puts us out of step with the crowd. Many have been ridiculed for walking away from the comforts of life to follow the Almighty. When called a fool for what he was doing, Oswald Chambers responded, "I am not many kinds of fools in one; only one kind, the kind that believes and obeys God."

Obedience does not require full knowledge of the game plan. It only requires confidence in the one you are following. When you come to the place where you believe with all your heart that God can be trusted, no matter how foolish it may appear, and you make a commitment to serve Him, someone will ridicule you and try to make you feel stupid.

Faith demands a commitment of the heart, but obedience demands a commitment of your feet. You see, faith has two parts. The first is intellectual. It concerns what you believe. The second is trust, and that involves actions. The Bible says of Abraham, "He obeyed and went."

For the child of God, obedience is not an option, it is a command. When we are confronted with a command, we have two choices: obey or disobey. There is no third option.

Abraham was not perfect, but he was obedient, and God rewarded his obedience. The same God will provide for you as you trust Him and walk in simple obedience.

RESOURCE READING: Hebrews 11:8–12

March 15

THE TESTING OF YOUR FAITH

George Mueller spent most of his life in Christian work, operating an orphanage in England that over the years fed, clothed, and housed more than ten thousand children. Despite the enormous costs of such an enterprise—more than eight million dollars in nineteenth-century currency—Mueller never asked anyone for money—not once. His secret was faith in God. He prayed, and God answered.

On the subject of faith, Mueller wrote, "Faith is the assurance that the thing which God has said in His word is true, and that God will act according to what He has said in His word. This assurance, this reliance on God's Word, this confidence, is faith."

How do we find the courage to act on what we already know? In the Bible we read dozens of wonderful promises, but for many of us, there is a gulf between what we believe theoretically and what we put into practice in our lives.

The real struggle is often a matter of will. We want to be completely in control of our destiny instead of trusting in the promises of God. No wonder God allows our faith to be tested, for only then can we be sure that God has met us at the point of our need.

We all want the blessing of God's deliverance, but it takes testing to help us see that God is there and that He keeps His word. Human nature being what it is, we'd just as soon skip the challenge. We want deliverance without going through the fire and flood.

During periods of testing, faith is holding on to what we know is true. We won't understand everything, but if we keep on trusting and awaiting God's provision and deliverance, we will see His power.

With God's demand for simple obedience comes His promise to provide and protect. For George Mueller, it was trusting God to provide for the orphans of Britain. For you, it may be trusting God for your daily bread, or the strength to get through another day. The good news is that Jesus Christ is the same "yesterday and today and forever." We can trust God. He fulfills His promises.

RESOURCE READING: Philippians 1

March 16

HOW TO GET GREAT FAITH

G. K. Chesterton tells the story of a yachtsman who set sail from England, determined to reach an exotic South Sea island. After many stormy days at sea, he sighted land. Beaching his boat, he ventured inland, where he discovered a pagan temple. Determined to claim it for England, he scaled the walls and planted the Union Jack at its pinnacle, only to discover that he was standing atop the Brighton Pavilion on England's south coast. He thought he had sailed in a straight line, but the storm had blown him off course. He had gone in a circle without knowing it.

We smile at the comedy of the error, yet more than a few people I know have launched out in the venture of faith, only to hit stormy waters and lose their way. How can we keep from becoming lost in the storms of life? The following guidelines will help you when the winds blow.

Guideline #1: Learn about the nature and character of God. Faith rests upon the character of God. What we know of God, we have gleaned from the Bible, which has been a map for pilgrims and travelers for centuries.

Guideline #2: The winds of testing will strengthen your faith when you remain steadfast. Some Christians seem to think they should never have to face problems. They are the ones who become disappointed. Remember, God never promised to exempt us from storms, but to be with us and to take us through the storms.

Guideline #3: God is still in charge no matter how hard the wind blows. Sometimes when the storm is raging, your heart cries out, "Why me?" Remember, every storm will pass, and God will never leave you in the lurch.

Guideline #4: The walk of faith is one step at a time, one day at a time, one problem at a time. God's will is like a flashlight in a dungeon: It doesn't shine around corners, but it gives you enough light for the next step. That's as far as you need to go for today.

RESOURCE READING: Philippians 1:12–30

March 17

WWJD?

By now you've no doubt seen the letters WWJD? on bumper stickers, bracelets, necklaces, and a variety of trinkets and jewelry. The letters stand for "What Would Jesus Do?" based on a fictional story by Charles Sheldon titled *In His Steps*. The author, who was a liberal Congregational minister and an advocate of "social reform," wrote of a variety of social situations in which the characters ask, "What would Jesus do?"

Not bad—or is it? In a recently published article in *Viewpoint* magazine, Gary Johnson suggests that most people don't know which Jesus we're talking about. Is it the One espoused by the Mormons, Jehovah's Witnesses, or the Jesus acknowledged by Muslims?

Johnson contends that most folks wouldn't like the real Jesus, the One who spent long periods of time in prayer and denounced the religious establishment of His day. Yet this same Jesus tenderly held little children in His arms and blessed them saying, "Of such is the kingdom of heaven."

I agree with Johnson's premise that a lot of us don't know much about the real Jesus, the One who lived among us for thirty-three years, who died at the hands of the Romans, but who broke the shackles of death and rose again after three days.

"What would Jesus do?" The question becomes even more poignant when we realize it was Jesus who taught that love is greater than hatred, that he who would save his life must be willing to give it up, that there is dignity in serving instead of demanding to be served, that there is virtue in touching the untouchables—the fallen of life, the poor and neglected, the not-so-charming.

Far too often, the real problem is not that we don't know what to do, but that we don't want to do it. What Jesus taught runs counter to our culture, our old nature, and the norms of modern life.

Knowing what Jesus did and then doing it is a clear reflection of what God wills. The two are synonymous. In one of his letters, John puts it so clearly: "The world and its desires pass away, but the man who does the will of God lives forever" (1 John 2:17). How could it be clearer?

Resource reading: 1 John 2

March 18

UNDERNEATH ARE
THE EVERLASTING ARMS

T he eternal God is your refuge," says Deuteronomy 33:27, "and underneath are the everlasting arms." What does that mean? Obviously, the first part means that God, who is without beginning or end, will always be a refuge, One to whom we can turn in times of trouble. But what does it mean that "underneath are the everlasting arms"?

"Underneath means underneath," says George Stormont, a British-born pastor now approaching his tenth decade. No matter how low you are, God will still be there beneath you, to support you and lift you up.

God is underneath your lowest emotions and your darkest night. What was the lowest point of your life? Maybe it was when your doctors diagnosed cancer and your spirits dropped. Maybe it was when you lost your job or your spouse left you. Whether or not you felt the strong hand of God, it was still beneath you. Never will you be in a pit so deep that God will not be there.

God will always be underneath your deepest loss. The firm hand of God can take the broken pieces of your life or business and put them back together again. God specializes in this sort of thing, and He's had lots of experience doing it, too.

Even underneath your most shameful act, the everlasting arms are there to pick you up and reestablish your feet.

There is a big difference between discipline and punishment. Because God loves you, He allows the circumstances of life to discipline you, but then His strong hands—the same ones that kept you from total destruction—pick you up, smooth away the hurt and pain, and help you get up on your feet again.

Whether your most shameful act is something known only between you and God, or it made the front page of the newspaper, God's grace covers the wrong, and His forgiveness will make the difference.

The promises of God are not reserved for a handful of saints ready for immediate promotion to heaven. God plays no favorites. Underneath are His everlasting arms. They are underneath your lowest emotion, your deepest loss, and your most shameful act. Mark in your Bible that great promise found in Deuteronomy 33. And put your name on it.

RESOURCE READING: Deuteronomy 33

March 19

HOW DO YOU RESTORE A CONNECTION WITH GOD?

H ow does a person restore a connection with God?" a friend of mine asked. Like so many who have drifted away from the warmth of the Father's love, this young woman had sustained a tragic loss. When her brother had been brutally murdered, her heart cried out, "God, why did You let this happen? Where were You when my brother needed Your help?"

Down in their hearts, people who blame God for the pain and disappointments of life know that He isn't the One who caused the problem. They've simply turned and walked away because He didn't step in to reverse the tide of evil or the wickedness that broke the tranquillity and order of their lives.

Then, perhaps, a little child begins asking about God, or a friend lies at the point of death, or in the darkness of their souls they begin thinking about how it used to be, how at one time the joy of the Lord was real and the presence of God seemed so close and meaningful.

How do we restore a broken connection with God? Just by asking the question and facing the issue we recognize the deep longing in our hearts to connect with God.

When David realized that the affair with Bathsheba had broken his connection with God, he prayed, pouring out his heart and honestly telling God how he felt (see Psalm 51). That's the first step. Realize that God is far more willing to embrace you and draw you to Himself than you are to be embraced or drawn.

Remember, God was not the One who moved. You did. So come back. As Paul told Timothy, "Even when we are too weak to have any faith left, he remains faithful to us and will help us, for he cannot disown us who are part of himself, and he will always carry out his promises to us" (2 Timothy 2:13 TLB).

Faithfulness is God's nature. His love never changes, and His desire for fellowship never lessens, despite your detour from His presence.

Draw a line and step across it. Leave the past behind and choose to walk with the Lord. Get back to church, dust off your Bible, and start reading it. Underline it, memorize it, and realize it's God's love letter to you personally. It's time to restore that broken connection.

RESOURCE READING: Psalm 51

PEACE WITH GOD

I have been producing *Guidelines* since 1963. Over the years, only God knows how many have responded, pouring out their hearts. Many of those who write tell about the unrest and discontentment of a broken relationship with God: the girl who feels estranged from God since she aborted her unborn child; the father who walked out on his wife and children.

"Dear Dr. Sala," wrote one young woman, "More than anything else, I would like to know that I have peace with God."

How do you make peace with God? In a war, both sides of the conflict draw lines and build fortifications with a no-man's-land in between. Sometimes we build fortifications in our lives and never allow the sunlight of God's love to penetrate. We raise the drawbridge and hurl our angry thoughts and words against God, as though He were the enemy. He's not.

God sent His Son, unarmed, to make peace with us. The Son walked across a vast no-man's-land—the dark valley between the mortal and the immortal that separates us from God—and was born at Bethlehem. Jesus made it clear that His Father is not an angry enemy who is out to get us. Jesus says, "Peace I leave with you; my peace I give you. I do not give to you as the world gives. Do not let your hearts be troubled and do not be afraid" (John 14:27).

First, we must understand that God wants us to have peace with Him. God's Son came to show us how to find His peace, to drive away the darkness of fear and the bitterness of loneliness.

The second step to peace with God is to understand that God made Christ to be sin for us so that we might be accepted, without guilt, in God's sight. This enables God to forgive our sins, our rebellion and our wrongdoing. Forgiveness, however, isn't automatic. We have to ask for it, confessing our sin. That's our part of the process—the equivalent of running up the white flag and surrendering.

Then what happens? God says, "I, even I, am he who blots out your transgressions, for my own sake, and remembers your sins no more" (Isaiah 43:25). That's good news, friend. When you know that God has forgiven you, His peace fills your heart.

RESOURCE READING: 1 Peter 2

March 21

PASSING THE TORCH OF FAITH

New Yorker Max Jukes neither believed in Jesus Christ nor the importance of Christian training. He never went to church, nor would he allow his children to go. Interestingly, of the 1,026 descendants who are traceable to this man, 300 were sentenced to prison for an assortment of crimes, 680 became alcoholics, and 190 of the women were known prostitutes.

At the same time, there lived a godly minister named Jonathan Edwards. His children were in church weekly. In their home the Bible was read daily, and family prayers were a common occurrence. Counted among his 929 descendants were 430 ministers, 86 university professors, 13 university presidents, 5 U. S. congressmen, and 2 senators.

When God talked about the influence of the fathers upon their children to the third and fourth generation, he was describing the cause-and-effect relationship between generations.

A generation ago, many people had parents or grandparents who were Christians. Though they didn't always live as they should, they were clearly committed to the principles of Scripture and identified with Jesus Christ. Families stuck together, and couples didn't divorce simply because they couldn't get along. They went to church, paid taxes, and supported each other in the family and the community. Many people today grow up in homes where there is no mention of God apart from profanity, no religious training, and no sense of moral right and wrong.

Though church attendance is still significant, godliness and righteousness run very shallow. We speak of freedom as though it means "freedom from," as in freedom from duty, responsibility, parenthood, or accepting the consequences of our behavior.

Are we so far gone that there is no hope of returning to the values of the past? Absolutely not! But the consequences of our failures can't be canceled with government spending, or by fainthearted messages about how to "feel good" about ourselves.

God's solution remains unchanged: "If my people, who are called by my name, will humble themselves and pray and seek my face and turn from their wicked ways, then will I hear from heaven and will forgive their sin and will heal their land" (2 Chronicles 7:14).

RESOURCE READING: 2 Chronicles 7:11–22

March 22

THE TEST OF
YOUR CHARACTER

When the British ship *Caravan* sailed into Rangoon Harbor on July 13, 1913, a young American couple, Adoniram and Nancy Judson disembarked with great anticipation. The welcome was not what they had expected. They were greeted by a minor official who told them they were unwanted in Burma, and that the best thing they could do would be to get back on the ship and go somewhere else. They decided to stay.

On the voyage over, Nancy's first child was stillborn, but a little boy was born during their first year in Rangoon. Six months later, they buried him. Then war broke out between Burma and Britain. The Judsons were Americans, but the Burmese didn't know the difference. Because he looked and spoke like an Englishman, Adoniram was arrested and placed in a death prison—a wretched place of disease and filth. Meanwhile, Nancy died after giving birth to another baby— and then the baby died as well.

After his release from prison, Adoniram Judson broke under the strain and suffered a nervous breakdown. On top of all this, during the first seven years he lived in Burma, Judson did not have one single convert to Christianity—not even a child. How do you suppose his supporters back home perceived his ministry? He wasn't exactly "knocking them dead" with success.

How much does it take for a man, even a stubborn man, to say, "Enough! I've had it," and go home? But the word *quit* wasn't in Adoniram Judson's vocabulary. He persevered and today we look back and call him the father of Christianity in Burma.

What would happen if we all had the strength to persevere? When Judson was not well received, people began scornfully calling him "Jesus Christ's man in Burma," thus unintentionally bestowing on him the highest compliment. The term *Christian* was first used to ridicule followers of Jesus Christ, but it became a badge of honor among believers. Jesus said, "Woe to you when all men speak well of you, for that is how their fathers treated the false prophets" (Luke 6:26).

The purpose of today's selection is to remind you that

the real test of your character is what it takes to stop you. Think about it.

RESOURCE READING: Galatians 6

March 23

IS GOD ON YOUR SIDE?

When the United States divided over the slavery issue, someone asked Abraham Lincoln if God was on his side. Lincoln replied candidly that he didn't know if God was on *his* side, but it made a great deal of difference whether or not he was on God's side. There is a great deal of comfort in thinking that God is on our side, but the question really is, "Am I on God's side?" We need to ask, "Is what I am doing, or what I intend to do, consistent with what God wants me to do?"

One of the games we play is pretending we are doing God's will when we are actually disobeying Him. People say things like, "God can't expect me to be miserable in my marriage. After all, God wants us happy, doesn't He?"

A long time ago, at the foot of Mt. Sinai, God confronted His people, who had been disobedient. After Moses had received the Law, he was coming down from the mountain when he heard voices singing and saw the people worshipping a golden calf. In anger, Moses destroyed the image and confronted his brother Aaron, who had created the idol. Aaron explained that he had taken gold jewelry from the people and "threw it into the fire," and "out came this calf."

Right. Who would believe an unlikely story like that? Certainly not Moses. In response, he cried out, "All of you who are on the Lord's side, come over here and join me" (Exodus 32:26 TLB). The Levites responded and stood with

Moses, who stood on God's side.

Are you on God's side? There is much to be said about standing where God stands. Though you may lose a few skirmishes, you will ultimately win the battle. In the meantime, peace will fill your heart, because you know that God cares about you and will not forget you as His child.

How do you know whether or not you are on God's side? Study and memorize God's Word. In the Bible, God clearly spells out the life principles that we need to find happiness and fulfillment. When we willfully violate God's Word, we must never, under any circumstances, allow ourselves to think that God is on our side. Think about it.

RESOURCE READING: Exodus 32

March 24

DELINQUENCY IS PREDICTABLE

D r. Sala, I was at a point of absolute desperation. . ."
As I read the letter of a young woman deserted by her husband, in poor health, and bearing the responsibility of a family without a means of support, I got to thinking about the number of people who came to Jesus at the same point in their lives: the woman rejected by society, who confronted Jesus at the well of Sychar; the politician Zacchaeus, who was despised and hated by his peers; the sisters Mary and Martha, whose brother Lazarus was dying. Most of the people who came to Jesus for help were driven there by their desperation.

Desperation has a way of stripping us of our pride, taking away our human resources, and forcing us to reach for the help that only God can give. Is that wrong? Is it cowardice to turn to God in the time of need?

When people turned to Jesus in desperation, He never rebuked them for coming to Him. He never said, "Why bother coming to Me when everything else has failed?" Instead, with compassion and kindness He reached out to them and said, "Come to me, all you who are weary and burdened, and I will give you rest. Take my yoke upon you and learn from me, for I am gentle and humble in heart, and you will find rest for your souls" (Matthew 11:28–29). No one was ever turned away empty-handed.

Why is it that we wait until we are desperate before we reach out for God's help? Ask the two-year-old who refuses his mother's help, saying, "I do it myself." Our fierce drive for independence becomes a stumbling block that keeps us from reaching out to Him who alone can change our lives.

Friend, are you at a point of desperation in your life? Why not close your door, turn off the TV, and humbly get on your knees before God and tell Him exactly where you are and what bothers you? You will make the greatest discovery of your life, the discovery that God is alive and will meet you as He has met men and women down through the centuries. Our desperation is God's opportunity.

RESOURCE READING: 2 Chronicles 32

March 25

DRIVEN TO THE ALMIGHTY

After a successful career in Hollywood, Milo retired, thinking that at last he would have time to enjoy life and do some of the things he had never had time to do. Then his wife of many years died, and the emptiness of his life grew more oppressive. He had everything that money could buy, but what he wanted most could not be bought for any price.

Day by day, Milo grew more lonely and depressed. He thought about ending his life, but was troubled at the prospect of meeting God as the result of suicide. Eventually pain overcame his reason. He closed the blinds of his little home and sat alone for a week in the darkness, crying most of the time, never going outside. Then he made his decision. Life wasn't worth living. *Surely,* he thought, *God will understand.*

He turned on all the gas burners on the stove and walked into the living room. Before he lay down on the sofa, he turned on the radio and scanned the stations. He heard the sound of organ music, and began listening to drown out the hiss of the escaping gas that would soon end his life.

When the organ music stopped, Paul Evans, the speaker on the *Haven of Rest* radio program, began to talk about an answer to the loneliness and pain of life. Milo was convinced that God was speaking directly to Him. At last there was hope. Milo jumped to his feet, ran to the kitchen, and turned off the gas.

Desperation can be a good thing if it strips us of our defenses, but not if it causes us to give up hope. One of the characteristics of Christianity is that God's promises give us a hope that drives away pessimism, despair, and desperation. Jesus promises us that "all that the Father gives me will come to me, and whoever comes to me I will never drive away" (John 6:37). *The Message* puts it, "And once that person is with me, I hold on and don't let go." That's good news.

Desperation can be a friend if it drives you to the feet of Him who loves you and died for you. Responding to God's love and compassion is the only thing that really makes sense.

RESOURCE READING: Matthew 11:25–30

March 26

YOUTHFUL JUVENILES

"Teenage Time Bombs" read the cover story of a recent news magazine depicting the growing problem of juvenile crime. The experts' gloomy prediction is that things will get much worse before they get better. By the year 2010, the number of juvenile criminals is expected to increase by one-third.

What's the answer? Treat juveniles as adults and impose harsher sentences? Build more substantial prisons and a lot more of them? Confronting delinquents with the reality and the severity of what they have done is something that should have been done years ago. Responsibility is something to be learned early in life. The older a person is before he learns the consequences of his actions, the more difficult the lesson.

Not only should we hold juveniles accountable for their actions, but I'd like to see society hold parents accountable as well. Why should they be absolved of responsibility for producing the delinquent in the first place? Why should a father who sires offspring and then walks away not be held accountable?

The great failure isn't the generation that has made gangs their families; it's the parents who abandoned these kids to the streets.

Every teenager has three basic emotional needs that must be satisfied: 1) to give and receive love, 2) to feel worthwhile to herself and to others, and 3) to have a sense of security. When parents are not there and cease to meet those needs, teens turn to each other, often in self-destructing patterns. When Daddy isn't there to provide hugs, a girl often reaches for love and affection from the wrong sources.

The sad thing to me is that the future of a teenager who runs headlong into the anger of society is pretty grim. With no sense of morality or right and wrong, and with practically no education—apart from the wrong kind—what chance does a kid have to earn a decent living and make something of himself?

Solomon told us long ago that when a child receives the training he or she needs, God would honor that. "Train a child in the way he should go, and when he is old he will not turn from it" (Proverbs 22:6). It's still true. May God help us get a handle on what counts and come to grips with the consequences of broken homes.

RESOURCE READING: Ecclesiastes 11

March 27

THE LOVE OF A FATHER FOR HIS WAYWARD SON

The New Testament calls David a man after God's own heart. If ever a man faced difficulties, yet kept his focus on the Almighty, it was the shepherd who became king. Among the great leaders of history—from Alexander the Great to Winston Churchill—none had any more greatness of heart than David.

Despite his weaknesses, his failures, and the dark chapters of his life, David consistently repented and laid hold of God as his fortress, his strength, and the source of his hope—even when tested by tragedy.

Following David's adulterous relationship with Bathsheba, the son that she bore to him died. Then another of David's sons, Amnon, raped David's daughter Tamar. When David didn't respond righteously, Absalom, Tamar's brother, killed Amnon. Absalom was banished from the presence of the king, and later led an ill-fated revolt against David.

When David's troops finally went into battle, he instructed them to "be gentle with the young man Absalom for my sake" (2 Samuel 18:5). Be gentle to the one who couldn't wait to be king, who undermined his father's authority, who had killed his own brother, whose word meant nothing. "Be gentle to him," said David.

Is it any wonder that every father and mother whose son is arrested for a crime, says, "He is a good boy; surely he could not have done this." But the facts bear out the truth of what happened.

Eventually Absalom's vanity became his undoing. As he was fleeing David's troops, his thick head of long hair caught in the low branches of a tree. Joab, David's chief of staff, quickly dispatched the young rebel, ending the revolt.

David, though, wept over his wayward son. "O my son Absalom! My son, my son Absalom! If only I had died instead of you—O Absalom, my son, my son!" (2 Samuel 18:33).

David's love for his son—unworthy as he was—only makes sense when we realize that God's love for us also defies explanation or understanding. God sent His Son to bring us—who like Absalom have undermined His authority and spurned His love—back into fellowship with Himself. Ah, what love, what unfathomable love the Father has for His children.

RESOURCE READING: 2 Samuel 18–19

March 28

THE PHONY DOCTOR

In 1979, pharmacist Gerald Barnes was sent to prison for three years on a manslaughter charge. It seems he had decided that *prescribing* medicine would be more fun than filling prescriptions, so he had changed professions and become a doctor. The only problem was he had never gone to medical school. By forging documents, he got a job as a doctor and got along quite well for awhile until he sent a patient home with diabetes who should have gone to the nearest hospital. Two days later, the man went into shock and died. That's when the medical examiners discovered that Dr. Gerald C. Barnes was an impostor.

Barnes was in his forties when he went to prison, and you'd think that after a stint in gray stripes, he would have learned his lesson. Not so. Not long after his release, the pretender Dr. Barnes was arrested again. Same song, second verse. He was found to be treating as many as twenty patients a day at an executive health center.

Although many people were duped by the bogus Dr. Barnes, I doubt that any of his patients decided to avoid doctors forever, saying, "That's it; I've had it with medicine. I'll never go to a doctor's office again." Chances are they looked for another doctor the next time they got a sore throat or a stomachache.

Yet I've heard people say with intensity, "I knew this guy who said he was a Christian, and he lived just like I do. Man, if that's what going to church does for you, I'll just stay home." Anyone who is honest would have to admit that more than a few individuals who are long on profession and short on possession have filled the pews in churches. That's to be expected.

Nobody counterfeits something that is common or worthless. You don't see a lot of phony pennies out there. They don't have much value. And nobody counterfeits brown wrapping paper. It's too common. So is it with those who pretend to be more spiritual than they really are.

"Brothers," wrote Paul, "if someone is caught in a sin, you who are spiritual should restore him gently. But watch yourself, or you also may be tempted. Carry each other's burdens, and in this way you will fulfill the law of Christ" (Galatians 6:1–2).

RESOURCE READING: Galatians 5:13–6:5

GIVING 'EM A DOSE
OF THEIR OWN MEDICINE

As Christians in a non-Christian world, we face a tough decision: Will we live by the laws of the jungle, treating others the way they treat us, or will we choose to live as God intends, and treat others accordingly?

Taking an "eye for an eye" and a "tooth for a tooth," harboring bitterness, carrying grudges, and waiting for the day to pay back our enemies goes clear back to the book of Genesis. But Jesus taught His disciples to meet harshness with kindness, stinginess with generosity, and hatred with love. In his paraphrase of the New Testament called *The Message,* Eugene Peterson puts it like this:

"Here's another old saying that deserves a second look: 'Eye for eye, tooth for tooth.' Is that going to get us anywhere? Here's what I propose: 'Don't hit back at all.' If someone strikes you, stand there and take it. If someone drags you into court and sues for the shirt off your back, giftwrap your best coat and make a present of it. And if someone takes unfair advantage of you, use the occasion to practice the servant life. No more tit-for-tat stuff. Live generously.

"You're familiar with the old written law, 'Love your friend,' and its unwritten companion, 'Hate your enemy.' I'm challenging that. I'm telling you to love your enemies. Let them bring out the best in you, not the worst. When someone gives you a hard time, respond with the energies of prayer, for then you are working out of your true selves, your God-created selves. This is what God does. He gives his best—the sun to warm and the rain to nourish—to everyone, regardless: the good and bad, the nice and nasty. If all you do is love the lovable, do you expect a bonus? Anybody can do that. If you simply say hello to those who greet you, do you expect a medal? Any run-of-the-mill sinner does that.

"In a word, what I'm saying is, *Grow up*. You're kingdom subjects. Now live like it. Live out your God-created identity. Live generously and graciously toward others, the way God lives toward you" (Matthew 5:38–48 TM).

The next time someone treats you rudely, ask yourself, "Will I lower myself to his level, or will I choose to treat him the way God wants me to?"

RESOURCE READING: Matthew 5:38–48

March 30

WHATEVER HAPPENED TO CIVILITY?

"Curtis, please stop doing what you're doing," the father said to his six-year-old son. The boy continued his activity as though he were deaf and never heard a word. The father repeated his request, and again his son ignored him. After the third request, the boy decided he should do something, so he walked over to his dad, doubled up his fist, and punched him in the stomach. And you know what? The father, an executive vice president of an aerospace company, choked on his cigar and almost apologetically said, "Now, please don't do that, Curtis. These folks will think you're not a nice boy!" Believe it or not, I witnessed this scene myself.

Children who dictate to parents, parents who thumb their noses at civility, and a society that takes out its hostilities on its weaker member—all these are symptoms of a sickness that is tearing us apart.

What is civility? Our English words *civilization* and *civil* come from a Latin word meaning citizen or government. According to Webster, civility came to mean "good breeding, politeness, consideration, or courtesy." It also means a "polite act or utterance." Civility is the glue that holds a society together, It makes our parks safe for children to play. It allows a woman to walk safely down the street without an escort.

The opposite of civility is rudeness, vulgarity, and profanity—all of which have become more common of late. Civility must be learned, and the sooner the better. It's a conscious choice. But for the many people today who have grown up without learning civility, respect for parents disintegrates, and eventually teachers, policemen, and the weak become targets of abuse.

What's the solution? It starts with you. You may not change the world, but you can change your own attitude, and the environment of your home, office, and classroom. You can chose to act with decency and civility regardless of how others respond.

Lately, our society has begun to associate civility with "right-wing Christianity." If the foundation of civility is treating others as you would like them to treat you, then Christians are guilty as charged. Jesus says, "In everything, do to others what you would have them do to you, for this sums up the Law and the Prophets" (Matthew 7:12).

RESOURCE READING: 1 Samuel 2:12–36

LIVING IN A
NON-CHRISTIAN WORLD

When Supreme Court justice Antonin Scalia spoke to a group of law-school students at a Christian university, he said that Christians are "destined to be regarded as fools in modern society" because of their belief in the supernatural.

Scalia's comments—though pretty much a statement of fact—were ridiculed and called "out of place" by critics.

Justice Scalia, a practicing Catholic, is strong enough to ignore his critics, yet the intensity with which individuals are attacked today who dare invoke the Almighty or assert that morality is a public issue is absolutely amazing. Profanity, vulgarity, and obscene remarks are pretty much accepted by today's society, but let someone mention God in positive terms and he becomes a target for criticism and an object of scorn and even hatred.

Yale professor Stephen Carter contends that there is a "long-standing tendency within the secular society to marginalize, ghettoize and belittle religious belief." In his disturbing book, *The Culture of Disbelief,* he writes, "We have pressed the religiously faithful to act as though their faith does not matter."

The lines are clearly drawn. A Christian should expect the same freedom to express his faith publicly as a non-Christian has to express his own worldview. But don't expect it. It doesn't work out that way.

We are caught in a spiritual battle against powerful forces that would silence the voice of anyone who expresses faith in God. But not to worry. Jesus said, "I have told you these things, so that in me you may have peace. In this world you will have trouble. But take heart! I have overcome the world" (John 16:33). The majority of people who support decency and morality must not be silenced by a few vocal critics.

When moral voices are silenced, our salt has lost its flavor and ceases to be of any worth. To flaunt moral convictions may be casting pearls before swine, but to silence those who speak from a platform of morality produces a society without conscience or moral fiber.

"All that is necessary for evil to triumph," said Edmund Burke, "is for good men to do nothing." And if Burke were alive today, he might add, "and to say nothing," as well.

RESOURCE READING: 1 Corinthians 1:18–31

April 1

OF COURSE, CHRISTMAS IS MORE POPULAR

It's now official. A survey has indicated that Christmas is more popular than Easter. Christmas vs. Easter? That's like asking people whether they prefer going to a baby dedication or a funeral. Of course Christmas would be more popular. And why not?

Who doesn't love a baby? With thoughts of peace and prosperity, enough to eat, the warmth of a fire, and the friendship of close friends and family, who doesn't enjoy the spirit of Christmas? Babies are nonthreatening. They smile, gurgle, and warm the heart. They laugh and make you laugh, too.

Easter is more like a rose with prickly thorns. No matter how beautiful the rose, it still has thorns. And Easter certainly has its thorns. There would be no Easter—no thought of resurrection—unless a crucifixion had taken place. A baby is God's way of saying that life goes on, but

Good Friday brings life to an abrupt halt. The Resurrection brings hope, but it also brings us face-to-face with our humanity and the weakness of our flesh.

The injustice of the Cross is another reason why Easter runs second in popularity to Christmas. No matter how you try to skirt the issue, Jesus paid a brutal penalty—and for what? For healing the sick and afflicted, for comforting the grieving, for touching the social outcasts of society? Which of His good works deserved death on a cross?

The Cross makes us uncomfortable because we sense a certain complicity, an involvement with those who perpetrated this evil. Who among us at some time has not chosen to come down on the dark side of an issue? Who among us is without sin? The apostle Paul says that the cross of Christ became "a stumbling block to Jews and foolishness to Gentiles" (1 Corinthians 1:23). In a very real sense, it is everybody's thorn.

The next several selections will focus on the power of the Cross, which resulted in the joyous resurrection of Easter. Take time to carefully read the accounts of the crucifixion in Matthew and Luke. Then read John 20 and 21, where the good news of the Resurrection touches our lives. Both Christmas and Easter are important, but Easter is forever.

RESOURCE READING: Matthew 26

April 2

WERE YOU THERE?

W ere you there when they crucified my Lord?" asks the old spiritual. "Yes, I was there," says Rembrandt van Rijn, the famous Dutch painter. In his masterpiece, "Descent from the Cross," Rembrandt shows the disciples gently lifting Jesus from the cross, their brows furrowed with anguish and questions. Among the spectators on that dark day, Rembrandt painted his own face, identifying himself with those who were at the cross.

"Were you there when they crucified my Lord?" For centuries people have avoided the issue, blaming either the Romans or the Jews for Jesus' death. But the real question is more fundamental than who ordered the Crucifixion or who carried it out. The real issue is, what brought Jesus to this point of crisis? It wasn't because His luck ran out. The cross of Calvary was part of a grand design, worked out far in advance by God, to correct something inside my old nature—and your old nature— that is badly flawed and corrupted.

If we were merely the product of evolution, we would be answerable to no one higher than ourselves. But, because we were created in the image of God, not only are we responsible for our choices, we're also accountable to our Creator. This truth changes everything radically.

As an individual, my record is flawed. I have fallen short of God's expectations by my choices and by nature. I have committed sins of omission as well as sins of commission. I'm a sinner, and when I include myself, as Rembrandt did, with those who were at the cross, I hear the faint sound of Christ's voice penetrating the hearts of men with joy as He cries, "Father, forgive them, for they know not what they do."

If I believe that I am merely a rational animal, I will continue to be offended by the Cross. But if I believe that I am a human being, created in the image of God, there is a powerful, magnetic attraction to the Cross, which is the antidote to all of my failure and all of my sin. In this I can glory, knowing that He paid a debt He did not owe so that I could receive the gift of the Father's love.

Count me in with the others who stood at the foot of the tree on that infamous day long ago.

RESOURCE READING: Matthew 27

"TAKE UP YOUR CROSS
AND FOLLOW ME"

A fundamental flaw in our thinking today is the illusion that God has done everything and we—doing nothing—can bask in His grace and goodness. This attitude has turned Christianity into a marketable lifestyle that costs nothing and demands very little. In the process, we have beautified the life of Jesus, ignored His death, and failed to understand the power of His resurrection.

In making the point that He had come "to seek and to save what was lost" (Luke 19:10) Jesus told parables about a lost coin, a lost sheep, and a lost son (Luke 15). His mission clearly was to do something about man's lostness, the source of our estrangement from God. But Jesus never suggested that by paying the price He gave us all a free ride.

He also said, "If anyone would come after me, he must deny himself and take up his cross daily and follow me'" (Luke 9:23). No wonder some people slipped quietly toward the edge of the crowd and quit. The cost of discipleship was too high; the demands were too great.

The disciples understood the significance of taking up a cross, because they saw its visible reality. In first century Palestine, the cross meant you were on the losing end of the argument—which was exactly what Christ had in mind.

In today's world, what does it mean to "take up a cross"? Obviously, we can't take it literally, because we don't crucify people anymore. But the significance hasn't changed. Taking up your cross is an act of self-negation, a sacrifice, a commitment with a price tag attached.

Taking up your cross means caring for the elderly, feeding the homeless, sheltering the kids who sleep on the street. It can mean as many different things as there are situations, but every "cross" has the same significance. It means you have yielded control of your life to the Father. The power of the Cross transforms lives, and society as well. No wonder Paul could glory in the Cross and boast that he had gained power over the world.

May God help you to leave your burdens at His feet, take up your cross, and follow in the footsteps of Jesus.

RESOURCE READING: Matthew 28

April 4

HAS THE CROSS FALLEN?

After China fell to the Communists, churches were closed and believers went underground to worship. Former houses of worship became factories, warehouses, stores, and apartments. In some cases, church windows were boarded up and gates chained shut.

In the city of Beijing, one church building in particular was singled out for a "statement" by the government. This cathedral, which had been designed by an English architect, had a magnificent cross adorning its graceful spire. Workmen were sent to the church to sever the cross and weld it back at an angle as though it were bowing before the onslaught of communism. I wonder what went through the minds of the men who broke the erect cross and made it appear to have fallen. In ancient days, the cross had but one purpose: to torture its victim and deprive him of life. It was a cruel and exacting means of execution. The criminal usually died of asphyxia, the result of pressure on the chest cavity finally taking its toll as the lungs burned with pain.

The use of the cross as a symbol goes back to the end of the first century, within a generation of Christ's crucifixion. For many centuries, crosses have adorned the graves of heroes, kings, and bishops.

Of course, the power of the Cross is not merely symbolic; it represents a powerful reality that took place on that Good Friday long ago. When Jesus cried, "Father, into thy hands I commend my spirit," he opened the way to the new life of resurrection.

The message of the Cross is that someone else—not the one being crucified—is in control. For Christians, the Cross says, in effect: "God wants to be in control of the circumstances of my life."

The cross on the Beijing church may never be mended, but we can be certain that the true Cross will never be vanquished or reduced to a leftover relic of an outmoded religion. The death and resurrection of Jesus Christ has done more to change the lives of men and women—bringing forgiveness, healing, and joy—than anything in all the world. No government, ideology, or philosophy will ever triumph over it.

RESOURCE READING: Luke 23:32–56

April 5

THE TRIUMPH OF THE CROSS

After a devastating typhoon battered Macao in 1825, John Bowring, the governor of Hong Kong, came to explore the damage. He found buildings smashed, homes devastated, and the territory in ruins. All that remained of the cathedral, which had borne the brunt of the storm, was the façade, with its cross standing tall on the pinnacle. Reflecting on this scene of destruction, Bowring later wrote, "In the cross of Christ I glory, towering over the wrecks of time." May it ever be!

Nothing is more central to Christianity than the Cross. The Cross represents the best and the worst of humanity. From this ancient symbol of a cruel and painful death— man's inhumanity to man—God brought redemption and forgiveness through the sacrifice of His only Son. The Resurrection is unique to Christianity. Buddhism, Hinduism, and Islam have no response to the simple story that Jesus lived, died, and rose again.

Take five minutes and read the account of Christ's crucifixion in Luke 23. Read on as the hopes and dreams of His disciples die as they place His bruised and broken body in a new tomb. Read the final chapter, when the light of dawn on Sunday morning shines into an empty tomb, proving that He is risen.

The Easter story is so simple that it could never have been fabricated.

The One who died came back to life, and forever changed the destiny of mankind. Christmas is wonderful— exciting and warm, but Easter is joyous and meaningful. There is no person whose life is not enriched by the knowledge that life is not an endless grind, a machinelike existence, but that every person is endowed with the breath of God and can find forgiveness and the hope of tomorrow.

Our culture substitutes Santa for the manger, and the Easter bunny for the empty tomb, but every graveyard, and every obituary reminds us that Good Friday and the Resurrection on Easter morning give us life and hope beyond the grave.

I heard recently that the old Macao cathedral is being rebuilt—a kind of testimony to the truth that the gates of hell will never prevail against the church.

RESOURCE READING: 1 Corinthians 15

CHANCE

Historians have pointed out some interesting parallels between Abraham Lincoln and John F. Kennedy. The two were elected one hundred years apart. Both were deeply involved in civil rights issues; both were assassinated on a Friday in the presence of their wives; both lost a son while living in the White House. Lincoln was assassinated in Ford's Theater; Kennedy was killed while riding in a vehicle made by the Ford Motor Company; both men were succeeded by men named Johnson, who were born one hundred years apart.

Because of the natural laws that God put into effect, certain things can be predicted according to the principles of probability. For example, if twenty-three people are selected at random, chances are at least two of them will have the same birthday.

Not everything can be figured by probability or dismissed as a coincidence, however. Psychiatrist Carl Jung spent a lifetime studying rare phenomena, and he coined the term "synchronicity" to describe his observation that "coincidences occur much more frequently than probability theories would predict."

For those committed to the truth of God's Word, divine guidance goes far beyond coincidence or chance. In the words of William Shakespeare, "There's a divinity that shapes our ends, rough hew them how we will!" This "divinity," better known as the providence of God, provides direction in ways we cannot fathom. The sure hand of God guides our will and sometimes overrides our decisions. God says, "I am the LORD your God, who teaches you what is best for you, who directs you in the way you should go" (Isaiah 48:17).

Viewing life as an intricate game of chance can leave

you feeling as though you're at the mercy of odds that are not in your favor. Viewing life from the perspective of the Bible, however, reveals the strong, sure hand of God guiding the affairs of our world, and our personal lives as well.

God's great promises are reserved for His children. He says, "I will instruct you and teach you in the way you should go; I will counsel you and watch over you" (Psalm 32:8).

For children of God, there's no such thing as chance or fate, only the loving guidance of our heavenly Father. There is never a coincidence—only an incidence wrought by the Hand of the Almighty.

RESOURCE READING: 2 Chronicles 32

April 7

COINCIDENCE OR THE WILL OF GOD?

I was eating dinner in a small hotel in Italy when I over-heard two Australians talking at the next table. After the meal, I introduced myself and asked where they were from. When I learned they were from Melbourne, I said, "That's interesting. For the past two weeks, prior to leaving on this trip, we've had house guests from Melbourne." We com-pared notes and soon discovered that this couple lived next door to our friends. Coincidence? Perhaps. But the chances of that happening are pretty slim.

How about this one:

Fifteen people were scheduled to attend choir practice at a little Baptist church, but at 7:15 P.M. when the prac-tice was scheduled to begin, nobody had arrived. Each member had a good reason for being late: a car wouldn't start, a radio program wasn't over, the ironing hadn't been finished, a conversation hadn't ended. As the result of their tardiness, not a single member of the choir, including the director, was inside the church at 7:25 P.M. when an explosion destroyed the building. Warren Weaver, the author of *Lady Luck,* says the chances that no one was hurt were one in a million.

Knowing what I know about God, I find it difficult to believe that the tardiness of the choir was just luck. "And we know that in all things God works for the good of those who love him, who have been called according to his purpose," says Paul in his letter to the Romans (8:28). Beyond chance or mere coincidence, the hand of God brings about His will and purpose in our lives.

God is aware of your needs, and He has a will and a purpose for your life. But Romans 8 makes it clear that while God's direction and care are part of His grace, they're not to be taken for granted or treated with presumption.

The protection and providence of God are not benefits of an eternal insurance policy that lets you do as you please under the umbrella of God's grace. God's purpose is revealed through the relationship you have with Him, when you are committed to His will and strive to walk in His way. God's will is not a coincidence.

RESOURCE READING: Psalm 5

April 8

THE BIG FROGS IN YOUR LIFE

John Redman tells the story of a farmer who came to town and asked the chef of a new French restaurant if he could use about a million frog legs. "Oui!" the chef responded enthusiastically, "but where in the world would you find so many frogs?" "I have a pond at home that is filled with them," replied the farmer. "They drive me crazy night and day."

A few weeks later, the farmer made his first delivery: four frog legs. With a red face he stammered, "I guess I was wrong. There were just two frogs in that pond, but they sure made a lot of noise."

That's often the way it is with the stress factors in our lives. Like a grain of sand in your eye, or a torn cuticle on your finger, a small amount of friction can produce a great deal of discomfort and irritation.

Here's the important question: How do you turn things over to God?

A lot of people want to use God like a parachute on a plane that is going down. Once they safely reach the ground, they want to disengage and go their own way. But the relationship that brings security in Jesus Christ is one in which you surrender your life to the sovereign will of God and become God's child. The Bible calls it "conversion" or "being born again."

Surrender means you acknowledge your inability to save yourself or help yourself. The gulf between you and God is called "sin." It's the rebellion of your heart that makes you want to live as though there is no God. But when you confess your sin and ask God to forgive your rebellion, you embrace God's Son as your Savior and Lord. He promises, "Never will I leave you; never will I forsake you" (Hebrews 13:5). This means that you aren't alone in your workplace, your marriage, your neighborhood. That knowledge alone takes stress out of your life.

Finally, it means you confess Christ as your Lord, asking Him to guide, direct, and empower you. Remember, "the battle is not yours, but God's" (2 Chronicles 20:15). With that understanding, you can cope with what bothers you.

RESOURCE READING: 2 Chronicles 20

KNOWING WHO YOU ARE

When he was putting himself through school, John Hagee worked at an orphanage. On the days when visitors were allowed, he noticed one young man who always came and stood by the gate. No one ever came to visit the boy. One day John asked him why he always stood by the gate when no one ever came to see him. "I'm waiting for my father," replied the lad. "Yes, but your dad never comes, so why wait?"

The boy wistfully replied, "I don't know my father, and until I know my father, I won't know myself."

Do you know who you are? Or, like the orphan at the gate, are you confused about your identity? Even if you've never met you natural father, you can get to know your heavenly Father and find your identity in Him.

Jesus was secure and confident, because He knew His Father. He knew where He had come from, and He knew exactly who He was. In John 2:25, the apostle makes an interesting statement about Jesus: "He did not need man's testimony about man, for he knew what was in a man."

Paul tells us that we "are all sons of God through faith in Christ Jesus" (Galatians 3:26). Paul goes on to say that when we trust Jesus Christ as our Lord and Savior we are adopted into the family of God, becoming His children with an inheritance that can never be taken away.

We've all heard the saying "Blood is thicker than water," and the same thing is true spiritually. The blood that Jesus shed on our behalf brings a fellowship forged by suffering that unites His children and gives them a love for each other which surpasses even the closest of human relationships.

Have you joined the family of God? It begins by trusting Jesus Christ as your Lord and Savior. Once you've been adopted by God, you life in Christ is enriched by worshipping with brothers and sisters in Christ, strengthened by studying the Word to find out who you are in God's sight, and sealed by God's great love for you. He provides strength for your weakness, riches for your poverty, and hope for your despair.

Don't stand at the gate waiting for a father who doesn't care. Join the family of God and discover your true identity.

RESOURCE READING: Psalm 23

April 10

YOUR RESPONSIBILITY TO A FRIEND

Your friend is about to make a serious mistake. Do you tell her, "You're about to ruin your life, and I'm not going to let you do it—you mean too much to me!"? Or do you sit back and think, "Who am I to tell her what to do? If she hits the wall and splatters, I'll be there to pick her up!"

Though we seldom admit it, the Bible makes it clear that we are responsible for each other. No less than fifty times, the New Testament uses the phrase "one another" to stress our mutual responsibility.

Too often, we think, "I'm not qualified!" and we turn our hurting friend over to a professional—a pastor or a counselor. "After all, they're trained to help," we reason. I wrote the book *Coffee Cup Counseling* out of a profound conviction that common, ordinary people can effectively help each other. Your friend can't fool you—you know his strengths and weaknesses. And unlike the counselor, you'll be there when your friend needs help and you can provide the necessary support to help him stay on the right path.

I believe that Paul had this idea in mind when he told

the Galatians, "Brothers, if someone is caught in a sin, you who are spiritual should restore him gently. But watch yourself, or you also may be tempted. Carry each other's burdens, and in this way you will fulfill the law of Christ" (Galatians 6:1–2).

There is a place for professionals and specialists, whose expertise goes far beyond what most of us can do, but the fact is, there are not enough professionals to help all the hurting people around us. The body of Christ must stand up and be counted!

The real business of the church, according to Paul, is not condemnation but restoration! Is that not the prevailing theme of the Bible? In a thousand ways, God reaches down to heal the hurt caused by sin. He reaches out to the fallen and helps them to walk again.

As Paul says, "God, who reconciled us to himself through Christ. . .gave us the ministry of reconciliation" (2 Corinthians 5:18). Yes, you can help people, and with God's help, you can make a difference!

RESOURCE READING: Galatians 6:1–10

April 11

CHANCE AND THE FATE OF A NATION

To what degree does chance or fate determine the establishment and removal of world leaders? Do men become leaders by power and charisma, or does God decree that one shall lead and another shall be set aside?

I'm reminded of King Ahab, the haughty, arrogant king of Israel who defied the counsel of the prophet Micaiah and flaunted his own authority.

In a strange alliance with Jehoshaphat, the king of Judah, Ahab declared war on Syria. To foil the negative words of Micaiah, who had prophesied his death, Ahab disguised himself as an ordinary soldier. King Jehoshaphat wore his royal robes—which made him a target for the enemy soldiers.

To make matters worse for Jehoshaphat, the chariot commanders of the Syrians had been told to fight with no one except the king himself. It wasn't until Jehoshaphat cried out in fear that the attackers realized he wasn't Ahab and turned back from their assault. Meanwhile, Ahab was concealed among the foot soldiers.

The enemy commanders may not have known the whereabouts of the king, but God saw through Ahab's disguise very clearly. Here's the record of what happened: "Someone drew his bow at random and hit the king of Israel between the sections of his armor. . . . The king died and was brought to Samaria, and they buried him there" (1 Kings 22:34, 37).

What are the odds of that happening? An archer fires an arrow at random, and it just happens to strike between the armor plates of the commander-in-chief and kills him.

Before Ahab went to battle, he had been warned. In fact, Micaiah told him, " 'If you ever return safely, the LORD has not spoken through me.' Then he added, 'Mark my words, all you people!' " (1 Kings 22:28).

What are we to say when a wicked individual comes to power and holds the lives of millions of people hostage? Is he in power by God's appointment?

When situations develop that bring jeopardy and suffering to humanity, God works through men, yet He is the One who puts one man aside and raises up another.

Never forget that those who walk across the stage of world leadership are there only by the grace of God.

RESOURCE READING: Psalm 75

THE FEAR OF DEATH

William Cullen Bryant once wrote of a person who lived his life in fear of death. Though invisible, the man's fear was as strong as the chains on a quarry slave, who was shackled and could never walk away from his captor.

Many people are chained to their fears today. That's why they buy health insurance. That's why health care is a thriving industry. Our society also attempts to soften the language of death and camouflage the reality of dying. Morticians are now called "bereavement counselors" and cemeteries are referred to as "memorial gardens."

Throughout the ages, the fears that haunt people have changed very little. The writer of Hebrews in the New Testament speaks of "those who all their lives were held in slavery by their fear of death" (Hebrews 2:15).

For those who fear death, survival becomes their number one goal. Gripped by selfishness that goes far beyond the natural instinct to preserve life, they become addicted to the cult of youthfulness. Women will spend a small fortune trying to smooth away the signs of aging, and men will do almost anything to forestall the effects of age.

Frankly, I can understand why people were afraid of death before Jesus came. I know I would have been. Read Genesis 5, the obituary page of the Old Testament. There you will find a roster of Adam's descendants who lived and died, followed by their sons and grandsons, who also lived and died. But when Jesus died and rose again, He broke the power of death forever.

A young man who was searching for meaning in life visited the Garden Tomb in Jerusalem and heard the story of the Resurrection. Going forward to talk to the man who had presented the gospel, he said, "Mister, if what you said is true, there should be singing and dancing at this spot every day of the year."

The finality of Christ's victory takes away the sting of death and drives away the sadness so that there can be singing and dancing in your heart.

RESOURCE READING: 1 Corinthians 15

April 13

A LITTLE CHILD SHALL LEAD THEM

Children often have a spiritual sensitivity and a big-as-life sort of faith. No wonder when Jesus held a little child in His arms He said, "Of such is the kingdom of heaven" (Matthew 19:14 KJV).

In her book *Images of Grace,* Dr. Diane Komp, a pediatric oncologist, tells how children influenced her spiritual transition from unbelief to faith in God.

"Many times," says Dr. Komp, "I listened politely to parents who groped for God in their most painful hour. I respected them all for their journeys, but I heard no convincing evidence in their revelations that challenged my way of thinking."[1] Then she met Anna, a seven-year-old girl who was fighting a losing battle with leukemia. One day, the young girl sat up in her hospital bed and exclaimed, "The angels—they're so beautiful! Mommy, can you see them? Do you hear their singing? I've never heard such beautiful singing!" And then she lay back on her pillow and died.

For weeks, the question haunted Dr. Komp: "Have I found a reliable witness?" Anna's choir of angels didn't result in a Damascus Road conversion experience for the doctor, but it started the process.

Over her many years of practice, Dr. Komp observed

that children, before they died, often experienced a vision or an appearance of Jesus or angels, and they described it in a simple, matter-of-fact sort of way. In some cases, these children came from homes where the name of Jesus was never spoken, other than in vain. Yet these children were able to describe very clearly what they saw before they died.

The loss of a child can be a bitter experience. It tears some couples apart, and others declare war on God. But for some, it's a window to heaven. During the final week of Jesus' ministry and life on Earth, He told His disciples, "Let not your heart be troubled; you believe in God, believe also in Me. In My Father's house are many mansions; if it were not so, I would have told you. I go to prepare a place for you. And if I go and prepare a place for you, I will come again and receive you to Myself; that where I am, there you may be also" (John 14:1–4 NKJV).

RESOURCE READING: Revelation 21

April 14

YOU SHOULD HAVE STAYED IN BED, KATSUO

"Dear Lord, so far today, I've done all right. I haven't lost my temper. I haven't said anything I regret, nor have I been greedy, grumpy, nasty, selfish, or overindulgent. But, Lord, in a few minutes, I'm going to get out of bed, and from then on I'm probably going to need a lot more help." Right!

If you've ever had one of those days, you'll appreciate this story about Katsuo Katugoru, a Tokyo subway commuter whose routine ride to work turned out to be the worst day of his life. Here's what happened:

All his life, Katsuo had a fear of drowning by tidal wave. To offset this phobia, Katsuo invented a kind of life jacket underwear made of rubber, which could be inflated by a pressure cylinder, such as you would use to quickly inflate a bicycle tire.

The problem came when something malfunctioned while Katsuo was on a crowded commuter train. Suddenly, his rubber underwear inflated, making him balloon up like the Michelin Tire man. A well-intentioned passenger remedied the situation by stabbing the inflatable underwear with a sharp pencil. The underwear, along with Katsuo's ego, were quickly deflated.

There are days when you feel like you should have just stayed in bed. But you don't have that choice. Do you ever wonder if God is trying to tell you something? Have you ever considered the possibility that you need to back away from your situation and see the humor in it?

If God is sovereign—and He is—and if you are His child, then nothing can happen to you beyond His knowledge and will. Nothing? Yes, nothing. With that single word, we can turn the corner and face our human inadequacy and the greatness of God's resources and power.

God usually doesn't override my blunders, but He does give me the courage to go on and the wisdom to learn from my mistakes. He doesn't change the immutable laws of cause and effect, but He does lift me up and set my feet on a straight path.

When you have one of those days, don't take yourself too seriously. Remember, this too shall pass. Still, it isn't a bad idea to consult God about what lies ahead even before you rise in the morning.

RESOURCE READING: 2 Corinthians 4

IT'S EASY TO BE A DAD. OH YEAH?

How important are fathers when it comes to a child's social, spiritual, and emotional development? Clinical psychologist Dr. Wade Horn doesn't mince words on the subject. He says, "The notion that single-parent households are just as effective and desirable as traditional families has caused an epidemic of violence, pregnancy, drug abuse, and suicide among today's teens.

"Our culture," he continues, "needs to replace the idea of the superfluous father with a more compelling understanding of the critical role fathers play in the lives of their children, not just as 'paychecks,' but as disciplinarians, teachers, and moral guides. And fathers must be physically present in the home. They can't simply show up on the weekends for prearranged 'quality time.' "[1]

"Being there" for your kids involves much more than merely being present in the home. It takes your involvement and your attention. I'm thinking of one dad who told me, "I know I should spend time with my son, so I take him to a baseball game occasionally. But when I'm there, I don't enjoy it. I'd much rather be home working."

I'll never forget the time I lauded a certain Christian leader as a man of leadership and compassion, because the organization he had founded had touched the lives of thousands of children around the world. After I finished my remarks, a young woman approached me. "You didn't know him like I did," she said. "I was Sharon's best friend." Sharon, the man's daughter, had taken her own life as a teenager.

A torrent of words poured from the woman's mouth. She told of being at her friend's house when this Christian leader came home from overseas trips physically and emotionally exhausted. He had nothing left for his own family, and everyone paid the price.

I could tell you countless stories of dads who had no time for their children, until their kids were gone. Dads, what does it take to be a promise keeper? What does it take to be there for your kids? It takes a conscious decision that your family is more important than your work, your love of sports, or playing around on the computer.

"Dad, act like a man," was Paul's advice. It's still the need of the day.

RESOURCE READING: Philippians 1

April 16

WHY ACCEPT THE AUTHORITY OF THE BIBLE?

E very week, men and women around the world gather to study a book written more than two thousand years ago—the Bible, the world's best selling and most widely read book. Why do so many accept the authority of this Book?

I accept the authority of Scripture because of the correlation between biblical prophecy and secular history. Also, the abundance of manuscript evidence convinces me of the purity of the text. More than 4400 ancient biblical manuscripts are in existence today, forty of which are more than one thousand years old.

Reason three is the findings of archaeology. Though not an exact science like chemistry or astronomy, archaeology is nonetheless a valid source of truth. The spade of the archaeologist uncovers the ruins of ancient civilizations and rolls back the centuries of time, confirming the existence of biblical figures such as David, Caiaphas the high priest, Pontius Pilate, and other figures who played major roles in the drama of Scripture.

The fourth reason I accept the authority of this Book is the uncanny way in which modern science has confirmed statements from the Bible that were completely out of synch with accepted theories of the writer's day. For example, Acts 7:22 tells us that Moses was schooled in the wisdom of the Egyptians. The Egyptian wise men believed that the world came from an egg, yet Moses wrote, "In the beginning, God created the heavens and the earth." Who taught Moses this truth? Not the wise men of his day, for sure.

The final reason that I accept this Book without reservation is that it changes people's lives for the better. Stories abound of individuals who were tempted to take their own lives until they found a Bible and began reading it.

Like medicine that lies unopened in a cabinet or drawer, the Bible can't impact your life until you read it and open your heart to its message. It's time to let this great Book touch your heart.

RESOURCE READING: 2 Peter 1

April 17

WHAT REALLY HAPPENED ON THAT DAY?

In 1883, a British general stationed in Palestine was sitting on the verandah of his home in Jerusalem. Studying the surrounding terrain, General Gordon was impressed with a limestone hill just across the Kidron Valley on the Mount of Olives. The more he looked at this promontory, the more he thought it resembled a skull. Gordon remembered that Jesus was crucified at Golgotha, or "the place of the skull." "Could this be the very place?" he asked himself.

Further investigation led him to the discovery of a nearby first-century tomb, which he believed could have been the one belonging to Joseph of Arimathea where the body of Jesus was placed. Gordon was killed in military action shortly thereafter, but his interest in the place began a movement which eventually led a British group to purchase the site known today as the Garden Tomb.

General Gordon believed that the traditional site of Golgotha, marked by the Church of the Holy Sepulcher, lay within the walls of the ancient city. Scripture made it clear that Golgotha was outside Jerusalem, conforming to Mosaic law. After Gordon's death, archaeologists determined that in Jesus' day the traditional site was outside the walls of the ancient city.

Over the centuries, the Church of the Holy Sepulcher accumulated an unbelievable number of incense pots, icons, and religious paraphernalia. When he visited the site in 1869, Mark Twain wrote, "When one stands where the Savior was crucified, he finds it all he can do to keep it strictly before his mind that Christ was not crucified in a Catholic Church. He must remind himself that the great event transpired in the open air, and not in a gloomy candle-lighted cell, upstairs, all bejeweled and bespangled with flashy ornamentation in execrable taste."

The real issue is not "where was Christ crucified?" but "How does that historic event relate to our lives today?"

Why did Jesus have to die? The apostle Paul put it like this: "God made him who had no sin to be sin for us, so that in him we might become the righteousness of God" (2 Corinthians 5:21). Simply put, God accepted Christ's death in place of ours. That's good news!

RESOURCE READING: Matthew 27:32–55

SEVEN STEPS TO
SPIRITUAL SURVIVAL

Is there a secret to staying on top of things spiritually?
Nearly one-third of the world's Christians now live in areas where the expression of their faith is restricted. For these followers of Christ, living a vibrant spiritual life comes at a cost, yet they seem to have learned secrets of spiritual survival that the rest of us vitally need. Every time I worship with Christians living under oppression, I come away feeling dwarfed, humbled, and reproved for my usual grumbling and complaining.

Since 1980, Paul Estabrooks has ministered to the suffering Church. He has traveled thousands of miles and met with thousands of ordinary men and women who have paid an extraordinary price for their faith.

In his book, *Secrets to Spiritual Success,* Estabrooks tells the true-life stories of men and women who learned to rejoice under difficult circumstances. He lists seven secrets to surviving joyfully:

Secret #1: Wholehearted love for God. Wang Ming
Dao, the father of the house church movement,
spent twenty-two years in prison. When asked,
"What can we in the West pray with you about?"
old Brother Wang replied, "Pray for us that we
will love the Lord more."

Secret #2: Wholehearted commitment to God.
Having taken up the cross of Jesus Christ, they
are committed. They have crossed the line and are
willing to pay the price.

Secret #3: Wholehearted service for God. C. T.
Studd once said, "If Christ be God and died
for me, then no sacrifice can be too great for

me to make for him."

Secret #4: They enjoy the trip. Filled with the Spirit of God, people who are so committed find a joy and happiness that others lack. Owning almost nothing, they possess nearly everything.

Secret #5: Spiritual strength for the battle. Taking the Word of God literally, suffering believers often see the power of God in ways that we only read about in the book of Acts.

Secret #6: A passionate love for people. Having first loved the Lord, they love their brothers and sisters and those who are lost.

Secret #7: Confidence that nothing can separate them from the love of Christ. With this confidence, they glorify Christ, whether by life or by death.

RESOURCE READING: Romans 8:31–39

April 19

A NEWER, MORE RESPECTABLE CROSS

Unannounced and mostly undetected," writes A. W. Tozer, "there has come in modern times a new cross into popular evangelical circles. It is like the old cross, but different: the likenesses are superficial; the differences, fundamental. First, from this new cross has sprung a new philosophy of the Christian life, and from that new philosophy has come a new evangelical technique—a new type of meeting and a new kind of preaching. This new evangelism employs the same language as the old, but its content is not the same and its emphasis is not as before. The old cross," he contends, "would have no truck with the world." [1]

Was Tozer perceptive or paranoid? Is the new evangelism simply a contemporary version of the old, or has its basic character changed, rendering it anemic and leaving it far short of the standard of God's grace? Has popularizing the message altered it so much that the essential meaning and purpose of the Cross have been nullified?

Jesus said, "If anyone would come after me, he must deny himself and take up his cross daily and follow me. For whoever wants to save his life will lose it, but whoever loses his life for me will save it" (Luke 9:23–24).

Paul believed in a personal cross—the price that believers must pay. In Galatians 2:20, he writes, "I have been crucified with Christ and I no longer live, but Christ lives in me. The life I live in the body, I live by faith in the Son of God, who loved me and gave himself for me."

One proof that the new cross is not the same as the old cross is the vast number of individuals who call themselves Christians, who go to church and carry Bibles, yet with no appreciable evidence of change in their lives.

Don't be misled. The contemporary cross—the one with no offense, no cost, and no shame—is not the Cross Paul was referring to when he wrote, "For the message of the cross is foolishness to those who are perishing, but to us who are being saved it is the power of God" (1 Corinthians 1:18).

RESOURCE READING: 1 Corinthians 1

April 20

THE HARVEST IS PAST

"The harvest is past, the summer has ended, and we are not saved" (Jeremiah 8:20). The prophet wrote these words at a time when Judah was surrounded by her enemies and it seemed there was no hope of deliverance. Jeremiah's sobering statement should cause us to ask ourselves, "Have I really got it all together? Or is it possible that after all the wonderful things I have done, I could fail to make it to heaven?"

Jesus shocked His hearers when He said, "I can see it now—at the Final Judgment thousands strutting up to me and saying, 'Master, we preached the Message, we bashed the demons, our God-sponsored projects had everyone talking.' And do you know what I am going to say? 'You missed the boat. All you did was use me to make yourselves important. You don't impress me one bit. You're out of here'" (Matthew 7:22–23 TM).

Is it possible that a person can go to church, give large sums of money to charitable causes, participate in community causes, and own several Bibles, yet die without the assurance of heaven? Not if entrance to heaven is based on what we do. But if entering the presence of the Lord depends on our response to what Jesus Christ did, then all our good deeds fall short.

The disheartening fact about trying to earn our way to heaven is that we just can't be good enough. In the heart of every person stirs rebellion against the Almighty.

When Jeremiah cried out, "The harvest is past, the summer has ended, and we are not saved," the next logical question should be, "All right, then, what must we do to be saved?"

I can sum up the answer in three simple but profound steps:

Step #1: Acknowledge your need for a Savior.
Step #2: Believe that God will save you according to the promise of His Word.
Step #3: Confess Jesus Christ as Lord of your life. "If you confess with your mouth, 'Jesus is Lord,' and believe in your heart that God raised him from the dead, you will be saved" (Romans 10:9).

Take your spiritual pulse. It's one of the best things you can ever do. Make sure that when the harvest is over, you're on God's side.

Resource reading: John 3

April 21

JUST A SMILE, PLEASE

For many years, Mother Teresa gave herself to the poor and suffering of India, working among the outcasts of society. This gifted and dedicated saint lived the example of Jesus with courage and commitment. As her reputation grew, people from around the world sought to visit her and catch a glimpse of this dedicated woman. To some she was a kind of religious icon; to others, a source of puzzlement. Why would anyone choose to do what she did?

On one occasion, a group of visitors had an audience with her. As they were leaving, one of them said, "Mother Teresa, please tell us something that will help us live our lives better."

Mother Teresa simply said, "Smile at each other—it doesn't matter who it is—and that will help you to grow up in great love for each other." Another member of the group quickly asked, "Are you married?" (knowing, of course, that she was not). Mother Teresa replied, "Yes, and I find it difficult sometimes to smile at Jesus." Wow! Talk about applied Christianity.

I've seen pictures of Jesus—at least as artists and sculptors have imagined Him—in the art galleries of the world. Most are sober, some reflect tenderness, compassion, and great love. But I cannot recall ever seeing a picture of Jesus smiling. Why not? Did He only drink vinegar, wear black, and reprove the disciples for laughing?

No, Jesus smiled. Does the text tell us that? No, but the context does. Who could hold a little child and not smile? Jesus no doubt laughed with His disciples and expressed the joy of His life.

People rarely smile when they are fearful, uptight, and full of stress. A genuine smile is an expression of an overflowing heart of love. Paul tells us that the fruit of the indwelling Spirit of God includes "love, joy, and peace." We can smile because we know that God is in charge of the world and our lives.

Mother Teresa was right. There are times when it is difficult to smile. But it is never impossible. Is there anyone in your life who makes it hard for you to smile? That person is God's challenge to you. Go on, relax and give that person a smile. You just might discover something really worth smiling about. Try it.

RESOURCE READING: Proverbs 15

April 22

WHAT'S YOUR PLAN?

A hardworking immigrant built his business the old-fashioned way. He put in long hours, made his customers feel important, and met the needs of everyone who came into his shop. His years of toil paid off, and he was able to send his son to college.

When the son came back to join the business, he was appalled by his father's antiquated bookkeeping system and urged him to computerize and do it the modern way. His father replied, "My bookkeeping plan works like this: When I started my business, I had $100 and a pair of pants. When

I want to know what I'm worth, I deduct the pants and $100, and what's left over is profit."

A generation ago, it might have been okay to keep your cash in a cigar box and use a yellow pad for accounting, but not today. Failure to adequately plan accounts for the majority of small business failures. A strategic plan is vitally important—for your business, your church, and your life.

Business advisor Dennis Waitley says, "Most people overestimate what they can do in a year and underestimate what they can do in five." He's right.

Jesus said, "Suppose one of you wants to build a tower. Will he not first sit down and estimate the cost to see if he has enough money to complete it?" (Luke 14:28). Any worthwhile plan starts with counting the cost to see if you have the resources to succeed. Then, along with your goals and objectives, you need an action plan to translate your ideas and dreams into reality. These principles apply to marriages, families, friendships, and businesses.

Another important factor in strategic planning is God's direction in your life. When asked about his five-year plan, Francis Schaeffer replied that he had none, because God had not yet revealed His direction for five years down the road. I've never forgotten that.

Wise is the person who makes God the senior partner. As the writer of Proverbs says, "We can make our plans, but the final outcome is in God's hands. We can always 'prove' that we are right, but is the Lord convinced? Commit your work to the Lord, then it will succeed" (Proverbs 16:1–3 TLB). What more needs to be said?

RESOURCE READING: Proverbs 16

STRATEGIC PLANNING AND GOD

S trategic planning is important, a vital key to business success. But where does the leadership of the Holy Spirit fit into the equation?

Scripture promises us that God is involved in the successes and failures of our lives. Take a concordance and notice how the word *success* is used in the Bible, especially the Old Testament. You'll discover a consistent relationship between God's blessing and man's success. For example, in Psalm 1, David talks about the blessings of the man who walks according to God's direction, then adds, "Whatever he does prospers."

On the flip side, failure is associated with ignoring God, leaving Him on the sidelines as we play the game of life. Stories of failure in the Bible are often preceded by the words "He consulted not the Lord."

Jesus saw no conflict between seeking the will of God and strategic planning in business. He refers to a man who wants to build a tower, which in those days was used for protection, storage, and refuge. Jesus said that the man would first sit down and count the cost.

You've no doubt heard it said, work as though everything depends on you; pray as though everything depends on God, and you will never go wrong. Far too often, we think of God as a court of last resort, a last-ditch effort to prevent failure. We wait until the ship is sinking before we pray for a miracle, but had we taken God into our confidence at the beginning, we might never have ended up in distress. God will be there in the day of disaster, but He is also there to guide your steps at the beginning of the journey.

Trusting God is never an excuse for doing less than your very best. It's never a substitute for hard work or supreme effort. But no matter how wonderful your plan or how hard you work, there are factors known only to God. Trust Him.

Don't think of God as your passport to health, happiness, and riches. But consider that He is a loving Father who walks with you through the ups and downs of life, including changing markets, successes, and failures. Trust your ways to the Lord. Remember, your heavenly Father knows best.

RESOURCE READING: Psalm 1

April 24

UNWELCOME SURPRISES

The sudden loss of a job, the death of a loved one, a storm that damages your town. How do you handle the unwelcome surprises of life?

Psychologists call it "coping." Some think of it as "rolling with the punches." Others say with resignation, "That's life!" But when unexpected surprises come our way, we respond in one of two ways: We either fight and become bitter, or we reach out for the grace of God and become better through what we endure.

What is this commodity of the heart called "grace"? In simple terms, it is the help of God that enables us to cope with the pain and unwelcome surprises of life.

The apostle Paul faced many unwelcome surprises, things he didn't deserve and certainly didn't ask for. As strange as it may seem, he welcomed these trials and tribulations. Responding to a persistent "thorn in the flesh," he says, "Three times I pleaded with the Lord to take it away from me. But he said to me, 'My grace is sufficient for you, for my power is made perfect in weakness.' Therefore I will boast all the more gladly about my weaknesses, so that

Christ's power may rest on me. That is why, for Christ's sake, I delight in weaknesses, in insults, in hardships, in persecutions, in difficulties. For when I am weak, then I am strong" (2 Corinthians 12:8–10).

God gives grace to help us cope with the surprises of life—those nasty turns we neither expect nor deserve. But though grace is always available, tapping into it or accepting it isn't always easy. Bitterness and anger bottle its flow. We need a certain measure of humility to say, "Lord, this surprise is more than I can handle. I need Your help!"

Poverty of spirit comes when we have depleted our resources, when our charm, our looks, money, and connections are no longer enough to get us out of our jam. That's when we know we need God.

"When I am weak," said Paul, "then I am strong." When unwelcome surprises confront you, learn about grace, God's grace, and you will also find strength to cope. It's worth discovering.

RESOURCE READING: 2 Corinthians 12

April 25

IT'S STILL "A"

Clyde McDowell told the story of a man who came to visit an old friend, a music teacher. As the man entered the studio, he asked, "What's the good news today?" The old teacher said nothing for a moment, then stood up and slowly walked across the room. He picked up a tuning fork and struck it a sharp blow. As the melodic sound filled the room, he said, "That is 'A'. It is 'A' today; it was 'A' five thousand years ago and it will be 'A' ten thousand years from now. The soprano upstairs sings off-key, the tenor across the hall flats his high notes, and the piano downstairs is out of tune." He struck the note again and said, "That is 'A,' my friend, and that's the good news for today."

God's good news is that His truth is the same yesterday, today, and forever.

But in a world that is hopelessly out of tune, the person who knows true "A" will always be out of step with society. Have you ever noticed that it is intellectually acceptable to pursue the truth as long as you don't find it? But once you say, "This is it!" you become a narrow-minded bigot.

God has revealed His truth through His Son and through the Bible. The writer to the Hebrews says, "In the past God spoke to our forefathers through the prophets at many times and in various ways, but in these last days he has spoken to us by his Son, whom he appointed heir of all things, and through whom he made the universe" (Hebrews 1:1–2).

The issue is clear. Either there is truth, or there is not. The note "A" is either true, or it ceases to be a reliable standard, in which case, those who sing flat are just as right as those whose pitch is perfect.

God's truth—ultimate truth—doesn't come in seventeen pastel colors. It has abrupt edges. It never says, "Well, maybe" or "It's a judgment call." May God help us to be as narrow as the truth and as broad and as loving as He is.

RESOURCE READING: John 17

April 26

PRAYER

Homicide detective Felix Jimenez spends most of his time looking for criminals, but when ValuJet Flight 592 plunged into the Florida Everglades, he found himself probing the alligator-infested waters looking for remains from the crash. Fifteen days after the plane exploded and crashed, the flight recorder still had not been found.

When Jimenez stopped for a break, he bowed his head and prayed, "God, so far I've prayed for You to keep everyone safe out here and I haven't asked for Your help in finding anything. Now I'm asking You to help us find this recorder." The next time he put his probe into the water, it hit the recorder. Talk about an immediate answer to prayer! "An amazing coincidence," some might say, but you would never convince Jimenez.

God answers prayer four ways. Sometimes He responds immediately and directly—and that's the kind of answer we all want. But many times God's timetable is different from ours. He sees the end from the beginning. He also works in the hearts of those for whom we are praying—sometimes softening, sometimes preparing a way that we can't see from a distance. We might say these answers are delayed.

The third way that God answers prayer is through disguised answers. I've found that the answers to many of my prayers fall into this category. God doesn't answer the way I think He should. He gives me something better. Sometimes, a situation that I hadn't even envisioned eliminates the burden or the problem. A disguised answer from the loving hand of the Father is better than our own solution.

The fourth way that God answers prayer is with a resounding, definite "No." Request denied. Our loving Father simply loves us too much to give us everything we ask for.

At this point we must learn to trust the heart of the Father who knows what we need far better than we do. As Jesus put it, "If you, then, though you are evil, know how to give good gifts to your children, how much more will your Father in heaven give good gifts to those who ask him!" (Matthew 7:11).

RESOURCE READING: Matthew 7:1–12

WHEN PLACED IN COMMAND, TAKE CHARGE!

General Norman Schwarzkopf is a "take charge" sort of person who leaves no doubt as to who is in command. But don't call him a "born leader."

"There's no such thing as a born leader," he says. "Most leaders are ordinary people who are thrust into positions of leadership and respond to the challenge. . . . The simple but most important thing in leadership is character."

When Schwarzkopf was a two-star general, newly assigned to the Pentagon, he met his superior officer in the hall one morning.

"I'm out of here," the man said, suitcase in hand.

"What am I supposed to do while you're gone?" Schwarzkopf asked. His superior replied, "Rule 13."

Schwarzkopf's mind went blank. He knew he should know Rule 13, but he couldn't remember. Finally he asked, "Excuse me, sir, but I don't remember. What is Rule 13?"

"When placed in command, take charge," his boss replied.

"Yes, sir," said Schwarzkopf. "But what do I do?"

"Rule 14," came the response.

Again Schwarzkopf's mind went blank. Was this guy playing games with him? "What is Rule 14?" he asked reluctantly. "Do what's right," said his boss as he walked away.

Whenever there's a parade of two or more vehicles, confusion reigns until someone decides to lead. It's the same in a business, a platoon of soldiers, a church, a team on the basketball floor, or in a marriage. Somebody has to lead.

An old Arab proverb says, "An army of sheep led by a lion is more powerful than an army of lions led by a sheep."

Today we are facing a crisis of leadership. We need both Rules 13 and 14, and we need them desperately.

Having no leadership in a family is as devastating as having a poor leader. Sometimes, by default, our kids end up leading the parade.

God's plan is for husbands to be leaders—not dictators or bosses—but as loving husbands, as shepherds who care for their own. Remember Rule 13? "When placed in command, take charge." Balance that with Rule 14: "Do what's right."

May God give us the courage to take charge and do right, regardless of the cost.

RESOURCE READING: Ezekiel 22

April 28

WE BELIEVE IN DIFFERENT GODS

On his second great journey through the Roman Empire, Paul came to the city of Athens, then the cultural center of the world. "While Paul was waiting for [Timothy and Silas] in Athens, he was greatly distressed to see that the city was full of idols. So he reasoned in the synagogue with the Jews and the God-fearing Greeks, as well as in the marketplace day by day with those who happened to be there. A group of Epicurean and Stoic philosophers began to dispute with him. Some of them asked, 'What is this babbler trying to say?' Others remarked, 'He seems to be advocating foreign gods.' They said this because Paul was preaching the good news about Jesus and the resurrection" (Acts 17:16–18).

What god do you serve? Everyone serves some kind of god. Even atheists, who say there is no god, live according to some force, some belief system, authority, or values. The Muslim suicide bomber, the hedonist who lives for pleasure, and the churchgoing, Bible-toting Baptist are all driven by religious convictions.

Can everybody be right? Does it matter whether you believe only in yourself or in the resurrection of Jesus Christ? Does it matter if you die as a Buddhist in your twenties, or live to be eighty and have a Christian burial?

If Christianity were mere religion, it would make little difference which religion you chose. But the one crucial issue that changes everything is the person of Jesus Christ.

The Bible leaves no room for compromise. Peter says, "Salvation is found in no one else, for there is no other name under heaven given to men by which we must be saved" (Acts 4:12). Jesus Himself says, "I am the way and the truth and the life. No one comes to the Father except through me" (John 14:6).

The bottom line is not which religion is best, but whether or not Jesus Christ is God, whether He was crucified at the hands of Roman soldiers, and whether He rose—literally and physically—from the grave. If so—and the preponderance of evidence supports Christ's claim—then the most powerful God is quite evident.

RESOURCE READING: 1 Kings 18

April 29

THE LAD WHO SAVED PAUL'S LIFE

After Paul had preached the gospel throughout Asia Minor, he came to Jerusalem and there gave his testimony. His speech went just fine until he mentioned that God had sent him to the Gentiles. That's when things exploded.

Things got so bad that the Roman commander of the

guard feared that Paul might be killed by his enemies. He intervened, taking him into protective custody. Forty Jewish men then took a vow to eat nothing until they had killed this rebel who claimed that God loved the Gentiles.

Once Paul was under the protection of the Roman army, getting close enough to kill him was a challenge. Of course, these men wanted to settle the matter quickly so they could start eating again. They convinced the high priest to lean on the Romans and ask them to return Paul to the Jewish council for more questioning. On his way to council they planned to attack him.

There was one big problem with their plan. A young lad, probably in his teens, heard about the plot. He happened to be the son of Paul's sister who lived in Jerusalem. This boy took it upon himself to inform Paul about the plot. He went to the garrison where Paul was being kept, and asked to speak to his uncle. When Paul heard the bad news, he asked that his nephew receive an audience with the commander of the garrison.

When the commander heard the details of the plot, he ordered an armed guard to assemble in the night and whisk Paul to safety in Caesarea. Luke never tells us whether the forty-man posse starved to death or went back on their vow, which also would have resulted in death.

One thing is certain. This teenager saved Paul's life. His moment in the spotlight is brief, but tremendously important. Regardless of his age, it took courage to expose the plot.

Exposing corruption or dishonesty always takes courage. Standing alone while others go along with the crowd often makes you an enemy. The real heroes are those who have the courage to abide by their convictions and do what is right. As Golda Meir once put it, "If not I, who? If not now, when?" The questions are still valid today.

RESOURCE READING: Acts 23:12–24

FORGIVENESS

S even centuries before Christ, the prophet Micah exclaimed, "Who is a God like you, who pardons sin and forgives the transgression of the remnant of his inheritance? . . . You will. . .hurl all our iniquities into the depths of the sea" (Micah 7:18–19).

The significance of Micah's statement was not fully understood until recently, when oceanographers and hydrologists began to explore the depths of the ocean and discovered that life as we know it ceases to exist only a short distance beneath the surface.

When Micah says that God hurls our sins into the depths of the sea, he paints a beautiful picture of forgiveness. We can rest assured that the issue is settled, finished, never to be discussed again.

No matter how good or evil we are, sooner or later we all face the issue of finding acceptance before the Almighty. Does forgiveness come because of what we have done, or is it because God credits us with what Christ has done?

This very issue confronted one of our *Guidelines* radio listeners who ended up in prison. He thought his life was finished, but God had other plans. Let me quote from his letter: "I was arrested on September 13, 1993. At the time I was looking at, the very least, thirty-six years in prison. I contemplated suicide and even went so far as to write my mother a suicide note. Then I found a pocket-size New Testament Bible and began reading. I had never read a Bible before. Then some Christians came into my jail cell, and I was baptized in the Holy Spirit and all my suicide thoughts vanished. I thank the Lord so much for bringing me out of the miry clay and making me a vessel of honor." He signed the letter, "A brother in Christ."

"Too easy!" you may be thinking. "Isn't there something

else we must do?"

The simple things are never easy. The most difficult thing we must do is acknowledge our personal need and realize that the solution to our sin is the grace of God, which brings forgiveness and restoration to everyone who believes.

RESOURCE READING: Isaiah 53

May 1

LEST WE FORGET

B efore written language was developed, parents passed on to their children orally the truths they wanted preserved. These oral traditions included God's dealings with people, family history, battles that were fought, marriages that produced offspring, and cataclysmic events such as earthquakes, famines, and floods.

Sometimes they were sung or chanted; sometimes they were told around the fire, but the stories were preserved and eventually passed on to the next generation. One of the great flaws of our present generation is that we are so consumed with the immediate that we have never learned what ought to be remembered. We depend on books, CDs, and computers to preserve our history. Meanwhile, we're watching TV or playing Nintendo. We've become a generation of spectators.

Our generational failure is far more dangerous than being unable to read or write. When I first encountered tribes that were considered primitive and uneducated— meaning they lacked a formal education—I was surprised to discover that these people are neither stupid nor ignorant. In fact, they know many things that we, in our educated so-phistication, have never learned: weaving baskets from fiber, making medicines from herbs and roots, crafting handmade tools, and weaving textiles and fabrics with intricate patterns.

The tragedy of our society is that we forget what should be remembered, and often remember what we should forget. We've neglected the Old Testament mandate to remember the Lord's deeds and to tell them to our children.

Psalm 78:4 talks about the works of the Lord, saying, "We will tell the next generation the praiseworthy deeds of the LORD, his power, and the wonders he has done." Moses instructed parents not only to remember the Lord's commandments but to "impress them on your children. Talk about them when you sit at home and when you walk along the road, when you lie down and when you get up" (Deuteronomy 6:7).

Why is our history so important? By remembering the good times, we are reminded of the grace and goodness of God. By remembering the bad times, we might avoid repeating our failures and mistakes.

By forgetting our history, we are condemned to repeat the same errors that brought us bondage and death. By remembering, we stay strong and healthy.

RESOURCE READING: Deuteronomy 6:1–12

May 2

THE POWER OF THE CROSS

Donald Peppard was a communications technician aboard the American ship *Pueblo* when it was taken captive by the North Koreans. He ended up in prison. One day as he exercised outside, he noticed an empty wooden box, which he casually picked up and took back to his cell. Using the two-inch blade of a small penknife, Peppard laboriously carved a cross and began praying for his family at home, and praying that he would soon be released from prison.

When his Communist captors routinely searched his cell, they found the cross. In a rage, they smashed it, scattering pieces of wood across the tiny cell, and proceeded to take out their anger on Donald Peppard. "This is not a church," they screamed.

On the other side of the globe, a young Frenchman was discovering the life-changing power of the Cross. After sowing his wild oats, his conscience began to trouble him. He sought out a priest and casually confessed his sins. The priest, recognizing the young man's lack of remorse said, "Here's what you must do. I want you to go and kneel before the great cross in the Cathedral of Notre Dame and say, 'Dear God, all this You did for me, and I don't [care]'."

The young man made his way to Notre Dame and found the cross in the nave of the church. Kneeling quietly, he began to pray, "Dear God, all this You did for me, and I don't—" He broke into tears. "Oh God, I do care. I do care."

What is the attraction—the power—of the Cross?

The answer, simply put, is what the cross represents. The New Testament says that Christ "humbled himself and became obedient to death—even death on a cross!" (Philippians 2:8). Paul explains that "in [Christ] we have redemption through his blood, the forgiveness of sins, in accordance with the riches of God's grace" (Ephesians 1:7).

Nothing is more central to our faith than the cross of Jesus Christ. When we remember its true meaning, we find the power that will sustain us, not only in prison, but in life's darkest hours.

RESOURCE READING: John 19

DARE TO BE A DAVID

W e took on Goliath!" bragged a small business whose product was overshadowed by a major manufacturer. It's the classic underdog story, pitting the little guy against the giant. Sometimes the little guy gets flattened like a stray cat in the path of a steamroller. But what's the real story of David versus Goliath?

To the west of Jerusalem, in the gentle rolling hills between the Jordan valley and the coast, two armies gathered who were bitter enemies. The Philistines, a fierce and savage people, wanted to drive the Israelis out of the land. Instead of wasting a considerable number of men in battle, the Philistines sent out a warrior who would have made Shaquille O'Neal look like a midget—well, almost. Goliath never played basketball, but according to the record he was at least nine feet tall.

David was a young shepherd who had taken a break from tending his father's sheep to bring provisions to his brothers in the Israeli army. When he saw the giant and witnessed the intimidation of the Israeli soldiers, David cried out, "Who is this uncircumcised Philistine that he should defy the armies of the living God?" Grabbing his slingshot, he felled the giant with a single stone and won the battle!

David's remarkable feat was marked by the following four qualities, which we desperately need today:

Quality #1: Competence. David had spent hours in slingshot practice while herding his sheep. He had experience knocking down bears and lions.

Quality #2: Courage. Others, no doubt, trusted the Lord but preferred to stay in the shade and pray. David had the intestinal fortitude to go for it. Real heroes are not individuals with superhuman courage; they're simply people who, when confronted with a situation demanding action, do what has to be done.

Quality #3: Commitment. This was not David's fight. He wasn't even a soldier, but his love for country and for God demanded that he join the battle. Edmund Burke once said, "All that is necessary for evil to triumph is for good men to do nothing."

Quality #4: Confrontation. Going one-on-one with the enemy is never pleasant; but apart from confrontation, evil is sure to triumph.

David learned that one plus God is always a majority, no matter how big the enemy. Every generation must learn this lesson.

RESOURCE READING: 1 Samuel 17

May 4

CHANGING THE BIBLE TO ACCOMMODATE OUR CULTURE

Who says we need a Bible so simple that even a pagan—someone with no religious orientation—could pick it up and understand it clearly? That's hardly a fair question, but how far should modern Bible translators go in their quest to simplify the language of Scripture? When they're finished, will we still have a Bible that is trustworthy?

The desire to provide a text that is clear and in contemporary language is a worthy goal, but not if we lose some biblical concepts that may always be incomprehensible to the uninitiated. Note in your English Bibles how terms such as redemption, grace, propitiation, and regeneration are being replaced with synonyms that cannot convey their true depth of meaning.

No one can translate without interpreting, and every translator has a bias. That's simply a statement of reality. For those whose bias is based upon the testimony of Scripture that every word of the Bible is God-breathed and given by the direction of the Holy Spirit, conveying the truth of every word is important.

The quest to simplify the Bible to the level of our culture and pagan understanding is like trying to write a chemistry textbook that is so simple I could understand it without having to study it. And that way I could skip the first year of chemistry and polish off the second year at the first try.

The Bible holds magnificent truths that will never be made so simple that a first-year student can grasp them. By changing the terminology, we also change the meaning, which leaves us with less than a full understanding of God's Word.

Shortly before his execution, Paul wrote to Timothy saying, "Study to shew thyself approved unto God, a workman that needeth not to be ashamed, rightly dividing the word of truth" (2 Timothy 2:15 KJV). Studying is hard work. It means digging out the text, checking the commentaries, reading the margin notes, and going beyond the headlines.

Forget the shortcuts. Rich rewards await the one who goes deeper into the Word, the one who really wants to know God's revelation of Himself.

RESOURCE READING: 2 Timothy 2

OVERCOMING A MAJOR BLUNDER

N o matter how loving or kind you are, sooner or later you fail. Do you admit it or deny the whole issue? The first major hurdle when you have violated your conscience is admitting you've done something wrong. Samuel the prophet outlined the steps beyond confession, which provide guidelines for us today.

Guideline #1: Don't fear that God will abandon you. (See 1 Samuel 12:20). God always hears the prayer of the person who is sincere in turning to Him.

Guideline #2: Don't give up, thinking that you have gone too far astray to come back. "For the sake of his great name the LORD will not reject his people, because the LORD was pleased to make you his own," Samuel told those who had turned their backs on God (1 Samuel 12:22). "As for me," he added, "far be it from me that I should sin against the LORD by failing to pray for you." Not bad. He wasn't there as a critic, but as a friend who wanted to help.

Guideline #3: Turn from what is wrong, and start doing what is right. When you blow it, fail, or violate your conscience, don't keep on doing the wrong thing. Turn back and pick up the pieces. Get going on the right path. Those who really love you will forgive you and stand with you.

Guideline #4: Realize that God wants to make you a person for Himself. He understands brokenness, human failure, and the sinfulness of the heart, and He's in the business of restoration and healing.

Guideline #5: Focus on the positive and remind yourself of what God has done in the past. Here's a word of encouragement from Scripture: "But be sure to fear the LORD and serve him faithfully with all your heart; consider what great things he has done for you" (1 Samuel 12:24). Redefining the point of your focus is vital. Get your eyes off your failure and remind yourself that God is faithful, He has met you in the past, and He will meet you today.

The future can be brighter despite the failure of the past, but only if you admit it, seek the help of others, and then let God's Holy Spirit restore you as His child.

RESOURCE READING: 1 Samuel 12:18–25

May 6

WHY BOTHER IF I CAN GET IT FREE?

I do not choose to be a common man," writes Dean Alfange. "It is my right to be uncommon. I seek opportunity to develop whatever talents God gave me—not security. I do not wish to be a kept citizen, humbled and dulled by having the state look after me. I want to take the calculated risk; to dream and to build, to fail and to succeed. . ."

In simple terms, Alfange is saying, "With the help of God, I'd rather do it myself, than to be dependent on the government or others to do it for me." Now, here's the tough question: Are such words admirable rhetoric, but impractical in today's world? Is self-sufficiency something for the history books but not for us today?

I'm reminded of the time a man came to me with a story of extreme difficulty. He was out of work, had a family to support, and couldn't get to where he wanted to go in life. "I think I can help you," I responded. Instead of simply giving him money, which would have been a quick but very temporary fix, I called a friend who readily agreed to employ him.

A few days later, I saw the man and asked how his job was going. "I didn't take the position," he said. "Why not?" I asked with surprise. "Well," he said, "I could get almost as much from the government for not working, so I said, 'Why bother?' "

Why bother? First of all, because God has decreed that man should earn his living by the sweat of his brow.

Why bother? There is a deep satisfaction in saying, "This with God's help, I have done." There is a joy in seeing the work of your hands come to harvest, whether it is in watching your bank account grow or seeing the garden you planted produce beautiful tomatoes and cabbages.

Why bother? Because there is dignity to honest labor, something which we deprive people of with government handouts and programs that emasculate men as breadwinners and family providers. The free handout often does more psychological damage than it helps with physical needs.

Why bother? The apostle Paul says, "If a man will not work, he shall not eat" (2 Thessalonians 3:10).

RESOURCE READING: 2 Thessalonians 3:6–15

May 7

A NICE
SEVENTEEN-YEAR-OLD MURDERER

Robert Knowles thought he had the perfect formula for raising children. Love your child, spend plenty of time with him, involve him in wholesome activities, help him get a good, balanced education, and everything will turn out fine. "Suddenly, after seventeen years of dedicated effort, something happened to my foolproof plan," Knowles told the press. "I found out I was the father of a murderer."

Martin Knowles, a high school honor graduate, is serving a life sentence for murdering Maria Louise Corsi, a sixteen-year-old acquaintance. "The shock, agony, and soul-searching are unbelievable," said Robert Knowles. "Everything you believe in is gone in one bolt of lightning that rips your heart out at the same time. What went wrong?"

The following guidelines will help to ensure that you will never have to ask yourself, "Where did I go wrong?"

Guideline #1: Lead your family spiritually. Most parental failures occur right here. Our behavior and our expectations don't match up. "Do as I say, not as I do," we tell our kids. But they reject our counsel and words of admonition and pick up the same flaws we have—and then we condemn them.

Guideline #2: Teach your children right from wrong. Fight the secular trends of our society by sharing Christian values with your children. As the apostle Paul told the Romans, "Be not conformed to this world" (Romans 12:2, KJV). We must resist the secularization that runs contrary to the attitudes and philosophy of the Word of God. Compare the number of hours your children spend in a secular environment with the number of hours of Christian training they receive. How do you expect a couple hours of church-related teaching to offset the influence of television and a secular education?

Guideline #3: Be a parent. Nobody can do this for you. Know who your child's friends are, where he goes, and when he's coming home. It isn't merely your right to know these things; it's your responsibility.

When a teenager gets in trouble, we become concerned. But we could avoid a tremendous amount of trouble by showing concern before the youngster gets into difficulty. "Train up a child in the way he should go," says Proverbs 22:6, "and when he is old, he will not depart from it" (KJV)."

RESOURCE READING: Ephesians 6:1–4

May 8

SCARRED PEOPLE ARE BEAUTIFUL

Charles Cooke writes of a conversation between a man and God. What he says expresses the feelings of a lot of people. It goes like this: "I've seen a number of movies lately, Lord, like *Romeo and Juliet*. The love of young people, at least in these movies, is beautiful. . .so simple. . .so total. . .so uncomplicated. They seem so natural, so free in their feelings. I wish I could be like that, Lord.

"But I can't be. I've been hurt, Lord. I have trusted and been betrayed at times. I have loved and received nothing in return. I have tried hard to care and failed—often. I have shared my secrets and heard them whispered to others. I have asked forgiveness and heard no response. I have been warm and received a cold shoulder. I've been through it, Lord. I've fallen on my face. I've banged my shins. I've been bruised. Look, Lord, I'm all covered with scars."

And then the Lord speaks: "Maybe you haven't understood enough. Maybe you haven't learned that human life is like that. All saints are scarred. Young love isn't the highest form of human love. The greatest love comes from scarred people. I know that many people stop loving so they won't be hurt again, but those people who do start over again, who continue in spite of all, who leave themselves open to the possibility of being hurt again, these people are able to love in a deeper way, a more understanding way, a richer way. . ."

The man ponders the words of God and says, "I think I know what you mean, Lord. I've met people like that—and knowing them gives me courage. The great people are those who continue to love with all their scars. I like scarred people, Lord. They are beautiful. . ."

How do you love when your love has been rejected? How do you confide when your confidence has been betrayed? How do you forgive when your forgiveness is scorned?

Through our failures, we learn patience; through rebuffs, we learn compassion; and through suffering, we partake of Christ's suffering. The crushed flower is the most fragrant, and a rose without thorns is really no rose at all.

RESOURCE READING: 2 Corinthians 4

May 9

THE LAPPIDOTH PRINCIPLE

You will not find the Lappidoth Principle in a physics book, though it sounds scientific. Neither will you find a discussion of the Lappidoth Principle in a psychology class, though it does affect human behavior. In fact, this may be the only place you'll ever hear about the Lappidoth Principle. Before I define it, let me give you some background information on Lappidoth.

Lappidoth was an Israelite who lived about 1280 B.C. during the period of the judges. That's about all I can tell you, because his real claim to fame is that he married a woman, named Deborah, who did make the history books.

The Lappidoth Principle finds its biblical framework in Judges 4:4: "Now Deborah, a prophetess, the wife of Lappidoth, was judging Israel at that time" (NASB). That's all the Bible says about Lappidoth, but from this brief mention we can derive an important principle that may one day make his name a household word.

Notice in this verse four facts about Deborah: She was a woman, a prophetess, and a wife—and she was a judge. This last detail makes some men today uncomfortable. Her ministry as a prophetess wasn't her own idea; the gift had been given to her by God. It seems from the order of mention that Deborah was established in her ministry before she met Lappidoth. Yet there appears to be no conflict between her home life and her God-given ministry. In addition to her work outside the home, she was also the wife of Lappidoth and probably the mother of his children.

God is the Author of balance, yet so often in our human relations we have anything but balance. We flit from one extreme to the other, and it seems to me that some husbands today could profit from Lappidoth's experience. Marriage should enhance individuality and personality—not nullify it or force one spouse into the other's mold. Jesus elevated the position of women to a new high as they played vital roles in the New Testament church.

The Lappidoth principle can be defined as follows: "Happiness in marriage is directly proportional to the ability of a husband to allow his wife to be her own person."

May God help us to respect our wives and allow them room to maintain the uniqueness that God intended.

RESOURCE READING: Judges 4

HANDLING YOUR WIFE'S SUCCESS

How can two people in a marriage blend their hearts and lives in oneness yet maintain their own individual uniqueness? Like cooking, when two flavors or spices are "married" together, a unique dish is created, something perhaps even better than the original ingredients. It sounds simple, but the blending of two lives is a challenge at best.

To increase your chances for success, here are a couple of guidelines for husbands:

Guideline #1: Let your wife be her own unique person. When you discover your own value and worth in God's sight, and recognize that He has placed you as head of your family under Him, you won't be overshadowed by your wife's accomplishments. In fact, you'll take pride in what she does, especially as she touches other lives for God. One of the truly beautiful things about God's plan for our lives is that, when we are in His will, two individuals can become one, yet maintain their own identity and uniqueness. Husbands and wives should complement and complete each other.

Guideline #2: Overcome feelings of competition by leading the way spiritually. Spiritual leadership is part of your job, according to God. Men who feel threatened by their wife's accomplishments are usually men who have defaulted in the area of leadership. I have observed that most successful, godly women have husbands who take the lead spiritually.

Now, here are few guidelines for wives:

Guideline #1: Don't forget; your husband and your children must be your number one priority. Any woman who gets so wrapped up in her business or ministry or whatever that she neglects her family is mixing up her priorities.

Guideline #2: Meet the needs of your husband and children. In the will of God, duties do not conflict; therefore, you have to determine how much time you can give to outside interests without wiping out your family. Some women have gotten so involved in church activities that their unsaved husbands told them, "Go live with Jesus, because you're never home with your family."

Guideline #3: Maintain a wholesome balance in your life. A woman can sense when her husband feels overshadowed by outside activities. When you sense that he's chafing, back up and take a good look at things together. Talk it over. For both men and women, this is a valid scriptural principle.

RESOURCE READING: 1 Peter 3

May 11

ENCOURAGEMENT— THE DIFFERENCE IT MAKES

You may have heard the story of the man who crawled out onto the ledge of a tall building and contemplated suicide. A friend, hearing of the dilemma, came to offer a word of encouragement. Joining the man out on the ledge, he said, "I've come to encourage you."

"It's no use. I'm going to jump."

"Before you do anything violent, let's talk this thing

over," said the friend. So the two men talked. . .and then they both jumped.

All jesting aside, don't underestimate the power of your words to influence another person. Encouragement is the act of bringing courage to another. However, if you study the topic of encouragement in the Bible, you'll discover that it is used almost as often to describe men who encouraged others to do evil as it is of those who used their influence for good.

Discouragement can be contagious, but so can a word of encouragement that lifts spirits and spreads goodwill to others. You might be a light in a pretty dark spot, perhaps in your office or shop. If you have been thinking of quitting to find a job where there aren't so many gloomy people, remember, God may have put you there precisely to be an encouragement to others.

Like the fellow I mentioned at the beginning, a lot of people are at the very brink, discouraged, wondering what to do. Perhaps you are one of them. What can you do when no one seems willing to offer a word of encouragement?

King David found himself in the most bitter of circumstances. His city had been destroyed with fire. His family had been taken captive by the enemy. His own soldiers were ready to kill him. "David was greatly distressed," says 1 Samuel 30:6, "for the people spake of stoning him, because the soul of all the people was grieved, every man for his sons and for his daughters: but David encouraged himself in the LORD His God (KJV)." The last phase—the upward look—is the only answer. *David encouraged himself in the Lord.* Remember this when you feel like saying, "Stop the world; I want to get off." The upward look dwarfs the circumstances that are pulling us down. Thank God for the power of encouragement.

RESOURCE READING: Deuteronomy 1

May 12

GOD, GIVE US A PROPHET!

When he was a young man, he saw Assyria invade and carry away much of northern Israel. Thirteen years later, he watched Samaria fall along with the rest of Israel. A few years later, the ruthless Assyrians raided and destroyed forty-six walled cities in Israel, taking away 200,000 captives. In 701 B.C., when he was an old man, he rejoiced when God sent an angel to destroy the Assyrian army of King Sennacherib as it camped outside the walls of Jerusalem.

Who was this man who witnessed so much history unfolding before his eyes? His name was Isaiah, and his response to his times is preserved for us in the Old Testament book that bears his name.

If you think the Old Testament is dry and boring, get acquainted with the book of Isaiah. It contains some of the most magnificent passages ever penned by human hand. Henry Halley says, "In some of his rhapsodies he reaches heights unequaled even by Shakespeare, Milton, or Homer." The book of Isaiah gave George Frederick Handel his inspiration for the score of *Messiah* as he put to music the majestic theme, "For He shall reign, forever and ever, and of His kingdom there shall be no end" (see Isaiah 9:7).

Isaiah's message centers around the theme that unless genuine, national repentance turned the hearts of God's people back to Him, He would send judgment and that the nation would fall. But Isaiah's message was not all gloom. He announced that God would preserve a remnant, and eventually the Messiah would come to redeem mankind.

Isaiah 53 pictures the passion and death of Jesus Christ as vividly as though the prophet had stood on the brow of Golgotha as an eyewitness. In this passage Isaiah writes, "We all, like sheep, have gone astray, each of us has turned to his own way; and the LORD has laid on him the iniquity of us all" (53:6).

Study the book of Isaiah. In its pages you will discover yourself. You will see your wandering heart and find there is an answer in returning to the loving Father who sent His Son as a Shepherd searching for lost sheep. Thank God for the prophets who point us back to the Father.

RESOURCE READING: Isaiah 53

May 13

COME ON,
LET'S REASON TOGETHER

Have you ever wondered why some people refuse to forgive, why they hold on to bitterness until it becomes a cancer that eats away at them? Medical research has proved conclusively that people who are free of bitterness and anger live longer and enjoy life more than those who refuse to forgive. There's no logic in living with bitterness.

The bottom line is that releasing bitterness, giving up your right to hurt someone else because that person hurt you, is not only good for your health, but good for your heart and soul as well. The best way to deal with those who hurt you is to forgive them, love them, and let God deal with them in His way, and in His time.

Forgiveness doesn't mean you give in, that you capitulate in a consummate show of weakness. But it does mean that you release the bitterness that has been gnawing at your innards, and you allow the process of healing to begin. The way that seems right from a human standpoint is the way of revenge, of getting even. But that's not God's way.

Long ago, God held out the olive branch of peace to

those who had willfully and knowingly turned against Him. He invited them to stop their willful disobedience and to think about the cleansing power of forgiveness. Forgiveness is not only reasonable; it is the only path to healing and restoration. Here's the famous text found in the first chapter of Isaiah: " 'Come now, let us reason together,' says the LORD. 'Though your sins are like scarlet, they shall be as white as snow; though they are red as crimson, they shall be like wool. If you are willing and obedient, you will eat the best from the land; but if you resist and rebel, you will be devoured by the sword' " (Isaiah 1:18–20).

Have you forgiven those who hurt you? Jesus said that unless we forgive others, our Father in heaven will not forgive us. So, since you are in need of forgiveness yourself, you had better learn to forgive. Say it, write a letter, make a telephone call—whatever is necessary—just do it. You'll be the winner when you do.

RESOURCE READING: Luke 16:1–13

May 14

THE GENTLE SHEPHERD

L ike a shepherd he takes care of his flock," says the prophet Isaiah. "He gathers the lambs in his arms. He carries them in his arms. He gently helps the sheep and their lambs" (Isaiah 40:11 GW).

Isaiah lived seven hundred years before Christ, yet the image of a shepherd is almost as powerful in the Middle East today as it was then. From the burning sands of the Negev to the gentle hills where the blue Mediterranean meets the shore, shepherds are still found in abundance.

King David, who spent his early years as a shepherd, wrote that "we are his people, the sheep of his pasture" (Psalm 100:3). Of all the creatures that God ever made, sheep are among the least intelligent. Lions roam the jungles. Alligators take care of themselves. Birds take to the air. But without a shepherd to protect them, sheep wander off into danger and soon fall prey to disaster.

Comparing the children of God to sheep, Isaiah says, "We all, like sheep, have gone astray, each of us has turned to his own way" (Isaiah 53:6). Both the Old and New Testaments picture God, our heavenly Father, as One who cares for His own. In spite of our failure and our wandering dereliction from what we know is right, He seeks us out, like a Shepherd searching for lost sheep, and gently leads us back to the fold.

Are you a lost sheep, estranged and cut off from the care of the Shepherd? The Good Shepherd is searching for you far more than you are for Him. God, at times, uses gentle persuasion to get our attention, sometimes difficulty, sometimes the pain of a broken relationship, sometimes the heartache of rejection. When we realize that the missing ingredient of our lives is a relationship with God, the Shepherd of our souls leads us back home.

The story that Jesus told of the prodigal son who rebelled against his father's authority and journeyed far into the world, is a picture of the Father's love for His children, who have strayed.

There's good news, friend. No matter where you are, how far you have strayed, or how great your pain, the words of Isaiah are still good news: "He gathers the lambs in his arms. . . . He gently helps the sheep and their lambs."

RESOURCE READING: Isaiah 53

May 15

THE FATHER'S LOVE

A reporter was interviewing a prostitute on late-night TV, when he noticed she was wearing a small cross on a gold chain around her neck. "Are you a religious person?" he asked. Somewhat embarrassed, she quickly said, "Oh, not at all. I got away from all that."

The attraction of the big city, the glamor of the lights, and the thrill of the moment has caused more than a few to pack their belongings in a duffel bag and run away from home. Most of them end up the same way—dirty, hungry, abused, and disappointed.

Jesus tells the story of a lad who "wasted everything he had on a wild lifestyle." When tough times came, he ended up feeding slop to pigs in the field. Talk about hitting bottom. Here's how the story ends:

"So he went at once to his father. While he was still at a distance, his father saw him and felt sorry for him. He ran to his son, put his arms around him, and kissed him. Then his son said to him, 'Father, I've sinned against heaven and you. I don't deserve to be called your son anymore.'

"The father said to his servants, 'Hurry! Bring out the best robe, and put it on him. Put a ring on his finger and sandals on his feet. Bring the fattened calf, kill it, and let's celebrate with a feast. My son was dead and has come back to life. He was lost but has been found.' Then they began to celebrate." (Luke 15:20–24 GW).

What was the turning point in the life of this young man? "Finally, he came to his senses." What stops you from coming back? Pride? Stubbornness? The refusal to admit that things were better, you were a lot happier, and you felt a lot better about yourself when you walked with the Lord?

It's never too late. You've never gone too far. You are never beyond the care of the Shepherd, but it's up to you to turn around and head back home.

The father who throws his arms around the son and weeps with joy is a picture of God's love for you. The same theme runs throughout the Bible. Jesus says, "Come to me, all you who are weary and burdened, and I will give you rest" (Matthew 11:28).

RESOURCE READING: Luke 15:11–32

May 16

SOUR GRAPES

How do you handle another person's victory? Are you happy, or do you detest their good fortune because it didn't happen to you? When your best friend marries the girl you dated, it's hard to get excited. When the man you hired gets promoted, leapfrogging over you, you may wish you could put a dagger in his back. Rejoicing in another's good fortune never comes easy!

There's a part of human nature that remains the same from generation to generation. It's called jealousy. The same problem confronted a young man years ago when his brother took half the family inheritance and headed for the big city. He blew it. He spent the entire bag of gold on wine, women, and song. Then things went sour, and he ended up working for a hog farmer. That's when he came to his senses and went home.

When we read the story of the prodigal son in Luke 15, it's easy to think of the young man as a loser. But the real loser in the story is not the son who strayed and came back; it's the son who never left but who resented the return of his brother.

When the wayward son came home and his father

killed the fattened calf and made merry, his brother was mad—disgusted, annoyed, and, yes, jealous. Why all the hoopla over a scoundrel who deserted the family and blew his inheritance? Why does he get treated like a hero? The brother takes issue with his father, saying "When this son of yours who has squandered your property with prostitutes comes home, you kill the fattened calf for him!" (Luke 15:30).

What should you do when you find yourself steaming over someone else's good fortune? First, acknowledge that your feelings of jealousy are wrong. Call it by the right name—sin. Then ask for God's forgiveness and help. Instead of being bitter, choose to rejoice. Does friendship count for nothing? Is money more important than a relationship? Will you allow yourself to stoop to the level of jealousy and harsh feelings?

"If you love those who love you," asked Jesus, "what reward will you get?" (Matthew 5:46). Pray for the one whose success annoys you. Learning to rejoice with those who find happiness only spreads the joy! It's something I've had to learn, but it works!

RESOURCE READING: Review Luke 15:11–32

May 17

TRUSTING WHEN THINGS DON'T GO WELL

What do you do when what you've prayed for doesn't happen? Maybe you don't turn your back on God and quit, but you put prayer on the back burner of your heart, reserved only for times of absolute desperation. I know the feeling. I've spent a lifetime trying to understand how God works. I don't have all the answers, but I have come to some conclusions.

1. Don't give up on God when He doesn't snap His fingers and make everything happen according to your plan and timetable. I serve and worship the Almighty because He is sovereign and Lord, because He is God, not because of what I get out of the relationship. No matter what the outcome, trusting God still makes for the smoothest path in life.

2. We live in an imperfect, broken world. Let's face it. Not everything makes sense. There's a lot I don't understand. There is no logic to explain why one girl aborts an unborn child when her neighbor would give almost anything to conceive. It's not fair and it's not right, but that's when we learn to "mourn with those who mourn" (Romans 12:15).

3. When things don't always come together, I remind myself that God has a plan and purpose beyond what I can see. We give up far too soon, and assign far too much importance to the immediate—something you can't always understand when you're young. I've also found that the promises of the Bible bring comfort when I lack understanding, because God's nature is goodness and love. I've learned that impatience is not a virtue, and most of my mistakes in life have come when I gave up on God and decided to do it myself.

4. When doors close, it may have nothing to do with my ability to get the job done, so I'm going to keep on trusting God and doing my very best. The path to the top is not a straight line. When my goals are what I think God wants done, I'm going to keep on knocking on doors, making

calls, and keep on believing in God, myself, and
my friends. Solomon was right when he affirmed,
"He will direct your path."

RESOURCE READING: Proverbs 3:1–12

May 18

DO YOU REALLY LOVE ME?

O ne of the weaknesses in popular Christianity today is
the overemphasis on God's love and an underempha-
sis on obedience on what He expects of those who follow
Him. Love and obedience are not antithetical to each other.
To the contrary, obedience—without hesitation—is the result of unconditional love.

Obedience is not a choice, an option that one may
select out of several possibilities or lifestyles. Either you are
obedient or you are disobedient. Just as a man is faithful to
his wife or else he is unfaithful, either you walk in obedience
to what God expects and requires or your love is less than
genuine and sincere.

Grudging obedience, the kind that is exacted by someone who is stronger than you or who will severely punish
your failures, isn't what brings pleasure to the heart of God.
Of course I will comply if my automobile is stopped and
someone with a gun asks for my money. Yet—and this happens all the time—I freely give money, time, and energies to
those whom I love, to those who are in need.

A certain woman badly in need of money answered an
ad for a housekeeper. The man who was employing someone to take care of his children and his home had lost his
wife and mother of the children. After the woman took the
position of housekeeper, it became apparent that this man

was no ordinary sort of person. He was a pain in the neck. On the first day of her employment, he presented her with a neatly typed list of responsibilities, and he was so particular that she almost quit after the first week.

Eventually her resentment began to subside and she began to see a softer, gentler side of the man who had employed her. In time, she grew to love the children and seemed to be able to overlook his idiosyncrasies of temperament and habit. Eventually, to the great delight of the children, he asked the housekeeper to become his wife and they were married.

Everything that she had so disliked now was no problem. The difference? She had come to know and love the man who had hired her as a housekeeper.

A faith that assumes because God does love you He will overlook anything you do is not true faith at all. It is a sentimental notion that God doesn't really mean what He says and that Jesus' words of reproof to those who knew the language but ignored submission to His will and plan can't really apply to us.

"Why do you call me, 'Lord, Lord,' and do not do what I say?" Jesus asked those who came for the bread and fish, the thrill of a religious experience, and a good time without cost (see Luke 6:46).

Jesus' question to Peter, "Do you love me?" is one that you can answer only by measuring your obedience to what He asks of you (see John 21:17). Listen to the quiet echo of that question which never goes away, "Do you love me? Then keep my commandments."

RESOURCE READING: Luke 6:43–49

GOD WORKS THE NIGHT SHIFT

Have you ever worked the night shift? Getting used to the schedule isn't much fun. It's different: eating supper at breakfast time; going to bed when everyone else is getting up; sleeping when others are working or playing; watching the moon instead of the sun; working in the dark instead of daylight. Not everyone can take it. For most of us, the night shift is too lonely, too dark, too much of a difficult thing.

The darkness of the night shift seems to intensify everything. It's quieter, it's lonelier, and it's longer. Sixty minutes at night can seem as long as an entire afternoon with daylight.

In his book titled *God Works the Night Shift*, pastor Ron Mehl says that we often hear the voice of God speaking to us in the quietness of the night. During the day, His voice might be drowned out by the din of traffic, the cries of children clamoring for our time, the demands of business and earning a living—to say nothing of the noise of TV and radio with their obnoxious commercials and empty chatter.

The absence of sunshine is not all that makes for darkness in our lives; it is also the difficulties, the suffering, the results of our stupid mistakes, the losses we sustain. But in the darkness of our lives, we hear God's voice bringing comfort, encouragement, and assurance. Listen for His voice in the darkness.

Long ago, David wrote, "Indeed, he who watches over Israel will neither slumber nor sleep" (Psalm 121:4). He could well have written, "He who pledged to keep you during the night shift will never get drowsy or forget you in the darkness that troubles your life." It's true, friend.

We learn some strong lessons about ourselves and about

God's care in the darkness, and when the dawn of sunlight begins to pierce the eastern sky, we're better men and women because of what we've been through.

I have a recommendation for you. Take a Bible concordance and look up the word *darkness*. It's amazing what the writers of Scripture had to say about darkness and how God views it. It's well worth your time.

RESOURCE READING: Genesis 1:1–27

May 20

WHEN YOU FORGET THAT GOD WORKS THE NIGHT SHIFT

What happens when you forget that God works the night shift? Do you stay awake at night, tossing and turning? Maybe you think, but it's usually negative, unproductive thinking. You ponder the future, but the darkness obscures everything. You probably see the worst case scenario. You worry, and worry, and worry some more.

At times like these, don't forget that the darkness intensifies everything—your fears, your worries, your feelings about failure and rejection. Remind yourself that God doesn't sleep on the night shift.

One night when worries overwhelmed my sleep, I got out of bed and found my Bible. I turned to 1 Samuel 30 and read about a time when David encountered some very difficult circumstances. While David and his men were away from home, the Amalekites had kidnapped their wives and children and burned the city. To make matters worse, David's men turned on him.

"But David encouraged himself in the LORD his God," it says in the King James Version (verse 6). He didn't say,

"Look, men, I couldn't help this. Don't blame me." He didn't say, "All right. Let's come up with a plan."

When trouble awakens you in the night, don't head for the refrigerator or click the power button on the TV remote. Instead, open the Bible, and get your eyes on the Lord—not on your circumstances. Feelings and emotions usually lie when you forget that God works the night shift. Simply put, things almost always appear worse than they are. The darkness of night makes you lose sight of how important you are in God's sight.

What does it mean to encourage yourself in the Lord? David redirected his focus from the darkness of his circumstances to what God had done in the past. He focused on the nature and character of God, not his own failure. He remembered what we usually forget, that God hasn't abandoned or forsaken us when all trouble breaks loose and the darkness seems to overwhelm us.

Friend, have you forgotten that God still works the night shift? Read 1 Samuel 29 and 30, and encourage yourself in the Lord. Remember, God neither slumbers nor sleeps. He's on duty twenty-four hours a day.

RESOURCE READING: 1 Samuel 30

May 21

HEARING GOD'S VOICE IN THE DARKNESS

When you're in a pit, you don't play games with God. You don't tell Him what a nice person you are or how much you've done for His cause. You go one-on-one with the Almighty, pleading your case, asking Him to intervene.

We no longer take people and throw them into pits, but in ancient days, it was a common practice. You may remember that Joseph was cast into a pit by his brothers, who later sold him into slavery. The prophet Jeremiah was dropped into a slime pit when his prophecies angered the king (see Jeremiah 38). In the remains of the House of Caiaphas, the high priest who condemned Jesus, you will see a kind of pit, a hollowed-out limestone cavern, where Jesus may have been kept while the council of the Sanhedrin was summoned.

The pits we find ourselves in today are more psychological—depression, anger, inadequacy, worry, addiction. Like a real pit, they are things you can't break out of; they keep you in darkness and make you feel as though you've been swallowed and you will never escape.

I'm reminded of some of the letters we've received at *Guidelines* from people just like you—people with education and culture; people who married with the greatest hopes, but now live with the most desperate fears; people who believe that God answered their prayers at one time, but now they wonder where He is and why He doesn't deliver them.

It's uncertain whether David was ever actually in a pit, but he talks about pits more than any other person in the Bible. Emotionally and spiritually, he was in the pits many times.

Sometimes David blamed God for the circumstances that put him in a pit, but David always credited God for every deliverance. God still delivers. He can still take us from the pit and put our feet on solid rock.

Would you admit to needing help in getting out of the pit? You've tried it yourself and failed. Why not ask His help? There's no need to strike a bargain with God. Just tell Him your need and trust Him completely. Deliverance from the darkness of the pit is a life-changing experience. You'll never be the same again.

RESOURCE READING: Habakkuk 2

LEAD, FOLLOW,
OR GET OUT OF THE WAY

L ead, follow, or get out of the way" might well be the
guiding principle for leadership in the secular world.
But from God's perspective, leadership is substantially different. God often picks individuals who have little natural
skill to recommend them and chooses them to lead. God
knows that he who lacks much, trusts much.

A leader needs to know where he is going, right?
From God's perspective, not necessarily. When the Lord is
leading, you don't need to see the whole plan, only the next
step. When Moses led the Israelites out of Egypt, he needed
to learn that a leader is also a follower. To make His point,
God gave Moses a visual aid: a pillar of fire by night and
a cloud by day. When the cloud or the pillar moved, all
Moses had to say was "Break camp; let's move," and two-
and-a-half-million people followed him.

Even when the way seems clear, a leader must continue
to trust God. A few days out of Egypt, Moses and the people encountered trouble. The pillar of fire and the cloud led
them into a box canyon, with the Red Sea on one side,
mountains on the other, the desert to the south and the
army of Egypt fast approaching in the rear.

God knew what He was doing, and He knows what
He's doing when He allows you to get boxed in by circumstances that look like disaster. Remember, when He leads,
no matter how grim the circumstances may be, all you have
to do is move when He moves, stop when He stops, and be
patient, very patient.

Leadership is an awesome task, nothing to be taken
lightly. Sometimes the hardest part of leadership is waiting until God says, "Move it!" No one can lead who has
not learned to wait. When something inside says, "Lead,

follow, or get out of the way," it's time to go before the Lord and ask for His direction. God leads; you follow. That's the difference.

RESOURCE READING: John 15

May 23

GOD, IF YOU WILL JUST GET ME OUT OF THIS MESS

God, let's make a deal. If You will just get me out of this mess, I'll. . ." In the military, they call it foxhole religion. You know what I mean. You've been there. You've knelt in the little chapel at the hospital and bargained with God. You've sat in the kitchen with your Bible on the table and fear in your heart. You've shed your tears and gone through your night of darkness, and now things have turned around. The infection is gone, your marriage has come together, and your night of danger is over. Now what? Do you go back to business as usual and live as though nothing ever happened? Or did it change your life when God met you and brought you through your dark night of distress?

Here are three things to do after you have seen God's deliverance:

1. Never forget that it was God who delivered you. After the crisis, it's easy to think that it was the antibiotics that worked and gave you back your baby, or that your luck—whatever that is— changed for the better, or that things just turned around. Don't believe it for a minute. The circumstances of your life are in God's hands.
2. Don't go near the edge. If alcoholism or addiction

was your darkness, give it a wide berth. After Hop Hadley was delivered from alcohol, he spent the rest of his life helping others who struggled with that addiction. But when Hadley walked down a street and smelled alcohol coming from a bar, he crossed the street to walk on the opposite side. He didn't trust himself. He gave himself enough space to handle the problem. When you hear an inner voice saying, "Don't worry; you can handle it," rebuke the devil's voice and cross the street.

3. Share your testimony with others who are facing their hour of darkness. Knowing that someone else has been through it and found God's help gives strength and hope to those facing trials. Paul writes, "No temptation has seized you except what is common to man. And God is faithful; he will not let you be tempted beyond what you can bear. But when you are tempted, he will also provide a way out so that you can stand up under it" (1 Corinthians 10:13). Share the good news.

RESOURCE READING: Psalm 73

May 24

GOD KNOWS

In times of difficulty or disaster, nothing is more comforting than meeting someone who knows how to help you. When the doctor says, "Yes, this is serious but we have a solution," or the financial advisor says, "There's a way we can work through this," or the trail guide says, "Don't worry. I know how to get us out of here," our anxiety begins to ease. It is when you find yourself overwhelmed and you don't know how to resolve your problems that you get sweaty palms, your heart beats rapidly, and sleep eludes you.

Years ago, God's people found themselves in a "no way out" situation. During the reign of King Uzziah, Egypt, Syria, and Babylon all wanted to control Israel, which was trapped in the midst of the three superpowers.

God saw their tears, felt their frustration, and responded saying, " 'For I know the plans that I have for you,' declares the LORD, 'plans for welfare and not for calamity to give you a future and a hope' " (Jeremiah 29:11 NASB).

"I KNOW!" The words resound with authority. This is the same God who spoke the world into existence. The same God who determined your genetic code at conception. The same God who knows what tomorrow holds. And the same God who says that His plans are for your welfare and not disaster to give you a future and a hope.

Just a minute, you may be thinking. *How can God bring any order out of this chaos?* Don't worry; that's His problem, not yours. If God has a plan (and He does), then His plan has to be better than yours because He knows the end from the beginning, and your vision is very limited. God's plan works when human logic and insight fail.

If God's plan is going to work for you, you must trust Him completely and without reservation. Following that great promise, God said, "Then you will call upon Me and come and pray to Me, and I will listen to you. And you will seek Me and find Me, when you search for Me with all your heart" (Jeremiah 29:12–13 NASB). Seek the Lord with all your heart. That's the answer.

RESOURCE READING: Jeremiah 29:10–14

WHEN TO SAY "WHEN!"

H ow do you know when it's time to hang 'em up and quit? Do you grasp the golden parachute, as they call a good retirement in business, or do you wait until they give you ten minutes to clean out your desk and a security guard walks you to the door?

For Tommy Lasorda, the dynamo of energy who managed the Los Angeles Dodgers for two decades, it wasn't until he was rushed to the hospital with a heart attack that he decided to step down. After several weeks of recuperation, Lasorda called a news conference to announce that it was best for both him and the organization for him to retire.

For Tommy Lasorda, the heart attack was a wake-up call, a clear indication that it was time to end his illustrious career. Others are more likely to "jump the gun" and quit too soon. Maybe they get hurt feelings, or get annoyed or irritated— or maybe they're just tired and tense. So they quit.

The following guidelines will help you know when it's time to say "when."

Guideline #1: It's time to go when timing, not emotion, drives your decision. If you're motivated to quit by a personality conflict, a single misunderstanding, or a few discouraging days, you're probably making a mistake.

Guideline #2: It's time to quit when you see trends that are clearly established. A clearly established pattern is one of the ways that God uses to help you know when it's time to say "when." Wisdom is having the good sense to recognize the changing seasons of life.

Guideline #3: It's time to go when your decision is confirmed by caring friends who will be honest with you. Talk over your decision with someone who is neutral, and carefully evaluate your options.

Guideline #4: When you openly and sincerely make the situation a matter of prayer, asking God to guide you, He will give you a sense in your heart that the time is right.

God promises that He "will instruct you and teach you in the way you should go" (Psalm 32:8). His promises are still valid today. Is it too much to expect that God can give you personal guidance? Not at all. Trust Him to show you when it's time to say "when."

RESOURCE READING: Ecclesiastes 3:1–12

May 26

PASSING THE TORCH

In 1991, a Soviet cosmonaut left Leningrad for a 313-day journey into space. By the time he returned, the USSR no longer existed, and the city of Leningrad had been renamed St. Petersburg. While he was orbiting the earth, everything had changed.

We resist change, but change is inevitable in our world. Today there are the young Trojans who are eager to change things and the old warriors who hold on to leadership, resisting change and often refusing to listen to new ideas. That's one of the reasons that young companies with aggressive leadership often make quantum leaps forward, while older, more conservative ones keep plodding on year after year. Young aggressive companies are volatile and may crash and burn while the older ones make less but are more stable.

Does the same principle apply to individuals? Absolutely.

Over the years I have seen men who resisted change ride out the storm while younger, very capable men grew weary with the status quo and left the organization. Other individuals, though, provide capable leadership for years, then wisely sense that it is time to pass the torch to a younger person, and become "President Emeritus" with embraces of love and affection. And the individual retires in a blaze of glory.

Is there no way that the wisdom of years can be synthesized with the dynamic "go get 'em" energy of youth? When it can be done, a company or an organization is the stronger for it. But altogether too often, pride and ego get in the way, and it is all or nothing.

Take time to read Deuteronomy 32 in your Old Testament and notice how God raised up a man eighty years of age to lead his people. For forty years Moses led God's people. Then the time finally came when God told Moses to pass the baton to Joshua.

God has a will regarding timing, and when God's time has come, whether it is for a younger man to take the torch of leadership and run with it, or for you to step aside and offer counsel and much prayer, you'd better know when it is time to say "when." Refusing to heed the voice of God saying, "Now!" has resulted in some organizations and businesses losing the ground that could have been gained by a more energetic, younger leader.

A final thought: Retirement isn't a biblical concept. Quitting just isn't in the book, but training a Joshua to take over or simply realizing that there are seasons to life and leadership, and knowing when to say "when" is as important as first hearing the voice of God and saying, "Yes, Lord."

On a personal note, I'm not sure that organizations should be sustained indefinitely simply because they are there, but I am most certain that God can give guidance in the sunset as well as in the exuberance of a new day.

RESOURCE READING: Deuteronomy 34

WHO SAYS THAT HAPPINESS IS ALL IN YOUR GENES?

What's wrong with this picture? The mother is shopping in the grocery store. The father is browsing at the magazine rack. In the stroller are two identical twins, about a year old, contentedly watching people walk by, occasionally yawning or stretching. Sounds too good to be true, right?

Maybe my kids weren't normal, but I can recall pushing the stroller through crowded aisles as they pulled stuff off the shelf, punched each other, and yelled like crazy.

Scientists say that contentment is all in your genes. Dr. Edward Diener, a psychologist at the University of Illinois, has proposed a concept that he calls the "happiness set point." He says that our ability to be calm, well adjusted, and happy comes primarily from our parents. I guess that's why my offspring were wound with a tighter spring than some. They can blame me and I'll blame my father. Why not?

The one thing that bothers me about these recent studies is the suggestion that whatever you are is primarily the result of heredity, and your ability to be happy is pretty much fixed. No matter how you're raised or what happens, you're bound to drift back into the same pattern with which you were born.

Although the results of the study make some sense, they overlook a powerful factor: the God dimension—the power of the Holy Spirit to change our outlook on life. Writing to the Corinthians, Paul makes a statement that runs counter to these research findings: "Therefore, if anyone is in Christ, he is a new creation; the old has gone, the new has come!" (2 Corinthians 5:17). A paraphrase puts it: "When someone becomes a Christian, he becomes a brand new person inside.

He is not the same any more. A new life has begun!" (TLB).

If there is no God, and He's not there to help us at the point of our weakness, then our best intentions will crumble and we'll drift back into our past failures and mistakes. But the good news of the gospel is that God can make a difference, my life can be different, and I don't have to be a victim of my heredity.

Has God made a difference in your life? If you were arrested for being a Christian, would there be enough evidence to convict you?

RESOURCE READING: Galatians 5:16–26

May 28

THE GOD DIFFERENCE

S tudies of happiness in several countries have found that money makes little difference to perceptions of happiness, except among the very poor," says Daniel Goleman of the *New York Times*. "Nor do education, marriage and a family, or any of the many other variables that researchers have sought to correlate with contentment. Each facilitator may make a person a little happier, but it has a minor impact, compared with the individual's characteristic sense of well-being."

Neurologists believe they have located a spot in the brain where pleasure or happiness is registered. They also discovered that unhappiness seems to be registered in the prefrontal lobes of the brain. Individuals with depression register more activity on the right frontal lobe.

One thing that the secular research doesn't take into consideration is what I call the "God factor," the about-face change that takes place when a person begins to live for God instead of himself.

For example, take Malcolm Muggeridge, the sharp-tongued editor of the British magazine *Punch*. This brilliant man of letters was a well-known cynic. During World War II, while stationed in Mozambique with a British intelligence agency, Muggeridge became depressed and decided to end his life. He planned to start swimming in the ocean and not come back. But something happened—something that changed his life. A bright light appeared before him. He didn't understand it. He only knew that God was there, and that God wasn't ready for him to die.

Later, this never-quite-happy fellow met Mother Teresa. He never spoke of it as a conversion, but that's what happened. His life got turned around. He became a believer and wrote about the regret he had for not making his discovery sooner.

You were born with a certain disposition, and the transformation of conversion will not change your personality type, but it will radically change your outlook on life. Muggeridge is one of millions who can say, "When I found God, He changed my life, and I wouldn't go back for all the gold in all the world." The researchers are right: Winning the lottery, seeing your dream come true, or reaching your goal is a momentary lift, but the God-lift is eternal.

RESOURCE READING: 2 Corinthians 6:1–10

May 29

"MY CONSCIENCE IS CLEAR!"

He died in prison at the age of seventy-two. The world knew him as Pol Pot, the Cambodian revolutionary who seized the reigns of political power in 1979, and turned his gentle land into the Killing Fields—sending some two million Cambodians to their deaths. Some died by execution, some through starvation; others were worked to death.

Shortly before his death, this man whose brutalities ranked among the world's worst, broke an eighteen-year silence and gave an interview. When asked whether he felt any remorse or sorrow for all those who had lost their lives, he replied, "My conscience is clear. Even now, you can look at me. Am I a savage person?"

The human conscience is a strange thing. Some say their conscience is clear, though they have committed horrible acts, while others experience horrible guilt over taking a postage stamp from an employer.

The prophet Jeremiah says, "The heart is deceitful above all things and beyond cure." Then he asks, "Who can understand it?" (Jeremiah 17:9). Jesus does. The One who came from heaven and became sin on our behalf, understands the treacheries of the unregenerated heart. Jesus candidly talked about the heart as the seat of our conduct. He said, "For out of the heart come evil thoughts, murder, adultery, sexual immorality, theft, false testimony, slander" (Matthew 15:19).

Though most of us would condemn Pol Pot, we sometimes refuse to accept responsibility for our own human failure. "I can't help it when I'm with that woman," a philandering husband recently told me, as though he were an animal in heat with no personal accountability.

"She took of the fruit," Adam told God, "and I did eat of it." In other words, "I'm not responsible." When I stand before God, I won't have to give an account for Pol Pot, but as sure as the sun rises in the east and sets in the west, I will have to account for myself. "You, then, why do you judge your brother? Or why do you look down on your brother?" asks Paul in the book of Romans. "For we will all stand before God's judgment seat. It is written, 'As surely as I live,' says the Lord, 'every knee will bow before me; every tongue will confess to God' " (Romans 14:10–11). We're all personally accountable to God.

RESOURCE READING: Romans 14

May 30

WHEN THINGS AREN'T GOING VERY WELL

H ow are things going?" you ask a friend.
    "Do you really want to know?"
"Sure."
"Things couldn't be much worse. If my business doesn't turn the corner in the next sixty days, I'm going under."

How do you respond? You probably wish you hadn't asked the question, but you say, "I'll pray for you," thinking that this will put an end to the conversation.

Your friend, though, has been praying, but he's starting to lose hope, wondering if prayer is supposed to work in the world of commerce. "Sure," he says. "Prayer is fine sitting in a church with beautiful music and no ringing telephones or creditors hounding you."

In the dark hours of the night, it's easy to begin to lose faith, to wonder if God really cares about you. Does it make any difference to Him whether you go under, or your business turns the corner and succeeds? Doubt creeps in and you say, "Maybe God doesn't care about me."

Malcolm Muggeridge said that atheists are the only ones on Earth who have no doubts. "The moment one believes," he said, "one automatically doubts, doubt being an integral part of faith." C. S. Lewis said that before he became a Christian there were times when Christianity looked terribly probable.

After he became a Christian, there were times when atheism looked quite probable. He believed that unless we tell our doubts where to get off, we'll dither back and forth with no confidence in anything.

Prayer brings us into confrontation with what God wants. It doesn't always change the circumstances, but it always changes the one who prays.

When it is hardest to pray, that's when you need to pray the hardest. Fight doubt by taking a Bible and marking the many promises of answered prayer. Underline them and take them to heart. Put a notebook in the back of your Bible and begin to jot down dates and what you are praying about, and then record how God answers.

Don't believe all your doubts and refuse to doubt all your beliefs. "Let God be true, and every man a liar" (Romans 3:4).

RESOURCE READING: Joshua 1

May 31

WHAT IS A BLESSING?

When Charles Stirling was imprisoned in North Korea, his captors caught him silently saying grace before a meal of rice, turnips, and a small piece of rancid pork. "What are you doing?" his guards demanded.

"I was praying, silently thanking God for these blessings," he told them.

"What did you say?" they wanted to know. So he told them. He had silently said, "Lord, we thank You for these blessings, and all of us ask for Christ's mercy. Amen." That was it. He had learned the prayer as a boy from his father. Not satisfied, his guards demanded that he repeat the prayer out loud several times.

Then they asked, "What is a blessing?" He tried to explain, but they couldn't understand. They ridiculed him as a fool and disciplined him, telling him never to pray again. "They told me that the food was a gift from the Korean people, not from God." Today, North Korea is in desperate straits, lacking food for its people. Most go to bed hungry at night, and some are literally starving.

"Blessed is the nation whose God is the LORD," says Psalm 33:12. The blessings of the Almighty are difficult for atheists to understand. They refuse to acknowledge that it is the hand of God that brings the sunshine and the rain, that gives us the strength to earn a living and enjoy life and health.

It was not without purpose that God saw fit to include Psalm 1 at the beginning of the ancient Hebrew hymnbook. It summarizes everything else in the book. Psalm 1:1 says, "Blessed is the man who does not walk in the counsel of the wicked or stand in the way of sinners or sit in the seat of mockers." The promise applies to all people of all races and all generations.

Notice the progression from walking to standing to sitting. It speaks of degrees of involvement of those who deny the blessings of God. First you walk, then you stand and talk, and finally you sit down and embrace the mind-set.

A farmer who was asked why he thanked God for his blessings, replied "It's the full heads of grain that bow low; only those whose heads are empty remain upright."

Bow your head and acknowledge God's blessings. Thank Him for what He has given to you.

RESOURCE READING: Psalm 1

THE POWER OF HOPE

Before the days when it was common to board a plane and cross an ocean in a matter of hours, passengers were confined to a ship. Rough seas, at times, made the crossing an ordeal. On a certain occasion, a passenger was clutching the rail of the ship, his face a sickly green from sea-sickness. The steward, trying to encourage him, said, "Don't be discouraged. No one ever dies of seasickness." "Oh, don't say that," replied the passenger. "It's been the hope of dying that has kept me alive this long."

We smile at the man's humor, yet few of us understand the power of hope to sustain life. James Hewett tells of the time a visiting artist became ill and could not finish the piano concert he was playing at a certain university. As the artist apologized and walked from the stage, a little-known music teacher from the school rose from his chair and sat down at the piano. Starting where the guest artist had stopped, he finished the work flawlessly without music.

"How did you do that?" he was asked. The teacher explained that he had been imprisoned in a concentration camp during World War II. "The future looked bleak," he said, "but in order to keep the flicker of hope alive that I might someday play again, I practiced every day. I began by fingering a piece from my repertoire on my bed board late one night. The next night, I added a second piece and soon I was running through my entire repertoire. I did this every night for five years. Constant practice is what kept my hope alive. Every day, I renewed my hope that I would one day play my music again on a real piano—in freedom. It so happens that the piece I played tonight was part of my repertoire."[1]

More than 150 times, the Bible talks about hope and how the strength of a person's faith in God, and His ability to sustain and deliver, makes the difference between survival and giving up. Are you at the point of giving up hope? The same God who sustained and strengthened the prisoner can give you help and encouragement.

It is little wonder that Paul describes God as the God of hope who fills us with joy and peace, and when that strength invades your life, you cope better.

RESOURCE READING: John 21

June 2

IS THERE ANY HOPE?

I s there any hope?" anxious relatives ask the doctor when a loved one is admitted to the emergency ward following an accident.

"Is there any hope?" a panicky caller asks the airline representative when a plane has gone down with a family member on board.

It's the same question we ask our friend when he tells us his marriage is hanging in the balance. "Is there any hope?" When hope dies, something dies inside that affects every part of our being.

Some would say, "Where there is life, there is hope," but that's not necessarily true. But where God is, there is *always* hope.

For a moment, stop thinking about the situation that concerns you and focus on God. The word *hopeless* isn't in His vocabulary. Jeremiah records a question, which is also found in two other passages in the Bible: "I am the LORD, the God of all mankind. Is anything too hard for me?" (Jeremiah 32:27).

"Is anything too hard for Me?" God asks.

How would you answer that question?

Many situations are too difficult for us to handle. There are those times when the doctor says, "There's nothing more we can do." There are times when the economic tide goes out and our situation becomes desperate. But these crises are the very opportunities God is looking for to demonstrate why He is "the God of all hope." When things are beyond our control, they move us into the realm where God alone is capable of dealing with them. I believe that God allows desperation so that, when the solution comes, we realize it wasn't because we pulled strings, or made things happen, or bribed or bought our way out of the problem. God had to do it.

Man's extremity is God's opportunity, and in this we hope. To have faith does not mean that we believe something that isn't true or hope for something that's hopeless. Faith is simply responding in obedience to the great and precious promises of the Bible.

Strike the word *hopeless* from your vocabulary. Where there is life, there is God, and where there is God there is no such thing as hopelessness.

RESOURCE READING: 2 Kings 4

June 3

JUST A HAIR'S BREADTH OFF

After a delay of nearly seven years, the Hubble space telescope was finally launched into its trajectory around the earth. Scientists had great expectations that this magnificent piece of machinery would be able to peer almost to the limits of creation.

Not long after the launch, disappointment struck. Photos from the telescope, which were supposed to be crystal clear, came back looking like they had been taken with your grandmother's old Brownie camera.

The problem was caused by a minor flaw in the grinding of the lens. Eventually, the telescope began to transmit the kind of astonishing images that the developers had promised, but not until the flaw was corrected.

Here's an interesting fact: The imperfection in the lens was one-fiftieth the width of a human hair. In your camera, that wouldn't cause a ripple, but when magnified by hundreds of thousands of times, that very slight blemish made a significant difference.

Nobody's perfect, right? Of course, but for some things to work as they should, the measurements must be precise and completely accurate. A pinch of this and a spoon of that may work fine for your grandmother's oatmeal cookies, but those kinds of measurements don't cut it when we're talking about a finely tuned piece of equipment. The lens on the Hubble telescope was so close to being perfect, so nearly right on target, but it fell short. It was almost there, but not quite. That's why correction was necessary.

Like the flawed telescope, we humans need outside help. Compared with our flawless God, even our very best isn't enough. We need correction to bring us back into conformity with God's will.

That's what the beautiful story of redemption is all about. Man's best isn't good enough. It's flawed. That's why God sent His best, His only Son, who said, "This is the way back to heaven. Follow me!"

When it comes to spiritual matters, God is as precise as the laws of the universe. He never says, "All roads lead to the same place, so it doesn't really matter what you believe!" Neither does He say, "Do the best you can and that should be enough!" Jesus put it bluntly when He said, "I am the way and the truth and the life. No one comes to the Father except through me!" (John 14:6).

RESOURCE READING: Romans 3

THE ATTITUDE OF GRATITUDE

The American poet Carl Sandburg said, "When a nation goes down. . .[or] a society perishes, one condition may always be found. They forgot where they came from. They lost sight of what had brought them along." What is true of nations is also true of individuals.

Millions of people pause on occasion to give thanks for their blessings, but often their expression of gratitude is so nebulous, so indifferent, it's hard to know who is being thanked and for what.

May I suggest three words that will help you define gratitude? They are the prepositions *to, for,* and *in.* Gratitude must be directed *to* someone or something. You are grateful to God for His blessings, or to your parents for what they did, or to the person who gave you a job. Gratitude without a connection is meaningless.

The second preposition, *for,* clarifies your gratefulness. Maybe you're grateful for your health, your family, your faith, or your hope of heaven. One little boy, when asked what he was thankful for, said, "My glasses!"

"Is that so you can see better?"

"No," responded the lad. "I'm thankful for my glasses because they keep the boys from fighting with me and the girls from kissing me." That kid had the right idea.

Finally, we must learn to be thankful *in* every situation. The apostle Paul says, "Give thanks in all circumstances, for this is God's will for you in Christ Jesus" (1 Thessalonians 5:18). This may well be the ultimate test of gratitude, because you cannot be thankful in every situation unless you have confidence that God is in control of your life.

When you accept that God is in control, you can relax and thank God that He is bigger than your loneliness, your pain, or your financial need. When a friend of mine finds himself in a hole too large to dig out of, he smiles and says, "God, You now have a great opportunity to do something really significant."

Gratitude, expressing appreciation, and saying "Thank you," are habits that must be learned. There's something about human nature that makes gratitude difficult to express, but gratitude is a sure sign of a man at peace with himself and his world. May God deliver us from the sin of being thankless.

RESOURCE READING: Psalm 107

June 5

GOING ONE-ON-ONE WITH GOD

Going one-on-one with God is not something to take lightly. In the hour of confronting your need, you must know that God can be trusted.

Jacob went one-on-one with God when he wrestled with the angel, and his cry was, "I won't let you go until you bless me." Moses went one-on-one with God when he pleaded on behalf of the people he was leading.

Going one-on-one with God isn't what a soldier does in a foxhole when he says, "God, let's make a deal. If You spare my life, I'll go to church when I get back home." God doesn't bargain, no matter how you weigh the odds in His favor. Here are some guidelines for going one-on-one with God:

Guideline #1: Come to Him in simplicity and candor, and throw yourself completely on His mercy.

Isaiah 64:6 says, "All of us have become like one

who is unclean, and all our righteous acts are like filthy rags; we all shrivel up like a leaf, and like the wind our sins sweep us away."

The Bible says that sooner or later every man bends his knee in surrender. When you go one-on-one with God, be completely honest, because God knows the thoughts of your heart. He knows your strengths and weaknesses, but He delights in hearing you confess your weaknesses as you throw yourself on His mercy.

Guideline #2: Stand on the promises of God's Word. The Bible says that whoever comes to God will not be rejected. Based on the promises of Scripture, ask God in simple faith to meet you and to prove Himself to you. More than a few times in Scripture we read about God doing something big and important so that people will know that He is God. He still shows His power today.

Guideline #3: Approach God on your knees in surrender and obedience. Going one-on-one with God is a Gethsemane experience. An encounter with the Almighty is not a party game or religious experiment. It's heavy stuff, but it is the only way to encounter the mighty power of God in your personal life. Once you have been there, like Jacob, you bear the mark and there is no going back.

RESOURCE READING: 1 Chronicles 21

BEARING THE MARK OF
THE DIVINE

I f you had cheated your brother out of his inheritance and had fled for your life, then learned a few years later that he was coming to see you with a small army of thugs, would you be concerned? You'd be scared silly, right? The fear of what might happen when Esau arrived drove Jacob to his knees before God.

You can read the full story in Genesis 32–33, but here's what happened when Jacob went one-on-one with God: "That night Jacob got up and took his two wives, his two maidservants and his eleven sons and crossed the ford of the Jabbok. After he had sent them across. . .Jacob was left alone, and a man wrestled with him till daybreak. When the man saw that he could not overpower him, he touched the socket of Jacob's hip so that his hip was wrenched as he wrestled with the man. Then the man said, 'Let me go, for it is daybreak.' But Jacob replied, 'I will not let you go unless you bless me.' The man asked him, 'What is your name?' 'Jacob,' he answered. Then the man said, 'Your name will no longer be Jacob, but Israel, because you have struggled with God and with men and have overcome. . . .' Then he blessed him there" (Genesis 32:22–29).

For the rest of his life, Jacob limped—he bore the physical mark of His encounter with God. Whenever you encounter God, you will never be the same. From that point on, you will bear the mark of the divine on your life.

Sound scary? Not for a moment. God is a loving God, and when He blesses your life, it is always for the better.

What are some of the results of an encounter with God? Your perspective changes. You realize how weak and incapable you are. Your priorities change. Holiness, not just happiness, becomes important. Living right becomes more important than living well. You become determined to trust God and do the right thing, no matter what the cost.

When Jacob met his brother, instead of a bloody battle, he made peace with him. That's the difference God makes.

Never fear to go one-on-one with God. It will forever settle the question of whether God cares about you.

RESOURCE READING: Genesis 33

June 7

THE GIFT OF LOVE

B roadway producer Eddie Dowling says, "When I interview actors and actresses for roles in my plays, I ask them to say only two lines: 'I love you' and 'I believe in God.' If they can read those two lines well, they can play the role."

Jesus also used a simple-sounding two-part test to answer a lawyer who tried to trick him by asking, " 'Teacher, which is the great commandment in the law?' " Jesus said to him, "You shall love the LORD your God with all your heart, and with all your soul, and with all your mind." This is the first and great commandment. And the second is like it: "You shall love your neighbor as yourself." On these two commandments hang all the Law and the Prophets' " (Matthew 22:36–40 NKJV).

Two great commandments: Love God with all your heart, and love your neighbor as yourself. In our day and age when the pressures of life push us apart instead of together, we need to rediscover what love really is. A good place to start is by reading 1 Corinthians 13.

Paul was writing to a group of immature Christians in the ancient city of Corinth—about forty miles from Athens.

The Corinthians were people who had been cut loose from their heritage when Corinth was overthrown by the Romans in 149 B.C. Nearly a hundred years later, the descendants of those who had been carried away in chains came back and rebuilt the city.

When Paul came to Corinth and preached, many were converted, but they still lived according to the surrounding culture. Paul wrote several letters to the Corinthians, instructing them how to live as Christians in a secular world. In one letter, he says, "If I speak in the tongues of men and of angels, but have not love, I am only a resounding gong or a clanging cymbal" (1 Corinthians 13:1).

The Corinthians were Greeks, who prided themselves on their great orators, men like Demosthenes, Plato, Socrates, and Aristotle. Paul is saying, "Even if I had their tongues and had the power to sway vast crowds with my oratory, even if I spoke like an angel—if I don't love God and my neighbor, my words are like a clanging cymbal."

Think about it.

RESOURCE READING: 1 Corinthians 13:1–3

June 8

LESS THAN A ZERO WITH THE CIRCLE RUBBED OUT

Writing to the Corinthians, Paul said, "If I have the gift of prophecy and can fathom all mysteries and all knowledge, and if I have a faith that can move mountains, but have not love, I am nothing."

The word that Paul used for *nothing* means "worthless, meaningless, of no value whatsoever." Was Paul merely being theatrical? No, he simply wanted to convey his message in the most powerful and graphic terms he could find. Think of it like this: If you have a very tiny amount of something, you can measure it, you can subtract from it or add to it, but when you are *nothing*, it means you do not even rate the dust of the ground. That is Paul's opinion of your life if you have no love—regardless of how important or brilliant you may be.

In case the Corinthians might still miss his point about the importance of love, Paul continues: "If I give all I possess to the poor and surrender my body to the flames, but have not love, I gain nothing."

For seventeen years, John Huss pastored Bethlehem Chapel, the most sophisticated church in the city of Prague. He preached in his native Bohemian tongue and the masses loved him. People waited for hours to hear him preach the gospel, and it revolutionized the city. But when he attacked the corruption of the aristocratic landowners and the abuses of the church, he made enemies. When Huss said that "every saint is a priest but every priest is not a saint," he was ordered to recant or be burned as a heretic. Huss gave himself to be burned. As the flames licked at his body, he said, "I have said the truth according to the gospel of Jesus Christ, so I'll choose to die—and gladly."

Paul's point is that even if we have the convictions of a John Huss, if we have no love in our lives, we are nothing! Paul's words have a way of getting under our skin. Still, we must realize that no matter what great charitable causes we support, even to the extent of giving away everything we have—or giving our bodies to be burned at the stake, without love, we are nothing. And that is pretty insignificant.

RESOURCE READING: Read 1 Corinthians 13:1–3 in a
    different version than you read yesterday.

KNOWING THE REAL THING

C artoonist Charles Schulz was dining in the home of a friend when the host remarked that he had just what Schulz needed to set off his dinner jacket. He disappeared for a few minutes before returning with a medallion on a chain. Across the face of the medallion were the letters L-O-V-E. Schulz fingered it for a moment before handing it back to the host. With a wry "Charlie Brown" smile on his face, he said, "It's just a little too much for me. Do you have one that says L-I-K-E?"

In his honesty, Schulz pointed out an important truth: Love is not easy. The apostle Paul gave us marks or descriptions to identify real love.

First, he says, "Love is patient." Patient love persists when your husband leaves his clothes on the bathroom floor or your wife leaves the cap off the toothpaste.

The second test of real love is kindness. Kindness is not weakness, softness, or inaction. It is the strength of character that lets you meet harshness with kindness or keep your mouth shut.

Real love "is not jealous" (NASB). With his seven hundred wives and three hundred concubines, Solomon knew something about jealousy. He says, "Jealousy is cruel as the grave" (Song of Solomon 8:6 KJV). The green-eyed monster of jealousy can destroy the warmth of a home, calling thoughts and motives into question. Jealousy is an enemy of real love.

"Love does not brag and is not arrogant" (NASB). Did you ever hear anyone say, "He's a self-made man and he worships his creator"? That is the way of arrogance.

Real love puts aside selfish motives and personal gratification, and puts the welfare of others above your own. This quality of love is described by Jesus when He says, "Greater love has no one than this, that he lay down his life for his friends" (John 15:13).

The fourth test of love is how you behave toward others. "Love. . .does not act unbecomingly," says Paul (NASB). I paraphrase it like this: "Love does not make a fool out of anyone." Measure your love against Paul's words.

RESOURCE READING: 1 Corinthians 13:4–7

June 10

REAL LOVE NEVER MAKES A FOOL OUT OF YOU

Three perspectives on love:

1. When Sir Ernest Shackleton was exploring the Arctic, he and his party faced a difficult hour when their rations became depleted. Finally, the last few biscuits were given out to the men. That night, Shackleton lay awake in his sleeping bag with their peril heavy on his mind. He knew that death by starvation was near unless something happened.

   As he lay there, from the corner of his eye he noticed movement by one of his men. A cold chill came over him when he realized that the man was stealthily reaching for another man's food bag. Shackleton's mind reeled; he could not believe what he was seeing from one of his most trusted men. Still, he knew that starving men sometimes acted like predators.

   His faith was restored, however, when he saw the man take his last biscuit and placed it in the other man's parcel. That is the sacrifice of real love.

2. George Bernard Shaw once said, "I was taught when I was young that if people would only love one another, all would be well with the world.

This seemed simple and very nice, but I found when I tried to put it into practice not only that other people were seldom lovable, but that I was not very lovable myself."

3. A gardener wrote to the U.S. Department of Agriculture: "I've tried everything I've ever heard or read—including all your bulletins—on how to get rid of dandelions, and I've still got them."

By return mail he received the last word on the subject:

"Dear Sir,
If you have tried everything and you still have dandelions, then there is only one thing left for you to do: Learn to love them."

Life is like a lawn full of dandelions. We want to be rid of them any way we can, but at times the dandelions hang in there, and God expects us to learn to love them. The alchemy of love can turn the dandelions of life into daisies. When Paul wrote to the Romans, he told them that God's love comes through the Holy Spirit who is given to us. The only way to love others is to have God's love within ourselves.

RESOURCE READING: Read 1 Corinthians 13:4–7 in a different version than you read yesterday. Compare the two.

June 11

LOVE ONE ANOTHER

As a young man, Pitirim Sorokin witnessed the violence and chaos of the Russian Revolution. When the

Communists came to power, he escaped and came to the United States, eventually becoming chairman of the sociology department at Harvard University. He says, "When all is said and done, the great need of the world is not more powerful armament or even better communication. It is not to bring about a zero population growth, or more food for the world. It is to begin to love each other with a simple but pure love that inevitably puts the welfare of the other first—whether it be a member of your family or the most insignificant person anywhere."

For centuries, people have tended to fight fire with fire. But Jesus says, "Love your enemies, do good to those who hate you, bless those who curse you, pray for those who mistreat you" (Luke 6:27–28). Peter says, "Love one another deeply, from the heart" (1 Peter 1:22).

And to the Romans, Paul writes, "Do not take revenge, my friends, but leave room for God's wrath, for it is written: 'It is mine to avenge; I will repay,' says the Lord. On the contrary: if your enemy is hungry, feed him; if he is thirsty, give him something to drink. In doing this, you will heap burning coals upon his head" (Romans 12:19–20).

A man discovered this truth when he bought a piece of property. When he met his neighbor for the first time, the neighbor bluntly said, "When you bought this land, you also bought a lawsuit with me. Your fence is ten feet over my property line."

Taken aback, the new neighbor forced a smile and replied, "Listen, friend, I'd like for you to be a friendly neighbor. Tell you what—move the fence where you want it, and send me the bill. You will be satisfied, and it will be fine with me."

Paul says, "Love. . .does not take into account a wrong suffered" (NASB). In other words, love is a poor mathematician and has an even poorer memory. Some folks have amazing memories when it comes to personal injury or harm done to them; others hardly remember when someone owes them a large sum of money. Love never counts the cost of helping those you really love.

RESOURCE READING: Luke 10:25–37

June 12

I KNEW IT ALL ALONG

W hen you hear that your bitterest enemy has really "gotten it in the neck," do you quietly—or perhaps not so quietly—rejoice?

Good! you think. *He got just what he deserved! I never liked him anyway.*

Your natural reaction is the opposite of how God wants you to respond. In the greatest passage ever written about love, Paul gives us some tough words of advice. He says simply that "love does not delight in evil but rejoices with the truth" (1 Corinthians 13:6).

When you learn to love the way God loves, you are saddened when a person falls in a moment of weakness. The King James Version says, "[Love] rejoiceth not in iniquity, but rejoiceth in the truth." The Living Bible says, "It is never glad about injustice, but rejoices whenever truth wins out."

Why are we quicker to believe a lie than the truth? Consider the following true story:

A staff member of a certain church became jealous and resentful of the senior pastor and decided he would "get him." He borrowed the church's mailing list and wrote a letter—which was totally untrue—accusing the pastor of sexual indiscretion with one of the secretaries.

When confronted, the disgruntled associate admitted he had lied and that the letter had been designed to settle a personal score. The church council promptly exonerated the senior pastor, and fired the associate. But that wasn't the end of it.

Despite the associate's retraction, the rumor about the senior pastor quickly spread. "Have you heard about so-and-so?" When his name came up in conversation, people whispered, "They said he didn't do it, but I'm not so sure." The damage had been done. Despite the pastor's innocence, his ministry was hurt so badly by the rumors that he quietly resigned and accepted an appointment to a church in another city.

The spirit of love asks three tough questions before it passes on charges involving character: 1. Is it needful? 2. Is it kind? 3. Is it true?

May God help us to learn to rejoice in truth and be saddened when someone stumbles and falls. May God also grant that those who are unsteady never stumble and fall because our feet were in the way.

RESOURCE READING: Ephesians 4:1–16

June 13

LOVE PROTECTS

Someone has said that marriage is the art of two incompatible people learning to live compatibly together. Anyone who has been married for more that twenty-four hours would agree that sustaining a marriage takes more than romantic feelings. It's costly, too. But its currency isn't monetary. We pay by repressing the desire to always be right, by giving up the desire to win every round. Yes, love learns to compromise and yield, but it triumphs in the end.

In the magnificent prose found in 1 Corinthians 13, Paul describes the characteristics of love. An intense study of this chapter can change your life, as it did mine many years ago.

Paul says that real love—the kind that makes incompatible people compatible—is patient, kind, free of envy, not boastful or proud; it doesn't insist on its own way; it is slow to believe wrong but quick to rejoice in good things.

Following these words Paul makes four statements about love: "[Love] bears all things, believes all things, hopes all things, and endures all things" (NASB).

Love bears all things. Another translation says, "Love protects." Another way to say it is, "Love covers all things." L. Huffman received a letter from a foreign friend, and the letter was filled with expressions that were quaint because the friend's knowledge of English grammar was quite poor. However, Huffman's heart was deeply touched as he read the postscript: "The mistakes you will cover with the coat of love."

Eventually, even the best of us will need the covering of love to hide his imperfections. The Living Bible says, "If you love someone you will be loyal to him no matter what the cost" (1 Corinthians 13:7). That is the picture of a real friend.

Love believes all things. This characteristic of love explains how a young man can commit a hideous crime, yet his mother will say, "He was always a good boy who could do no harm to anyone." That is the great quality of *agape* love.

Love hopes all things and endures all things. With almost unbelievable tenacity, love suffers long, is kind, and endures all things. Nowhere in all of life's relationships is love more important than in our homes, where we train incompatible people to be compatible.

RESOURCE READING: Ephesians 4:17–32

LOVE IS WHERE IT'S AT

The Wizard of Id comic strip one Sunday showed a clergyman standing in the pulpit, proclaiming to his congregation, "My children, love is where it's at!" The next several panels show him driving home his point, saying, "Love thine enemy. Love thy neighbor. Love one another. Love is the way." The final panel showed the minister standing at the door shaking hands with the people. He's thinking, *This is the part I hate the most.*

The humor underlines a sober truth. It's one thing to talk about love and another thing to live it in the everyday world where we rub shoulders with people we don't always like. *Agape* love—the kind that keeps peace in a relationship—is more than a meaningless shibboleth. It is a way of life, whereby God touches other people through our lives.

The apostle Paul says, "Love never fails." What a claim! Was Paul merely swept away with poetic license? No, he is simply stating a fact: Love has power that transcends human logic. The word translated "fail" is the same word used of a Greek actor who muffed his lines. Paul is saying that on the stage of life, love is bound to win. It is certain to succeed, and those who would practice it will never be defeated, no matter how poorly they appear to be playing their parts.

Love is more powerful than the attitude that says, "If you hit me on the cheek, I'll punch you in the nose!" When love is put to the test, it always succeeds—in your marriage, your family relationships, and at the office, shop, or factory where you work.

One day everything you possess will fall away, but love will live on. Paul is saying that the effect of love lives far beyond the moment when our frail, mortal bodies are placed in a grave. Love in our lives is endowed with an eternal quality, because God is love (see Romans 5:5 and 1 John 4:7).

Perhaps you loved someone and your love was not returned. Maybe it was even rejected. You are hurt. You do not understand what happened or why. If this is your life, remember what Paul says: Your love was not offered in vain. Love never fails.

RESOURCE READING: John 13:34–38

June 15

THE TRIUMPH OF LOVE

W hen I was a child," wrote Paul to the Corinthians, "I talked like a child, I thought like a child, I reasoned like a child. When I became a man, I put childish ways behind me" (1 Corinthians 13:11).

Have you ever seen two children playing who just couldn't get along? Before you know it, one of them is shouting, "Okay, I'll just take my toys and go home!" As adults, we act like children when we threaten to walk out on our marriages rather than facing issues, learning to communicate, and resolving conflict. Quitting is always easier than facing our childishness. We need the courage to allow the persistence of love to win out.

Paul says that love is a mystery we will never fully understand until we cross the threshold that separates us from the God of love. "Now we see in a mirror dimly, but then face to face; now I know in part, but then I shall know fully just as I also have been fully known" (1 Corinthians 13:12 NASB).

No one is born with love in his heart. It is learned, and

the longer you wait to let God's love fill your heart the more difficult it becomes for you to be willing to let Him love through you.

Your capacity to love may have been damaged by something that happened in the past; but the Great Physician can perform surgery on your heart, erase the scar tissue of unpleasant memories, and bring the touch of love into your loveless life.

"And now," concludes Paul, "these three remain: faith, hope, and love. But the greatest of these is love." On a scale of 1 to 10, how would you rate your ability to love? Has the fire of love in your heart gone out? Let God's love touch your heart and overflow to those around you. It still works just that way.

RESOURCE READING: 1 Corinthians 13:8–13
   (Memorize verse 13.)

June 16

GO TO THE SOURCE
FOR THE REAL THING

T he great rivers of the world begin on cold, frozen slopes high in the mountains. From a trickle of crystal-clear water, a stream begins to flow and eventually a cascade of water plummets down the mountain. In the valley below, the stream becomes a river, sometimes a great river like the Nile, the Amazon, the Ganges, or the Rhine. By the time these massive bodies of water reach the ocean, however, they are filthy, muddy, and grossly polluted.

The same principle applies to the love of God. The further we are from Him, the more polluted is our understanding of love.

For the past several days, we've focused on Paul's great chapter on love in 1 Corinthians 13. But any discussion of the subject would be incomplete without a few words of encouragement for those whose river of love has either evaporated in the desert of life, or become so polluted that you hardly know what it is.

When God touches your heart, your life changes, and the mud and filth of sin is washed away. When the pollution of sin is eliminated, love flows freely. This miracle of conversion is the answer to the lovelessness and the selfishness that destroys marriages, homes, and relationships.

Three guidelines can make the difference:

Guideline #1: Acknowledge your need for God. Confess that sin has stopped the flow of love in your life. Instead of pointing your finger at someone else, say, "God, I need You. Forgive me and touch my life."

Guideline #2: Ask God's forgiveness and invite Him to be your Lord and Savior. Jesus promises to help us: "Here I am! I stand at the door and knock. If anyone hears my voice and opens the door, I will come in and eat with him, and he with me" (Revelation 3:20).

Guideline #3: Begin loving in simple steps. When you fail and fall back into old habits and loveless ways, quickly admit your mistake and ask for God's help. Until you go back to God—the fountain of love, you'll never lay hold of the real thing. Go back to the Source. It's the only way to fill your cup of love to overflowing.

RESOURCE READING: 1 John 4

I LOVE YOU, YOU'RE PERFECT, NOW CHANGE

"I love you, you're perfect, now change" is the name of a humorous play—a parody on how we fall madly in love and then strive to remake our spouses. Sometimes we nag. Sometimes we cajole or manipulate or threaten. But it just doesn't work.

I often tell a bride that there will be three words on her mind when she marries. One is the *aisle* she will float down on her father's arm. The next is the *altar* where she will kneel. And the third is the *hymn* that will be sung during the ceremony. After the ceremony, her thoughts will move to three similar sounding words: "I'll alter him."

I love you, you're perfect, now change. In all honesty, do you find yourself trying to change your spouse? If you really want change, try these simple guidelines, which are guaranteed to work:

Guideline #1: Love your spouse "as is." Stop trying to get your mate to change. Love begins where you are right now. Change is the result of God's Holy Spirit working in a person's life. Your nagging doesn't help.

Guideline #2: Strive to be the person that God wants you to be. If you spend too much time getting your spouse to change, you'll forget to become the person you ought to be. Focus on being the right person, not making the other person right.

Guideline #3: Pray that God will do His work in your spouse's heart. "My husband's not a Christian," I often hear.

"Well, have you prayed for him, asking God to bring him to Himself?" "Oh, yes!"

Then say, "My husband hasn't *yet* become a Christian," reflecting the expectancy you feel in your heart that God has heard your prayer and in His own time will do His work in your husband's heart.

I love you, you're perfect, now change. It just doesn't work. But as we conform to what God wants, as we love our spouse and strive to please him or her, change will happen. I love you. You're perfect. Let's grow together and change as God works in our lives. That's the better way.

RESOURCE READING: Ephesians 5

June 18

THE OLDEST PERSON ALIVE

At age 85, Jeanne Calment took up fencing. At 100, she was still riding her bicycle. At age 110, she decided that living alone was too hard and moved into a retirement home. At age 121, the *Guinness Book of World Records* crowned her queen of all living beings—the oldest person alive. When she celebrated her birthday, they baked a cake and put more than ten dozen candles on it. I hope the fire extinguisher wasn't far away!

Whenever I hear about someone who has beaten the odds and lived well beyond the "threescore-and-ten" years Moses talked about long ago, I always ask, "What's the secret? What allows a person to outlive her contemporaries?" How do some folks develop a positive attitude, whereas others die in their bitterness and strife? Jeanne Calment attributed her longevity to olive oil and port wine.

One quality that distinguishes people who live to a ripe

old age: Nothing really gets to them. No matter what goes wrong, they've lived long enough to know that life goes on.

There's a connection between the way people live and how long they live. Of King David it was written, "He died at a good old age, having enjoyed long life, wealth, and honor. . . ." (1 Chronicles 29:28). Then God promised Solomon, his son, "If you walk in my ways and obey my statutes and commands as David your father did, I will give you a long life" (1 Kings 3:14).

Live right, eat right, and think right and you'll have an edge over the person who debauches himself, abuses his body, and suffers the consequences.

Christians are not immune to the physical consequences of ignoring the rules. I remember one highly respected Christian leader whose life was ebbing away in his early sixties. As he lay dying, he told a friend, "I've abused my health; I've never taken time to eat right, and now I'm suffering the consequences."

When Paul wrote to the Romans, he told them to give their bodies as a "living sacrifice" to the Lord, because God indwells His children. That's still good advice today.

RESOURCE READING: 1 Corinthians 6:12–20

June 19

ABRAHAM—THE MAN OF FAITH

There's nothing new under the sun. The struggles and battles we face are much the same as those fought in the hearts of men and women centuries ago. The good news is that we can learn from those who have gone before us.

Take Abraham, for example.

God made a promise to Abraham: "You will have a

son!" But God's promise was challenged by three factors: the flesh, the world, and the devil. Or, put another way: the promise was challenged by biology, society, and spiritual forces. Anytime you make a decision to follow God completely, you will be challenged. Here's how God met Abraham at the point of doubt and failure.

Abraham was an old man. His wife was an old woman, way past the normal time for bearing children. Do you believe the impossible? God scoffs at the impossible. He made the rules and has no problem setting them aside to accomplish His purpose.

The second factor that challenged God's promise was society. It's here that Abraham demonstrated how completely human he was. "If you are going to have a son," said Sarah, "then you had better take my maid and let her be the mother of the child." This, of course, was how Abraham had a son by Hagar, Ishmael, who became the father of the Arab world. Resist the temptation to help God out. It always compounds the problem.

Finally, Abraham waged a spiritual battle as well. "Who would believe such a preposterous story?" Abraham must have asked himself. "Me—a father at age ninety-six? Yes, of course!"

In time, God kept His word, precisely and completely. Abraham learned that simple obedience, no matter what your heart or your emotions may tell you, is necessary at the level of daily life. It requires the commitment of simple faith.

Friend, what Abraham struggled with—the world, his own failure, and the antagonism of the enemy, who is out to defeat you spiritually—are the same things we must battle every day. Faith was Abraham's weapon. It must be ours as well. As the songwriter put it, "Faith is the victory which overcomes the world."

RESOURCE READING: Ephesians 6:10–18

A TRIBUTE TO DAD

W hen it comes to parenting, most research focuses on the mother-child relationship, relegating the father to the task of bringing home the paycheck and paying the bills. But dads are more than providers. They can make all the difference in the world. Many of us would never have accomplished what we have in life had our fathers not set an example for us.

Father's Day is a time when we pause to pay tribute to our dads and their influence in our lives. Today's selection is a tribute to the man who was there when I needed him. I owe my father a debt of gratitude. Allow me to share some thoughts with you about how he influenced my life.

At Dad's memorial service, I mentioned four characteristics that imprinted the lives of his three children.

The first was his fierce determination. As one of nine children, Dad's early life was tough. But he desired to get ahead and worked his way through college. His "no excuses; you can do it" attitude refused to quit. Still, his drive to succeed was always tempered with integrity. "Think big; act big; be big," he often told us. I never knew him to distort the truth or to be less than fair—even with his competitors. *Guidelines* would not exist today if Dad had not taught me how to work and given me goals worth working for.

The second remarkable characteristic of my father was his commitment to righteousness and justice. There were only two ways to look at an issue: his way and the wrong way. His opinion of right and wrong was freely extended to preachers, fellow drivers on the highway, and—of course—politicians.

Dad was passionately loyal to his family. Some thought of him as proud and arrogant, and undoubtedly his accomplishments got in the way of his relationships at times. But he was proud of his three kids with a passion.

I also remember his love for God. My dad was an inspiration, a friend, an encourager, and a mentor. Whenever my radio or TV program was aired, he played it loud and in its entirety. For almost thirty-three years, he and my mother listened to my radio broadcasts. Though I can't prove it, I'm reasonably certain he's still listening today. Yes, Dad, I hope you are.

RESOURCE READING: Ephesians 6:1–9

June 21

WHAT DRIVES YOUR LIFE?

The fisherman who casts his line or net into the water knows his exact purpose: to catch fish. The athlete knows that the purpose of the game is to move the ball across the goal line and defeat his opponent. The doctor who scrubs for surgery knows exactly why he is there. He intends to save the life of his patient. But amazingly enough, when it comes to knowing their purpose in life, most people don't have a clue what life is all about.

Every person is driven by something. Whether it's money; the desire to be recognized; the hope that life will provide leisure or fun; the anticipation that you can reach the top; guilt, fear, greed, or whatever, something drives your life. Do you know what it is?

Sports and games are governed by an association, a rule book, or a referee. When questions of purpose or conduct come up, someone is there to say, "This is the way it is," whether people like it or not. Is it possible that so many folks today are uncertain about their purpose in life—apart from having fun—because they have ignored the rule book and have closed their minds to the counsel of the Creator?

Why did God put you here? What are you supposed to accomplish while you're here on Earth? Obviously He has some purpose, some intention, something for you to do. But until you bring God into the picture, you will never fully understand what life is about. He's the missing ingredient, the key to life's purpose that many people have never found.

The following three guidelines can help you bring the whole issue into focus:

Guideline #1: Recognize what drives your life today. "Be very careful, then, how you live—not as unwise but as wise," advised Paul (Ephesians 5:15). Take inventory.

Guideline #2: Realize that God has a purpose for your life. You are no accident, no chance happening.

Guideline #3: Receive the fullness of life that God intends you to have. "For to me, to live is Christ and to die is gain," wrote Paul to the Philippians (1:21). He knew what made His life worth living. How would you define your life purpose? You have one. Find out what it is.

RESOURCE READING: Philippians 1

June 22

CHOICES OR SINS?

A cartoon showed a man standing at the gates of heaven confronted by an angry looking St. Peter. Peter is holding a long list of the man's sins. With a look of bewilderment on his face, the man responds, "Sins? What do you mean sins? I thought those were lifestyle choices!"

Dr. Laura Schlessinger is a commonsense talk show host who refuses to let people get away with irresponsibility. Recently she wrote, "Every day on my radio program I talk with people who have gotten into all sorts of troubled, unhappy, and unworkable situations because they put aside questions of what was sensible, good, right, legal, moral, or holy, and turned instead to what they thought were worthy, viable alternatives. And always, they have excuses—excuses that may sound good, but that don't stand up to careful examination. 'This is the 1990s, you know. Things are different now,' people say to me."

"I have sinned," is a phrase used seldom today in accounting for our misdeeds. Interestingly enough, it was Pharaoh, during his battle with Moses over the Exodus, who first used the phrase, "I have sinned" in the Bible. He wasn't the only one. Tracing the use of the phrase chronologically, the next person to say "I have sinned" was Balaam, a sort of New Age guru before his time, whose donkey had more sense than he did. It was also used by King Saul and his successor, David, who cried out, "I have sinned greatly." In the New Testament, both Judas Iscariot and the prodigal son confessed, "I have sinned."

It may be difficult to acknowledge your personal responsibility for wrongdoing (which the Bible calls sin), but confession opens the door to forgiveness and life. Reflecting on his affair with Bathsheba, David cried out, "But there is forgiveness with thee, that thou mayest be feared" (Psalm 130:4 KJV). God forgives sin, but the stupidity of refusing to acknowledge your personal responsibility is unforgivable. "For the wages of sin is death," said Paul, quickly adding, "but the gift of God is eternal life in Christ Jesus our Lord" (Romans 6:23).

Forgiveness is the solution to our human failure, but until we are forthright and honest enough to admit we have sinned, we continue to walk in darkness. Think about it.

RESOURCE READING: Romans 6

TAKE A LESSON

As an occasional golfer, my game isn't very good. Finally, I got so disgusted that I decided to either get some help or quit. I enjoy getting together with friends, so rather than quit golf, I decided to take a lesson.

The pro took one look and began to point out little things I was doing wrong. He told me to close the face of the club, take an easier swing, loosen up, keep my head down and my eyes on the ball. Really profound, right? Not at all. It was all simple stuff I'd heard a long time ago when I took golf in college. I knew it all in theory, but I wasn't doing it. And I couldn't fix it myself without someone saying, "Here's what you need to do."

Businesses do the same thing. Corporations pay lots of money to bring in experts to tell them what they're doing wrong. Most of the time, the pros tell us what we already know and simply aren't doing.

I'm convinced that everyone needs to be spiritually accountable to someone. Periodically, we need someone to ask the tough questions and help us see our flaws. Paul says, "Brothers, if someone is caught in a sin, you who are spiritual should restore him gently. But watch yourself, or you also may be tempted" (Galatians 6:1).

Is your golf game more important than your relationship with God? Is your job more important than keeping your marriage together, or being a dad who is there making a difference in the lives of his kids?

I paid hard-earned money to get a golf lesson. It was worth it. I suspect, however, that a trusted friend could help me spiritually if I had the strength to say, "Right now things aren't going very well. Something is wrong, and I'm not sure what!"

What we can't see ourselves is usually obvious to those

who are close to us. They can tell us when our priorities need adjusting. Chances are you wouldn't have to pay more than the cost of a cup of coffee for that advice. It will make a difference.

RESOURCE READING: Galatians 6

June 24

CLOSURE

Item #1: A busload of Korean mourners gathers at the spot where a giant 747 crashed. They sprinkle flowers on the barren, desolate ground and offer prayers.

Item #2: A father kneels by the grave of his twenty-one-year-old son and cries, "I never got to tell you how proud of you I've been and how much I really loved you."

Item #3: The family of a young woman whose daughter was abducted as she drove home late one night wants to watch the execution of the murderer.

All of these people are seeking the same thing: closure. In simple terms, closure means putting something behind you and getting on with your life. In recent days, closure has become a kind of movement. World War II veterans are returning to the battlefields where they lost buddies, trying to come to terms with the guilt and anger they have carried for a lifetime. People who have lost loved ones attend memorial services, light candles, and spread flowers.

Closure can also mean finding God's grace and strength to go on, to discover His power and forgiveness. God has given us the means of applying closure to the sins of our past, and He wants us to know that when He forgives, the issue is closed.

In Isaiah 43:25 God says, "I, even I, am he who blots out your transgressions, for my own sake, and remembers your sins no more." Micah 7:19 tells us that God hurls our sins into the deepest sea, and Psalm 103:12 talks about our sins being as distant from us as the east is from the west.

"Do you mean I will never have to answer for the abortion I had?" asked one mother of three who didn't want another child. Not when we seek God's gracious forgiveness and forgive ourselves.

Closure is part of the healing process. Thank God that closure enables us to go on and to find His grace and strength. Aristotle once said, "A whole is that which has a beginning, middle, and end." The "end" part is also part of the whole. He's right.

RESOURCE READING: Psalm 103

June 25

BAD EXPERIENCES AT CHURCH

Where do you go to church?" I asked a young man recently.

"Oh, I don't go to church anymore," he said. "I had a bad experience and dropped out. I still believe in God, and stuff like that, but I don't go to church anymore."

"Someone did something or said something that offended you, right?"

"Exactly," he replied, relieved that I seemed to understand. He'd been hit by "friendly fire," which is how the military says, "We shot one of our own!"

"Let me tell you about an experience of mine," I began. I told him about having a meal in a fast-food restaurant in

Latin America. It was a beans-and-chicken sort of place, and my wife and I enjoyed the ambiance and the food—at least for a couple of hours. Then we both started coming apart at the seams. I mean, really sick. Believe me, it was no fun. As the result of that bad experience at a restaurant, I vowed never to darken the door of a restaurant again. Right? Of course not. We got a good dose of food poisoning, but it wasn't fatal and you can be sure we haven't stopped eating out.

Do you see the connection? "Let us not give up meeting together, as some are in the habit of doing," says Hebrews 10:25, "but let us encourage one another—and all the more as you see the Day approaching." In other words, when things get tough, we need each other all the more.

"I don't need church. I can do it on my own!" I will concede that going to church doesn't make you a Christian any more than going to a garage makes you an automobile. But think of Christian fellowship in terms of a campfire. Together, the logs feed off each other, but take one of those brands out of the fire and it begins to go out. People are much the same. Worshipping with others not only allows your soul to be fed from the Word, but rubbing shoulders with others strengthens your life.

Don't give up on church because of a bad experience any more than you would give up on eating out because of one greasy spoon that serves spoiled chicken.

RESOURCE READING: Hebrews 10:19–39

June 26

I'M SITTING DOWN OUTSIDE BUT STANDING UP INSIDE

One of the most confusing and misunderstood biblical concepts is how God wants husbands and wives to relate to each other. In Christian circles, most men remember Paul's directive that women are to be submissive—ah yes, how could they forget?—and women are quick to remember that husbands are to love their wives as Christ loved the church—a task at which most men are grossly negligent. Amazing, isn't it, that we always remember what the other is supposed to do, but we forget our own responsibility.

In many cultures of the world, women are treated as inferiors and often reduced to the level of servitude. In some countries even today, bride prices are paid to a woman's family, reducing her to the level of chattel—not much different from purchasing livestock. In China, as the result of amnio-centesis, by which the sex of the unborn child can be determined, far more baby boys are born than baby girls. By and large, many female babies are aborted.

Although many cultures and religions strive to repress women, Christianity elevates them to the status of joint "heir[s] of the grace of life" (1 Peter 3:7 NASB). It is for this reason—an outgrowth of the influence of Christianity in law and culture—that women in the West are treated as equals, not as inferiors. Paul directs men to love their wives as Christ loved the church—not to treat them as property or to repress them and keep them ignorant, allowing them only to learn to cook, clean, and sew, or do menial labor. The notion that women are supposed to knuckle under to their husbands, who treat them as domestic inferiors, is simply not biblical. Husbands and wives are to submit to each other, though wives are to allow husbands to lead the family.

The farther we move from the biblical model and pattern, the more out of kilter society is going to be. It's high time we returned to the timeless principles found in God's Word, for only then will the war between the sexes come to a halt and we will begin to find the happiness and harmony that God, the Creator and Architect of the family, designed for His children.

RESOURCE READING: 1 Corinthians 13

WHEN YOU ARE THE GUY SHOVING

A shopper with a four-year-old in tow was standing in line to make a purchase. As the line grew longer, tempers grew shorter, but the fellow with the little boy calmly said, "Take it easy, Albert. We'll make it okay. Don't get upset." The little boy waited patiently. An older lady, noticing that the little boy seemed reassured by his father's comments, leaned over and said, "Sir, you handle Albert very well. He's a fine little boy." Somewhat sheepishly the man replied, "Thank you, but his name is William. My name is Albert!"

"I thought that when I became a Christian," wrote one friend of *Guidelines*, "everything would be okay. But I find that sometimes I'm not any nicer than I was before." Sometimes our greatest failures become our most potent learning experiences.

Okay, you blew it. You know what you said or did was wrong. "If we claim we have not sinned, we make him out to be a liar and his word has no place in our lives," writes the apostle John to young believers. But he precedes these words with a solution to the problem: "If we confess our sins, he is faithful and just and will forgive us our sins and purify us from all unrighteousness" (1 John 1:9–10).

After my father's conversion at age forty, he still had some of the same character flaws, particularly profanity. As a teenager, what spoke to my heart was his immediate sense of conviction, and his determination to stop the habit. "I'm sorry; I shouldn't have said that" became part of his vocabulary after he met Jesus Christ.

The Bible calls this ongoing work of God in our lives *sanctification,* or becoming Christlike. When you fail, don't give up, don't rationalize it, and don't accept it as merely part of being human. One of the great undiscovered truths of the gospel is that along with God's forgiveness comes His strength to get on top of a situation or a habit.

Read 1 Corinthians 6:11, where Paul catalogues human failure and adds, "And that is what some of you were." The Christian life is an ongoing walk where you can grow stronger with each experience. That's God's plan.

RESOURCE READING: 1 Corinthians 6:1–11

June 28

IF THE GOOD LORD'S WILLING

There's a line from a barbershop quartet song that goes, "If the Lord be willing, and the creek don't rise." Those words weren't written by an English major or a theologian, but they bring a powerful question into focus: To what extent does God will that the creek doesn't rise? And why doesn't God stop it when the creek turns into a river, which turns into a flood?

Dick Johnson, a pastor and police chaplain, called me recently to ask if I had any insights that would help him handle a tough funeral. A young man, seventeen years old and a star athlete, was killed when his motorcycle went out of control. The young man riding with him was thrown seventy-five feet, severing an arm.

Why didn't God prevent this? Where is God in times of need? The Bible says simply, "The Lord is good. When trouble comes, he is the place to go! And he knows everyone who trusts in him!" (Nahum 1:7 TLB).

We live in an imperfect, broken world, and there will always be a tension between God's love and the natural laws of cause and effect that control our world. God is a refuge and strength to His children, but this does not save us from ourselves and our own mistakes.

When the creek rises, and you face tragedy, one of two things happens: The circumstances either drive you to God, or drive you away from Him. When you turn to Him, you find solace and strength, the kind that David discovered in the valley of the shadow of death. When you turn away from God, you deprive yourself of the only real help there is. I've never quite understood why God gets blamed for the consequences of living in a human world.

It's okay to tell God how you feel, how crushed you are, and how much you wish something hadn't happened. The prophet Habakkuk certainly questioned God when He seemed to be standing aloof and silent when disaster struck. Then God answered him. Listen for the answer, friend, and you will learn that God is not silent in times of trouble. He's very much there, speaking to us about the brevity of life and the importance of including Him in our lives. Sometimes through sorrow, His quiet voice comes through the loudest.

RESOURCE READING: Psalm 23

June 29

THE TROUBLE WITH THE WORLD

The British journalist G. K. Chesterton was a big man in more ways than one. Not only was he a heavyweight in the literary world, but he had a voracious appetite and weighed nearly 300 pounds. He also had a keen grasp of human nature and a sharp tongue, which often cut to the bone. When a magazine ran an article entitled, "What's Wrong with the World?" Chesterton responded with two words: "I am." Then he signed it,

"Yours truly, G. K. Chesterton." Wow! It takes a big man in the truest sense of the word to admit, "What's wrong with the world is *me!*"

Avoiding personal responsibility isn't something new. In the Garden, Adam begged off responsibility, pointing a finger at Eve as he explained, "She gave me some fruit from the tree and I ate from it." Husbands for generations have followed in Adam's footsteps, blaming their wives. Wives blame husbands, too. We blame our siblings and we blame our bosses. At times, we all place responsibility for our personal failure on someone else.

It's refreshing to hear someone like G. K. Chesterton say, "*I* am what's wrong with the world." Of course, God said that a long time ago through the prophet Isaiah: "We all, like sheep, have gone astray, each of us has turned to his own way; and the LORD has laid on him the iniquity of us all" (Isaiah 53:6).

What's right about recognizing when you have been wrong? Plenty. Only when you acknowledge failure and sin is there hope that it can be forgiven and overcome. Acknowledging responsibility is the key to becoming a different person.

One more thing needs to be said, and it's powerful. With our confession, followed by God's forgiveness, comes His help and strength to get on top of a situation that previously has controlled us. It's the promise of Scripture which says, "If we confess our sins, he is faithful and just and will forgive us our sins and purify us from all unrighteousness" (1 John 1:9). With that purging and cleansing comes healing and wholeness. Chesterton was right. What's wrong with the world is me! But God has the solution!

RESOURCE READING: 1 John 1

June 30

THE DIFFERENCE BETWEEN
VALUE AND COST

There's often a vast difference between the cost of something and its value. For example, the father who insists that his son drop out of school and get a job because of the cost of tuition, demonstrates that he doesn't know the value of an education. If you were stranded on an island and needed lumber to build a ship, you wouldn't quibble with a merchant over the price of the materials. You would know their value.

Many of us have become so cost conscious that we've lost sight of the value of things—whether it's the energy that goes into a friendship or the time it takes to be a good parent. When our values become distorted, we fail to recognize those things that are truly worthwhile and important.

How do we separate value from worth? In the world of commerce, education, computers, and E-mail, how can we tell the difference?

Part of the answer is perspective! Taking time away from your schedule gives you perspective and helps you separate value from cost. Look at the larger picture, not the short-term one. A child who gets an education will not only earn more over the span of his career, but he will also be better adjusted and able to cope out of a sense of well-being. Certainly there's value beyond the cost of the tuition.

The Gospel of Mark tells us of the time a woman named Mary anointed the feet of Jesus with precious ointment. Judas criticized her act of devotion and complained about how much better it would have been for the spices to have been sold and the money given to the poor. The truth is, what Mary did cost Judas nothing. Her gift was something meaningful and valuable to her. Jesus saw the value. He knew that costly acts of devotion and gifts of love have tremendous value.

Friend, when you begin to look at life only in terms of what it costs, you have become warped, and the flywheel of your life is out of balance. Take time to think through the difference between cost and value. There's a great difference.

RESOURCE READING: Mark 14:1–11

July 1

THE CRITICS PAY NO PRICE

Adrian Rogers tells the story of a man who found five new brooms in the closet of a certain church, and immediately began to complain. "What a waste!" he grumbled. "The janitor can only use one broom at a time." When the treasurer of the church heard about the flap, he retorted, "Yes, but think how you would feel if you found out that everything you had given to the church in the past five years was invested in five brooms."

Interesting, isn't it, how much criticism is rendered by folks who have no investment in the program. It's like the 50,000 spectators in the stands who always see the plays more clearly than the referee who is only a few feet away from the action.

Critical attitudes aren't a new phenomenon. When Mary came and knelt at the feet of Jesus and anointed His feet with spices, Judas objected loudly. "Could not this have been sold and the money given to the poor?" he said. Of course, it wasn't his money, and it wasn't any of his business what Mary did with it.

Jesus responded to Judas by saying, "She has done what she could" (Mark 14:8 NASB). What a powerful commendation. Few people truly do what they can. Seldom does someone give until it hurts. When someone does, and it's an act of devotion to their Lord, go easy with the criticism. Remember, it's their act of worship or devotion. It's their sacrifice—not yours.

On a certain occasion, I spoke in a very poor part of the city of Manila. After the service, a young woman approached me and warmly said, "I have a gift for you and your work." Later, when I opened the gift, I found a small bar of hand soap and a package of instant soup. At first I thought, "Is this a joke?" Then, realizing that the gift had come from a house girl, who lived with practically no income, I understood she had given the kind of gift she would present to her best friend. I was humbled and blessed at the same time.

May we so live that we hear the words someday, "She has done what he could," or "He has done what he could."

RESOURCE READING: Mark 12:44–44

July 2

FINDING JESUS

A visitor to Copenhagen would be shortchanged apart from a visit to the cathedral and the museum that feature the work of Bertel Thorvaldsen, the great Danish sculptor, whose works are so lifelike it seems you should be able to command them to speak.

The museum houses the prototypes of Christ and the twelve apostles. The image of Jesus is particularly striking. He stands with arms outstretched, reaching gently for the hand of the person who is in need. Thorvaldsen patterned his work after the text where Jesus says, "Come unto me, all ye that labour and are heavy laden, and I will give you rest" (Matthew 11:28 KJV).

After the finished sculpture was placed in the cathedral,

a European art critic came to see what Thorvaldsen had done. The man entered the nave and stood in the rear, gazing with skepticism at the image of Christ. As he turned to leave, a boy—probably one of the choirboys—saw the man's disappointment and said, "No, mister. That is not the way to see Jesus." Tugging at the man's coat sleeve, he said, "Follow me and I'll show you how to see Jesus." To humor the lad, the critic followed. Reaching Thorvaldsen's Christ, the boy knelt in front of the statue. "Come on. Kneel down," he said. Reluctantly, the man knelt and then looked up at the image of Christ. What a difference! Now he realized that Thorvaldsen had purposely designed the work to be seen best from a kneeling position.

In talking about their conversion experiences, people often say, "I found Jesus," but the reality is the opposite. It is He who finds *us,* who searches for us as a Shepherd looks for a lost sheep. Jesus is the One who lifts us out of the gutter, who redeems us when we are at the point of quitting. Jesus said simply, "For the Son of Man came to seek and to save what was lost" (Luke 19:10).

If you have never had an encounter with the living Christ who rose from the dead, start by reading the Gospel of John. If you search for Him, He'll meet you with open arms. The real Jesus is worth meeting. He'll change your life and your future.

RESOURCE READING: Acts 9

July 3

WHY STUDY THE BOOK?

T he world's best-selling and most loved book is more than 1900 years old and has been translated into more languages than any book ever written. Talk about an ongoing winner! Though it has been maligned, slandered, and condemned, the Bible is still important and worthy of study. Here are six reasons why:

Reason #1: No other book gives us knowledge of God like the Bible. Nature reveals something of God's power. Cults and other religions promise insights to the nature of God, but the Bible alone introduces the Creator who loved the world enough to send His Son in the flesh.

Reason #2: The Bible is a source of faith. Paul says that the greater your knowledge of what God says, the greater will be your faith (see Romans 10:17). It's just that simple. Want to know more about what God will do for you? Read the Book.

Reason #3: The Bible tells us how to live and convicts us of wrong when we violate God's standard. This conviction is based on God's standard of right and wrong—something which is missing in the lives of many today.

Reason #4: A knowledge of God's Word is the key to living a holy life. The word *holy* means pure and separated from defilement and corruption. It's the way God wants His children to live in a sinful world—untainted by the ravages of sin. Knowing how God wants you to live comes with the promise of His presence to help you live that kind of a life.

Reason #5: The Bible keeps us from error. Before we can tell what a crooked line looks like, we must know what a straight line is. We may not always live up to God's expectations, but when we know right from wrong, we are in a position to do right. Ignorance of the Word of God produces amoral individuals who don't know right from wrong.

Reason #6: The Bible commands us to know and study the Scriptures. Here it is, straight from the pen of the apostle Paul: "Study to shew thyself approved unto God, a workman that needeth not to be ashamed, rightly dividing the word of truth" (2 Timothy 2:15 KJV).

Do you read and study your Bible? If not, why not?

<small>RESOURCE READING</small>: 2 Timothy 3

July 4

THE E-MYTH

The E-Myth, by Michael Gerber, has been widely read by business owners who would like their companies to grow. The "E" in the title stands for entrepreneur, a word that wasn't even in the dictionary I used in college. It means one who is innovative, who takes advantages of opportunities, and who sees the possibilities when others don't even grasp the outline.

Gerber says that every person who goes into business wears three hats: One is the Entrepreneur, the visionary, the one who sees the big picture and dreams the big dreams. But he doesn't make it happen. That task is left to the Technician, the nuts-and-bolts person who takes the dream and translates it into steel and concrete.

The third person necessary to make things work is the Manager, the pragmatic person who operates like a symphony conductor, bringing little things together to support the structure of the dream.

Gerber believes that people launch businesses not simply for material reward, but for the sense of fulfillment that comes from accomplishing their dream or goal.

How does this apply to your life? Whether you realize it or not, every mother, every pastor, every businessperson, every teacher is three persons: the entrepreneur, the manager, and the technician. In too many cases, the dream has vanished, overcome by diminished expectations, losses, and disappointments. We become managers and technicians, trying to keep the family organized, the church from falling apart, the kids from ending up without clean clothes on Monday morning.

In the process, we've lost the dream and forgotten why we're here and what it's all about. "What's your motive?" asks Chuck Swindoll. Why are you doing what you're doing?

Our guideline for today comes from the pen of Paul, who was writing from prison: "Whatever you do, work at it with all your heart, as working for the Lord, not for men, since you know that you will receive an inheritance from the Lord as a reward. It is the Lord Christ you are serving" (Colossians 3:23–24).

Suddenly, the little picture becomes bigger, the technician becomes a conductor, and the routine and commonplace are endowed with the touch of the divine.

RESOURCE READING: Colossians 3:18–25

July 5

THE REAL MYTH

It's an old story but one worth repeating. Following the devastating Great Fire of London in 1666, the English architect and scientist Sir Christopher Wren designed many of the eighty-seven churches that needed rebuilding.

When Wren was visiting one of the buildings under construction, he asked several workers what they were doing.

One replied, "I'm a stonemason. I'd think that's obvious."

Another man was perched on a scaffold above the floor of the building. Wren called out, "You, up there. What are you doing?" and the man called back, "I'm helping Sir Christopher Wren build a cathedral."

Both men were working on the cathedral, but only the second man saw the big picture. Seeing the big picture is always the challenge, whether you're a CEO, a mother, or a secretary.

If you are a child of God, your faith becomes a framework for the big picture. Your life is framed by God's promises, which should bring encouragement to your heart.

" 'For I know the plans I have for you,' declares the LORD, 'plans to prosper you and not to harm you, plans to give you hope and a future,'" says Jeremiah 29:11. God's word through the prophet is echoed by Jesus when He promised, "Never will I leave you; never will I forsake you" (Hebrews 13:5).

At times it will seem that your work is unnoticed and unappreciated. At times you'll feel that what you do doesn't matter. Don't lose sight of the big picture. Remember, you are doing something for God and He notices. Our reward ultimately comes from the Lord, says Paul in his letter to the Philippians.

Bottom line: Be your own person and don't listen to the popular myth that you don't count, that you are unnoticed and forgotten. Find out what God says about you by reading the promises of Scripture. Hold on to the truth and starve your doubts to death.

High in the rafters of one of the cathedrals of Europe, there's a meticulous carving by an unknown craftsman. No one will ever see it. No one will ever care. But God saw and God cared.

Don't be overwhelmed with the details and fail to see the big picture. Don't just set stones. Help build a cathedral.

RESOURCE READING: Ecclesiastes 3:1–8

EMPOWERMENT

I f Rip Van Winkle awakened today, he would discover more than a few words he didn't know. Some are scientific, others are technical, and some are social. For example, the word *empowerment*. Newer dictionaries define the term as giving "official authority or legal power" to someone or something.

Simply put, empowerment means that individuals want part of the action. They are tired of being unrecognized, and they want some say in what happens.

Empowerment has spiritual ramifications as well, although the definition is somewhat different. God's empowerment, which He promised to His children long ago, opens the door to a new dimension of spiritual life for any who are willing to receive it on God's terms, not their own. It's the last three words that cause us trouble.

When individuals demand empowerment, it is usually on their own terms. But empowerment with God—the real thing—only comes through Jesus Christ. Peter tells us that "[Christ's] divine power has given us everything we need for life and godliness through our knowledge of him who called us by his own glory and goodness. Through these he has given us his very great and precious promises, so that through them you may participate in the divine nature and escape the corruption in the world caused by evil desires" (2 Peter 1:3–4). Reflect for a moment on what Peter has said. "His divine power has given us everything we need for life and godliness." That's all you need.

Jesus Himself promised us empowerment right before He went to heaven. He said, "But you will receive power when the Holy Spirit comes on you; and you will be my witnesses in Jerusalem, and in all Judea and Samaria, and to the ends of the earth" (Acts 1:8).

Spiritual empowerment isn't some "bells and whistles" sort of spiritual jazz to make our drab lives exciting. It's how God chooses to work through us to touch the lives of other people. God's power is there for the healing of our world and to enable us to overcome temptation and difficulty. Empowerment comes when we meet God's terms and ask Him to fill us with Himself.

May God give us a thirst for spiritual empowerment.

RESOURCE READING: 2 Peter 1

July 7

BREAKING THE BONDAGE OF YOUR OLD NATURE

Are you ever torn between what you know is right and what you really want to do? If your answer is "no," either you're not telling the truth, or the battery on your conscience has gone dead. The struggle is an old one. Even Paul experienced the conflict. He candidly tells of the battle that waged in his heart: "When I want to do good, I don't; and when I try not to do wrong, I do it anyway" (Romans 7:19 TLB).

God's Word is very clear. When you are born again, God accepts what Christ did and applies it to your account. Paul writes, "For he has rescued us out of the darkness and gloom of Satan's kingdom and brought us into the Kingdom of his dear Son" (Colossians 1:13 TLB). That in itself is pretty awesome. It means you have been transplanted spiritually.

Does that mean that you will automatically do the right thing? Not for a minute. In a sense it means that you begin the most ferocious battle of your life. Yes, you are God's child. Yes, the Holy Spirit has come to indwell your life. Yes, you belong to Jesus Christ, *but* you are still in the world and your old sinful nature wars with your new spiritual nature.

God doesn't take away your free will. Yes, the Holy Spirit can and does give you strength and help, but you are the one who has to decide the path you will take.

If you are fighting the battle of the two natures, take to heart the following three guidelines:

Guideline #1: Keep your relationship with the Lord warm and personal. Take time to fellowship with other Christians, read God's Word, and spend time in prayer.

Guideline #2: Keep the right company. If you are involved in a wrong relationship, break it off, once and for all. Don't try to justify it.

Guideline #3: Form the right habits. Someone once said, "The chains of habit are too weak to be felt, until they are too strong to be broken." Replace wrong habits with right ones.

God is still in the business of breaking our bondage and setting us free through the power of His Spirit. That's the real answer.

RESOURCE READING: Romans 7, 8

July 8

BLESS YOU

A businessman bought a Lamborghini and phoned the local parish priest to ask if he would bless it. Hesitating, the priest asked, "What's a Lamborghini?"

"Never mind," the man replied and hung up. Next, he

called a Baptist preacher and asked him to bless the sports car. The pastor immediately responded: "Wow? A Lamborghini? Best-engineered sports car in the world." He paused, then said, "What's a blessing?"

A lot of people come to God wanting a blessing, but they don't seem to realize that the blessings God gives are not a sprinkling of instant happiness and success.

What is a blessing? Modern translators have fumbled some words in the Bible, trying to make them meaningful to people today. In so doing, they miss something vital and important. In relationship to God, a blessing is a gift of His grace, the touch of His hand upon your life, the breath of His presence in such a way that you are enriched, strengthened, helped, and enabled. Does happiness mean the same thing? No way!

The English word *happy* comes from the same root word as *happenstance,* which means "good luck, chance, or fortune." Good luck is not the same as a blessing from the Lord.

The blessings of God often come disguised—sometimes as difficulties, or something we would never choose for ourselves. In retrospect we're able to see how God's loving hand gave guidance and direction in such a way that our lives were enriched, strengthened, and enlarged.

When you make happiness your goal, it never lasts, but when you seek blessing from the Almighty, He provides an ongoing source of encouragement. Like a spring that bubbles forth and will never cease, God's blessings continue to touch our lives from birth to our homegoing.

Friend, don't let the world do its number on you by convincing you that happiness is the greatest thing in life. Happiness is a by-product of being blessed by the Father, the realization that no matter what the circumstances, God is in charge.

The next time someone casually says, "God bless you!" you can reply, "Ah, yes. I am blessed every day."

RESOURCE READING: Matthew 5:1–11

LISTENING

After twenty-two years of marriage, the man and his wife reached an impasse. She moved out, and after months of striving to put things back together, he gave up and took his own life. In his suicide note, he urged the remaining members of his family to pull together and help each other, knowing he wouldn't be there himself. When problems developed, the family stopped going to church, and things went from bad to worse.

I can't help but wonder how different things might have been if someone had only listened to the husband and wife who were hurting. When no one listens, we pull back into our shells and bury our pain.

Our failure to really listen to each other is a serious injustice. The man who took his life left behind a wife and three children, ages sixteen, eighteen, and twenty-two. He also left behind shattered hopes and dreams, and robbed those he loved of his presence at graduations, weddings, and births.

Suicide has become a major social problem, and I believe these massive tragedies could be avoided if only we learned to listen to each other. Listening doesn't always fix everything, but it lets others know you care. When someone is convinced that at least one person cares, all sorts of situations become tolerable.

I never cease to be amazed when people say after we've talked, "You don't know how much you've helped me." My immediate response is, "All I did was listen," but that's precisely how I helped. I listened. There was no TV blaring, my head wasn't buried in a newspaper, I wasn't indifferent, and I gave the person my total attention.

Dr. Paul Tournier, the Swiss psychiatrist, wrote, "Listen to all the conversations of the world, between nations as well as between individuals. They are, for the most part, dialogues of the deaf."[1]

Listening is a skill that can be learned, and one that pays great dividends. Everyone needs someone to listen to them—kids, teenagers, husbands, wives, and seniors. By listening, we communicate compassion, love, and care. That's the way God made us.

RESOURCE READING: Job 1

July 10

THE FAITH DIFFERENCE

D r. Harold G. Koenig is both an internist and a psychiatrist. When he started working with elderly people, he noticed that individuals who were religious handled sickness better and recovered faster than those who had no faith.

Koenig analyzed the available research in the field of psychology and religion. He also began his own study in a dozen settings, ranging from prisons to hospitals to private homes. Koenig concluded that, indeed, religion makes a big difference when it comes to mental health. He found that individuals who had a God connection in their lives not only were healthier—lower blood pressure and less coronary heart disease—but they were also happier.

In reporting Dr. Koenig's results, the magazine of the American Psychological Association asked the question, "Given findings like these, why does religion continue to have a bad reputation among some psychologists?" Dr. John Gartner, an assistant professor of psychiatry at the Johns Hopkins University Medical School attributes it to professional prejudice—not opinions born out of scientific research. Gartner offered research to back up his opinion that some psychologists and psychiatrists—not all of them, of course—are biased against religion in general, and God in particular.

I think that the research merely certifies the obvious. Any doctor or nurse who works with the elderly and dying will tell you that those who have faith in God die far more peacefully than those who wonder what's on the other side of their last breath.

What psychologists think of religion is academic, but what you think of God, and what He thinks of you, is very important. Dr. Kenneth Pargament, a psychology professor at Bowling Green State University, says, "You can measure the footprints left by faith. But you can't measure God."

All the research in the world cannot measure the importance of intangible variables in our lives. When it comes to facing the unknown, the touch of God's finger on your life brings comfort, peace, and assurance. The faith factor resides in the human heart and isn't subject to charts and graphs. How can we measure the assurance that comes from knowing that God will never abandon us or leave us in a moment of crisis?

RESOURCE READING: Psalm 48

July 11

HOW MUCH IS YOUR PASTOR WORTH?

He marries your children and buries your dead. He counsels troubled souls and visits the sick and afflicted. He baptizes, advises, befriends, and listens. He's the pastor or priest in your church, the one whose phone number you reach for when you are in trouble or hurting.

What's his true worth?

His professional training usually ranks with doctors and attorneys—an undergraduate degree followed by three years of seminary. He begins his career with earnest aspirations of making a difference in the lives of men and women. But far too often he is taken for granted, overworked, and underappreciated. Seldom does anyone notice when he's there—day after day, week after week, year after year, but let him come up short just once and he hears about it loud and clear.

One young pastor customarily stood at the door after each service shaking hands with his parishioners. One rather successful businessman started saying, "You know, young man, you're really something else." The young pastor felt complimented, but there was something in the man's tone that made him wonder what he really meant. Finally the young pastor countered, "You say the same thing every week. What do you mean?" "Well," drawled the man, "You aren't much of a preacher, so you must be something else."

The rate of attrition among spiritual leaders continues to grow, and understandably. What bothers them the most is not the salary, which is usually substantially lower than most parishioners'; it isn't the long hours, or the demands on their time at all hours of the day and night. It isn't even the sacrifice of privacy that they make along with their wives and children. What bothers them the most is the feeling of being taken for granted, of not being appreciated.

What can you do if you have taken your pastor for granted? First, make sure that he receives adequate financial compensation. Is your pastor's salary comparable with those whom he serves in the congregation? Almost never is a pastor paid more than he deserves.

Learn to express appreciation—personally and collectively. An occasional note of encouragement is always in order. Remember, he might accept less than he's worth financially, but he can't handle being unappreciated. I've been there. I know.

RESOURCE READING: 1 Corinthians 9

WHERE IS ZEBEDEE?

W here is Zebedee?" asks George Stormont. "I've been looking for him for nearly fifty years. The New Testament is haunted by his name. You read of his sons, his wife, his hired servants, his fishing; but you never meet him."

To understand his question, you need to know that Zebedee had two sons, James and John, who were tending their father's nets near the fishing village of Bethsaida, when Jesus walked by and challenged, "Follow me!" Along with Peter and Andrew, they walked away from their nets to become disciples of Jesus.

We read of Zebedee's wife, who—in looking out for her sons' welfare—asked Jesus if her two boys could sit on Jesus' left and right in heaven.

But what about Zebedee? He's mentioned but never introduced! "Where is Zebedee?" Stormont answers his own question: "Busy. . .busy. . .busy minding his boats and mending his nets. . . He did not keep his wife or his boys from following Jesus. He [just] did not follow Jesus himself."

One of the great social tragedies of our day is the missing father. Whether he's gone to work or just gone, he's not there for his child. A father's involvement helps his children understand who they are, what it means to be male or female, and how to relate to our heavenly Father.

The sad fact is that the number of kids growing up in homes without a dad is almost as great as those living in two-parent homes. I always think twice before asking the question, "Where is your child's father?" I know that most single moms, more than anything else, wish the father were there— for them as well as for the child. These men need to be challenged, and in some cases reproved, for their irresponsibility and neglect.

Are you a Zebedee? Take a look at your appointment book and see how many days these past six months were spent with your son or daughter. How many weekends were you out of town, or golfing, or doing something apart from the family?

Where was Zebedee? Busy. Too busy. Occupied. Absent. Everything he missed could never be balanced by a few more fish, a few more coins in his purse, or a larger business. Some things just aren't worth it.

RESOURCE READING: John 1

July 13

FINDING AN EXTRA HOUR
EVERY DAY

Mothers have been working twenty-five hours a day since the Garden of Eden. Now a Dallas clockmaker has designed the perfect timepiece—guaranteed to give you an extra hour every day. Who wouldn't like that? Well, actually, he cheated. You see, this clock operates on a 57.6-second minute. Believe it or not, if you trim 2.4 seconds off each minute, multiplied by sixty minutes per hour, and twenty-four hours per day, you'll come up with a twenty-five-hour day.

This new clock may never be more than a novelty, but who wouldn't like an extra hour every day? It's amazing how those few seconds out of every minute add up to a pretty significant chunk of time.

For many things, I've learned that you don't *find* time. You have to make it or take it. If you don't determine how to use your time, others will do it for you in interruptions. Without a plan, time dribbles through the hourglass a few seconds here and a few minutes there. Would you like an extra hour a day? Then compress some of the wasted time in your schedule and take time for what's important. Want some suggestions?

1. Take time for your spiritual development. I list this first, because if you fail here, you'll fail everywhere else. You don't find time for this; you've got to take it. I've learned that getting up thirty minutes earlier every day to spend time in the Word and in prayer makes my entire day go better.
2. Take time for what counts—your wife and children. They depend on you for more than your paycheck. Whether you think much about it or not, your presence and involvement is important to your marriage and the development of your children. Standing at an open grave, I've heard scores of people say, "If we had only known we had so little time together, we would have played more."
3. Take time for yourself. "Dear God," prayed a little boy. "Please take good care of Yourself, because if anything happens to You, we're in big trouble." Dad—the same could be said of you. Take time to guard your health.
4. Take time for God. Worship as a family, do His work, reach out to someone who is hurting. Take time.

RESOURCE READING: Revelation 21

July 14

KNOWING HOW TO
EXPRESS YOUR LOVE

Maybe you grew up in a home where your dad never expressed his love. He worked hard and brought home his paycheck. He provided for you, but he never said,

"Son, I'm proud of you. I love you." He never signed a birthday card, "Love, Dad," or picked you up in his strong arms and comforted you when you fell and hurt yourself. More than a few times you asked yourself, "If he really loved me, why didn't he let me know?"

Saying, "I love you," is something some dads never do. Now that you're a dad yourself, do you repeat what you grew up with, or do you choose to learn how to express love? You can say it, write it, or hire a plane to skywrite it. But find a way to tell your kids you love them.

It's important to express your love, but it's equally important to show it. A father comes home and picks up the newspaper. When his five-year-old daughter thumps the paper and says, "Daddy, come in my room. I want to show you something," she's asking for the gift of time. If the mother quickly says, "Don't bother Daddy. He's had a busy day," the message that gets communicated is, "Reading the paper is more important than seeing what you have in your room."

Other gifts can be an expression of love, but they never count the same as the gift of yourself—time spent together.

I'm reminded of the story of the young boy who went into the den, where his father was working on a project. Seeing his son sitting on the floor, the father brusquely asked, "What do you want, son?" The little boy replied, "I don't want anything, Dad. I just wanted to be where you are."

The whole business of parenting is pretty much like spending a coin at the candy store. Once it's done, it's over, and there's no second time around.

The greatest mission field today is our children, and our greatest failure is when we bring a child into the world and give him or her almost everything but the gift of ourselves. Think about it. Only you can remedy the deficiency.

RESOURCE READING: Ephesians 6:1–4

CHOOSING YOUR RESPONSE
TO SUFFERING

Does God owe you health, wealth, soundness of mind, and loyal friends? All this, and heaven too? Or is His commitment to sustain and strengthen you, even when life isn't fair?

I've been thinking of some of the situations I've encountered recently, and how some of God's choicest servants have been on the receiving end of tough times. Like Jacob Walter, my missionary host in Papua New Guinea, who was pulled from his car by a gang of young thugs and pistol-whipped. He would have been killed had one of them not taken pity on him because he was a missionary. "In all of this," said Jacob, "I still had peace, because I knew they could do no more than God would allow."

What does God owe His children? Has He failed us when difficulties arise? We know that God could step in and overcome cause and effect. He could allow disease to strike only the wicked and send angels to protect believers.

Here's where our faith comes into focus. The promises of Scripture are not to spare us from the evils of a sin-cursed world, but to be with us as we pass through the valley and face the fire and the flood.

How well we respond to difficulties is usually the measure of how well we know God's Word. For some, whose knowledge is based on misconceptions, deep depression and anger result. They are the ones who feel that God failed them, that God should have stepped in and kept evil at bay, or protected them from sickness. But for those who know the Word, there's a deeper trust and understanding.

When Joseph confronted his brothers who had sold him into slavery, he said, "You meant it for evil, but God meant it for good." Because our vision is so limited, we often cannot see how good can come from evil. That's where the power of faith—often tried by pain and suffering—makes the difference. Sometimes we can clearly see the rhyme and reason of difficult or tough times, but some situations defy human logic, where asking the question, "Why?" is only an exercise in futility. Someday we might understand, but by then, perhaps, it just won't matter.

RESOURCE READING: Romans 8

July 16

WHEN YOU ARE IN THE VALLEY

Is trust in God really enough to take you through the dark hours of the soul? When your life is ripped apart by a bolt of lightning, your light suddenly turns to darkness, and your mind is reeling from a blow so severe you can't comprehend it, is God really enough? This shocking question penetrates the darkness when you lose a loved one, your business fails, or something tragic happens that you didn't expect.

Philip, a Chinese businessman, had spent years building his manufacturing business. Then a two-hour fire turned his dreams, and his $3 million investment, into ashes. In the darkness of his loss, he found God. Looking back, he can see that the fire was necessary for him to realize he needed a relationship with Jesus.

When Paul wrote to the Corinthians, he talked about the losses he had sustained, yet he was able to say, "We do not lose heart."

The issue is not whether you or your circumstances win, but how you fight the battle and whose side you're on. Far better to be on the side of righteousness and ultimately triumph than to be on the side that wins the battle but loses the war.

Hebrews 11 contains the stories of individuals who were certified by God as men and women of faith, yet even they endured trials: "Some faced jeers and flogging, while still others were chained and put in prison. They were stoned; they were sawed in two; they were put to death by the sword. They went about in sheepskins and goatskins, destitute, persecuted and mistreated—the world was not worthy of them. They wandered in deserts and mountains, and in caves and holes in the ground. These were all commended for their faith, yet none of them received what had been promised. God had planned something better for us so that only together with us would they be made perfect" (Hebrews 11:36–40).

When you are tempted to feel sorry for yourself or give up, stay focused on God and keep trusting Him. As David says, "Even though I walk through the valley of the shadow of death, I will fear no evil, for you are with me; your rod and your staff, they comfort me" (Psalm 23:4).

RESOURCE READING: Psalm 23

July 17

GOING BEYOND THE BARRENNESS OF AN EMPTY LIFE

When God challenged Moses to change his direction in his life, He asked, "What is that in your hand?" When Moses replied, "A staff," God said, "Throw it down." Sometimes we hold onto things so tightly that their grip on us is never broken. Corrie ten Boom used to say that our treasures should be held lightly because it hurts too much when God pries them out of our hands.

"What do you have in your hand?" Every person—regardless of age, rank, or status in life—has three things:

resources, time, and abilities. God wants them all. Acknowledging that they are His frees you to lay hold of that for which God has laid hold of you (see Philippians 3:12).

The following guidelines will help you gain new purpose in life:

Guideline #1: Acknowledge that everything you have —including your resources, time, and abilities— are a stewardship, not a possession. God has blessed you so that you might bless others.

Guideline #2: Discover how your gifts and aptitudes can punch holes in the darkness of human misery. You may not be able to devote full time to an overseas ministry. But could you carve out a few weekends or two or three weeks for ministry somewhere?

Guideline #3: Realize that your resources (including your money) are morally neutral. As God provides for your needs, you must confront the issue of lifestyle in answering the question, "How much do we need? How much is enough?"

Guideline #4: Don't limit God with small thinking. "If you could do anything in the world, what would it be?" I'm challenging you to think beyond the "I've never done that before" mentality. "Why not?"

Guideline #5: Do it now. Always waiting for the "perfect time," which never comes, leads to doing nothing. Don't wait until you can do *everything* before you do *something*.

Years ago, I penned these words in the flyleaf of my Bible: "I am only one, yet I am one. I cannot do everything, but I can do something. And what I can do, by the grace of God, I will do." You may be amazed at what can be accomplished as you stumble forward, trusting God day by day. I know. I've been doing it for years.

RESOURCE READING: Ecclesiastes 1

CAN YOU TRUST
YOUR CONSCIENCE?

How do you think a restaurant would fare if the customers were allowed to pay as much or as little as they thought the food was worth? Gene and Grace Valian, owners of the Great American Breakfast and Barbecue House, decided to try a pay-what-you-want experiment. It ended in failure. Some people have "no conscience at all," they said, though most people paid "just a shade under what they would have normally paid."

Have you ever wondered why one person can do something with apparently no conscience, while another person would struggle with the same issue? Does one person's conscience allow what someone else's conscience condemns? Strange as it seems, the answer is yes.

The My Lai incident in Vietnam illustrates the polarity of conscience that exists between different people. The sad and grim account of the slaughter of innocent women and children by a group of U. S. soldiers came to light because a soldier's conscience convicted him.

Until the beginning of the twentieth century, mothers in India would take their firstborn infant to the Ganges River and throw the innocent newborn into the waters, which were thought to be sacred, as a sacrifice to a pagan god. The very thought of this is abhorrent to most women in the world, especially those whose empty arms would desperately like to hold and cherish an infant.

If you can get away with it, does that make it okay? Many people would say "yes." The fact is that your conscience is only as good as your knowledge of right and wrong. What we call a "conscience" is more accurately defined as "guilt feelings." Can a person actually be guilty of something and have no feelings of remorse or a troubled conscience? Definitely. But when you know that what you have done is wrong before God, then your conscience becomes activated.

An understanding of how God wants you to live is the only thing in the world that will give your conscience the data it needs to be trustworthy and accurate. The bottom line is not what you think, or what your culture will allow, but how does God view your life? Remember, He has the final word in determining right and wrong.

RESOURCE READING: John 8

July 19

HAVING IT ALL

C an you have it all? Before you answer, listen to your heart for the next three minutes. Balancing home and family responsibilities with business requires the skill of a diamond cutter and the balance of a tightrope walker. Knowing when to prioritize, of course, is the key to the whole matter. But I, for one, am convinced that it is impossible to have it all and do it all. There are not enough hours in a day, nor enough emotional energy to measure up to the unrealistic expectations placed upon us by society, the work-place, and our consciences.

We must make tough decisions about what is important in life, especially in the long run. Of course, there will always be specific needs at work and in our social lives that demand extra hours and energy, but deciding what is important and then making long-range decisions in light of those major goals helps you to decide where to draw the line.

A word of warning. Affirming long-term values comes at the cost of short-term losses. OK, you don't get the promotion, or the pay increase, or the special bonus, but you do live without as much stress. And perhaps you get to see your daughter take her first step or be there when your son hits the ball out of the park. Surely that counts for something.

Who is in control of your life and destiny? You or your employer? Which is more important to you—realizing your dreams, or fulfilling the expectations and pressures of the corporate world? When you finally acknowledge that your life has been a rat race, with the rats winning, it's time to back off and ask yourself, "What's important to me?"

Having it all is an oxymoron—a contradiction of terms. It's what you really want that will eventually determine what you get. Yes, life is a matter of balance, but like the juggler who has crystal balls in the air, which won't bounce on the pavement, you must realize that there are no second chances, no returns to "go" on the boardwalk of your life. That's why careful, prayer decisions will produce long-range dividends. Forget about having it all. Decide what you really want and go after it.

RESOURCE READING: Proverbs 31

July 20

IF GOD HAD VOICE MAIL

We have all learned to live with voice mail," wrote an unknown pundit, "as a necessary part of modern life. But you may have wondered, 'What if God decided to install voice mail?' Imagine praying and hearing this: 'Thank you for calling My Father's House. Please select one of the following options: Press 1 for requests. Press 2 for thanksgiving. Press 3 for complaints. Press 4 for all other inquiries.' Or suppose you got the recording that said, 'All our angels are busy helping others right now. Your call is important to us. Please stay on the line for the first available operator.' "

Nothing is more irritating to me than calling long distance—especially from overseas—urgently needing to talk to someone, and getting a recorded message that puts me on hold. Thank God, that never happens when you need God's help. If there is one consistent theme down through the centuries, it is that God is always there to meet you at your time of need.

When Jesus prayed, the disciples discovered that the words flowed out of His heart. He didn't wait to pray until He found a cathedral with sunlight filtering through stained glass windows, nor did He wait until the Sabbath when He went to the synagogue. He prayed anywhere, and whenever there was a need. When the disciples presented Him with the little boy's lunch to feed the crowd, He lifted His voice in thanksgiving; when confronted with sickness and disease, He took control over it; when the raging hostile winds of nature threatened to sink the boat they were in, he prayed and calmed the seas.

Because God has no voice mail, you will never hear a recorded response such as, "At the tone, please leave a message. We'll get back to you as soon as possible. Meanwhile, may you be blessed and have a good day."

No concern is too small and no need is so great that you cannot take it to the Lord in prayer. As the apostle John has written, "This is the confidence we have in approaching God: that if we ask anything according to His will, He hears us" (1 John 5:14). And when we know that God has heard us, we can leave the rest to Him. Communication complete!

RESOURCE READING: John 17

GENESIS

When all else fails, read the directions." That's about the only logical explanation for the recent surge in secular interest in the book of Genesis, which has resulted in newsmagazine features, television documentaries, and talk show discussions.

Genesis is a book of beginnings. It records the beginning of our universe, man, marriage, sin, salvation, human government, nations, and the rise of a people who became Israel. In this book, you read the story of a man named Abraham, the father of both Arabs and Jews, and you find the historical background of the dispute that has divided the Middle East for centuries.

Whenever I receive a letter, I'm always interested in knowing who the sender was. Then I check the date and postmark. After scanning the letter quickly to see what it's about, I go back and read it carefully. The same procedure applies to reading the Bible.

And who was the author and when did he write? For centuries, both Jews and Christians have believed that Moses wrote the book of Genesis about 3400 years ago. Though some liberals today deny that Moses wrote the book, Jesus, Paul, and Luke all cite Moses as the author.

Luke, writing the book of Acts, says, "Moses was educated in all the wisdom of the Egyptians and was powerful in speech and action" (Acts 7:22). A lot of what Moses wrote about was completely contrary to what was believed and taught in the universities of Egypt. Moses began by saying simply, "In the beginning, God created the heavens and the earth." The Egyptians of Moses day believed the world was hatched from an egg, the fertility symbol that adorned ancient tombs and monuments. "Not so!" says Moses. "God did it!"

A resurgence of interest in the book of Genesis is nothing but good. It answers the questions of how we got here, who were our forebears, and how they ordered their lives. In this book, we see both the problems of people today and the answers to their questions about life. Read the book and listen to its message. You will be a better person because of it.

RESOURCE READING: Genesis 1

July 22

A RENEWED INTEREST IN GENESIS

"An evil soul producing holy writ is like an apple rotten at the core; outwardly beautiful, but inwardly full of deadly worms," wrote William Shakespeare.

Not long ago, *Time* magazine made the book of Genesis its cover story, showing planet Earth with a light shining from the heavens. The headline reads, "And God said. . ." with a subcaption below that says, "Betrayal. Jealousy. Careerism. They're all in the Bible's first book."

Around the same time, Bill Moyer produced a ten-part documentary series on Genesis for television. He explained the interest, saying, "At this moment of post-cold war confusion about where we're going as a civilization, with all kinds of murky religious ferment, it makes sense to do some stocktaking. Let's go back to the book that started the whole shebang."

Is this renewed interest in Genesis good or bad? No one would deny that we need to go back to the blueprint. From a human-interest standpoint alone, no other book in the world records the dreams and hopes, the sins and failures, and the foibles of human nature as does the Bible, and the book of Genesis in particular.

Unquestionably, some observers have attempted to use the book to justify our modern moral failures, portraying Moses' treatment of God as a kind of parable, not to be taken literally. They interpret the events in Genesis as a kind of existential "there is no real meaning to life" story, which then justifies our misdeeds.

The book of Genesis contains all the sordidness of man's base nature: murder, adultery, rape, war, and plunder. But the real issue is, did the people have a sense of morality, an understanding of right and wrong, which was violated? Focusing on single events could lead to the conclusion that the whole book is a collection of "anything goes" moral anarchy. Nothing could be further from the truth. Here's where an understanding of the context of Genesis in the whole Bible makes a remarkable difference. If the book of Romans, which talks about the law of conscience written on the hearts of men, was read alongside the stories of Genesis, one's conclusions would be vastly different.

RESOURCE READING: Genesis 16–18

July 23

INTERPRETING GENESIS

Should we interpret the Bible in terms of our culture? Or should our culture be interpreted in terms of what the Bible says? The answer depends on your view of final authority. Is man the measure of all things, or is God the ultimate reality?

Much of the current interest in the book of Genesis is based upon an interpretation of the events that relates our human failures and dysfunction to characters who had the same problems long ago.

Did these individuals who slept with each other's wives and murdered and plundered do so without a knowledge of right and wrong? Were they laws unto themselves, or did they have consciences marked by a sense of shame and conviction?

Let's go back to the book itself. Do you remember when our first ancestors chose their own will over God's? They ate the forbidden fruit in the Garden and then hid themselves from God. Why? In shame they saw their own nakedness and knew they had done wrong.

When Cain killed his brother Abel, God asked, "Where is your brother?" Cain shot back, "I don't know. Am I my brother's keeper?" His reply indicates a knowledge of wrongdoing. Where did this sense of guilt come from? The only answer is that God gave mankind a conscience, a sense of right and wrong ,which acts as a moral compass.

The conscience can be silenced by lust and desire. Paul speaks of false teachers whose consciences are dead. He writes, "These teachers will tell lies with straight faces and do it so often that their consciences won't even bother them" (1 Timothy 4:2 TLB). If you do something wrong often enough, eventually you'll justify your wrongdoing and continue without the slighted prick of conscience.

A British pastor once told me of a man who came to him and said, "Pastor, you just don't have it anymore. When I first heard you preach, I trembled with fear, but now you speak and it doesn't bother me in the least." The difference was not the pastor. It was the man's seared conscience. Enough said.

RESOURCE READING: Romans 2

WHO TOLD OL' HAMMURABI?

I n 1901, the science of modern archaeology was just coming into its own when archaeologist M. De Morgan began digging at ancient Susa, which is in modern-day Iran. He found a slab of black diorite measuring slightly larger than seven feet by six at the base, tapering to five-and-a-half feet at the top. At the top of this rounded stele was a depiction of Shamash, the Babylonian sun God, giving the law to Hammurabi. The writing on the stone is in Semitic Babylonian.

This code of law, adapted by Hammurabi for his subjects in Babylon, was written about the time of Abraham. It contains nearly 300 legal provisions, including such items as false accusation, witchcraft, military service, land and business regulations, family laws, tariffs, wages, trade, loans, and debts.

A study of these ancient codes reveals some common themes: the value and worth of the individual, personal rights that should not be violated, and prohibitions and regulations ensuring the safety of families and property. Where did these ideas of right and wrong come from? The answer can only be the universal law of God, affirmed by a moral sense of right and wrong, which, at first, was enforced by an individual's personal conscience.

Ultimately, these moral standards had to be written and codified, because the voice of conscience can go dead and mislead individuals. What one person's conscience may approve, another's condemns. Written laws take away the ambiguity.

Although you may have never thought much about it, it was exactly for this reason that God wanted you to know clearly what He expects of you and how you can find fulfillment and happiness. That's why He gave us a timeless book, the Bible, which spells it out for men and women of all cultures and all ages.

Laws spell out clearly what is right and wrong, and specify the punishment for wrongdoing. The Bible also does that, but it doesn't stop there. It speaks of mercy and forgiveness. "For the wages of sin is death, but the gift of God is eternal life in Christ Jesus our Lord" (Romans 6:23). The common theme is that God sent His Son, Jesus Christ, who became the penalty for our sin, so that we might be brought back into fellowship with the Father forever.

RESOURCE READING: Romans 3

July 25

QUIET YOUR HEART

Have you noticed how noisy it is lately? In addition to the din of traffic, the roar of jet engines, and the blare of radios, TVs, and stereos, there's the endless chatter of meaningless conversation. Someone figured out that the average person has at least thirty conversations a day, spends one-fifth of his life talking, and speaks enough words in a year to fill sixty-six 800-page books. Yet at the end of the day, we can seldom look back and remember a really meaningful conversation.

We're missing something, too—something creative and meaningful. It is stillness. Absolute quiet gives time to think, listen, ponder, and plan. God says in Psalm 46:10, "Be still, and know that I am God." I like the way a modern paraphrase puts it: "Step out of the traffic! Take a long, loving look at me, your High God, above politics, above everything" (TM).

"Be still." That means shut off your engine. Don't just

turn down the volume. Shut it off. Put the kids to bed, go out in the backyard and look at the stars. It's amazing how difficult it is to find a quiet place. Nature has its own kind of noise, though one that's restorative rather than numbing.

Being still isn't all that God wants us to learn. He says, "Be still, and know that I am God." We hear His voice most clearly when we silence our hearts before Him.

When people came to church a generation ago, they came to worship. In preparing their hearts, they usually sat in silence for a few minutes as the organ played a prelude. At the conclusion of the hour, they sat there, presumably thinking about what they had heard and how it could be applied to their lives.

You will never learn the benefits of stillness without reprogramming yourself. Try turning off your radio or TV for an evening. Maintain an hour of absolute silence. It isn't easy, is it?

There is strength in quiet and solitude. Isaiah 30 contains an interesting phrase: "In quietness and trust is your strength" (Isaiah 30:15). Yet the prophet notes that the people would not quiet their hearts before God. May we learn a lesson from their failure.

RESOURCE READING: Psalm 46

July 26

IF YOU ONLY KNEW

If you knew you had only sixty days to live, what would you do? That was the question I asked our staff at a Monday morning staff meeting. For a few seconds, it was very quiet and sober. Then the ice was broken. "Well, for one thing," said one man, "I'd stop paying my bills!" We all laughed, because the man who spoke would never leave a bill unpaid.

Mark Twain once said that he wished he knew where he was going to die, because he would never go near the place. We're all like that to a degree. We even tend to avoid the subject, ignoring the fact that the only thing certain about life is that you won't get out of it alive.

Long ago, Moses sat around a campfire in the desert and said, "We live out our years like one long sigh. Each of us lives for 70 years—or even 80 if we are in good health. But the best of them bring trouble and misery. Indeed, they are soon gone, and we fly away." Then he cried from the heart, "Teach us to number each of our days so that we may grow in wisdom" (Psalm 90:9–10, 12 GW).

How would you answer the question? If you had sixty days to live, would you ask forgiveness of someone you hurt? Clear your conscience by returning what you took years ago? Make sure to tell your spouse, your children, or your parents how much you love them?

If these things are important, why wait? Mark Twain once said that you should live every day so that even the undertaker will be sad when you die.

I know one thing for sure. A lot of people would make peace with God if they knew their time was running out. The sad thing is all the joy and happiness they're missing in the meantime.

Wise is the person who doesn't leave the important things in life for the last minute. Paul says, "Now is the time of God's favor, now is the day of salvation" (2 Corinthians 6:2). Why wait?

RESOURCE READING: Romans 10

WHEN YOU THINK,
"THERE AIN'T NO LIGHT!"

In 1953, country singer Hank Williams was riding the crest of his popularity, but he was far from a happy man. A few days before his death from drugs and alcohol, Williams and Rosemary Clooney were riding together, and Rosemary said, "Hank, let's sing."

"Whatcha wanna sing, Rosemary?"

"Let's sing your song," meaning, "I Saw the Light."

The two of them began to sing, and then Hank put his head in his hands and sobbed, "Aw, Rosemary, there ain't no light; there ain't no light!"

Can you relate to the darkness of his soul? Alone, frustrated, and confused, you wonder where to go, where to turn. Destiny in life is not the product of chance or fate; it's the result of your decisions, the direction you choose, and your determination to reach your goal.

Many people identify with the words of Isaiah 59: "We look for light but all is darkness; for brightness, but we walk in deep shadows. Like the blind we grope along the wall, feeling our way like men without eyes" (Isaiah 59:9–10). How do you know which way to go with your life when there are so many options? Two clear guidelines will give you the light you need:

Guideline #1: Recognize that Jesus Christ is the Light of the world. He said, "I am the way and the truth and the life. No one comes to the Father except through me" (John 14:6). You'll never go the wrong direction following His life and teaching.

Guideline #2: God's Word will give your life direction and purpose. David says, "Your word is a lamp to my feet and a light for my path" (Psalm 119:105).

The Bible gives direction for your life, your marriage, your relationships, and your future. But it's only as good as your willingness to follow its counsel and direction.

What do you do when you've started on a journey and discover you've take the wrong road? It happens all the time. Chances are you don't go back to your starting point. You make a change of direction to correct your error. That's how it is with God's will for your life. It begins anew every day when you discover your need for Him to redirect your life.

RESOURCE READING: John 8

July 28

COULD GOD EXIST, THEORETICALLY?

I'm an atheist; I don't need any religion to help me," a young pilot said as he brushed off the chaplain's invitation to attend chapel. Not to be turned aside so easily, the chaplain, J. Edwin Orr asked, "Could I ask you a couple of questions?" Thinking this would be easy, the pilot said, "Sure, go ahead and shoot."

"First," asked Orr, "do you happen to know everything?"

"Of course not." Trying to impress the chaplain, he explained that even Einstein said that all scientists were on the fringe of knowledge. "And I'll admit that I'm on the fringe of the fringe."

"Good," remarked Orr, knowing he had won the first round.

"Now the second question is this. Is it conceivable that God could exist outside all that you happen to know?" The pilot hesitated. Orr continued, "How much do you know, in relation to total knowledge—ten percent?"

"Ten percent!" exclaimed the pilot. "Less than one percent!"

"Well, said Orr, "let's say one percent. Is it possible that God could exist outside your one percent of knowledge?"

"Yes," acknowledged the pilot. Then Orr, who had debated some of the world's outstanding agnostics and atheists, said, "You are a most remarkable atheist then. A few minutes ago you stated that there was no God, and now you say it's possible that there is one."

J. Edwin Orr wasn't interested in simply winning an argument, but he did want to make a point: Only those who possess a knowledge of all the truth in the universe could be absolutely certain that God does not exist. Atheism appears to be in decline. Studies indicate that the number of young people today who believe in God—at least in a general sort of way—is greater than a generation ago.

To believe in God is one thing. To have a relationship with Him is entirely another matter. "Anyone who has seen me has seen the Father," said Jesus to a skeptical Thomas. The Gospel of John says that Jesus is the *ikon* (to use the Greek word) or express image of the Father.

Let God be judged on His own merit. Yes, let God be God.

RESOURCE READING: John 14:1–14

July 29

CAN YOU REALLY BELIEVE THE BIBLE?

Are the Bible's Stories True?" asks a recent *Time* magazine article. "Was Abraham a myth? Did the Exodus happen? Did Joshua conquer the city of Jericho? Was there a Moses?"[1] Typical of so many secular articles that focus on biblical history, the author cites recent archaeological finds but leaves the reader with the impression that until science can document events in the Old Testament, the Bible is better left in the category of religious myth. Statements such as "There is no direct evidence, other than the Bible, to suggest that Abraham's exploits. . .ever happened," reveal the mindset of the writer. Unless there is undeniable archaeological evidence, some scientists and theologians refuse to accept any part of the Bible as history.

Do these learned men know something we don't? Or is it the other way around? Is faith blind? Or do blind men refuse to accept evidence no matter where it's from? Here's their logic: An inscription on a tablet that has been buried for 2000 years is more reliable than a document that has been preserved for the same period of time by dedicated scholars.

How careful were the scribes who preserved Scripture? According to the Old Testament, when the Law was given, it was immediately placed in the Ark of the Covenant and considered holy beyond anything a human hand had ever written.

When Christianity threatened the existence of Judaism, a group of scribes and scholars known as the Massoretes, formed schools in Tiberias, Jerusalem, and Alexandria to collect and preserve ancient manuscripts. These dedicated scholars added vowel points to the text, codified it, and unified it. They counted the exact number of words, noting the middle word and middle letter of each book, and recorded other minute details that helped others who were copying the text by hand. They also gave the world a tremendous amount of information, which helped to accurately preserve the texts of Scripture. Both Christians and Jews owe the Massoretes a tremendous debt of gratitude.

Is the Bible historically accurate? Or can it be rejected as religious myth until "proven" otherwise? Frankly, until the past century, scholars—both believers and nonbelievers—never considered the Bible to be anything but accurate history. May God deliver us from the assumption that the Bible is untrue. The evidence just doesn't support the premise.

RESOURCE READING: Isaiah 40:1–8

July 30

WHAT A WAY TO GO

Eighty-three-year-old Peter Sedore got a hole in one at the Panorama Village Golf Course where he often played. Actually, it was his eighteenth career hole in one. But Peter didn't realize it would be his last. One hole later, he collapsed from an aneurysm in his brain, and was pronounced dead on arrival at a local hospital. "Maybe God wanted him to do it one more time before taking him," said Sedore's son, Dennis. What a way to go—bagging a coveted hole in one!

Since my father died, at age eighty-eight, I've thought a lot about the way people respond to death and dying. A lot of folks live in complete denial. They never mention death, even when it comes to making provision for their families. They fear that talking about it might make it happen, so they avoid the subject with a vengeance.

If we believe that matters of life and death are important to our heavenly Father—and part of the cycle of life—there's no reason not to talk about them.

If I were going to Buckingham Palace for an audience with the queen, I'd talk about it—what to wear, what to say, and how to conduct myself. Should we be less concerned about our entrance into the presence of the King of Kings and Lord of Lords?

If you believe the Bible, you know that God has a purpose and will for every person. When your life is purpose-driven, you can say with Paul, "I have fought the good fight, I have finished the race, I have kept the faith" (2 Timothy 4:7). The driving force of Paul's life was not to be remembered for his exploits and achievements, but to accomplish everything God wanted him to do.

Like sand quietly slipping through the hourglass, the days of our lives go by. Eventually, time runs out, whether we've made our first hole in one, or never had time to golf. "Dost thou love life?" asked Benjamin Franklin, "Then use time wisely, for that's the stuff that life is made of."

RESOURCE READING: 2 Timothy 3:10–4:5

July 31

THE GOD FACTOR
IN STRESS MANAGEMENT

I never cease to be amazed at amount of money spent on research that only certifies the obvious. Take, for example, this recent headline: "Stress Called Key Factor in Heart Risk." Obviously when someone is so stressed that he turns red in the face and the veins in his neck stand out like steel cables on a suspension bridge, his ticker has gone into turbo drive, and that's not healthy.

We live in a stress-filled world. With traffic, busy jobs, illness, and financial worries, stress is everybody's problem today.

How do we combat stress? Research has also demonstrated that those who believe that God is in control of their lives, and trust Him to do what they can't, live with less stress and have fewer heart attacks.

Who is in control of your life? Trusting God doesn't eliminate the problem you have with your difficult boss, or erase the other stress factors in your life, but when you take what the New Testament says literally and apply it to your life, it makes a big difference.

For example, read Matthew 6 and notice what Jesus says about how God cares for the birds of the air. Then ask yourself the question, "Are you not much more valuable than they?"

Memorize Philippians 4:6, which says in The Living Bible, "Don't worry about anything; instead, pray about everything; tell God your needs, and don't forget to thank Him for His answers."

Begin each day by taking at least fifteen minutes to read and meditate on Scripture, perhaps starting with the Psalms, and then commit the needs of your day to the Lord, asking Him to deal with those difficult situations that create stress in your life.

Knowing that God is your heavenly Father helps you to put life in perspective. Fifty years from now, the cares of today won't matter. But your relationship with God will count even when the stars have burned themselves out and become cinders. Because God loves you and is in control of your life, a lot of what causes stress isn't worth the worry.

RESOURCE READING: Matthew 6

August 1

IS DOOMSDAY
JUST AROUND THE CORNER?

About 1875, a French scientist wrote these words in his diary: "The time will come when man will not only toy with the atom but will split the atom itself. When that time comes, God with his long beard will come to Earth and say, 'Gentlemen, it's time to close up shop!' " On December 2, 1942, an Italian scientist who had left his native Italy to escape the oppressive Fascist regime, began bombarding atomic piles with neutrons. Without fully realizing what he had done, Enrico Fermi was the first to split the atom, ushering in the Atomic Age.

Now, some fifty years after Fermi's breakthrough, a strange array of bedfellows are talking about an impending apocalypse. Recently, a handpicked group of experts on religion met at Fermi's old university to talk about the end of the world. Although these individuals differed theologically, there was a consensus that time is running out.

What sparked this latest interest in the end of the world? Many factors come into play, including uncertainty about the future, the end of the millennium, the breakdown of the family, the rise of Israel and conflict with her Arab neighbors, and the proliferation of atomic weapons far more powerful than scientists could imagine in 1945.

What does the Bible say? The book of Revelation talks about the coming battle of Armageddon and the end of government as we now know it, but the clearest statement of an impending apocalypse is found in the book of 2 Peter.

Limited space does not allow me to describe all the factors that should force us to lift up our heads with anticipation that our redemption draws near. But the big issue is this: If what the French scientist so graphically predicted is true, how should this prospect affect our lives? That is the very issue that Peter addresses. He says, "So then, dear friends, since you are looking forward to this, make every effort to be found spotless, blameless and at peace with him" (2 Peter 3:14). Notice he says that our lives should be without spot—untainted by the corruption of the world, without blame—a reflection of genuine integrity, and at peace with God. Even so, come quickly Lord Jesus.

RESOURCE READING: 2 Peter 3

THE SOVEREIGN OF THE UNIVERSE

Is God sovereign? I looked up the word *sovereign* in an encyclopedia and found this definition: "The name sovereign was first applied to kings. Everyone in a kingdom was a subject of the king. The king himself was usually sovereign, which means subject to no one."

Is God sovereign? To whom does He answer and give an account? And if God is sovereign, how does this affect our lives?

God's sovereignty creates some binding consequences for our relationship with Him. If He is sovereign, then I am His subject. If He is fully in control, then what I think about Him is not nearly as important as what He thinks about me.

Many people prefer not to think about God's sovereignty, or consider their relationship to Him. For those who have never learned about God's nature—His mercy, kindness, grace, and goodness—the thought that God is absolutely in control would be rather frightening. Then, too, a lot of a misunderstanding stands between some people and God: "Where is God when people suffer?" or "Why didn't God do something when my baby needed help?" Most of the questions that form a dark cloud and obscure the sovereignty of God involve issues completely beyond our understanding. Even if God were to explain them to us, we wouldn't fully comprehend.

Based on the thousands of letters we have received at *Guidelines,* it seems to me that the real issue separating mankind from the grand and comforting truth of God's sovereignty is that we are fearful of losing control. We want to hold onto the notion that we are masters of our fate, that we are in control, and that we are at the helm of the ship called destiny. This, of course, is a sad illusion. If only we would acknowledge our dependence upon this loving and mighty

God, we would enter into a Father-child relationship, where the care of the Almighty becomes personal and intimate.

Understanding the nature and character of God is the key to knowing Him. When you really know Him, you will love Him; and when you love Him, your fears will dissipate.

RESOURCE READING: Ephesians 1

August 3

A SOVEREIGN GOD AND MY WILL

I s God a divine accommodation, Someone we have invented to make us feel good about ourselves, particularly when we know we have done wrong? Can God be manipulated to get what we want? Can we can turn to Him when we need a good cry, and trust that He'll tell us, "What you have done is okay. You're not nearly as bad as some people"?

Guy Duffield writes: "To many, God is simply a divine accommodation. He exists just for them. He is the great Santa Claus of mankind. Many will only believe Him if He pleases them. The moment He asks them to do something contrary to their wishes, they part company with Him. There seems to be, on the part of so many, little sense of any personal responsibility to Him, or realization that all men must give account to Him as the Judge of all the earth."[1]

What we choose to believe or disbelieve about God doesn't change who He really is. Is it possible, friend, that you have formulated a smorgasbord concept of God, taking the qualities you prefer, and rejecting those you disdain? If so, are you not just as guilty of fashioning your own god as those who worshipped the golden calf?

Why are you afraid to embrace what the Bible says

about God's sovereignty? Pure fear, right? Are you afraid that God may impose His will on you in a way you won't like? It's the age-old battle of who is in control. Whether or not you admit it, there are very few factors that you can really control. You can't control your health. A heart attack, a stroke, or an accident can radically change your future. You can't control the weather, the economy, or the government either.

God works all things after the counsel of His will, says Paul. Furthermore, what God wills stems from His loving nature as an extension of His sovereign plan for this world.

Want to have your eyes opened? Look up the phrase, "O Sovereign Lord," in the Bible and notice the hundreds of times it appears in the prayers of God's people. Then ask yourself, "Why haven't I had my eyes opened to this great truth?" Jesus says: "Then you will know the truth, and the truth will set you free" (John 8:32).

RESOURCE READING: Ephesians 2

August 4

WHICH OF US, O LORD, SHALL BE SOVEREIGN?

"O Lord, who shall be sovereign—You or me?" I seriously doubt you'll ever hear someone voice that line in his prayers, but I can tell you that the issue of sovereignty has confronted everyone at some point in his spiritual walk.

Even Jesus struggled with this tremendous issue in the Garden of Gethsemane. Never before had He been separated from the presence of the Father. Seeing the black cloud overshadowing the cross, He prayed, "Let this cup pass from me; nevertheless, not my will but yours be done!"

Some—mistakenly, I believe—contend that because God is sovereign, He will do exactly what He pleases, regardless of our prayers. I recall the time I spoke at a Bible conference on prayer. My message was based on four New Testament passages where God makes certain promises, each of which is prefaced with the word *if* as a condition that must be met on our part. The next morning, the president of the host group confronted me saying, "Your message last evening was totally unnecessary." Somewhat taken aback, I asked, "And why is that?" "Oh," he said, "if God wants something done, He is going to do it whether or not we pray about it."

What would happen if a farmer applied the same theology to his crop? "If God wants me to have a good crop this year, He'll give it to me, no matter what I do." No way. The farmer cultivates the soil, plants the seed, then prays that God will send the necessary rains to bring the crop to fruition. Obviously, some elements are subject only to the will of God. The gentle rain, which delights the farmer, could turn into a torrent of water and wash away the crop. The sunshine, which produces germination, could burn out his crop.

Obviously, our Sovereign God sends the harvest, but the farmer toils in harmony with his heavenly Father, praying and working, fulfilling his responsibility to be a good steward.

If you want to align with Scripture, then pray as though everything depends on God, and work as though everything depends on you. Prayer will bring your will into harmony with the will of your Sovereign Father. Then you can pray with intensity: "Lord, may Your will be done."

RESOURCE READING: 2 Samuel 7

WHICH OF US, O LORD,
SHALL BE SOVEREIGN? — PART 2

"Dear Teacher," read the message on a get-well card from her class. "We wish you a speedy recovery by a vote of fourteen to thirteen." Yes, indeed. In a democracy, the majority carries the day. But with God, no votes are taken. His kingdom has no elected officials. God is sovereign, and what He wills is absolute. If God is sovereign, and I am His child, what are the benefits of knowing that He rules the day?

I would need far more than the space available to fully answer the question, but allow me to point out four major benefits:

Benefit #1: The responsibility for running the world—even my own personal life—has been lifted from my shoulders. That's good news. Paul sums it up when he says, "And we know that in all things God works for the good of those who love him, who have been called according to his purpose" (Romans 8:28).

Benefit #2: Wholeness and peace become my inheritance. I may not understand everything God does, but I can rest in the confidence that He is in control. If God is sovereign, we can be confident that the world is not out of control, no matter what the papers tell us.

Benefit #3: God's sovereignty gives me a sense of security both spiritually and emotionally. Ephesians 1 says that God chose you before the foundation of the world. You are no accident, no slip of fate. You are uniquely created in the image of God, and He chose you to be His son or daughter. You are a child of the King, and no one can rob you of your birthright.

Benefit #4: God's sovereignty gives me confidence when I pray. As God's child, I come boldly into the presence of the Father. He understands my frailties and weaknesses. Best of all, He sorts out the dumb things I ask for and gives me what I really need, because of His great love for me as His child. Take time to read Romans 8, especially the last half where Paul so beautifully tells us that nothing can separate us from the love of this sovereign, loving God, neither now nor for all eternity. Yes, thank You, Sovereign Lord.

RESOURCE READING: Romans 8

August 6

WHEN ANXIETY TURNS TO WORRY

One of the reasons we tend to worry is that life can quickly get out of control. When the cause of our concern is a teenager, an aged parent who depends on us for help, or a family business that seems to be going the wrong way, we can't simply walk away from the situation. Quitting isn't an option.

What do we do? One woman, who was the primary caregiver for her elderly parents, both of whom were in failing health, quoted Philippians 4:6, which says, "Do not be anxious about anything, but in everything, by prayer and petition, with thanksgiving, present your requests to God." Then she added, "It seems to me that anxiety is inevitable. We love people, and because we love them, we care for them when they cannot care for themselves. At some point, we realize we cannot make them happy or even comfortable, let alone meet all of their needs. Love and responsibility combine to become concern, then worry, and then full-blown anxiety. In some cases, our anxiety is fueled by a lack of appreciation for what we are doing—the 'never enough' syndrome."

Life has its moments of anxiety and concern. So what do you do? Start by asking yourself the following questions:

- What is my responsibility before God in this situation? How much is enough?
- Am I doing what I'm doing out of love or a sense of duty?
- Am I depending on a show of appreciation to feel good about what I'm doing, or am I working as unto the Lord, without expecting thanks or appreciation?
- What part is mine, and what must I leave to God to handle? This is a judgment call, and it isn't always easy to determine.
- Could I enlist the help of others?

When anxiety turns to worry, ask yourself these questions:

- Am I turning this over to the Lord?
- Am I praying with thanksgiving every time I feel anxious?
- Have I focused on the fact that God cares for me?

We have the great privilege of being able to cast our anxiety, our worry, our cares upon God. He is both powerful and loving, and He is in control of what you cannot control. God's sovereignty makes the difference.

RESOURCE READING: Philippians 4:10–23

INTERVIEW GOD

In 1889, a dam broke on the South Fork Reservoir, twelve miles east of Johnstown, Pennsylvania, in a valley of the Allegheny Mountains. Raging waters surged down the valley and swept over the town, taking twenty-five lives and causing $50 million in damages, a considerable amount for those days. The editor of a Pittsburgh paper sent a young reporter to cover the story. "This is a break for you, kid," said the boss. "Give it all you have!" He slapped him on the back and sent him scurrying out the door.

Hours later the wire dispatch came back, "God sits brooding on the hillside overlooking the disaster and desolation of Johnstown. The roaring waters seem but to echo the mind of the Creator. . ." Without bothering to read further, the editor wired back, "Don't bother with the flood; interview God!"

We smile at the humor, but seldom do we think about interviewing God or finding out about Him. Unless we are at the point of death or badly in need of something that prompts us to pray, we don't even think much about Him.

If you were to interview God, what would you ask Him? "Why is there suffering in our world?" "Why don't You strike down the wicked and eliminate the evil in our world?" "Why must a childless woman desperately wish for a baby when millions of unwanted children are aborted every year?" "Why do You allow wars and strife?" Supposing you got an answer to your questions, would you really understand? Probably not.

Conducting an interview consists of asking questions and recording answers. Beyond that, there's no personal involvement. An interview and a relationship don't have the same degree of involvement and intimacy. Knowing *about* God—which few people really do—is only the beginning.

Knowing God involves a relationship of communication, interaction, and commitment. Why is knowing God important? Only when you know God will you love Him. Only when you love God will you obey Him. Only when you obey God will your soul rise on the wings of faith.

Get to know God. It's the most important knowledge you will ever have, and an absolute necessity if you intend to spend eternity in His presence.

RESOURCE READING: John 17

August 8

WHAT IS GOD LIKE?

A child's approach to God must still have something of heaven intertwined in it—something we tend to lose as we grow older, more skeptical, and more secular. It is no wonder that Jesus said, "I tell you the truth, anyone who will not receive the kingdom of God like a little child will never enter it" (Mark 10:15).

When my son Steven was about five years old, I had to fly to San Francisco. As I was negotiating rush-hour traffic, trying to figure out where I was going and hoping that I wouldn't miss a critical turn, I wasn't carrying on much of a conversation him. Suddenly, without any prologue, Steve blurted out, "Daddy, what is God like?"

His question caught me off guard. We often talked about God at home and had daily devotions, and Steven was in Sunday school and church, and obviously he had been thinking about the issue. A sober dialogue about what God is like wasn't what I was expecting on the way to the airport. It made me realize that kids often think about what adults ignore.

What is God like? I fumbled for words, trying to satisfy

the curiosity of a little boy. I explained that God was never born, unlike us. He has always existed and always will exist. I said that God loves us very much, so much that He sent His Son to give us eternal life; that God is faithful and just. He is always the same and never changes or grows old. He can always be counted on, and because we are His children through faith in Jesus Christ, we can pray to Him and He answers our prayers as He sees best.

An understanding of God—the God of the Bible—will do more to influence your lifestyle and behavior than anything in the world. It does more to shape your morality and integrity, including your value system, than anything else.

It is when we don't really know God that we assume we can make our own rules and get away with it. Many folks wrongly assume that the ever-loving, beneficent, gray-bearded Father of the Universe will say, "That's okay. You're only human."

Make getting to know God a priority in your life.

RESOURCE READING: John 1

August 9

NOBODY KNOWS WHAT GOD LOOKS LIKE. OH YEAH?

It's an old story, but one that bears repeating. A little girl was drawing a picture with bold strokes in bright colors when her teacher, viewing the child's work of art, said, "Tell me about your picture." The little girl responded, "I'm drawing a picture of God!"

"Hmm, I see," said the teacher. "But nobody knows exactly what God looks like!"

"They will when I'm finished," the little girl said authoritatively. Ah, for the spiritual insights of a little child.

The God of the Scriptures is a Person with all the characteristics we identify with personality—He thinks, He feels, He wills, He loves and hates, He shows mercy, demands justice, and He acts independently of the consequences.

But God is no mere mortal. He expresses His transcendence through the prophet Isaiah, saying, " 'For my thoughts are not your thoughts, neither are your ways my ways,' declares the LORD. 'As the heavens are higher than the earth, so are my ways higher than your ways and my thoughts than your thoughts' " (Isaiah 55:8–9). Because God's viewpoint is different from ours, which is limited by time and space, it can only follow that some of the things God does won't make sense.

A god so small that you could predict his every whim and fancy would never be one before whom you would bow. But the real question is this: Can this God—the One who spoke the word and brought our world into existence, the One who took clay and breathed into it the breath of life— can this God be known? Had Jesus never been born at Bethlehem, had He never laid aside His divine power as the Son of God, it would be difficult to answer that question, but He did come. He did walk among us. He did say, "He who has seen me has seen the Father!" And by His life, His instructions, His sacrificial death, and His triumphant resurrection, He showed us what the Father is like.

RESOURCE READING: Psalm 2

August 10

GOD IS. . .(PERIOD!)
(ATTRIBUTE #1: THE ETERNALITY OF GOD)

Shortly before his death, A. W. Tozer wrote the following: "In this hour of all-but-universal darkness, one cheering gleam appears: Within the fold of conservative Christianity there are to be found increasing numbers of persons whose religious lives are marked by a growing hunger after God Himself. They are eager for spiritual realities and will not be put off with words, nor will they be content with correct 'interpretations' of truth. They are athirst for God, and they will not be satisfied till they have drunk deep at the Fountain of Living Water."[1]

When someone says, "Tell me about God" or "What is God like?" I turn to the pages of God's Word, for there alone will I discover what God is like. The selections for the next nine days will deal with the attributes of God.

Attribute #1: God is eternal. You and I had a birth-date, and someday we will die, but God has no beginning or end. There was never a time when He did not exist. The Bible says, "In beginning, God. . ." And Moses in his psalm cries out, "Before the mountains were brought forth, or ever You had formed the earth and the world, even from everlasting to everlasting, You are God" (Psalm 90:2 NKJV).

In 1888, when astronomers were beginning to fathom how far the stars and planets are from Earth, they devised a measurement known as a light-year. Simply put, a light-year is the distance that light travels in one year in a vacuum, or about 5.9 trillion miles. The nearest star in the universe is 4.5 light-years away, and that's just the beginning.

God, who created these things, preceded the work of His hand. Don't be frightened by the reality of such an awe-some God; take heart. He never faints nor grows weary. As Moses says, "The eternal God is your refuge, and under-neath are the everlasting arms" (Deuteronomy 33:27).

At the height of the counterculture movement in the 1960s, someone scribbled on the wall of a New York subway: "God is dead!" and signed the name Friedrich Nietzsche, the

European philosopher who challenged God's existence. A few days later, a passerby noticed that someone had crossed out those words and written, "Friedrich Nietzsche is dead!" signed, GOD. Touché!

RESOURCE READING: Philippians 3:1–14

August 11

GOD NEVER CHANGES
(ATTRIBUTE #2: GOD'S IMMUTABILITY)

Change can be threatening—and often for good reason. In a chaotic world that is constantly changing, nothing is more comforting than having a secure relationship with a God who never changes.

No one would deny that our generation has seen more changes than any other generation in history. Ask your grandfather about the world when he was growing up. Ask about the medicines that were prescribed during his childhood, and the length of time it took to go somewhere or do something.

People change, too—so very quickly. The glow of a woman's beauty passes, as does the strength of the man who wooed and won her hand. The beauty of youth yields to the aging of the years. Seasons change, nations rise and fall, men rise to power and fall aside—but God remains the same.

God Himself has declared, "I am the LORD, I change not" (Malachi 3:6 KJV). The Bible says that He is the Father of lights with whom there is no change or variation (James 1:17). God will never be less than He is now, nor will He ever be different from what He has already revealed Himself to be. His essential characteristics or attributes are always the same.

God is without beginning or end. He is all-knowing, all-powerful, ever-present, holy, faithful, loving, and just. God is unchanging in His wisdom and in His counsel.

In the grand old hymn "Great is Thy Faithfulness," by Thomas Chisholm, there is a line that goes, "Thou changest not, Thy compassions, they fail not; As Thou hast been Thou forever wilt be."

A. W. Tozer writes, "God never changes moods or cools off in His affections or loses enthusiasm. His attitude toward sin is now the same as it was when He drove out the sinful man from the eastward garden, and His attitude toward the sinner the same as when He stretched forth His hand and cried, 'Come unto me, all ye that labor and are heavy laden, and I will give you rest.' "[1]

No wonder the songwriter Henry Lyte wrote, "Change and decay in all around I see; O, Thou who changest not, abide with me." Yes, abide with me. Thank God, He never changes.

RESOURCE READING: Psalm 90

August 12

GOD KNOWS IT ALL
(ATTRIBUTE #3: OMNISCIENCE)

In his book *God Works the Night Shift*, Ron Mehl recalls the first time his Bible school team played Cal Tech. "[They] may not have been the most talented basketball team in our league," he says. "But they were the smartest."

At halftime, Ron's coach asked the Cal Tech coach if he could see the shot chart. "Sure," replied the coach, pointing to a student sitting in the bleachers. "He's got it." Ron's coach sent him to get it. When Ron asked the Cal

Tech student if he could see the shot chart, the young man replied, "Look, I haven't made up the chart yet, okay?"

Ron was rebuffed. "Why not?"

"When the game's over, I'll sit down and recall in my mind every shot that was taken, where on the court it was taken from, and circle it if it was a score. . . Okay? Any other questions?" That kid had every shot in the game stored in his head. And he was as obstinate as he was brainy.[1]

If a bright college student could plot the shots made in a basketball game from memory, should we be surprised that God can keep track of everything we do on planet Earth?

The Bible says that God is all-knowing. *Omniscient* is the term scholars use. God knows everything we do, and everything we think. The letter to the Hebrews puts it like this: "He knows about everyone, everywhere. Everything about us is bare and wide open to the all-seeing eyes of our living God; nothing can be hidden from him to whom we must explain all that we have done" (Hebrews 4:13 TLB).

God's omniscience would be pretty scary were it not for one powerful truth: There is forgiveness with God. David says, "But there is forgiveness with thee, that thou mayest be feared" (Psalm 130:4 KJV). God isn't a spy in the sky, recording your every failure and transgression, but He knows, and He remembers. The good side of omniscience is that God also knows and understands your needs, your heartache, your pain, and your cares. He also remembers when others forget and take you for granted. Thank God. He never forgets. What an awesome, marvelous God.

RESOURCE READING: Revelation 21

THE GOODNESS OF THE LORD
(ATTRIBUTE #4: GOODNESS)

The goodness of God is something you can experience individually and personally. "Taste and see that the LORD is good," says David in Psalm 34:8. "Surely goodness and mercy shall follow me all the days of my life" (Psalm 23:6 KJV).

On August 23, 1961, about four o'clock in the morning, I came to grips with the issue of God's goodness. My wife had been in labor with our first child for more than twenty hours. Finally the doctor decided that in order for the baby to survive, he had to take the struggling infant without delay. The baby's heartbeat had suddenly jumped to more than 200 beats a minute when the umbilical cord wrapped itself around her neck. Never have I been more alone than when they rolled the gurney into the operating room and the doors closed.

As I stood in the hospital corridor, my heart filled with fear. Then I remembered the little New Testament and Psalms I had tucked into my shirt pocket. A single light bulb overhead gave me just enough light to see the small words. Turning to Psalm 27, I read, "I had fainted, unless I had believed to see the goodness of the LORD in the land of the living. Wait on the LORD: be of good courage, and he shall strengthen thine heart: wait, I say, on the LORD" (Psalm 27:13–14 KJV). Earnestly my heart cried out, "God, just as You were good to David, please show me the same goodness and spare my wife and baby." God saw us through that crisis, and I knew I had tasted of the goodness of the Lord.

God's goodness is the only one of God's attributes that the Bible challenges you to find out for yourself. It doesn't say, "O taste and see that God is powerful," or "O taste and see that God is sovereign." But it does say you can taste the goodness of our loving God.

Have you learned that God is good? Are you rushing through life, oblivious of what God has done, yet complaining about your circumstances, or blaming God for your failures and mistakes? The bottom line of all theology is that God is good.

RESOURCE READING: Job 42

August 14

THE GOODNESS OF THE LORD, 2
(ATTRIBUTE #4: GOODNESS)

When you look at a piece of furniture and see the beautiful grain in the wood, what you see is only the polished surface, but the grain runs deep inside the wood. God's essential attributes are somewhat like the grain of a polished piece of wood. The intertwined veins blend together and glow with a deep radiance and beauty that reflect the inner depth of God's character.

We can say that God is faithful, or just, or all-powerful, but no attribute—with the possible exception of God's faithfulness—speaks more to my heart than the goodness of God. It isn't that I question God's goodness. I'm simply confounded that I would be the recipient of this goodness. After all, I am the problem—not our gracious and kind Father.

How is God's goodness revealed? Most reliably through the testimonies of men and women who tasted of God's goodness. In times of difficulty, they turned to God, and God met them. The Bible is our primary source for understanding what God is like. In simple but strong terms, the men who penned this grand old Book contend that God is good. God's goodness is cited more than one hundred times in the Bible.

Goodness, as opposed to evil, stems from the very essence of God. This is not syrupy sentimentality, but a strong reflection of purity and kindness. Goodness should never be regarded as weakness. A study of other religions reveals that goodness is only associated with the God who created our world and sent His Son to show us the way back to heaven. Pagan deities are generally thought of as angry gods who must be appeased.

When we stop to think about what God has done, we are quickly reminded that this great and good God has touched our lives for the better. How do we respond? In some cases, we grasp for more, never satisfied with what we have. But the truly grateful person can only respond with thanksgiving and gratitude.

Long ago the psalmist cried out, "Oh that men would praise the LORD for his goodness, and for his wonderful works to the children of men!" (Psalm 107:8 KJV). The need is even greater today. O that we would praise the Lord for His goodness and for His wonderful deeds to us.

RESOURCE READING: Psalm 107

August 15

THE JUSTICE OF GOD
(ATTRIBUTE #5: GOD'S JUSTICE)

Let's suppose that a certain judge in your city faces an indigent man who is accused of a crime. This unfortunate individual has a court-appointed attorney. Furthermore, the defendant has a surly disposition—just by looking at him, you "know" he committed the crime. Sure enough, the judge says, "Guilty!" as he slams down his gavel and pronounces a harsh sentence.

On the flip side, when someone with money, education, family connections, and good attorneys faces the judge, he either beats the charges, or if he's found guilty, he receives a lenient sentence.

"We want justice!" we scream. But where does our notion of justice come from? Our ability to distinguish between justice and injustice is a reflection of our creation in God's image. The farther we move from God, the more warped our concept of justice becomes.

God could not be righteous or upright if He were unjust or inconsistent. Though He is a God of mercy, He is also a God of justice. The Bible tells us that God is no respecter of persons. Romans 2:11 says, "God does not show favoritism." In Colossians, Paul says, "But he who does wrong will be repaid for what he has done, and there is no partiality" (Colossians 3:25 NKJV).

Our Western concept of justice is based on Judeo-Christian principles; namely, that man is accountable to a supreme judge of the universe; and certain issues are right and wrong, and those who violate the standard pay the ultimate consequences. In civil law, someone must judge right from wrong, but we have become hesitant to make sharp moral pronouncements, lest we offend someone.

The reality that God ultimately enforces justice is both comforting and disconcerting. When I see so much injustice in the world, it's comforting to know that God will have His payday someday. But I must realize that I, too, am accountable to God, and He knows my actions and thoughts better than I do.

Longfellow was right when he wrote, "Though the mills of God grind slowly, yet they grind exceeding small; though with patience He stands waiting, with exactness grinds He all." Yes, God will have His day.

RESOURCE READING: Revelation 20

THE WRATH OF GOD
(ATTRIBUTE #6: GOD'S WRATH)

D ear Dr. Sala," wrote a friend, "Being raised in the Baptist denomination, I always heard that people who did not meet the biblical requirements of being saved would burn in a literal hell after death. . . . Does God get some kind of revenge or satisfaction from seeing persons. . .suffer in burning anguish forever and ever?"

In essence, the writer was asking, "How can a God of love ever send someone to hell?" God does love you very, very much. The heart of the gospel is John 3:16, "For God so loved the world that he gave his one and only Son, that whoever believes in him shall not perish but have eternal life." But in this simple expression of God's purpose is found both life and death.

What most people don't know is that "there are more references in Scripture to the anger, fury, and wrath of God, than there are to His love and tenderness," says theologian Arthur Pink. I never cease to be amazed at the conspiracy of silence when it comes to letting people know that God's love is not accompanied by indifference to wrongdoing.

When have you heard these passages from the New Testament quoted or used as a text for a message: "It is a fearful thing to fall into the hands of the living God" (Hebrews 10:31 KJV). "The wrath of God is being revealed from heaven against all the godlessness and wickedness of men who suppress the truth by their wickedness" (Romans 1:18). "Let no one deceive you with empty words, for because of such things God's wrath comes on those who are disobedient" (Ephesians 5:6). "Because of these, the wrath of God is coming" (Colossians 3:6).

The Bible says very clearly that the door of mercy is still open. God's wrath is not poured out indiscriminately on the weak or downcast, but the sinful and wicked, regardless of wealth or status, are the ultimate targets of His wrath.

God is not only a loving God but also a God whose patience will ultimately end. If I were outside the fold and not God's child, I would run to Him and plead for His mercy and His forgiveness. "Knowing therefore the terror of the Lord, we persuade men" (2 Corinthians 5:11 KJV).

RESOURCE READING: Romans 14

August 17

GOD—EL GRANDE SUPREME
(ATTRIBUTE #7: OMNIPOTENCE)

You walk into a taco shop and scan the menu. Least expensive is a plain bean-and-cheese burrito. A step above that is my choice: the *carne asada* burrito, with meat, beans and cheese. But at the top of the menu is El Grande Burrito Supreme! It's the works—the best there is with everything thrown in.

In describing God, theologians at times grasp for words, sometimes falling back on Latin terms, like omniscient, omnipotent, and omnipresent. I rather like Arthur Pink's term: God's supremacy! God is supreme! I understand the idea, if I don't fully grasp the reality.

Our understanding is challenged because we're so limited. We're human; God is not. We came into the world kicking and screaming, and someday we will die. But God has neither beginning nor end. We grow weary and tired. God never does. As I've grown older, I've come to grips with the vastness of my limitations. But God is unlimited, and He never changes.

Is there anything that God cannot do? You've no

doubt heard the old conundrums: Could God make a rock so big that even He couldn't move it? or, could He create something greater than Himself? There are some things our Supreme God cannot do. He cannot lie, for example, because He is absolute truth. He cannot violate His nature, because His nature never changes. He cannot create evil, because He is ultimate goodness.

Greatness and bigness are not the same thing. Our universe is vast, yet God is greater than the work of His hand. As one writer puts it, "Yours, O LORD, is the greatness and the power and the glory and the majesty and the splendor, for everything in heaven and earth is yours. Yours, O LORD, is the kingdom; you are exalted as head over all" (1 Chronicles 29:11).

This God Supreme is never too busy to listen to your cry and reach down to touch your life when you have lost your way and need His help. What an awesome, overwhelming thought! Never settle for a beans-and-cheese sort of God when you can worship the El Grande Supreme God, the Maker of all heaven and Earth.

RESOURCE READING: Isaiah 40:21–31

August 18

THE FAITHFUL GOD
(ATTRIBUTE #8: FAITHFULNESS)

T he better I know some people, the more I love my dog!" goes a bit of doggerel. Why? Dogs are faithful: They love you no matter what. The same cannot always be said of people, ourselves included. Though man is made in the likeness of God, when it comes to faithfulness and commitment we are vastly different. One of the great differences between our fickle flesh and God's unchangeable nature is His faithfulness. "If we are faithless, He remains faithful; He cannot deny Himself," said Paul to Timothy (2 Timothy 2:13 NKJV).

Moses, a man who knew something of the mercurial nature of humankind, wrote, "Know therefore that the LORD your God is God; he is the faithful God, keeping his covenant of love to a thousand generations of those who love him and keep his commands" (Deuteronomy 7:9).

God is faithful to His promises in Scripture. He plays no favorites. God allows me to come boldly into His presence, fully assured that, what He has done for others, He will do for me. I like the way Paul puts it when he says, "For no matter how many promises God has made, they are 'Yes' in Christ. And so through him the 'Amen' is spoken by us to the glory of God" (2 Corinthians 1:20). Paul is saying that when God honors His promise, we smile and say, "Amen, God! You did it again!"

All that God does is in perfect accord with who He is, but it is here that we sometimes go wrong. Naturally, we like to receive from God, but we often divorce the reality of who God is from what we want. Sometimes we think of God only in terms of what we can get out of Him, rather than in terms of our relationship with God, worshipping Him for who He is.

God is faithful in responding to the needs of His children. Many people find this hard to understand because their father was not there when they were growing up. Human unfaithfulness clouds our view of our faithful Father. Still, He abides faithfully. God is faithful to execute justice upon the wicked and mercy upon those who seek Him.

RESOURCE READING: Psalm 89

August 19

KNOWING A HOLY GOD
(ATTRIBUTE #9: HOLINESS)

I t's a good thing that our image of God doesn't come from a Steven Spielberg movie where God is portrayed as dwelling in a dark cave surrounded by smoke and vapors, loud claps of thunder, and flashes of lightning. When we really confront God, our image of Him as a cosmic policeman, a beneficent but powerless old man, or even a disinterested spectator, quickly vanishes.

When Isaiah, the prophet, had an encounter with God, he cried out, "Holy, holy, holy is the LORD Almighty; the whole earth is full of his glory" (Isaiah 6:3). Then the next thing he did was fall on his face, decrying his own sinful condition.

Holiness is sometimes equated with someone who is out of touch with life. But the English word *holy* comes from the Anglo-Saxon *halig,* or *hal,* meaning "well" or "whole." And that is exactly how God is: complete in Himself, untainted and undefiled by the corruption of our world.

When the Bible speaks of God's holiness, two concepts emerge: One is the idea of purity, and the other is separation from sin or defilement. But those thoughts seem to put distance between us and God. Yet Peter, a man who had a temper and was a very ordinary, blustery, say-it-with-your-fists sort of man, writes that God wants us to be holy because He is holy. The writer of Hebrews says that without holiness no man will see God.

How do we bridge the gulf? God reaches out and touches our lives with His presence. His Spirit washes away our sinful nature and changes us into His image. Renewal is also part of nature's way of restoring the beauty of creation. The rain washes away the footprints in the sand and brings the spring flowers. Even forest fires purge the dead wood and prepare for new life.

God never asks you to be all-powerful. Nor does He ask you to know everything as He does. But He does ask you—no, He commands you—to be holy, just as He is. Part of that is God's work, and part of it is your work as you put distance between you and the corruption and defilement of your culture and society.

RESOURCE READING: 1 Peter 1

August 20

HOW KNOWING GOD SHOULD CHANGE YOUR LIFE

On the streets of Manila, dirty, brash, young entrepreneurs—called cigarette boys—dash between the cars, jeepneys, and buses, competing with each other to sell cigarettes, Stork throat lozenges, and Chiclets. One such lad was struck by a vehicle, catching his display board and throwing the contents on the dirty pavement. In a moment, a man stepped quickly from the crowd of onlookers, helped the boy to his feet, and began to pick up the fallen wares.

Somewhat dazed and not sure what to say, the boy looked intently and blurted out, "Is you Jesus?"

When Paul wrote to Titus, he urged him to teach indentured servants to be trustworthy and loyal to their employers or masters, "so that in every way they will make the teaching about God our Savior attractive" (Titus 2:10).

When your neighbors and friends look at your life, what do they see?

When God touches your life, something should rub off: the mark of the Divine. God's attributes should be evident in the lives of His children. The image of the Father should, in some way, be reflected in the visage of the son.

Peter says that God's divine power has given us everything we need for life and godliness. He says we are to add to our faith "goodness; and to goodness, knowledge; and to knowledge, self-control; and to self-control, perseverance; and to perseverance, godliness; and to godliness, brotherly kindness; and to brotherly kindness, love." Then he adds, "For if you possess these qualities in increasing measure, they will keep you from being ineffective and unproductive" (2 Peter 1:5–8).

Making the gospel attractive isn't accomplished by making it easy; it is done by making it desirable and authentic.

A certain woman seeking membership in her local church, talked with the pastor. He asked, "Which one of my sermons brought you to the Lord?" "Oh," she quickly replied, "your messages are fine, but none of them really impressed me. What touched my heart was a woman in your congregation who is my neighbor. When I was sick, she brought me food. She befriended me and helped me. She was always so cheerful. I said to myself, 'When I get well, I want to find out what makes that woman different.' I did. It was her faith in God."

RESOURCE READING: Titus 2

August 21

DENY HIM, IGNORE HIM, OR ADORE HIM

Albert Einstein, one of our century's leading intellectuals, not only reflected on the theory of relativity, but on the meaning of life itself. Einstein believed that there was a God, but he believed that God was unknowable.

Some people deny God altogether. Perhaps they think that their colleagues in the university or the hospital may think them anti-intellectual if they recognize God's existence. Most atheists, however, are practical atheists. They simply don't want to acknowledge that they will ultimately be accountable for their personal lives.

Some people simply ignore God. They would never go so far as to deny His creative power. But, by and large, they completely ignore Him, which is the highest form of insult.

Some people adore God, falling on their knees before Him in adoration and worship. God told Jeremiah, "'For I know the plans I have for you, . . .plans to prosper you and not to harm you, plans to give you hope and a future. Then you will call upon me and come and pray to me, and I will listen to you. You will seek me and find me when you seek me with all your heart'" (Jeremiah 29:11–13).

King George V of Britain once walked into the dining room of a hunting lodge where he had been entertaining some of his friends. Out of respect, the friends of the king stood to their feet. "Be seated," said the king. "I am not your Lord."

"Yes, Sire, we know," replied one of the men. "If you were our Lord, we would not rise to our feet but fall on our faces and worship you!"

When Jack Hayford was in Britain on a certain occasion and saw the pageantry and preparation for an appearance of the queen, he began thinking of the soon-coming appearance of the King of Kings. Moved with emotion, Hayford quickly wrote the words, "Majesty, majesty! Worship His majesty. Unto Him be all glory, honor, and praise."

RESOURCE READING: Revelation 5

THE POWER OF A FORTY-SIX-TEN

A certain businessman's world was coming apart. When he shared his difficulties with a friend, the man said, "What you need is a dose of forty-six-ten!"

Forty-six-ten? This was new stuff to him. He knew what a .357 was, and a .38—both are powerful handguns. "What's a forty-six-ten?" he asked. Instead of replying directly, his friend said he would send him something in the mail.

A few days late, the businessman received a padded envelope. When he opened it, he found a wooden plaque with an engraved inscription that read 46:10. He turned the plaque over and found these words of explanation: "Be still, and know that I am God" (Psalm 46:10).

I'm amazed how many people find greater strength in the power of a weapon than in the promises of God.

My family will never forget the experience we had shortly after we moved to Manila. One night, thieves broke into the house immediately behind ours. With a knife to the throat of our neighbor, they gently shook him awake and relieved him of his money and valuables.

The thieves then crawled across the wall separating our house from our neighbors. Our teenage daughter woke up to the sound of voices under her window whispering, "Americanos!" My call to security brought five policemen with guns drawn, but all they found was an empty backyard.

We wondered if this episode had frightened our children. The next day Bonnie picked up her Bible and read Psalm 4:8, the words of King David: "I will lie down and sleep in peace, for you alone, O LORD, make me dwell in safety."

What's the source of your protection when the enemy is crouched under your window? God says, "Be still, and know that I am God." The New American Standard Bible translates the verb *to be still* as "cease striving." The root of the Hebrew word means to let your hands drop. Think for a moment what would happen to a boxer who let his hands drop. Nevertheless, God promises that He will protect and sustain you. Quiet your heart, stop trying to defend yourself, and let God be your strength. Forty-six-ten is a powerful defense.

RESOURCE READING: Psalm 46

August 23

THE GOD OF JACOB

Heroes can be larger than life itself, and it doesn't take a public relations firm to turn a rascal into a hero. Jacob, the grandson of Abraham, was just such a character.

Jacob is mentioned at least nine times in the book of Psalms, and when the writers refer to him, they use the expression, "the God of Jacob." Why is this important? Well, first of all, not once in the Bible will you find the expression, "the God of Daniel," or "the God of Moses," or "the God of Elijah." These individuals were giants of epic proportion, yet Jacob is the one mentioned twenty-two times in the Bible.

Who was Jacob, anyway? After his marriage to Rebekah, Abraham's son Isaac desperately wanted a son of his own. Finally, as the result of earnest prayer, Rebekah conceived twins. When the first boy, Esau, came into the world, before the women attending the birth could lift him to his mother's breast, the second child was born, holding on to the heel of his brother. This second child was named Jacob, which means "heel catcher," as in someone who purposely sticks out his foot to trip another.

Was the name a self-fulfilling prophecy of what was to come? You will no doubt remember that Esau became a hunter, and a good one. But one day, he came in exhausted and famished with hunger, just as Jacob was preparing lunch for himself. Stupidly, Esau bartered his birthright as the first son for a bowl of stew. Later, when Isaac was old and ready to pass on his estate, Jacob remembered his deal with Esau.

In order to get the larger portion of the inheritance, however, Jacob had to lie to his dad, and deceive him, by passing himself off as Esau. We're talking about someone who was less than a role model, less than a benchmark, not exactly someone you would hold up as an example for your son to follow. Yet he is identified with God in the phrase, "the God of Jacob." How can this be?

When Jacob was absolutely desperate, he finally turned to God, and God changed his life. I'm glad that God chose to be identified as "the God of Jacob." It gives me hope, because if God could change Jacob's life, He can change mine—and yours as well.

RESOURCE READING: Genesis 25

August 24

WHITE-WATER RAPIDS

Have you ever been on a white-water rafting trip? What an experience! I remember my first trip. (Come to think of it, it was my last trip as well.) I'd been around water ever since I was a little kid, and when they gave me a life jacket and cinched it about as tight as the saddle on a horse, I thought, "I don't need this thing." After all, we were putting the raft into water that was placid and calm.

In a few minutes, the water started flowing more rapidly. *Great stuff!* I thought. After a few curves, the current became swifter. Glancing up, we could see the raft in front of us wafting like a potato chip in the wind. *So that's what they call white-water,* I thought, as I realized our boat was next.

The helmsman, who, thank God, knew what he was doing, yelled for us to paddle left, then right, then hard left, then—whoosh! I found myself in the water, fighting for breath, trying to get my feet pointed downstream.

It didn't matter that the rapids were not rated very high on the scale of difficulty. I didn't care that other rafters would laugh at me. When you've been thrown from the boat and are gasping for air, others' opinions don't matter.

White-water rafting and life are similar in that you don't know where the rocks are or what's around the corner, and there's no going back for another run. When you get dunked and are gasping for breath, you want help and you want it now.

Have you ever found yourself in a desperate situation? Maybe you're on the wrong end of a lawsuit, the recipient of slander, or the loser in an argument with your spouse. Perhaps the doctor just said, "We've done our best, but the outlook isn't good."

When life turns into a white-water experience and you're tossed from the boat, what do you hold on to? Turn to Psalm 46 and read what the psalmist did when he faced the white waters of life. When God is your refuge, the intensity of the rapids isn't all that important.

RESOURCE READING: Psalm 46

August 25

THE RAGGED EDGE OF REALITY

Joe Stowell calls it "the ragged edge of reality." That's the place where your life is out of control, and you don't know what to do about it. When the ragged edge of reality closed in on the psalmist, he wrote, "God is our refuge and strength, an ever-present help in trouble. Therefore we will not fear, though the earth give way and the mountains fall into the heart of the sea, though its waters roar and foam and the mountains quake with their surging" (Psalm 46:1–3).

He's describing big trouble. Mountains quaking and cascading into the sea is pretty graphic. But the impact is no less unsettling than hearing the doctor say, "We've done everything we can to save your little boy," or hearing the one you expected to grow old with say, "I don't love you and I'm tired of pretending. I want out of this marriage."

The ragged edge of reality can be painfully devastating. I don't have to describe it further. You've been there. But you may need encouragement to let the Lord be your strength and help.

Anyone who would say, "I'm not going to turn to God now. I don't want Him to have to bail me out," probably hasn't gotten to the ragged edge of reality yet. When there's an avalanche, you don't waste time putting wax on your skis. You move. Shipwreck survivors will grasp anything that will keep them afloat, right?

What I'm about to say sounds hard, yet it's true. Sometimes God allows us to face the ragged edge of reality so we'll stop playing games with Him, and get desperate enough to let Him help us.

Self-reliance may be an admirable trait in our society, but when it comes to the ragged edge of reality, there are things that only God can do. The psalmist says, "For in the day of trouble he will keep me safe in his dwelling; he will hide me in the shelter of his tabernacle and set me high upon a rock" (Psalm 27:5).

Because God is good, and a help in times of trouble, you can reach out for Him. When you search for Him and seek Him with all your heart, you'll find Him, and when you do, the ragged edge of reality will become your friend.

RESOURCE READING: Nahum 1

TURNING LOOSE THE NET

Tell me what's important in your life, and I'll tell you who your God really is. How you spend your money and your time reveals what you really consider important—whether it's your family, your hobby, or your work.

The tension between work, family, and God isn't new. It's the other things that crowd your schedule and keep you from prioritizing your time and energy. Maybe you feel like a juggler, tossing more and more glass balls into the air until it becomes certain that something is going to crash. How do you balance all the demands? Jesus says, "Seek first my kingdom and my righteousness and all these other things will be given to you as well" (see Matthew 6:33).

Have you ever noticed that the very last thing Jesus said to Peter was exactly what he said at their first encounter? "Follow me." That was it. That's all Jesus wanted from start to finish.

"Just a minute," you say. "These guys had to make a living and so do I." True. When Jesus called Peter and Andrew, they had their fishing nets in their hands. They were about to throw the net into the sea.

I wonder if Peter thought, *Hey, maybe we can make a deal. I'm willing to follow You, but I'd like to keep my fishing nets handy, and when things slack off a bit, I'll still fish on the side.*

We hold onto our nets when we want to cut a deal with God. But it doesn't work. "If anyone would come after me," said Jesus, "he must deny himself and take up his cross daily and follow me" (Luke 9:23). Dietrich Bonhoeffer called it "radical discipleship."

Does leaving your nets mean walking away from your business or work? Not necessarily. But it does mean making Jesus the Lord of your life, your home, your leisure, and your thoughts. Jesus promises to add the other things when you make Him first in your life. Turn loose the net, friend, and you'll discover that God will fill it more times than you can count.

RESOURCE READING: Matthew 4:18–22

August 27

WHOSE FAULT IS IT?

When British rock star Liam Gallagher's father took a hammer and struck his mother, Liam blamed God. "I stopped believing in God because of what happened to me," he said. He and his mother and two brothers were forced to move into an apartment and start another life.

Blame God. I've never quite understood why God becomes the whipping boy for all human failure, instead of the refuge we seek when people fail us and adverse circumstances envelop us.

The fact is we live in an imperfect, broken world. A very good friend of mine has been given four weeks to live. Two other friends face surgery for cancer. The two-year old daughter of a family friend drowned in a swimming pool accident. Another respected friend, a capable writer and pastor, fell from a ladder and was pronounced brain dead, leaving behind his wife and two daughters.

A Christian musician tells kids that if they pray, God will send an angel to protect them. True, the Psalms tell us that the "angel of the Lord camps round about them that fear him," but this is not to suggest that believers have a safety net that protects against human failure and accidents.

Nearly 3,000 years ago, David struggled with the issue of human suffering and concluded, "Do not fret because of evil men or be envious of those who do wrong; for like the grass they will soon wither, like green plants they soon die away" (Psalm 37:1–2).

David had many reasons to try to hold God accountable for trouble. He could have said, "Look, God, Samuel anointed me as king, something You asked him to do; and ever since, Saul has hunted me as an animal and sought to kill me." No, instead, David turned to the Lord and cried, "The LORD is my rock, my fortress and my deliverer; my God is my rock, in whom I take refuge." (Psalm 18:2).

In times of trouble, your attitude and your posture make all the difference in the world. Instead of blaming God, run to Him and pour out your heart to Him in prayer. Let Him bring the comfort of His presence and speak to your troubled heart.

RESOURCE READING: Psalm 37:1–9

August 28

IF YOU COULD ASK
BUT ONE QUESTION

If you had an opportunity to ask God just one question, what would it be? Would you ask how old the universe really is—a question that would put to rest once and for all the debate about the age of the earth? Or would you ask a theological question—say, about free will versus the sovereign will of God?

I suspect your question would be more like one of these: "Why can't I have a baby when other women abort children they don't want?" or "Why was the life of my son cut short?"

Some questions will never be answered this side of

eternity. There are a lot of things we don't understand. When we confront evil, no matter how it is packaged, we are shocked and reminded that we live in a sinful, broken world. The consequences of sin touch the lives of the just and the unjust, the good and the evil, the young as well as the old.

David cries out, "From the end of the earth will I cry unto thee, when my heart is overwhelmed: lead me to the rock that is higher than I" (Psalm 61:2 KJV). When his strength was failing, my father-in-law, Guy Duffield, often quoted the words of Connie Libbey: "Sometimes on the Rock I tremble, faint of heart and weak of knee, but the steadfast Rock of Ages, never trembles under me."

When your heart cries out, "Why?" remember these three guidelines:

Guideline #1: God's nature is loving and kind—not harsh and capricious. Kindness is often misjudged as a weakness, but someday God will right the wrongs and even the score with evildoers.

Guideline #2: God is sovereign. Isaiah says, "Yet, O LORD, you are our Father. We are the clay, you are the potter; we are all the work of your hand" (Isaiah 64:8).

Guideline #3: God cares what happens to His children. Nothing escapes His sight. Your tears and cries never are ignored. When darkness seems to surround your life, realize that God experienced darkness when His Son faced death at Calvary. God knows. He's been where you are and He's with you now. And someday He'll answer your question: "Why?"

RESOURCE READING: Habakkuk 1

INASMUCH AS YOU
DID IT TO ONE OF THESE

A Southern Baptist pastor with no criminal record was facing jail. His crime was that he had allowed homeless people to sleep on the church property and use the rest rooms, in violation of local zoning ordinances. The jurors felt sorry for him, but nevertheless came back with a verdict of guilty. May God help the district attorney sleep at night.

How did Wiley Drake get into this mess?

It began, he explained, "on a cool November morning [when] I arrived at the church [to do my] sermon preparation. As I walked around the. . .property, I noticed what appeared to be a person curled up in our covered walkway."

Drake nudged the man with his foot. But the man didn't move. He nudged harder. Then, he said, "I bent over, grabbed him by his dirty, damp lapels. . .and said, 'How dare you come on to God's property, drunk, and desecrate these holy grounds.'" Drake got the man to his feet and unceremoniously propelled him in the direction of the street. As the man staggered, Drake hoped he wouldn't fall and end up suing the church.

After this encounter, Drake stormed into his office to study for his message. His Bible fell open to the words of Jesus in Matthew 25:40: "Inasmuch as ye have done it unto one of the least of these my brethren, ye have done it unto me" (KJV). Drake's conscience began to trouble him for what he had just done.

"I heard no audible voice," he said, "but Jesus said to me, 'You just kicked me off your church property.'"

Drake promised the Lord that he would never again kick anyone off the church property, and that he would become a shepherd to the lost, whether they wore a suit and a tie or brought their possessions in a plastic bag.

Drake began taking in the homeless, letting them stay on church property which eventually landed him in court where he was convicted of zoning violations; however, three of the jurors who convicted Drake attended his church service the following Sunday. Perhaps they got the message after all.

RESOURCE READING: Matthew 25:31–46

August 30

THE WORLD'S MOST MARRIED MAN

G lynn Wolfe found a niche in the *Guinness Book of World Records* as the world's most married man. Twenty-nine times he went to the altar, and twenty-nine times he divorced. But when he died, not a single one of his former wives attended the funeral—and only one of his reported nineteen children and forty grandchildren was there. He was buried in a pauper's grave, and when the dirt covered the donated casket, his descendants hoped to cover their dark memories of the man and get on with their lives.

Newspapers and magazines picked up on the story and tried to contact some of his former wives. In an article titled "Most Married, but Little Missed," one paper said, "The man whose family tree sent branches and sub-branches into every direction, the man who married more often than Zsa Zsa Gabor, Elizabeth Taylor and Henry VIII combined, the man who made twenty-nine different till-death-do-us-part promises was singularly alone at the end."[1]

A number of marriage and family therapists offered

their comments, trying to explain how anyone could fail so miserably at relationships yet keep on trying. Wolfe himself was once asked why he changed marriage partners so often. He replied that after a while he just got bored and wanted to find something new and exciting. It didn't work. He died almost broke, homeless, and alone, with a wedding dress reportedly hanging in his closet, just in case he found bride number thirty.

He should have taken the advice of Henry Ford, who was once asked how he could stay married to the same woman for so many years. "I've treated marriage just like the automobiles I've built," said Ford. "Just stick to one model."

You get out of a marriage what you put into it—fulfillment, excitement, joy and happiness, or indifference, trouble, and boredom. If he had worked things right, Wolfe might have made the rounds of the late night talk shows or written something for a gossip magazine. Instead, when he died, he left nothing but bad memories to his wives and children. The small inheritance he had went to a stranger who ran the photocopy business where he took his divorce papers for reproduction. How's that for being a loser!

RESOURCE READING: Proverbs 31

August 31

THE POWER OF TIME

What can bring down empires, humble the mightiest of men, crumble a craggy granite peak, yet has the power to heal a wound and change a life? Described as the greatest power on Earth, that force is TIME. Benjamin Franklin once wrote, "Dost thou love time?

Then use time wisely, for that's the stuff that life is made of."

There are many inequalities in life. But when it comes to time, everybody gets the exact same allotment: twenty-four hours a day, no more and no less. Suppose that every morning 186,400 dollars, pesos, lira, or whatever your coinage, was deposited in your bank account, but every evening whatever was left in the account was canceled out. What would you do? You can be sure that you would withdraw every coin before the bank closed each day—just to avoid losing anything.

You have such an account and its name is *time*. Every morning you are credited with 186,400 seconds, and it's up to you to use it or lose it. At the end of the day, whatever you haven't used is lost forever. Time does not come to us in days or even hours; it comes to us in moments. The fragile nature of time led Moses to pray, "Teach us to number our days, that we may apply our hearts unto wisdom" (Psalm 90:12 KJV). That's another way of saying it's the use, not the length, of our days that really counts.

Life can be full of meaning at age thirty. Others have lived three times as long with little meaning or purpose. Jesus was only on Earth for thirty-three years, but only eternity will measure the impact of His work.

What is the impact of your life? How have you used the time that God has given you? God has given each of us a measure of time, and when we are done, He will ask us to account for how we used it. While we are bound within time, we must make preparation for eternity.

We do not lose time; it slips through our fingers in lost moments, seconds at a time. It is time to harness the tremendous power of time.

RESOURCE READING: Psalm 90

BRINGING OUT
THE BEST IN PEOPLE

C harles Schwab, the one-time president of Bethlehem Steel, once said, "I have never seen a man who could do real work except under the stimulus of encouragement and the approval of the people for whom he is working." Encouragement brings out the best in people, but there are so many things that push us down and discourage us, rather than lifting us up. Discouragement is one of the weapons the enemy uses to blunt our effectiveness in Christian service and to hinder our progress in our Christian discipleship.

Want to become an encourager? Put the following guidelines into practice in your life:

Guideline #1: Be sure that your source of strength is great enough to share with someone else. How can we encourage someone else when we need so much encouragement ourselves? First, get your own heart right. Find God as your total Source of encouragement. To be an encouragement to another person, you must believe in the ultimate outcome of what you are laboring to achieve.

Guideline #2: Look for the best in people. Thank God for the largeness of heart that looks beyond skepticism and doubt and sees genuineness and sincerity. When I think of this attribute, I think of Barnabas from the New Testament. His name means "son of consolation." When Saul, the bigoted persecutor of the faith, was converted, most in the church were skeptical. He was known to be a murderer and a rascal. Who would believe his conversion was genuine?

Barnabas was so convinced that he sought out the former enemy of the faith and brought him to the church at Jerusalem.

Guideline #3: Get your focus off your own problems and look for someone you can help. This is perhaps the most important step of all! All of us face challenges and problems. We can either be engulfed by them or break through our problems and minister to others. By encouraging others, we lift ourselves. Nothing is as small as your own little world and nothing is as large as being part of someone else's.

The writer of Hebrews says that we are to encourage one another daily as we see the day of Christ approaching. Encouragement isn't something you practice. It is something that you are! Think about it.

RESOURCE READING: Deuteronomy 31:1–8

September 2

HISTORY REWRITTEN

Have you seen the World History Revisions compiled by Richard Lederer, a teacher at St. Paul's School? Here are a few choice excerpts, reportedly written by his students. "Adam and Eve were created from an apple tree." "Jacob, son of Isaac, stole his brother's birthmark." "The inhabitants of Egypt were called mummies. They traveled by Camelot." "Moses led the slaves to the Red Sea, where they made unleavened bread, which is bread made without any ingredients." "In the Renaissance, Martin Luther was nailed to the church door at Wittenberg for selling papal indulgences. He died a horrible death, being excommunicated by a bull."

History rewritten. A more sobering type is when individuals with purpose and intent decide to rewrite the sordid details of the past. For example, Saddam Hussein now purports to be a direct descendant of Mohammed. He is attempting to use history to support his claim as the legitimate sovereign of Syria, Iran, Kuwait, Saudi Arabia, Jordan, and, naturally, Israel. Unfortunately for him, the history books in those countries don't support his version.

Twisting the truth, or fabricating it, isn't new at all. For centuries, men and women have tried to make themselves appear bolder, more courageous, more important than they really are. I'm thinking of old King Sennacherib, whose army was trounced when his forces came against the Angel of the Lord and 185,000 died overnight. He omits that encounter from the Assyrian chronicles, but he was sure to leave us a relief on the wall of his palace showing himself as a great conqueror.

Have you ever tried to rewrite your own history? Perhaps you do it by what you tell your friends, or what you include on your expense account. Perhaps you rewrite history at tax time when you deliberately overlook those cash transactions.

What's wrong with rewriting history? The same thing that's wrong when a doctor cheats in medical school, or a husband lies to his wife. When God says, "Enough!" and you stand in His presence, the record will be straight, unadulterated, and precisely accurate. People who try to rewrite history are kidding themselves. As Jesus put it, "You will know the truth, and the truth will set you free" (John 8:32).

RESOURCE READING: Revelation 20:11–15

WHEN YOU ARE
TAKEN CAPTIVE BY TROUBLE

O n the night of March 31, 1994, missionary Ray Rising was riding his motorcycle back to Loma Linda, his group's headquarters in Colombia, when he was captured by a band of armed guerrillas. For the next 810 days, his life was on hold.

Moved from place to place in the Colombian jungle, at first Ray was angry and fearful. Then he began to realize that God was still there, and He was still working in his life. Life went on, just differently from what he had planned. He later wrote, "God was making me into something on the inside that my captors needed to see on the outside."

Ray was finally released on June 16, 1996. Before they let him go, the guerrillas lined up and shook hands with him, which gave Ray an opportunity to express verbally the faith he had demonstrated for two-and-a-half years.

I shall never forget a conversation I had with Wang Ming Dao, the father of the Chinese house church movement, shortly before his death. This saintly man had been in prison for twenty-two years at the hands of the Communists who sought to drive every vestige of religion from the country.

In his book, *A Stone Made Smooth,* Wang explains how God uses persecution and difficulty to polish our lives like water wears down a stone in a riverbed. "Brother Wang," I said, "many years ago I read your book." He smiled and quickly responded, "Stone still not yet smooth." Though well into his eighties, this godly man knew that even in this season of life, God was still polishing the stone.

There is no human rhyme or reason why God allows us to face the tough hours, but I am certain that God walks through the dark valleys with every one of His children. He keeps working on the inside of us so that our enemies can see the outward changes. When you are taken captive by tough times, remember Ray Rising's powerful words, "God was making me into something on the inside that my captors needed to see on the outside."

RESOURCE READING: Isaiah 43:1–6

September 4

GOD'S REMODELING PROJECT

Theologians call it sanctification. George MacDonald, the man who greatly influenced C. S. Lewis, would have called it remodeling. It's what happens when you have made your plans for your future in vivid detail—and then God pushes them aside, surprising you with something different.

In *Mere Christianity,* Lewis quotes MacDonald, who wrote, "Imagine yourself as a living house. God comes in to rebuild that house. At first, perhaps, you can understand what He is doing. He is getting the drains right and stopping the leaks in the roof and so on: You knew that those jobs needed doing and so you are not surprised. But presently He starts knocking the house about in a way that hurts abominably and does not seem to make sense. What on earth is He up to? The explanation is that He is building quite a different house from the one you thought of—throwing out a new wing here, putting on an extra floor there, running up towers, making courtyards. You thought you were going to be made into a decent little cottage: but He is building a palace. He intends to come and live in it Himself."

Frankly, I haven't faced the traumatic experiences (those ones that "hurt abominably") that some have gone through. But I have walked through the valleys with more people than I can remember. I've noticed the very thing MacDonald was writing about. When God remodels a life—no matter how painful the interruptions are in the process—the end result is always an improvement.

A person is more sensitive, more Christlike, more understanding. There is less arrogance, more compassion. Less glamour, more gold.

I have had some experience with remodeling, and about the best thing that I can say about it is that I like it best when it is finished. Who likes the sawdust on the floor or the noise of hammers and drills? But when the task is finished, we say, "Ah! It was worth it."

The writer of Hebrews described life's remodeling as a kind of spiritual discipline. He wrote, "Endure hardship as discipline; God is treating you as sons. For what son is not disciplined by his father?" (Hebrews 12:7). Notice that he says it is hardship or difficulty which we are to consider as discipline—not punishment. Punishment is for wrongdoing, and the focus is on the past. But discipline focuses on the future in producing something different, something better, something of quality.

RESOURCE READING: Philippians 1

GETTING BACK UP
WHEN YOU STUMBLE

A nyone who watched the 400-meter semifinals in the
1992 Olympics will never forget it. During the race,
Derek Redmond, a British runner, tore a hamstring and
collapsed on the track, his hopes for a medal dashed into a
thousand pieces. His dream and his years of training had
been betrayed by the weakness of his body. For a few seconds, he lay on the track, then slowly got to his feet and
began dragging himself toward the finish. Every step was
painful agony.

Derek's father, thinking that his son was trying to get off
the track, came out of the stands, ran to the track, and put his
arm around his son. But Derek wasn't about to quit the race,
even though he could not win. Instead, with his dad sup-
porting him, he slowly began to hobble toward the finish
line. The crowd, sensing what was happening, began to cheer.

God doesn't prevent the torn hamstrings of life, but He
loves us enough to support us in our pain and problems. In
Hebrews 12:7, the writer says, "Endure hardship as discipline." In other words, "Stand your ground, hold out, persevere in trouble, affliction, and persecution." Don't quit
just because you're down and can't win the gold.

Difficulty either causes people to stumble, or to gain
strength and put their lives together again. God says, "Make
straight paths for your feet," or don't yield to the temptation
to quit. Keep moving, and go straight ahead, so that those
who are weaker than you won't stumble over your example.

When someone falls into trouble, many are quick to
say, "Isn't it terrible?" But the ones who really get hurt are
those who watch from a distance, who never say a word, but
reason, "If he or she can't make it, neither can I." This is the
weak brother—the one who stumbles over your example

and becomes spiritually disabled.

When you are felled by something in life, get back up, and start making tracks toward the finish. You'll discover the strong arms of your heavenly Father will be there to support you and keep you from being a stumbling block to a weaker brother or sister.

RESOURCE READING: Hebrews 12

September 6

GETTING THE BIG ROCKS IN FIRST

Stephen Covey tells the story of a seminar where the instructor was lecturing on the importance of planning our time. To impress his audience with the point he was making, the instructor took a widemouthed jar and filled it with fist-size rocks. Then he asked, "Is the jar full?" Noticing that no more large rocks could be placed in the jar, the audience nodded their heads.

The instructor reached beneath the podium and took a bucket of gravel and poured it over the large rocks, shaking the smaller rocks down into the cracks, and asked again, "Is the jar full?" This time, everyone hesitated. Finally someone said, "Probably not!"

Right! Next, the instructor took a container of sand and poured it over the gravel until it sifted down and filled the remaining space. Same question: "Is the jar full?" No one responded.

Then he took a pitcher of water and poured it in, filling the entire jar with water. With finality, the lecturer turned to his students and said, "Now, what's the point?" Someone responded that the obvious moral was that you could always get more into your life. "No," the teacher countered, "the real moral is you'd better get the big rocks in first."

What are some of the foundation stones upon which we should build our lives? Try these six for a solid foundation:

1. Commitment
2. Care
3. Communication
4. Cohesiveness
5. Constraint
6. Conveying what really counts—faith and values.

Your commitment as a parent is of utmost importance. Though my heart goes out to every single parent who lays a foundation alone, kids need two parents to keep up with them. Parenting is a two-person task, and when two individuals love each other and are committed to their offspring, they provide the environment that enables growth and nurturing.

The best thing parents can commit themselves to is each other. Husband, love your wife. Wife, love your husband. Next, commit to a set of values. Decide what's important and what is nonnegotiable, then live out your values. Finally, commit to serve the living God; bring a taste of heaven into your home. "Seldom if ever," wrote a juvenile court judge in a personal letter, "do I see a boy or girl in my court who has had the benefit of religious training."

Get the big rocks planted in the foundation first.

RESOURCE READING: Psalm 127:1–2

LAYING THE FOUNDATION

According to John Drescher, in his book *Signs of the Times,* children go through three phases of development: from the organization of childhood, through the disorganization of youth, to the reorganization of adulthood. Drescher calls the first stage the age of regulation, from birth to about age six or seven. The second period is the age of imitation, from age seven to twelve, when a youngster begins to notice that being different makes you stand out from the crowd, and peer pressure kicks in. Then comes the challenge: phase three—the age of inspiration during the teen years.

Parenting teens is the most challenging stage, but the most important stage, without question, is the early years, when the foundation is being laid. Parental care is the foundation upon which respect, understanding, and values can be taught. Because you love your child, you should establish your authority as the parent. You've got to love your child enough to require him to eat his vegetables, brush his teeth, and look you in the eye and say, "Yes, Mom," not just "Yeah." Love also provides the foundation of the teaching-learning process, including discipline. You can discipline a child without love, but you can't really love your child without discipline.

No matter how busy you are, love demands the gift of yourself and your time. What do you really owe your youngster? Not computer games, music lessons, skateboards, or bicycles. But you do owe every child an undivided portion of old-fashioned love—the spanking kind, the kind that cares enough to teach a child right from wrong and respect for authority and adults.

When newspaper columnist Ann Landers asked her readers if they had it do all over again, would they have kids?

Of 10,000 who responded, 70 percent said "No!"—a reaction she described as both surprising and disturbing. A lot of parents feel that way, but I can tell you one thing for sure: When you include commitment, love, communication, constraint, and values in your formula, you will be among the minority who consider parenting one of the most rewarding tasks in all of life. It's easy to become a parent, and tough to be a really good one, but it's worth the time and effort.

RESOURCE READING: Ephesians 6

September 8

IF YOU CAN'T TRADE 'EM IN, BETTER CARE FOR THEM!

I f we paid no more attention to our flowers than we do to our children," said botanist Luther Burbank, "we would be living in a jungle."

If you are about to drop your child off at a day care center, are late for work, or feel like taking your youngster back and trading him in for another model, you might be tempted to skip this page. Let's face it. There are days when our precious little jewels are semiprecious, and those sweet little ones are bittersweet.

"Nobody told me that being a parent would be this tough," said a young mother. I've been there. But take heart and hang in there. When you win the battle by not running up the white flag when your children are small, you'll enjoy them as teenagers a whole lot more.

The foundation of a building is the most important part of the entire structure, and so it is in parenting. We've looked at the importance of commitment to a game plan and old-fashioned parental care, and today I want to stress the importance of communication in a child's foundation.

That little guy or little girl who came into your life as a baby is just as much a real person as you are. The only difference is twenty or thirty years of experience, which he or she will get the same way you got yours—one day at a time. It's been proven that children whose parents talk to them, read to them, and communicate with them develop faster and are more intelligent than their counterparts who don't get that special communication.

Kids respond to the level of input we give them. Every parent impacts the life of his child—either negatively or positively. When you are positive and upbeat, your children embrace the same attitudes. When you succumb to stress, you convey the same thing to them. Are kids a mirror of ourselves? Far more than we would like to admit. Remember, raising positive kids in a negative world begins with you and ends with you, too. It's a fact.

RESOURCE READING: Colossians 3

September 9

THE FOUNDATION-HEIGHT FORMULA

Philip Recto is one of Asia's leading architects. His name and signature are on the building plans of scores of high-rise structures in Manila, Hong Kong, Singapore, and Kuala Lumpur. When I had breakfast with this outstanding man and his lovely wife, I couldn't resist taking advantage of his professional expertise. "I have a question that I've always wanted answered by someone who knows what he's talking about. How do you know how strong to make the foundation of a building?"

Philip smiled knowingly and said, "The height of a building is always in direct proportion to the strength of the foundation." The foundation of a building is the most important part of the structure. In the same way, the height of a child's accomplishments may also be determined by the strength of the foundation laid by the parents during the child's formative years.

Helping your child understand that he is a person of value and worth helps lay the foundation of self-esteem. Helping your child understand that he or she is a person of great worth in the sight of God gives him the largeness of heart to serve others and not feel threatened by doing the small tasks. Surrounding your child with an environment of security helps him or her sleep at night and rise in the morning ready to accomplish something.

When your youngster knows that you are behind him, he's far more confident, more determined, and better able to handle failure. Watch the kid who strikes out in a baseball game. Notice how he glances at the stands to see what Dad's reaction is—whether he feels acceptance or rejection. The parent who is laying a strong foundation is shouting encouragement at the games, attending school functions, and going to church with the family. Strong families hang together, establishing perimeters that allow for growth and development.

The next time you look at the skyline and see a skyscraper towering in the clouds, remind yourself that the height of the building is always in inverse proportion to the strength of the foundation. The next time you get discouraged in the task of parenting, remember: Your influence in the life of your child will outlast the skyscraper on the horizon. Think about it.

RESOURCE READING: Read Psalm 127 in a contemporary version.

THE FOUNDATION STONE
OF FAITH

A Harvard University professor, pressed to complete a writing assignment, placed a large tape player with his tape-recorded lecture in the center of the table, and wrote a message on the blackboard explaining his absence and asking the students to take notes. Toward the end of the hour, the professor dropped by the classroom. To his surprise, he found the room was empty, except for six small tape recorders on the table, all making a copy of his recording. "Monkey see, monkey do."

There is a vast difference between letting your kids grow up taking the path of least resistance, and growing kids God's way with purpose and direction. No other building block is more important than faith in God, faith in each other, and faith that we can achieve our goals.

As God's children were about to march into the land of promise, He instructed, "Hear, O Israel: The LORD our God, the LORD is one. Love the LORD your God with all your heart and with all your soul and with all your strength. These commandments that I give you today are to be upon your hearts. Impress them on your children. Talk about them when you sit at home and when you walk along the road, when you lie down and when you get up" (Deuteronomy 6:4–7).

How do you do this? In a certain home, the first son ran away and joined the navy. The second became a lifeguard, and the third got a job on a fishing boat. "I don't understand why my three sons all had a fascination with the sea," said their mother to a friend. The friend responded, "Have you ever taken a look at the picture in their bedroom?"

"No. Why?"

"Take a look at it!"

On the wall of the bedroom was a gigantic seascape with a square-rigged schooner cutting through the waves, sails billowing in the breeze, salt spraying. Is there a relationship between what we see around us and what we do? Absolutely!

God tells His people, "Be careful that you do not forget the LORD" (Deuteronomy 6:12). We still need that message today.

RESOURCE READING: Deuteronomy 6:1–19

September 11

THE DARK SIDE
OF HUMAN FAILURE

M arriage counselors agree that infidelity rears its ugly head in the majority of broken homes. Though filmmakers and TV producers make it look so natural, so romantic, and so free, its consequences are devastating beyond description.

Fidelity to the one who stood by your side at the marriage altar is considered passé. But what the filmmakers don't show you is the guilt, the heartache, the loneliness, and the emptiness of a life plowed under by infidelity. The truth, it seems, doesn't fill theater seats or demand primetime exposure.

No relationship in the world can be compared to that of two people who love each other, who have gone public with their commitment by marrying, giving themselves to each other sexually. This relationship is not only blessed by God Himself but involves the emotional, the physical, and the spiritual components of the total person.

How far we have come in only a generation! The proliferation of sex in the media today has gone far, far beyond what film producers in their wildest thoughts could have imagined putting on the screen a generation ago.

In the 1960s, morality began to change, and for a time sexual license was applauded as being free and beautiful. Eventually, people began to realize that the marriage bonding cannot be broken apart without anger, hostility, and jealousy. Sharing your husband or wife with someone else cannot be done without tremendous emotional upheaval, which more often than not results in rejection and divorce.

What the moviemakers don't tell you, David learned long ago: Infidelity is horrible, and its consequences of anguish and pain reach beyond the darkness of a sleepless night. Take time to read Psalm 51 in your Bible, where David cries out to God asking for forgiveness and restoration.

"I thought I was doing what I wanted to do," writes one friend of *Guidelines,* explaining why she became involved with another man, "but now I realize that I was destroying the very thing I really wanted." Some people just have to learn it the hard way.

RESOURCE READING: Psalm 51

September 12

PLAYING GOD

When scientists recently cloned sheep, goats, and monkeys, voices were raised in protest, warning against "playing God."

What does it mean to "play God"? Are we not doing this when doctors operate on a ruptured appendix? Are we not playing God when we give someone an antibiotic to fight the infection that would otherwise take his life?

Those things are okay, we reason. Now let's go one step further. Recently *Scientific American* magazine reported that a team of researchers isolated the human gene that produces a protein causing blood to clot—something that is very important following surgery, and something that promises hope for millions of hemophiliacs. Researchers were able to insert this bit of DNA into the embryo of a mother pig. When her piglets were born, they carried the human DNA factor—the one causing blood to clot—in their genes. These pigs produced this valuable protein which can be harvested and used by humans, thus making the pigs a kind of living laboratory, manufacturing drugs that can save human life. Is that not okay?

When are scientists "playing God" and when are they making noble advances for the cause of humanity? The issue isn't resolved easily. From a biblical perspective, God gave mankind a considerable amount of room in which to maneuver when He commanded that the earth should be subdued. Should we include in that mandate DNA-altered substances that resist disease and blight? Because God is the Author of life, what we can do to sustain life through surgery, antibiotics, and anesthesia must also be okay. It's consistent with sustaining the gift of life, which came from God.

But at some point, man must recognize that humankind is not merely a higher form of mammal. Created by the direct act of God, brought forth in His image, humankind is different, and it is this knowledge which has to be taken into consideration..At some point, we "play God" in ways that our Creator never intended. Where the line is drawn is no easy matter and the issue will never be without controversy, but the fact that man has a soul has to be part of the equation. It is the human soul that separates man from lower forms of life and lifts him into the realm of the heavenly. This fact must never be denied or ignored.

RESOURCE READING: 1 Samuel 1:1–20

DON'T JUST SIT THERE, GOD

Junk mail either grabs your attention or it gets thrown away unopened. That's why American Family Publishers produces those multicolored envelopes proclaiming that you are a "finalist" for the $11 million top prize. You have about as much chance of getting struck by lightning as you do of winning the jackpot, yet millions of people dutifully fill out the enclosure and mail it back, hoping to win the big one.

Bill Brack is the pastor of an Assembly of God church. He got a chuckle when a contest computer database picked the word God from the name of his church for one of their sweepstakes mailings. Pastor Bill opened the envelope and read: "God, we've been searching for you. . ." Pastors like to know someone has been searching for God. The letter touted all the benefits of winning and then encouraged the recipient to respond immediately: "Don't just sit there, God." Yes, don't just sit there, God, do something. Put a stamp on that envelope and mail it back, fast.

I wonder how God would feel if He won the sweepstakes—all $11 million of it. I'm reminded of the time one of my children—then about three or four years old—wrapped a couple of coins in a piece of paper and gave them to me as a gift. The money was insignificant; the love behind it was priceless.

Does God really need anything you can give Him? Yes and no. He doesn't need your money. He owns the diamonds in the depths of the rocks, the veins of gold deep within the earth, the oil beneath the oceans and deserts. Our gifts to the Almighty are like small coins from a child to his father.

So why does the Bible encourage us to give a tenth of our income to the Lord? Tithing demonstrates our understanding that everything we have belongs to the Father.

There is something that God wants, which only you can give and money can't buy, and that is your love and devotion. "More love to Thee, O Christ, more love to Thee," says the old hymn. God doesn't need to win the sweepstakes, but He wants the devotion of our hearts that overflow with praise and thanksgiving.

RESOURCE READING: Isaiah 40

September 14

WHEN THE BATTERY OF CONSCIENCE GOES DEAD

I was standing on the corner of Hollywood and Vine on my way to a radio interview. With me was a missionary, Bill Carne, who had gone into the highlands of Irian Jaya and brought the gospel to a Stone Age people.

Bill and I were commenting on some of the weird people we observed on the streets of Hollywood, with their tattoos, earrings, makeup, chains, and bizarre outfits. As we talked about changing morality, Bill said, "You know our people in Irian Jaya have a far stricter moral code than we have today." This struck me as rather strange, because where he had been, women wore grass skirts and men wore gourds—nothing more. "How is that?" I asked.

He explained that in their tribe, they had prescribed morals that determined what was right and wrong. Few people would deny that in western civilization morality has changed in the past generation. What our grandparents talked about in hushed tones, our parents did with troubled consciences, and our generation is doing without a troubled conscience.

Alexander Pope once wrote, "Vice is a monster of such frightful mien/As to be hated, needs only to be seen/But seen too often, familiar with face/We first endure, then pity, then embrace."

If society says, "It's OK," does that really make it OK? Not for a moment. What may be lawful isn't necessarily moral or right in the sight of God. Your conscience is only as good as your understanding of what is right and wrong. If you shut out the voice of God and ignore His Word, your conscience won't give you much trouble. That's why Paul says that continued wrongdoing sears the conscience as with a hot iron (1 Timothy 4:2). But the issue of guilt before God remains unchanged no matter how acceptable something may be in the eyes of the world and society.

A final thought. The laws of God are given—not to take the fun and excitement out of life—but to provide the joy and happiness of fulfillment in life. Recognizing this and abiding by those timeless guidelines, your conscience is trustworthy. Go with it, and heed its voice.

RESOURCE READING: Hebrews 9

September 15

TAKING THE PATH LESS TRAVELED

T he president of a manufacturing company learned that his company had produced a product that was badly flawed. A television reporter requested an interview to ask about the problem. The executive had three choices: He could deny the problem (which is what his subordinates encouraged him to do). He could duck out the back door and let a subordinate try to smooth over the problem. Or he could face the music, acknowledge the problem, and outline a solution—which is what he chose to do. That's integrity.

A real estate executive was offered a substantial bribe for pushing a certain project. As it happened, the decision to proceed with the project had already been made. For a fleeting moment, the man realized that he could take the bribe and no one would know. Instead, he refused the money and reported the bribe attempt. That's integrity.

A visit to a fast-food drive-through netted far more than tacos for one man. Included with his order was the cash receipts for the previous day in a bag just like the one the food came in. When the man discovered the mistake, he promptly turned around, drove back to the restaurant, and returned the money. That's integrity.

Our English word *integrity* comes from a word that means "uprightness." At times, integrity is neither appreciated nor rewarded. Doing the right thing because you might be rewarded isn't true integrity. Integrity means doing the right thing because it's the right thing to do.

I've spent a lot of time in Communist countries and former Communist countries, where God has largely been left out of life's equation. I've come to the conclusion that integrity is part of the moral fabric of a society that recognizes our ultimate accountability to God. Honoring God in turn makes me accountable to you as my neighbor or friend.

Doing right only when it's rewarded creates a Pavlovian response. But when we are motivated by integrity, we do the right thing because our conscience demands it. The quick fix, the shortcut, the feeling that we can get away with something that feels good or is profitable is what drives societies to moral bankruptcy. The pathway of integrity is the one that honors God.

RESOURCE READING: Mark 8

JESUS, FULL OF JOY

H ave you ever had the experience of reading something in the Bible—even something you have read many times before—and suddenly it leaps out at you? Like blinking neon, it cannot be ignored, and you say to yourself, "Funny, I never saw that before." I've never had quite the same experience reading the newspaper or a chemistry textbook, but it happens all the time with the Bible.

Here's an example. In Luke's account of the gospel, he says that Jesus was full of joy. Recently, as I was reading Luke 10, that phrase took me captive. Jesus—full of joy.

I read several different translations and all said about the same thing. Then I decided to research how the word was used elsewhere in the New Testament and in the writings of the early church fathers.

Here's what I discovered. The word means exactly what the text says. It means "to be glad, to rejoice."

Peter uses the same word when he writes that "you will also be full of joy" (1 Peter 4:13 GW). That's pretty clear. In Acts 16:34, Luke uses the same word to describe a man who was "filled with joy because he had come to believe in God."

Peter uses the word another time to say that joy was unspeakable, or indescribable. Luke says that the source of Jesus' joy was the Holy Spirit. There was a God connection. It was the Holy Spirit who caused the joy.

Joy is the by-product of a God-connection, which results in the Holy Spirit indwelling us, driving back the darkness of circumstances, going far beyond the quest for happiness that consumes so many. Paul says that joy is the fruit, the outward manifestation, of God's indwelling spirit.

Many of God's children settle for far less than God intended. Forgetting that God is far greater than their worries, they struggle through life with frustration and turmoil. Instead, we who are Christians should taste joy and relish it as part of our birthright.

If joy is missing in your life, drop to your knees and say, "Lord, I'm short on joy. Please, Lord, fill my cup to overflowing." He will.

RESOURCE READING: Galatians 5

September 17

MULTITASKING

The word "multitasking" can only be found in the most recent dictionaries, but chances are quite good that you're familiar with the concept.

Kevin Maney defines multitasking as "doing as many things simultaneously as possible." Brushing your teeth at the same time you put on your shoes and listen to the morning news would qualify, but usually the term is applied to more technical applications like driving and talking on your cell phone at the same time.

Isn't it wonderful that technology allows us to do so many more things—all at the same time? Forgive the sarcasm, but I'm not fully convinced that modern technology has done much to make life easier. Technology allows us to accomplish more, but our expectations have risen commensurately.

Do we really need to talk on the phone, send E-mail via wireless modems, and receive faxes in our cars while we're stuck in traffic? Has technology made life better, or just faster? Does it improve my relationship with my wife or does it drag me away from my family to sit in front of the computer trying to figure out why the modem won't work with drive Z?

Lest I sound too cynical, let me say that technology is here to stay. Technology can be very useful, if we make it our servant, but not if we end up serving technology. We must be the ones who learn to pull the plug and say when enough is enough.

As I watch people driving to work putting on their makeup, curling their lashes, shaving, and downing a mug of coffee as they head for the office, I'm inclined to think that meandering across a meadow with a friend, looking for a fishing hole with your son, or taking your daughter by the hand and walking along the beach tossing pebbles in the surf might be far more productive in the long haul than winning a gold medal for multitasking. "This one thing I do," wrote Paul to the Philippians (KJV). Not two things, or three, or half a dozen, just this one thing. Only you can decide how to keep the main thing the main thing.

RESOURCE READING: Philippians 3

September 18

I HAVE NO FAITH IN RELIGION

I have no faith in religion," read a sign in the home of Madalyn Murray O'Hair, arguably the best known atheist of the century, along with Bertrand Russell. O'Hair probably did more to remove God from the public awareness than any other person in the twentieth century.

"I have no faith in religion," she says. Though I would not agree with her on much, I must admit the truth of her statement. Faith in religion isn't the answer. But faith in God, the Maker of heaven and Earth, the One who put the stars in the sky, and the One who loved us enough to send His Son to die for us—that's an entirely different matter.

Perhaps O'Hair's dismissal of religion explains her

ultimate rejection of God. Religion is a broad generic term. It includes everything from Buddhists in jewel-adorned pagodas, to Muslims making the long pilgrimage to Mecca, to hucksters who peddle their brand of the gospel for great personal gain.

Is it any wonder that people have become skeptical of religion? No matter how wrong she may be, Madalyn Murray O'Hair was right not to have faith in religion. Whether she would admit it or not, Mrs. O'Hair was a believer. Her faith was in atheism, which is just as much a religion as Islam or Buddhism, though sort of a no-faith faith.

A stanza from my favorite hymn reads, "My soul has found a resting place, not in device or creed. I trust the ever-living One, His wounds for me shall plead. I need no other argument. I need no other plea. It is enough that Jesus died, and that He died for me."

What is the object of your faith? Yourself, a cult, a religion, or the living God? If the Bible is true, if God has revealed Himself to us through His Son, Jesus Christ, then Christianity has distinguished itself from the religions of the world. When I respond to what God has told us about Himself, I enter into a relationship with a living person, and that faith changes my life. Not believing in religion is a step in the right direction, but what really counts is what you *do* believe in.

RESOURCE READING: Hebrews 11

September 19

ATHEISTS AND MIRACLES

When atheist Madalyn Murray O'Hair disappeared, her comfortable five-bedroom home fell to her associate, Oren Tyson. But when the taxes were not paid, the authorities confiscated the house and set Tyson's belongings out on the street in cardboard boxes. He was indignant. In response, he fashioned a sign that defiantly read, "Homeless Atheist, Nam Veteran, Will Wait for a Miracle."

Now there's a contradiction in logic for you: an atheist waiting for a miracle. Whoa! Perhaps it's a matter of definition, but atheists don't believe in miracles unless a miracle is simply a stroke of luck. True miracles involve the supernatural, the suspension of normal laws by a higher being.

I'm convinced that most of the people who describe themselves as atheists are really lifestyle atheists. They prefer to live their lives with no accountability to God and no recognition of moral and spiritual laws.

I once encountered a young man who described himself as an atheist. As we talked about creation and the laws of cause and effect, he finally admitted, "Well, I can't live the kind of life I want to live and believe in God." Of course, refusing to acknowledge God's existence doesn't make Him go away any more than burying our heads in the sand makes our problems disappear.

It's interesting to note that when Madalyn Murray O'Hair's son, William, became an adult, he concluded that atheism had no answers for the tough questions of life, such as Who am I? Where did I come from? and, Where do I go after death? Consequently, he renounced atheism and embraced Christianity, choosing to serve the living God.

I suspect that many who describe themselves as atheists would do an about-face if they opened their eyes to the realities of life. Atheistic Communism in the former Soviet Union ultimately collapsed because man cannot live without God. If you really want to know more about God, read the original source Book, the Bible, starting with the Gospel of John, C. S. Lewis's *Mere Christianity,* and Josh McDowell's *Evidence That Demands A Verdict*. These books can give you further insight. God gives us a promise: "You will seek me

and find me when you seek me with all your heart"
(Jeremiah 29:13). It's still true. God is as close as the cry of
a sincere heart: "Lord, show me Yourself."

RESOURCE READING: John 1

September 20

WHEN GOD TURNS YOUR LIFE AROUND

By the age of thirty, Howard Ball was a successful businessman—not wealthy, but moving steadily toward his
career goals. He was happily married and had a family. But
in the process of moving up the ladder, he had closed the
door on God. As an agnostic, he considered God irrelevant
and unknowable. Nonetheless, he still went to church, taught
a Sunday school class, and served on the stewardship com-
mittee of a large church. Ball played it safe. He was making
the right moves, getting good connections. His world was
coming together, but what he didn't know was that his life
was about to take on a new dimension. God suddenly
became real in his life when a friend introduced him personally to Jesus Christ.

Soon after his conversion, Howard learned that the
fruit of God's Spirit brings love, joy, peace, and other God-
like qualities in our lives. *That explains why I'm different,* he
thought. Two years later, he almost gave up on the whole
business. Why?

He explains it like this. When he first found Jesus
Christ, he was short on knowledge and long on joy. He
knew practically nothing about the Bible or God's plan for
his life. He only knew that he had found an intense joy and
satisfaction in living which he had never had before. Then

things gradually began to change. He began to study the Word and became deeply involved in activities. Before long, he was so busy doing things, serving on boards and committees—doing things for God—that He had little time to be with God, nurturing his relationship and walking with Him day by day.

The Christian life can be a lively and vibrant friendship with Jesus, or it can become a ritual, a routine, a lifestyle without much life. There's nothing wrong with serving on boards and committees, but we must never forget that what counts is the ongoing, day-by-day relationship with Jesus Christ. Howard Ball didn't give up, but he had to learn how to keep the main thing as his top priority. Paul was right. When a person is in Christ, he is a new creation. God's purpose is for you to keep that joy for the rest of your life.

RESOURCE READING: John 3

September 21

POWER TO ENDURE

F orget about climbing Mt. Everest or Anapurna, or bicycling through the Sahara Desert. "God, just help me get through this day." If that's how you feel, you've got lots of company. But, frankly, when you're under a heavy load, you aren't much concerned about the next guy; you only want help with your own load—and fast. That's the way it is with life.

It's interesting to note that when Paul prays for the Colossians, he doesn't ask God to remove their burdens. Instead, he prays that they would be "strengthened with all power according to his glorious might so that" they might "have great endurance and patience, and joyfully give thanks to the Father" (Colossians 1:11–12). Talk about something practical! Think about Paul's prayer for a moment. He asks for strength, endurance, patience, and the ability to give thanks to God.

Human nature being what it is, we usually ask God to remove the burden. "God, change my circumstances," we pray, thinking that removing our problem will bring happiness and joy. Not so, according to Paul's perspective. He knows that it's better to have endurance and patience, and learn to be thankful in the process.

God's Holy Spirit responds to our needs when we resolve to trust Him to take us through the problems that confront us. When we reach out for the Father's hand, we feel His strong arms around us, helping us to stay the course. Yes, God, give us patience and endurance and help us to thank You. Give us stronger backs and greater resolve, and help us to trust You for the strength that we lack. Help us to walk through the darkness, knowing that You walk with us, even when we cannot feel Your hand.

There are times, friend, when you have to trust the Father's heart even when you cannot see His hand or feel His presence. Jesus has promised us that, "'Never will I leave you; never will I forsake you. So we say with confidence, 'The Lord is my helper; I will not be afraid. What can man do to me?' " (Hebrews 13:5–6).

RESOURCE READING: Psalm 91

September 22

GOOD NEWS: FORGIVENESS

To err is human; to forgive is divine," said the wise man long ago. It's true, but of all the transactions that take place between people, none is more difficult than seeking and offering forgiveness. Forgiveness is the key to emotional and spiritual healing and the passport to future happiness. It's God's way of eliminating the cancer of hatred and anger that rips apart the fabric of relationships.

When David had a sexual relationship with Bathsheba, and sent Uzziah to his death, he could have said, "I couldn't help it. I was just overwhelmed with Bathsheba's beauty." Even though he was king, he wasn't exempt from the consequences. His conscience convicted him and he knew that his sin was not only against Bathsheba and her husband; he had sinned against God. "My sin is always before me," he said. "Against you, you only, have I sinned and done what is evil in your sight" (Psalm 51:3–4).

Do you want to silence that inner voice that accuses you when you have done wrong? Then do what David did. Admit your wrongdoing and ask God to forgive you. David cries out, "'O LORD, have mercy on me; heal me, for I have sinned against you" (Psalm 41:4). It takes strength to confess, but with repentance comes the reward of peace and joy. The New Testament says that if we confess our sins, God is faithful and will forgive us and cleanse us from all unrighteousness or wrongdoing (see 1 John 1:9).

When David asks for forgiveness, he also asks for healing. Can you relate to that? Frankly, it's often easier to accept God's forgiveness than it is to forgive ourselves and to get on with the process of putting our lives together after a hideous failure. The third step in the process of restoration is cooperation with the Lord in bringing healing to your life and the lives of those whom you have hurt. My definition of forgiveness is this: "I give up my right to hurt you because you hurt me." The process of giving up something means I have to release the bitterness and the pain as well as forgive myself. Thank God, David was right: There is forgiveness with God, which allows us to forgive ourselves as well.

RESOURCE READING: Psalm 41

THE ONGOING WORK
OF RESTORATION

S uppose you found a painting in your attic covered with dust and grime. As you gently wipe it off, you begin to see a beautiful picture obscured by the dirt that has accumulated with the passing of time. Sensing that this portrait might be worth a great deal, you take it to an art dealer for an appraisal. In a few days, the art dealer calls back, almost breathless with excitement as he informs you that the painting is a masterpiece worthy of hanging in one of the world's great art galleries.

I will never forget my first visit to the Sistine Chapel. Michelangelo's paintings were profound, but they were dark and dingy. The grime of several centuries covered their beautiful tones. Then came the restoration by several of the world's leading experts. On my next visit, the paintings had come alive. The restoration and cleansing made all the difference.

Restoration, of course, does not come without a price. It's much easier to leave something alone than to go to the work of restoring it, applying cleansers in just the right amounts, with just the right pressure so as not to permanently destroy the original.

In a real sense, spiritual restoration is the great work of Jesus Christ, a work so important that God sent His Son to accomplish the cleansing and healing of the masterpiece that God had made at creation.

Jesus showed us what God intended us to be, and His ministry, which cut to the core of human nature, began stripping off the veneer of hypocrisy and the superficiality of religion that had built up over the centuries. What man had corrupted, Jesus restored.

Jesus showed us what God is really like: a loving Father

who wills restoration for all creation. The restoration of humankind continues today through the great work of the church, touching the lives of people wherever they are. God's Holy Spirit removes the grime and brings restoration and healing.

No one is ever beyond restoration and reconciliation with a loving God. Regardless of what your conscience tells you, or what others may tell you, God considers you a person worth saving. There's hope, friend. That's what restoration is all about.

RESOURCE READING: John 3:1–17

September 24

MAKING YOUR SICK BED SOFTER

On his sickbed prior to death, Charles Spurgeon said, "If you do not wish to be full of regrets when you are forced to lie still, work while you can. If you desire to make a sickbed as soft as it can be, do not stuff it with mournful reflections that you wasted time when you were in health and strength."

Spurgeon was talking about coming to the sunset of your life, then looking back and realizing you took the wrong road and wasted a lot of years.

Here are four guidelines for living a life without regrets:

Guideline #1: Do it now. Don't wait until you retire to start a hobby, take a trip, or remodel the house. Also, make peace with your enemies and get rid of the bitterness that makes enemies out of friends.

Guideline #2: Plan it now. Some things you can't do right now. Some things take preparation and planning, but good intentions are not enough. A goal, someone said, is a dream with a timeline attached.

Guideline #3: Say it now. Tell your wife and your kids that you love them. Look up the teacher who influenced your life and tell her how much you appreciated what she did. Tell your dad how much you love him. Don't wait. Say it now.

Guideline #4: Live it now. Make your peace with God now, not on your deathbed. "True conversions are seldom made on the deathbed," said Matthew Henry. Writing to the Corinthians, Paul penned these strong words: "I tell you, now is the time of God's favor, now is the day of salvation" (2 Corinthians 6:2).

Sometimes hardworking, thoughtful people—the kind who have been very successful in business, education, and industry, who got to the top by skillful planning, hard work, and ingenuity—ignore God until they are felled by a stroke or a heart attack. Suddenly, they find it difficult to do much straight thinking.

Find out what the Bible says about making peace with God so that when you stand at the door of God's heaven and knock, your knees won't be making more noise than your knuckles. Good advice to make your sick bed softer.

RESOURCE READING: Isaiah 38

September 25

EARTHQUAKES CAN SCARE YOU TO DEATH

It's now official. Earthquakes can scare you to death. Is that news? Everybody knows that some people literally die of fright during earthquakes, but now scientists have discovered that the stress following an earthquake can suppress your immune system and make you physically ill. The study done by psychiatrists at UCLA indicates that "natural disasters such as an earthquake not only cause emotional distress, but they also can create negative physical effects."

UCLA psychiatrist Dr. George Solomon says, "Psychological well-being and physical well-being are inextricably intertwined." The doctor is right, but he should have added a third dimension—spiritual well-being. Your emotional, spiritual, and physical beings are so intertwined that whatever happens in one dimension vitally affects all three. That's the way God made you.

Dr. Solomon was an earthquake victim himself. His laboratory was destroyed by an earlier California earthquake. Workers at the hospital lost their jobs. Children couldn't sleep. People were reminded of the trauma every time there was an aftershock, even a mild one. "The light bulb went on that this was a major stressor," he said.

Dr. Solomon discovered that some people adopted the attitude of, "Okay, this happened, but life isn't over. Let's get on with our business." These people grieved, vented their emotions, then picked up the pieces of their lives. They rebuilt and were basically okay. But others became hysterical and were filled with fear. Their immune systems became depressed. Their blood counts dropped and a variety of physical illnesses occurred, which Dr. Solomon attributed to the immunity suppression caused by the earthquake.

Here's where the spiritual factor enters the equation. When you believe that God is in control, that He can meet your need whether you lose your home, or your home is the only one left standing, you have an anchor that sustains you through the stressful period. The Bible says emphatically that what happens to you as God's child is not a matter of mere chance or fate. God walks with you through the valley, the fire, the flood, and even the earthquake.

Faith in God's providence makes a powerful difference

when your world starts to collapse. When the earth starts quaking, people who have remained close to God have an ever-present place of refuge. Don't forget it.

RESOURCE READING: Nahum 1

September 26

ACTS OF GOD

What constitutes an "act of God"? Is an earthquake an act of God? How about a tornado, a typhoon, or a hurricane? Is it an act of God when my car stops running, or I get a cold and have to go to the doctor? How about when my house burns down? The answer to that question may determine whether your insurance company pays to replace your house if it is destroyed. "Acts of God" are usually excluded.

The controversy gained notoriety when tornadoes destroyed thousands of homes in Arkansas and took the lives of twenty-five people. Insurance policies describe tornadoes as "acts of God." Governor Mike Huckabee, who is also a Baptist minister, disagreed. When a disaster relief bill used the term "acts of God," the governor asked that the phrase be changed to "natural disasters." He said, "I refuse to walk through tornado damage and to say that what destroyed it was God and what built it back was human beings." He added, "I saw God protect a lot of people, save a lot of people. That's an act of God, too."

The Bible doesn't use the phrase "acts of God." Since the Fall in the Garden of Eden, God has made it clear that the natural world is under the curse of sin. Man must earn his living by the sweat of his brow, and women bear children with pain. Though God is still entirely sovereign, He has set natural laws into operation, which result in cause and effect disasters, such as blizzards, typhoons, hurricanes, tropical storms, tornadoes, and even wars. Someday, God will step in and eliminate all of these situations, but until He returns and redeems the earth from the curse of sin, we'll have to cope with these natural disasters.

Instead of calling natural disasters "acts of God," we should give God more credit for the acts He does perform, like the birth of a baby, the salvation of a drunk, the rehabilitation of an addict, the blossoming of a flower, the rising of the sun, and the appearance of a comet in the sky.

God is a good God. He has placed into operation natural laws that govern our daily lives, and every so often He lays aside natural laws to do something supernatural.

RESOURCE READING: 1 Corinthians 15:20–58

September 27

TAKING DEATH BY FAITH

As she anticipated traversing the valley of the shadow of death, Catherine Booth, one of the cofounders of the Salvation Army, said, "One of the hardest lessons I have had to learn in my career, and one that I think I have been learning more effectually the last few years, is to discern between faith and realization. They are entirely distinct, the one from the other. . .

"All our enemies have to be conquered by faith, not by realization, and is it not so with the last enemy—death? Therefore ought I not be willing, if it be God's will, even to go down into the dark valley without any realization, simply knowing that I am His and He is mine, and this repeat in the last great struggle my life lesson? Yes, if it please the Lord to deal with me thus, I am quite willing, I can accept it; and however blessed it would be to see His face, if He deprives me of that sight I am willing it should be so. . . . And if His precious, blessed face does become visible to me, as to the martyr on the road who shouted out, 'I see Him,' then I shall be grateful, and you will know that faith has overcome; but if He does not appear it is all the same."

Shortly before her homegoing, Booth sent this message to her colleagues in the Salvation Army: "The waters are rising, but so am I. I am not going under but over. Don't be concerned about your dying; only go on living well, and the dying will be all right."

As she drew her last breath, her face became illuminated and she exclaimed, "I see. . ." and never finished the sentence.[1]

Perhaps it is just as well that she was not able to describe what she saw, for then each of us would perhaps expect exactly the same experience. "Dear friends," wrote the aged apostle John toward the end of his sojourn on Earth, "now we are children of God, and what we will be has not yet been made known. But we know that when he appears, we shall be like him, for we shall see him as he is" (1 John 3:2). That is good enough for me.

RESOURCE READING: Romans 2

September 28

LOVELESSNESS TODAY

Nobody loves me! Nobody loves me!" All of us at one time or another feel like that. While the cry of loneliness may not come from a prison chimney, it still rises from the prison of a lonely heart. As Howard Whitman once wrote, "Lovelessness is a prison wherein most of us are inmates at some time or another." Psychologists are uncertain why love is so important in life, but they know it is.

Dr. A. Brill, a psychiatrist, says, "It is quite as essential for a person to have love as to have pure air and food to sustain him. Love is to human beings what magnetic attraction is to molecules. It is the glue that holds the human race together and checks it from drifting into the estranging salt sea of loneliness."

Lovelessness plays a major part in the woes of life today. Psychiatrists who treat emotional illnesses such as schizophrenia, depression, neurosis, and other spiraling mental disorders, will tell you that a lack of love is one of the taproots of mental illness.

Is it possible that a lack of old-fashioned love—the spanking kind of love—is the real cause for today's juvenile delinquents? Is this the real reason for a generation in rebellion? We need the kind of love today that Paul talked about in 1 Corinthians 13. An eleven-year-old girl caught the meaning of it all when she paraphrased what Paul wrote. Here are her thoughts:

"Though I speak softly and sweetly, if I don't have love, I'm just making a bunch of noise. And though I'm very talented and very smart, if I don't have love, I am like an empty shell. And though I give away everything to the poor, and give my body to be burned at the stake for what I believe, and don't have love, it doesn't do me any good. Love can stand a lot of hurting and still be kind. Love doesn't act smart, doesn't think bad things about people, isn't happy when someone does wrong, but is happy when they do right. Love can put up with anything, hopes everything will turn out good. Love never lets a person down."

RESOURCE READING: 1 Corinthians 13

LEARNING TO LOVE

L ove begins with God, not man. When you open your heart to Jesus Christ, God invades your life and gives you the capacity to love the people in your life who are not very lovable. You learn to love in a dimension you have never known before.

Love that comes from our relationship with God can be expressed by a capital letter L. Love begins with God at the top. Through faith in Jesus Christ, man enters into a new relationship with God that allows His love to flow into your life. Then that love can flow through you in a horizontal relationship to others.

In New Testament times, three words were commonly used to express love. The first is *eros* (from which we get our word erotic), which never appears in the New Testament. It refers to a sensual, sexual kind of love, the *Playboy* kind that we see today in movies and on television. Another word for love, *philea,* is used forty-five times by the New Testament writers. The ancient Greeks used this word to express an emotional or brotherly kind of love.

The word used most often to describe love in the New Testament is the word *agape.* In the New Testament it means something different from its usage in the writings of the ancient Greeks. The writers of the New Testament wanted to express a different kind of love—a higher concept of love than was previously known.

Love is not sentimental slush—it is not wishful think-ing. It is not sexual expression. It is the glue that holds our lives together in meaningful relationships and makes life worth living. Without it, we are nothing and life becomes a weary treadmill of survival.

Take inventory. Are you short on this business of love? Has your capacity to love been bottled up because of an inadequate relationship with God? Love begins with God and until you make peace with Him through His Son, you will never know what love is all about. John writes, "This is how we know what love is: Jesus Christ laid down his life for us. And we ought to lay down our lives for our brothers" (1 John 3:16).

RESOURCE READING: 1 John 4

September 30

THE IMPORTANCE OF NOW

Four men were arguing about the best time to cut an ash stick. One man said that the best time was in the spring when the sap was rising. Another said, "No, summer is the best time, because then the wood is at its height." The third disagreed entirely. "The fall," said he, "is the best time to cut the ash stick, because the sap has matured and seasoned the wood." The fourth argued that winter was best because then there was not any sap at all and the wood could be cut smoothly.

Finally, the four decided to ask the local agricultural expert. He listened to their arguments, and then they pressed their question. "When do you say is the best time to cut an ash stick?" He thought for a moment and then replied, "The best time to cut an ash stick, gentlemen, is when you see one, because it may not be there the next time you pass by."

The most important time of your life is not in the future, nor is it in the past. Believe it or not, it is right now. Today is the only part of time and eternity that really belongs to you. Yesterday is history; tomorrow may never come. The present is the only time you can do anything about.

Strange as it may seem, God places greater emphasis on the present than He does the past or future. He tells us in strong simple terms that the time to do something about eternity is *now*. God pleads with men, "Today, if you hear his voice, do not harden your hearts" (Hebrews 4:7). Paul writes, "Now is the day of salvation" (2 Corinthians 6:2). Friend, may I ask what preparations you have made for the moment in your life when your watch becomes meaningless and time becomes eternity? All your accomplishments will be summed up in what you decided about Jesus Christ.

Jesus says, "I tell you the truth, whoever hears my word and believes him who sent me has eternal life and will not be condemned; he has crossed over from death to life" (John 5:24). Ah, yes, thank God for today!

RESOURCE READING: 2 Corinthians 6

October 1

IF I HAD IT TO DO
ALL OVER AGAIN

"If you could live your life all over again, what would you do differently?" I often ask this question when I interview people, including politicians, theologians, missionaries, and elderly people with varied backgrounds. Responses have varied from, "I'd have gone to school and better prepared myself for life," to "I wouldn't have sown my wild oats that I've come to regret." Most people, however, have thought pensively and then replied, "I wouldn't do a thing differently."

What would I do, if I could do it all over again?

For one thing, I'd spend more time playing with my three kids growing up. They are now adults and raising the most wonderful grandchildren in the world. Yes, we took time off and enjoyed camping, skiing, hiking, fishing, Monopoly, and poking fun at each other. But like a kid who spends a coin at the candy store, once you've spent it, it's gone and there are no second chances.

Another thing that I would do is strive to be less judgmental and more understanding with people. John Calvin spoke of a "learned ignorance," and perhaps that would describe my hesitance to draw such clearly defined lines and help out God by putting people on one side or the other of nonimportant issues.

A third thing I would do is strive to focus more on what is really important. You can't fight and die on every hill, so you'd better find out what God wants you to do and make the main thing the main thing. Spreading yourself too thin means you fail to do some things as well as you might have done them.

Also, I would strive to glorify God more and care less what people thought about me and about whether anyone ever remembered my name.

No, I would not live any differently, and God knows I would never compromise when there is offense because of the gospel, which comes with the call of God. No, I would not work fewer hours or travel less or try to save more money.

What about you? What would you do differently? Why not start doing the very thing you would do, if you could live your live over again. It's not too late.

RESOURCE READING: Job 38–42

October 2

REJOICE AND GIVE THANKS

Some folks just don't seem to get it! When things are really dark and dismal, they talk about rejoicing and giving thanks! Annoying, aren't they? After all, when the lights go out, we're supposed to weep and howl, right?

I never cease to be amazed at the insights Paul had into suffering and difficulty, which gave him the strength to survive the darkness of a prison cell and the difficulties he constantly faced. In his letter to the Corinthians, he tells of beatings, rejection, and hostilities that he faced. Clinging to floating debris after your ship goes down isn't exactly a Mediterranean cruise. He experienced all of these trials, yet he called them "light and momentary troubles" (2 Corinthians 4:17). He made what I gripe about seem pretty insignificant.

At times, Paul despaired of life itself, but he never lobbied to legalize euthanasia to eliminate life's difficult situations. No way! Instead, he steadfastly held on to the conviction that "He who had begun a good work" in his life would bring it to completion. From a prison cell—not a resort hotel on a white sandy beach—Paul wrote, "Rejoice in the Lord always. I will say it again: Rejoice! Let your gentleness be evident to all. The Lord is near. Do not be anxious about anything, but in everything, by prayer and petition, with thanksgiving, present your requests to God. And the peace of God, which transcends all understanding, will guard your hearts and your minds in Christ Jesus" (Philippians 4:4–7).

In every situation, says Paul, I can praise and thank Him. God is above these difficulties and can and will use them for His glory. Others may mean it for evil, but God means it for good.

The knowledge that God is in control and that you belong to Him are tremendous attitude adjusters. They lift you out of the dungeon of self-pity and despair and help you to trust Him for today. "Before you know it," says a paraphrase of Philippians 4:6, "a sense of God's wholeness, everything coming together for good, will come and settle you down. It's wonderful what happens when Christ displaces worry at the center of your life" (TM). The dimension of faith makes all the difference.

RESOURCE READING: Philippians 4

CHARACTER

Reputation is what others think of you, while character is what you really are. Your character is revealed by what you do, but Ralph Waldo Emerson said that character is defined by what you think. He wrote, "People seem not to realize that their opinion of the world is also a confession of character."

Convictions produce character, which may account for its scarcity today. Without firm convictions of right or wrong, a person's moral life becomes a replay of uncertainty, a combination of trial and error. When beliefs are put to the test, character—or the lack of it—reveals how much integrity a person possesses.

Conflict is the real testing grounds for character. When your views of right and wrong are challenged, you have to make a decision: Either compromise and violate your sense or right and wrong, or face the consequences.

That was exactly the situation years ago when a Persian queen named Vashti was asked to dance before a banquet of rowdy military officers. Women in those days didn't challenge their husbands' requests, but Queen Vashti knew that a debauched and drunken group of men would be leering at her. She also knew that the consequences of standing for principle could mean divorce and even banishment from the throne. The conflict produced a costly decision. In the event you don't remember the story from the book of Esther, it was Vashti's refusal that cost her the throne. Character comes with a price.

Conflict or crisis reveals our true character. We either have it or we don't. As Senator Dan Coats puts it: "Character cannot be summoned at the moment of crisis if it has been squandered by years of compromise and rationalization. The only testing ground for the heroic is the mundane. The only preparation for that one profound decision which can change a life, or even a nation, is those hundreds of half-conscious, self-defining, seemingly insignificant decisions made in private. Habit is the daily battleground of character."[1]

The following verse from an anonymous source puts it well: "Be careful of your thoughts, for your thoughts become your words. Be careful of your actions, for your actions become your habits. Be careful of your habits, for your habits become your character. Be careful of your character, for your character becomes your destiny."

RESOURCE READING: Titus 2

October 4

THE GRACE OF GOD
WHICH BRINGS FORGIVENESS

One of the anomalies of creation is that man, though created in the image of God, is so different from His Creator. God's nature is loving. Ours is often anything but that. It is His nature to forgive, ours to demand vengeance. His to bring healing. Ours to destroy. Yes, we can blame the serpent that tempted Adam and Eve and write all of this off as the result of sin, but it's still a fact that what God does and what we do are worlds apart.

Anthropologists have discovered that many pagan or non-Christian cultures have no word for "forgiveness" in their language. Only by God's example of sending His Son into the world to die can we understand what God has been striving to show humankind—that to demand vengeance is human, but to forgive is divine. The grace of God can touch us at the point of our need—no matter what it is.

Nothing is so counter to my culture and to my old

nature than to forgive. Forgiveness means that I give up my right to hurt you even though you hurt me first. Our society is more apt to say, "Do it to him because he did it to you first." Okay, so your husband betrayed you. You are confronted with two choices: vengeance or forgiveness. "But I'll lose face if I let him get away with this," you say. In reality, nobody gets away with wrongdoing. Seldom is a person's conscience so deadened that its accusing voice is completely stilled. But that isn't the issue as much as what *you* gain when you forgive.

What's in it for the person who forgives? In some cases, you have saved your children from the effects of growing up without a father. You have also rid your system of the bitterness that takes its toll on you physically. But most important of all, you have allowed the grace of God to bring healing and restoration to your relationship.

"It was his wrongdoing that destroyed my marriage!" Not necessarily. Was it not also your pride that demanded vengeance? Taste of the grace of God and forgive. Leave vengeance to the Almighty. He can handle it better than you can.

RESOURCE READING: Genesis 37:12–36

October 5

SHOULD I FORGIVE HIM?

He had betrayed his vows by having a fling with a woman from work, and now he realized what he must do. Confessing his wrongdoing to his wife was the hardest thing he had ever done, but he knew it was time to face the music. Would she forgive him? He wasn't sure.

His wife, of course, was shocked. She had never thought

that her husband was capable of doing this to her and their four children. Something inside kept saying, "Throw the bum out. He violated a sacred trust. He betrayed you. How can you ever be sure that he won't do it again?"

Heartbroken, she turned to an older woman, a trusted friend. "What should I do?" For years, Margaret had counseled and worked with women. She had seen the effects of broken homes, the bitterness of vengeance, and the loneliness of estrangement. She had also seen restoration and healing which can come when someone seeks forgiveness, both from God and from a mate. Margaret tried to help her see the implications of either choice. Wise counsel is a gift from God.

The choice was not easy, but the wife decided to forgive her husband. Of course, it took time for the relationship to mend and heal. Bones can be set in a matter of a few minutes but the pain subsides slowly. The therapy, which follows gradually, strengthens the hurting limb. So it is with the process of forgiveness. Saying, "I forgive you" doesn't automatically take away the momentary feeling of panic when your husband isn't home on time, or the phone rings and you hear an unfamiliar woman's voice asking if your husband is home.

The wife who forgave her husband is now a grandmother. Her children have married and have children of their own. She doesn't traipse from seminar to seminar telling how she learned to forgive. Only four people know the dark secret. The incident was dealt with and gradually the grace of God brought restoration and healing.

God not only demonstrated forgiveness in sending His Son, but He also commanded us to forgive just as He forgave our sins. Is forgiveness good medicine for the hurts of the world? There is none better.

RESOURCE READING: Ephesians 4

FORGET THE TEN SUGGESTIONS

"Forget the Ten Commandments," read a small sign displayed in a novelty store. "I'm looking for a religion based on Ten Suggestions." It was intended to be funny, but there's a lot of truth behind the attempted humor. We don't like being told what to do. Commandments are imperative. They don't ask me how I feel or make suggestions for my consideration. God never gave us multiple choices, or lifestyle options. He simply said, "Do this and live."

God's purpose is not to make you feel good about yourself, but to make you right, to keep relationships normal and healthy, and to make your town or village a safe place to live. If God's commandments were heeded, you would give no thought to the safety of your wife and children when you have to be away, or wonder whether your plow or tractor will still be there when you return home. But the days of going out without the deadbolt in place and the alarm system activated are history, at least in most places.

A Communist official from China once told me, "We have villages in China where almost everyone is a Christian, and we have no crime in those villages." I kept my mouth shut, but I felt like saying, "Doesn't that make a statement?"

Ten Suggestions or Ten Commandments? At some point, you must come to grips with two powerful issues.

Issue #1: Doesn't the Creator know me better than I know myself? Is it possible He knows better than I do what is in my best interest?

Issue #2: Are the mandates of Scripture motivated by a heart of holy love?

These questions are not difficult to answer when you come to an understanding of God's nature and character.

Long ago Isaiah said, "'For my thoughts are not your thoughts, neither are your ways my ways,' declares the LORD" (Isaiah 55:8).

Ten Suggestions may be fine for spending leisure time, but they are no good for finding your way when you are lost. The only way to find the path which leads home is to hear the voice of God saying, "Not over there; over here!" When you're lost, that's the voice you want to hear.

RESOURCE READING: Psalm 1

October 7

NO PIT SO DEEP

Things did not look good. Terrible cold, insufficient food, and no medical help at the infamous Ravensbruck concentration camp for women made Corrie ten Boom wonder if she and her sister Betsie would survive.

Built to accommodate 6,000 women, by 1944 Ravensbruck's population had swelled to 36,000. During the Second World War, some 50,000 women had died in that camp. Eventually Corrie's fears about her sister's health grew. As her fever soared, Betsie became too weak to stand. Her cough brought up blood. Corrie knew she couldn't live for more than a few days.

As her frail body was placed on a stretcher to make the one-way trip to the infirmary, Betsie turned to Corrie and whispered, "We must tell the people what we have learned here. We must tell them that there is no pit so deep that He [Jesus] is not deeper still. They will listen to us, Corrie, because we have been here." Within hours, Betsie was liberated by death.

Corrie continued to survive the brutal conditions. Then,

seven days before she was scheduled to be executed, she was freed, for no apparent reason, on New Year's Day, 1945. A fluke? Good luck? No, the details were all part of God's sovereign plan. He cared that the ten Boom sisters had shown love to some of the six million Jews who were sent to their deaths at the hands of the SS guards in the death camps.

After the war, Corrie traveled all over the world with the message of forgiveness and redemption. "We must tell them," said Betsie, "that there is no pit so deep that He is not deeper still."

We still need to hear the message that there is no pit so deep that God is not there. In the darkness, Corrie and Betsie learned what God had promised: "When you go through deep waters and great trouble, I will be with you. When you go through rivers of difficulty, you will not drown! When you walk through the fire of oppression, you will not be burned up—the flames will not consume you, for I am the Lord, your God, your Savior. . ." (Isaiah 43:2–3 TLB). It's still true.

RESOURCE READING: Isaiah 43

October 8

THE NATURE OF JEWISHNESS

Would a Filipino who studied the life of Jose Rizal, the hero of the Philippines, lose his essential Filipino character? Would a Russian who studied the life of Peter the Great cease to be a Russian? Would an American who studied Abraham Lincoln or Thomas Jefferson cease to be American? Of course not. So where is the logic in suggesting that a Jew who becomes a follower of Jesus Christ loses his Jewishness?

Of course, if Jesus Christ were an Egyptian, or a

Syrian who grew up in turbulent, first-century Palestine, the issue would be more complex, but Jesus was unquestionably Jewish.

His mother was a Jewish virgin—pure, sincere, and devout. Growing up in Nazareth didn't enhance Jesus' social standing. People from Nazareth were considered low-class. Galilee, a short distance away, was the breeding place of hotheads, revolutionaries, and individuals who didn't quite fit into the social structure of Jerusalem.

Jesus moved freely within the circle of life which was exclusively Jewish. He was circumcised like all Jewish male babies. He went to the temple and astonished the doctors of the law at age twelve. He was accepted as a rabbi, a teacher of the faith, and participated in Jewish synagogue services. No one with questionable heritage would have been afforded this kind of status.

Question: Have we Christians removed the essentially Jewish element from the fabric surrounding the birth and life of Jesus Christ? Have we attempted to give His culture and heritage a neutral, nondescript background? Perhaps. Go to the art galleries of the world and notice how Jesus is usually portrayed as Anglo-Saxon with His blue eyes and fair complexion, a reflection of the one who painted the picture. The Jesus commonly worshipped by Christians is One who has been transposed into another culture and age, not the Jesus described by the writers of the New Testament.

If Jesus was the Messiah, the fulfillment of what Isaiah and the prophets foretold, then any Jew who follows His teaching and embraces His life is as Jewish as he was on the day of his birth. Of course, Jesus Christ transcends race and culture, and men and women of all ages and cultures proclaim Him Lord, but let's not forget that God chose to send His Son through Israel, His chosen people.

RESOURCE READING: John 1

NOBODY KNOWS. WANT TO BET?

A few years ago, a friend sent a telegram to ten trusted individuals with the message: "All is discovered; flee at once!" All ten left the country immediately. That practical joke may not have been funny to the victims, but I've often wondered what was in their minds as they hastily packed and fled.

Technology being what it is today, there are few secrets. Perhaps you have an unlisted phone to protect your privacy, but if you give your home phone when you purchase an airline ticket or fill out a credit application, your phone number is no longer private. It goes into data banks that can be accessed on the Internet in about three keystrokes. Furthermore, if you have ever been involved in a lawsuit, that information is readily accessible to the general public. Technology is not always your friend.

Of course, God has always had instant access. The writer of Hebrews says, "Nothing in all creation is hidden from God's sight. Everything is uncovered and laid bare before the eyes of him to whom we must give account" (Hebrews 4:13). Someday, even the secrets of the heart will be revealed by God, who will then judge us according to our works. That thought would send shivers down my spine apart from the understanding that when God forgives, He clears the slate; He even removes the offense from His memory.

Is there anything in the data bank of your memory that God hasn't dealt with because you have never sought His forgiveness? If the answer is yes, you need to ask God to deal with that, to forgive you, and to blot it from His memory. Does God do that? Isaiah 43:25 says, "I, even I, am he who blots out your transgressions, for my own sake, and remembers your sins no more."

The grace of God embraces forgiveness, which allows

me to be completely whole and forgiven. The nagging worry of "what if this should be discovered?" vanishes when you learn what the Bible says about God's forgiveness. Paul says that in Christ "we have redemption through his blood, the forgiveness of sins, in accordance with the riches of God's grace" (Ephesians 1:7). That's very good news.

RESOURCE READING: Ephesians 1

October 10

MANY ACQUAINTANCES; FEW FRIENDS

The golfer Bobby Jones once told a young admirer, "Always remember, you never know who your friends are until you lose." Amazing, isn't it, that when you're on top, everybody knows you, wants to be with you, and wants to be your friend, but when you don't make the cut, you suddenly have a lot more elbow room. The writer of Proverbs addresses this very subject: "There are 'friends' who pretend to be friends, but there is a friend who sticks closer than a brother" (Proverbs 18:24 TLB).

What are the marks of genuine friendship? Three are worth noting.

Mark #1: Genuine friendship is not affected by notoriety.
Mark #2: Genuine friendship is not affected by personal failure.
Mark #3: Genuine friendship is not affected by time.

Lasting friendships are usually forged on the basis of genuine affection, common interests, mutual respect, and an indefinable bond at a deep, heart level. Deep friendships can be forged between people of quite different ages, back-grounds, cultures, and races. A real friend is not a mirror image of yourself.

When someone is a real friend, though months or even years may elapse without contact and a lot may happen in your personal lives, when you are together again, you pick up where you left off.

Genuine friendship is not affected by notoriety or obscu-rity. When your phone is ringing and you are in demand, you don't have the same amount of time as when nothing was going your way, but a real friend communicates his love and acceptance no matter how busy you both may be.

Joseph Scriven learned through adversity that there is one who will never leave you or forsake you. He wrote the song "What a Friend We Have in Jesus" after his fian-cée drowned in a Canadian lake. When you discover that those you thought were real friends turn out to be acquain-tances who walk away when you are no longer in the win-ner's circle, remember that Jesus is a Friend who stays closer than a brother. I have yet to meet a friend of Jesus who was disappointed. Get to know Him through the pages of the your Bible.

RESOURCE READING: Psalm 39

October 11

REWRITE THE SUCCESS SCRIPT OF YOUR LIFE

A re you a success or a failure?
That's a pretty blunt question, but today we are bombarded with messages in the media—radio, television, movies—and society in general, that says you are not a success

unless you get to the top, unless you are surrounded by beautiful people, unless you reach the top rung of the ladder. The tyranny of the urgent demands our constant, immediate attention—the ringing telephone, the urgent plea for help, the incessant demand to meet deadlines and balance schedules. An addiction to urgency can quickly lead to depression and feelings of failure. If you buy into that mentality, you are being brainwashed and are heading for big disappointment.

Actually, success and failure are determined by our own definition. In most cases, we fail to find the happiness we want in life because our definition of success has only two dimensions: ourselves and our goals. True success, however, is three dimensional. God, and His purpose for our lives, must be included in any definition of success.

Was Jesus' life a success? He made statements such as, "I must be about my Father's business" (Luke 2:49 KJV), and "My food. . .is to do the will of him who sent me and to finish his work" (John 4:34). His agenda included a third dimension that gave Him a purpose beyond accomplishing certain objectives in life. Should we not have the same perspective?

The secret of success—real success—doesn't come through better management principles, doing more, producing more, or earning more so you can spend more. It's relational. It has to include your family, your God, and yourself. David, who lived for years with the cloud of danger hanging over his life, cried out, "Show me, O LORD, my life's end and the number of my days; let me know how fleeting is my life" (Psalm 39:4). And Moses writes, "Teach us to number our days aright, that we may gain a heart of wisdom" (Psalm 90:12).

Friend, it may well be time to rewrite the script for your life. Focus on what God says about your roles in life and your purpose for each role. You may be far more successful than you've ever realized.

RESOURCE READING: Psalm 1

WOULD JESUS BLOODY
HIS KNUCKLES?

Norm Evans, a former lineman for the Miami Dolphins, writes the following about Jesus in his book, *On God's Squad:* "I guarantee you Christ would be the toughest guy who ever played this game. . . . If he were alive today, I would picture a six-foot-six-inch, 260-pound defensive tackle who would always make the big plays and would be hard to keep out of the backfield."

If Jesus were on Earth today, would He be a tough football player? I'm not so certain. I do know that whatever He did, He would do with all His heart, mind, soul, and strength.

A popular pastime these days is searching for statements in the Bible to support our "God wants us to win" mentality. We point to Psalm 18:29, where David cries, "With your help I can advance against a troop; with my God I can scale a wall." In simple terms, we want Jesus on our team, energizing us, enabling us to succeed.

While it's true that God gives us the strength to do things we might never accomplish any other way, that isn't the same as asking God for the strength to overcome the other team. Down through the ages, men and women have called on the Lord in times of trouble, and God has met them and delivered them; but when Paul talked about doing all things through God's strength, he was talking about persevering through difficulty—facing hunger, enduring derision, and surviving persecution, not sacking the quarterback or winning a football game. This new perspective changes the situation dramatically. Every competitor does not win, but every person facing difficulty—the negative side of the ledger of life—can find God's power to cope, to endure, to survive the attacks of those who would injure you. Paul emphasizes that no matter what your circumstances—

good or bad—you can learn to be content and you can find God's help to overcome adversity.

God wants you to go for it, to do your best, to strive for excellence. "Whatever you do, work at it with all your heart, as working for the Lord, not for men" (Colossians 3:23) was Paul's advice to the Colossians. But, frankly, I can't imagine Jesus as a "six-foot-six-inch, 260-pound defensive tackle who would always make the big plays and would be hard to keep out of the backfield."

RESOURCE READING: Philippians 4

October 13

WHO SAID I COULDN'T DO IT?

Don't ever tell a kid, "You can't do that!" unless you want him to try to prove you wrong. When you tell a person that something can't be done, something explodes inside that says, "Oh, yeah? Just watch me!"

Before the 1997 Masters golf tournament, defending champion Nick Faldo told the press that the up-and-coming Tiger Woods couldn't win, because he hadn't had enough experience. After all, the twenty-one-year-old Woods was barely old enough to shave, let alone conquer one of golf's most prestigious championships, and the Masters is played on one of the world's most challenging courses.

I don't know whether Tiger Woods took Nick Faldo's remarks to heart, but he proceeded to break nine Masters records on his way to winning the tournament by a record twelve strokes. There wasn't a happier young man anywhere when he finally sank the last four-foot putt on the eighteenth green.

Watching as Woods donned the trademark green blazer

that is awarded to every Masters champion, I began to think about how many people are stopped short of their potential by someone who tells them, "You can't win. You can't do that!" For some, instead of being a challenge, those words become a death sentence.

Tiger Woods has parents who were encouraging mentors, and who were always there for him. But a lot of parents are neither there for their kids nor do much to bring out their potential. Consequently, these kids flounder in uncertainty, never realizing what they might have been.

Telling a youngster, "You can't do that!" can also backfire if the child in anger and rebellion strives to prove you wrong. Much better is the parent who says, "I know you can do this. Be patient with yourself and keep trying. You are making great headway!" That's the spirit that helps a child become a real winner, whether or not he ever wins the Masters and dons the green blazer.

You as a parent can make the difference in producing a winner who will grow up to make you proud, adopt your values, serve God, and take his or her place in society. I believe that Tiger Woods's parents would tell you, "It's well worth what it takes to raise a winner."

RESOURCE READING: Luke 2:41–52

October 14

RAISING POSITIVE KIDS
IN A NEGATIVE WORLD

In his book *Raising Positive Kids in a Negative World*, Zig Ziglar says that the key to successful parenting isn't what parents do, but what they are. Ziglar is right. "That kid's a chip off the old block," we sometimes say of a youngster who resembles his dad. Or we say, "Like father, like son." What we are as parents results in what we do; and what we do—or what we model for our children—influences how they turn out.

Two sets of parents can raise their children in the same basic environment and culture, yet some kids go straight and make their parents proud and other kids get derailed, often mortgaging their futures and blighting their hope of getting anywhere in life. What's the difference?

I'm convinced that one powerful factor is how parents help their children to think of themselves. A positive self-image gives children enough strength to stand alone when they need to, to have the strength to walk away from bad situations and withstand negative peer pressure.

Three ingredients go into the formula of producing positive kids in a negative world:

Factor #1 is self-esteem—an understanding of who the child is in relationship to his parents, God, and family. This involves handling failure situations, knowing how to be independent, and having the proper tension between our lives and the pressures of conformity

Factor #2 is self-assurance. The world is no friend to your children. It's not only the neighborhood bully who is the enemy out there. Your child may also fight racial prejudice, poor education and training, and a host of other factors. He needs faith in God and in himself, which becomes an anchor.

Factor #3 is motivation. Proverbs 22:6 talks of the path that a child should go. You as a parent must help him get started on the right path and provide motivation to make the right choices. This is also where God's will comes into the picture

You must guide your youngster morally and spiritually, and teach him or her to honor God.

Raising positive kids in a negative world is one of the greatest accomplishments of life.

RESOURCE READING: Proverbs 3

October 15

LONG-SUFFERING

Have you ever faced a difficult situation when your heart cried out, "God, where are you? Why don't you do something?" Habakkuk voiced the same plea when he saw the Babylonians punishing Israel. He cried, "How long, O LORD, must I call for help, but you do not listen? Or cry out to you, 'Violence!' but you do not save?" (Habakkuk 1:2).

The Jews no doubt quoted those words as they disappeared into the death camps of Nazi Germany. Christians suffering under the iron grip of tyranny ask the same question, "God, how long will this continue?"

The Bible speaks of long-suffering seventeen times. Most of those references are to God's gracious patience with His people. But even though God is long-suffering, He is not weak. God's patience is not the result of His inability to step into a situation and correct it immediately. God will have His payday someday. Just because God is being gracious and patient with you, don't think for a moment that He ignores wrongdoing forever. Paul said that we should count God's long-suffering as salvation (2 Peter 3:15).

God's long-suffering should never be considered as indifference. If you believe what the Bible says about God's care for His children, you know that nothing escapes His knowledge. He knows when prison doors open for innocent men and women. He knows when doctors say, "There's nothing more we can do."

God's long-suffering is not a mark of stupidity. Isaiah says that God's thoughts are not our thoughts, His ways are above our ways (see Isaiah 55:8). Ours is a strange mentality today. We often think that the real hero is the one who gets away with wrongdoing, who doesn't get caught, who rips off the establishment and beats the system. No, that's one to be pitied, not one to be admired. We can be thankful, very thankful, that God's timetable is different from ours; otherwise, who among us would be safe from getting what we really deserve?

Friend, thank God that He is long-suffering, but realize there is an end to His patience. Read the last chapter of Habakkuk's encounter with God. God is God and He's in control, no matter how insane the world may appear.

RESOURCE READING: 2 Peter 3

October 16

WHO'S RESPONSIBLE?

An eighteen-year-old boy fathers a child and then walks away. A husband and father of three children abandons his family, saying, "I don't want to be married anymore!"

Whatever happened to personal responsibility? Has it gone out the window, overwhelmed by our desire for personal happiness, instant gratification, and immediate pleasure? As long as we're satisfied, does it really matter how others are affected?

Winston Churchill called responsibility "the price of

greatness." But having fun seems to be more important in our generation than greatness. Personal responsibility is challenged by three enemies today: individualism, relativism, and secularism.

There's no question that we live in the age of special interest groups who all demand their rights. The emphasis today is on me and my rights. Frank Sinatra summed up the individualism of our day when he sang, "I did it my way!" Have you ever considered what kind of mess we would be in if everybody got to do it his or her way? Having your own way may be very costly for others whose lives are impacted by your selfish choices. Everything you do affects other people.

The second enemy of personal responsibly today is relativism. "I'm not responsible. I'm a victim of my heredity, my culture, or the society that produced me." I was on my way home when the traffic came to a halt rather suddenly and I noticed a vehicle turned crossways ahead of me, obviously in trouble. Stopping to help, I approached the second car, which had caused the collision. In the driver's seat was a woman whose head had broken the windshield from the impact as her car had smashed the other vehicle. "Can I help?" I asked. "I'm an alcoholic," she cried, "I'm not responsible for what I did." The lives of two men in the truck were in the balance because of her irresponsible decision to get behind the wheel when she was drunk.

Secularism is another enemy of personal responsibility. To acknowledge that you will ultimately give an account to God Himself makes you think soberly and thoughtfully about your decisions and your obligations. Your choices determine your measure of responsibility for which you must ultimately be accountable.

RESOURCE READING: Ezekiel 18:19–32

YES, I AM RESPONSIBLE

I acknowledge my responsibility and accept the full blame for what happened!" You don't hear these words very often. It's usually, "Well, I'm really not responsible," or "I can't help what took place. I was a victim of circumstances."

In his book *The Purpose Driven Life,* Rick Warren points out that the word "fool," which is often associated with being stupid, really means "one who is irresponsible."

Are you interested in learning how to cultivate personal responsibility in your life? Then make the following guidelines part of the fabric of your life.

Guideline #1: Develop personal responsibility for your decisions. You can't control the weather, the economy, or the political climate, and you may not have much control over your job, but you are responsible for how you respond to the world around you. Your decisions affect your family and your own life.

Guideline #2: Be accountable to someone. It's at this point that we often fall prey to bad thinking. "It's my life. I should be able to do whatever I please—as long as nobody gets hurt." Nonsense! Like climbers linked together by a rope on the face of a cliff, every decision you make affects someone else. Be humble enough to make yourself accountable to another person.

Guideline #3: Make every decision on the basis of its implications. Everyone is entitled to an occasional splurge—whether it's chocolate or buying something a bit beyond your budget. Those acts of dereliction won't sink your ship. But if we counted the cost before we made most of our decisions, we would make them differently.

Remember the law of the harvest: You reap what you sow.

Guideline #4: Acknowledge that ultimately, you are accountable to God. In his letters to the Romans and the Corinthians, Paul emphasizes that we are accountable to God for our decisions and choices. "For we must all appear before the judgment seat of Christ, that each one may receive what is due him for the things done while in the body, whether good or bad" (2 Corinthians 5:10). Notice that this is not all bad. It also means that your responsible choices and decisions will be acknowledged and rewarded.

When Paul talks about assuming responsibility, he looks at the entire spectrum. That's also the way that God sees our lives, and the way we should see things as well.

RESOURCE READING: Romans 14:1–12

October 18

ACCORDING TO YOUR FAITH

You've heard the old saying, "Seeing is believing." From God's point of view, the opposite is true. Believing brings spiritual vision, which clears the brain of fuzzy negative thinking. I'm reminded of the incident that took place as Jesus was on His way to Jerusalem, where He knew He would be betrayed. A sense of urgency drove Him toward the Holy City. Jesus knew that what would take place in Jerusalem was the very purpose for which He had come.

As Jesus was leaving Jericho, on his way to Jerusalem, He encountered two blind men, who cried out, "Have mercy on us, Son of David!" When Jesus heard this, He stopped. The blind men had heard that He could heal the sick and deformed. "Do you believe that I am able to do this?" Jesus asked them, and they replied, "Yes, Lord." According to Matthew, who was an eyewitness, Jesus touched them and said, "According to your faith will it be done to you!"

So often, Jesus did things that were the opposite of human logic. The Jews placed a premium on action, but Jesus required faith. He tells a blind beggar to believe in something he has heard about but never seen. Thousands of people had seen Christ perform miracles, yet still had trouble believing. Nevertheless, Jesus tells blind men to believe!

Why were these two blind men—social outcasts with no real education—able to believe when some of the real intellectuals of Jesus' day stumbled over unbelief and came up empty-handed? Perhaps I have answered my own question.

Look again at the question that Jesus asks: "Do you believe that I am able to do this?" Well, what's your answer? Faith is simply believing what the Word says. It doesn't attempt to understand how God does it. It just believes that He can and He will.

Faith will carry you up to a new plane of living. It does not deny the problem. It just believes that God is powerful and that He will honor the simple promises He has made.

"Do you believe that I am able to do this?" God says, "According to your faith will it be done to you!"

RESOURCE READING: Matthew 9:27–38

October 19

THE JESUS WE NEVER KNEW

In *The Jesus I Never Knew,* Philip Yancey shatters many of the cherished ideals and images we have of Jesus Christ. Yancey says, "The Jesus I got to know in writing this book is very different from the Jesus I learned about in Sunday school. In some ways He is more comforting; in some ways more terrifying."

Yancey doesn't come up with preprogrammed answers or quick-fix solutions. He has an openness, a candor, and an honesty that prompts you to look within your own heart and soul. How did he rediscover Jesus? Through new, never-before revealed manuscripts? No. Through a mystic encounter with a great guru? No again. Through some vision or trance? Not so.

His book was a partial outgrowth of a study he did with a small group focusing on the life of Jesus Christ. The group also used video clips from almost every film ever produced on the life of Christ. But the Jesus we never knew, according to Yancey, is the one found in Matthew, Mark, Luke, and John. By saturating himself in the Gospels, Yancey was able to strip away the old varnish of images he had grown up with.

Philip Yancey is a gifted individual who has given us something of great importance, yet the Jesus that he never knew is the same One whom believers have worshipped for centuries.

Knowing Jesus as He really is can be complex and difficult because of the lives we live—not just the misconceptions and the wrong images we have grown up with. We get so busy that we have little time to read the four Gospels and digest them. Instead of feasting, we "taste" portions of Scripture, usually in short sound bites that tell us what we want to hear—that God loves us, forgives us, and helps us to succeed.

Does your restless heart want to break through the spiritual gloom and the pain of living in a broken world to see Jesus as He really is? Read Philip Yancey's book and saturate yourself in the Gospels. Ask the Lord to lift the blindness of prejudice and bias and help you to see Him as He really is. When you meet Him, you will never be the same.

RESOURCE READING: Philippians 3

October 20

WHEN YOUR HEAD AND
YOUR HEART DON'T AGREE

What do you do when your head and your heart don't agree? I'm thinking of several letters I've received from different parts of the world. The circumstances vary, but the theme is the same. A young Christian woman—either married or looking for the right person to marry—meets an older, married man, and he begins to give her attention. He makes her feel important, tells her how attractive she is, and says she is exactly what he has been looking for all his life. Then the bottom drops out.

Extricating yourself from an emotional entanglement isn't easy, but it must be done. The first bit of advice I would give is to tell you that men and women view affairs from a vastly different perspective. Men are physical; women are emotional. Men will feed a woman a line to break down her resistance. Lust, not love, is the basis of attraction. The attention that women receive, on the other hand, meets their need for validation.

I'm convinced that the main reason why God said relationships outside of marriage are wrong is because our deep emotional needs can never be met this way. A woman searching for real love, who settles for sex, ends up with shattered dreams and emotions.

The first step back is to realize that what has happened is wrong, and it will never result in the happiness or fulfillment you want out of life. God calls it sin. Painful as it may be, you've got to break off the relationship once and for all, closing the door forever. This may mean a change of jobs, certainly a change of phone numbers. It means saying "No" and not even leaving the door open an inch.

Once you've confessed your wrong before the Lord, the next step is to forgive yourself. Stop playing the "stupid-me-I-should-have-known-better" game. It wasn't that you didn't know better. You just didn't want to believe what you knew. Hence the battle between your head and your heart.

Ultimately, you have to get on with your life. The good news is that the past doesn't have to be a blight on the future. Your future is as bright as the promises of God.

RESOURCE READING: John 8

October 21

VENGEANCE OR WEAKNESS?

I am from mainland China," writes a friend of *Guidelines,* "and I find it impossible to love my enemy and pray for the person who hates me. My culture teaches me to pay an eye for an eye and a tooth for a tooth. But Jesus says, 'Do not resist an evil person. If someone strikes you on the right cheek, turn to him the other also.'"

Then he got to the bottom line. When he ended a relationship with a young lady, she began slandering him. "She couldn't forgive me," he said. "She perceived me to be weak and faint, so she kept on insulting and hurting me. I hated myself for not retaliating. My coworkers mocked me as a coward. I lost my self-respect. I wanted to get even. Please help me: I want to love as Jesus tells me."

This young man is not the first to feel torn between vengeance and doing what God wants. Three times the Bible tells us that vengeance is God's prerogative—not ours. For example, writing to the Romans, Paul says, "Do not take revenge, my friends, but leave room for God's wrath, for it is written: 'It is mine to avenge; I will repay,' says the Lord" (Romans 12:19).

Why did Jesus tell us to leave the revenge to Him? First of all, as the Judge of the world, He knows the full story. God is far more worthy to mete out impartial judgment than we are. The gristmill of God's justice grinds exceedingly fine. Nothing goes unnoticed; nothing goes unpunished.

Another reason is that there is no end to vengeance. One misdeed produces another. Family feuds go on for generations, inflicting more wounds and more pain. Jesus knew that bitterness is destructive.

"I want to get even to redeem my worth as a man," wrote our young friend. But forgiving someone, releasing the bitterness, putting the whole issue in God's hands, is actually redeeming our value as a person. Christ died to redeem us from the curse of our old natures, including the desire to inflict pain on others.

Vengeance never restores your loss or mends your broken heart. It only results in more pain, heartache, and bitterness. Yes, vengeance belongs to God. Let Him handle the situation.

RESOURCE READING: Romans 12

October 22

THE BURDEN OF UNDERSTANDING

Dear Dr. Sala, I am enlightened by your five-minute television talks. I oftentimes ask myself, what is life for? Why should one person be more hurt than others? Why must one's life be lived until you succumb to death? Why can't one evaporate, vanish on one's command, if life is untenable? Can you give some answers to these questions?"

Wow! Those are not simple questions. I'm reminded of the professor who asked his class to write a history of God, man, and the devil in one page. Why does God not control the typhoons that rage? Why does He allow some to be born beautiful and others to be ugly? Why suffering? Why should babies die?

The question "Why?" is endless and it echoes down through the centuries. But God never gave us the burden of understanding. Instead, He gave us the responsibility of obedience. If you want answers to the issues you struggle with, start by studying the Bible seriously. It's the only Book that answers the tough questions of life: Who am I? Where did I come from? Why am I here? Where do I go five minutes after my death? Only God can give purpose to an imperfect, confusing world.

I've discovered that what I do understand gives me far more trouble than what I don't understand. I have a choice: I can go through life making excuses for myself because "this is not fair" or "that is not right," or I can focus on a single issue: "What does God want me to do?" Obedience brings God into my life and adds a third dimension. "Understanding why" is something I have to leave with God, believing that He is faithful and that He is a God who loves me and cares about my life.

Moses says that God keeps covenant with those who love Him and keep His commandments—which means obedience. "Know therefore that the LORD your God is God; he is the faithful God, keeping his covenant of love to a thousand generations of those who love him and keep his commands" (Deuteronomy 7:9). It's just that simple. Don't make life too hard by trying to understand what only God can fathom. Obedience is the path of joy and happiness.

RESOURCE READING: 2 Peter 1

MAKING IT THROUGH THE VALLEY

Discouraged? Does the valley seem so long and dark that you'll never make it to the next peak? Ever wonder if it's worth it?

Helen Roseveare was a doctor who spent most of her life ministering in Africa. She set out with unrealistic expectations of what she could accomplish and what God was supposed to do. Through failure and disappointment, she learned about real faith in the real world. In her book, *Give Me This Mountain,* she writes, "I have often felt that my life was rather akin to mountaineering, with a clear goal to reach the highest peak. There may be a fairly long journey to reach the foothills before the real climb can be started. . . . I found frequently that I climbed in glorious sunshine, warm and invigorating, my face set determinedly for the nearest peak I could see. As I reached it, I reveled in the sense of achievement and victory."

Then she continues, "As I went down from the present peak into the valley between the mountains, I was often shadowed by the very peak I had been enjoying. This I interpreted in a sense of failure and this often led to despair. . . . I see now that I was wrong in this 'feeling.' The going down was merely an initial moving forward toward the next higher ground."

Did you grasp what she is saying? When you stand and look at a range of mountains, you see the peaks, not realizing that between them are long valleys, sometimes darkened by the shadows of those same peaks. In the valleys, we learn the importance of plodding, of taking another step, of facing another day, of finding God's grace to get the kids off to school, to handle the traffic, and to cope with frustrations at the office.

There are few real mountain peaks in life, where the air is clear and you are heady with success. It's in the valleys where we live and raise our families, where we find that God's grace is sufficient and we learn to trust Him for our needs. There is more to life than the thrill of reaching the top. It includes the satisfaction of the journey, knowing that He who has already scaled the peaks walks with us.

RESOURCE READING: Psalm 23

October 24

LET US GO ON

Life is full of ups and downs. Good days and bad days. Times of joy and times of sorrow. What would life be like with no valleys, no shadows, no tough times? Isn't it the challenge of the climb and overcoming difficulties that make reaching the top meaningful and important? Still, the effort of the climb can be exhausting.

The writer of the book of Hebrews, gives us three guidelines for overcoming discouragement and weariness.

Guideline #1: "Let us draw near to God with a sincere heart in full assurance of faith, having our heart sprinkled to cleanse us from a guilty conscience and having our bodies washed with pure water" (Hebrews 10:22). This first word of exhortation and encouragement is good news. Got troubles, pain, or misunderstanding? Then beat a path to the throne of grace and tell God how you feel.

Some people feel they are never good enough to warrant God's care or concern. But because of what Christ did on the cross, you can come just as you are and reach out for His help.

Guideline #2: "Let us hold unswervingly to the hope we profess, for he who promised is faithful" (Hebrews 10:23). In other words, hold on tenaciously to the promises of God. Don't let anyone, the devil included, talk you out of them by making you think you aren't good enough. God cares about you. His promises include the assurance that your sins are forgiven, that you have been brought into the family of God, that you are indeed His child, and that nothing or no one can ever separate you from God's love.

Guideline #3: "Let us not give up meeting together, as some are in the habit of doing, but let us encourage one another—and all the more as you see the Day approaching" (Hebrews 10:25). When people become isolated from each other, it's like taking a burning piece of wood from the fire: The fire in the wood begins to go out. We need each other for encouragement, for strength, for help. Study Hebrews 10 in your New Testament and keep on climbing.

RESOURCE READING: Hebrews 10

October 25

LET US CONSIDER ONE ANOTHER

When people struggle and give up, it often has less to do with the pressures "out there" than it does the lack of encouragement from the folks "in here." "Living with the saints above may be glory," someone once said, "but living with the saints below is quite another story." When our brothers and sisters stumble, they need help, not criticism.

A man stood up recently in a new church fellowship in Moscow and told how he had once been a KGB agent, but God had changed his life and now he wanted to serve the Lord. Cause for rejoicing, right? A fellow churchgoer didn't think so. Pointing his finger at the man, he said, "This fellow is lying. He is not a Christian, but a spy in our midst who still works for the KGB." Believe it or not, this situation occurred after the fall of Communism.

In his book *The Jesus I Never Knew,* Philip Yancey tells of a man working in the inner city who encountered a woman who had been a prostitute. She was in "wretched straits, homeless, her health failing, unable to buy food for her two-year-old daughter." The Christian worker asked her if she had thought about asking the church for help. "Church!" she cried, "Why would I ever go there? They'd just make me feel even worse than I already do!" Sadly enough, in many cases she would be right.

We have largely forgotten the instruction of the Word that says, "Let us consider how we may spur one another on toward love and good deeds. . . . Let us encourage one another—and all the more as you see the Day approaching" (Hebrews 10:24–25).

Consider how you can make a difference! What you do or say may give someone the strength to get up after he has fallen, to pick up the pieces and go on, to turn to the Lord—and to His people in the church—for the help they can give.

The world is full of critics, who are quick to point out our mistakes. But I strive to be included in the ranks of the encouragers. Hey, friend, you can make a difference in someone's life. "Let us encourage one another, and all the more as you see the Day [of Christ's return] approaching."

RESOURCE READING: 1 John 3

THE FEAR OF THE LORD

I don't know how it could have happened," a friend lamented. "They were one of the most spiritual couples I knew. Reading their annual Christmas letter," he said, "made me envious. Their lives were filled with so much; they were helping so many; they were involved in so many good causes."

What caused his distress? The woman had just left her husband for another man.

It would be easy to excuse such things by saying, "Those things happen, you know!" But we know that a lot of what happens is displeasing to our heavenly Father.

Have we lost sight of personal responsibility? Have we forgotten that God holds us accountable for our choices? Does it matter? If forgiveness comes easy, we're apt to say, "Okay, this isn't good, but God will forgive me."

Our quick fixes and easy solutions often produce estrangement, loneliness, and profound pain—and we have forgotten something important. God hasn't let us off the hook. "It is a fearful thing to fall into the hands of the living God," says the writer of Hebrews. I urge you to ponder the consequences of your decisions, because God's forgiveness never relieves you of the consequences of wrongdoing. You're stuck with them.

"Are you afraid of God?" I would answer both yes and no. No, in the sense that I love and trust Him. To the extent I know how, I've chosen to serve Him and walk the path of right living. That's what theologians call "a reverential trust." But to be perfectly honest, I'd be mortally afraid to think that I could turn my back on what I know to be true and hope to get away with it. "You may be sure," Moses told the Israelites, "that your sin will find you out" (Numbers 32:23). Those words are just as true today.

Some things never change, no matter how far our attitudes and morals shift or slide. God's faithfulness never changes, either. He is still a refuge, a strength, and a help, and He can be counted on to help us resolve the issues that tear us apart and turn what could be a disaster into a good relationship. He still makes the difference.

RESOURCE READING: Proverbs 1–2

October 27

THE FULL EXTENT OF FORGIVENESS

Archibald Hunter says that forgiveness is "surrendering my right to hurt you because you have hurt me." Richard Smith, a missionary and counselor who has made a lifetime study of cultures and relationships, says it isn't quite that simple. Forgiveness is not merely letting the offender off the hook. A lot of people mouth empty words of forgiveness, glossing over acts of wrongdoing, while holding on to bitterness in their hearts.

"Forgiveness means releasing the other person from your judgment and trusting God to handle it, even to the point of extending mercy, if that is His choice," Smith says.

We make statements like, "He's only human," or "It was as much your fault as mine." Sometimes we ignore the problem, which continues to fester and grow. We decide not to talk about it, because every time we get into a discussion, we get angry and say things we shouldn't say.

After I spoke once on the importance of forgiveness, a woman told me about the brutal murder of her son. He had been cut down in the prime of life, and she was angry. Even when the young man who had killed her son was sent to prison, her heart was filled with rage. As a Christian, she knew that she had to forgive, but she just couldn't do it.

The more she thought and prayed about it, the more she began to see the issue from God's perspective. What had happened was horrible. Not just to her son, but to her as well. Somehow, she began to realize that vengeance wasn't her responsibility. It was God's. And that's when she began to realize that God would deal with the murderer.

"That kid in prison doesn't know about God," she thought. Eventually, she sent him a Bible along with a long letter, explaining how she felt. She told him that God, the Author of forgiveness, would also forgive him.

"Don't do this," the warden at the prison urged her. "You're wasting your time." But she persisted. "And when I did that," she said, "the burden lifted and only then could I forgive him."

Forgiveness is more than giving up my right to hurt you because you hurt me. True forgiveness means trusting God to handle the situation. Nothing less will do.

RESOURCE READING: Ephesians 4

October 28

GETTING FOCUSED AGAIN

Anyone who has gotten away for the holidays or taken a vacation knows how difficult it can be getting back in the harness, going back to work, or tackling the routine again. If you are struggling with the blues trying to get back into the routine of life, may I suggest some guidelines that will help you refocus your energies and get moving again?

Question #1: "Why am I here?" Chances are that

your answer involves some sort of relationship. You're someone's mommy or daddy. Someone is depending on you to open the office, to get the bus running, to meet the customers. This is the part of life that links us to reality.

Question #2: "What's my motive?" In other words, "Why am I doing what I'm doing?" If you have trouble answering, you may be in the wrong place and need to consider a change. When you focus on your motive, the answer has to go beyond just getting a paycheck. For God's children, who take the teaching of the Bible seriously, there has to be another motive.

The Bible instructs, "Whatever you do, work at it with all your heart, as working for the Lord, not for men" (Colossians 3:23). Frankly, it's when we forget this principle that life gets boring and our tasks become drudgery.

Question #3: "To whom do I belong?" A popular talk show host often quips, "I am my kid's mom." If you are married, you belong to your mate. If you have children, you belong to your family. Most important, if you are God's child, you belong to Him and ultimately answer to Him. Five of the most powerful words in the New Testament are found in Paul's letter to the Corinthians when he reminds them, "You are not your own." Then he adds, "You were bought at a price" (1 Corinthians 6:19–20).

Who is counting on you today? A family is a series of interlocking relationships. Someone is counting on you— whether it is your children, your employer, or the rest of the people in the car pool.

Vacations and holidays are great, but they just aren't the stuff of which life is really made.

RESOURCE READING: Colossians 3

October 29

HEADED THE WRONG WAY IN LIFE

The problem with driving in an area where you haven't been for a long time is that the old landmarks disappear, and everything looks different. I learned this lesson firsthand when I attempted to go to an appointment in Manila, twenty years after I had last lived there. As I rounded one corner, I knew something was wrong from the quizzical stares I got from passersby. I was going the wrong way down a one-way street. I quickly hit the brakes, threw the car in reverse, and backed up to the first intersection.

Forgive the moralizing, but I'm reminded of the conversation I had with a woman whose husband is a workaholic. She had become involved in an affair that she just couldn't seem to break. She realized that her marriage, her kids, and her relationship with God were all in deep trouble. She was headed the wrong way down a one-way street, and a head-on collision with disaster was inevitable.

I'm also thinking of a person who has been siphoning off company funds, excusing herself because she isn't paid enough for what she is doing. Taking the money puts her on a one-way street to disaster. "There is a way that seems right to a man," says Proverbs 16:25, "but in the end it leads to death."

When you are headed the wrong way, you've got to make some changes, and fast. Nobody wants to face the consequences—the shame, the sorrow, the loss, the pain, and all the embarrassment that comes with discovery—but you can't just pretend that all the other cars are going the wrong way. When the prodigal son got to the end of his rope, "he came to himself," in the words of Luke. It was a rude awakening. Things hadn't gone as he had planned, but once he saw which way he was heading, he said, "I will return to the house of my father."

Going back is the toughest part. It requires humility, confession, and repentance. But it's worth it. Coming back to God when you have gone the wrong way is the only way back home. Only a fool continues down a one-way street the wrong way.

RESOURCE READING: 2 Corinthians 5

October 30

PRINCE AND THE PAUPER

I f you don't believe that truth is stranger than fiction, let me tell you the pauper-to-prince true story of American pilot Pete Peterson. In 1966, his aircraft was shot down over Vietnam's Red River Delta. For years until he was released, Peterson's identity was reduced to a POW number, an unknown prisoner subjected to ridicule, deprivation, and hardship.

In May 1997, Peterson returned to Vietnam as the U.S. ambassador. During the war, he had been held at the infamous prison known as the Hanoi Hilton, but this time he was greeted at the airport by Vietnamese dignitaries and escorted to the American embassy. The newly renovated and redecorated French-style home was a far cry from the wretched filth of the vermin-infested prison where he had lived during his captivity.

Any thoughts of righting old wrongs had been dealt with long ago. Ambassador Peterson believed that the only hope for the future was to bury the past and get on with life. He's right. Winston Churchill once said, "As long as the present is at war with the past there is no hope for the future." Nearly 58,000 Americans and 3 million Vietnamese died during the war. But now Peterson is a peacemaker, and he hopes to restore trade and economic growth in Vietnam.

Life has some interesting twists and turns. The prince becomes the pauper, and the pauper takes the place of the prince. Wise is the man who treats others the way he would want to be treated if the tables were turned.

Jesus says, "In everything, do to others what you would have them do to you, for this sums up the Law and the Prophets" (Matthew 7:12).

If roles were reversed, and your assistant became your boss, or your subordinate became your supervisor, would he or she seek revenge? Or would life go on pretty much the same? Arrogance and pride become a cancer that poisons relationships. Scores of people harbor bitterness and anger because of wrongs done to them. Pete Peterson has every reason to be bitter, but he is not. May God help us to live with the same graciousness and understanding, and to treat others the way we would like to be treated.

RESOURCE READING: Romans 12

October 31

HALLOWEEN

For many, October 31 is strictly Halloween, an evening of ghosts and goblins, of youngsters going from door to door asking for a "trick or treat." For some, it is an evening of reckless mischief.

Some churches, wishing to downplay the ghosts and goblins, focus on the saints of bygone ages, encouraging their youngsters to dress as heroes of the faith and have a good time. Some people ignore the reality of the spirit world and the devil and allow their children to dress as devils and spooks.

Are demons real? They're as real as angels, as real as the forces that resulted in World War II, and the evil that put 14 million men and women in concentration camps. Demons are as real as the unseen forces that lead people to murder, rape, and steal.

Perhaps you are thinking, *Aren't you getting carried away with this?* No. I've been there. I've seen these forces of evil in the world. I've had to deal with some of them firsthand.

Demons and devils are nothing to be toyed with. They are powerful, and they are real. On Paul's third missionary journey, he came to the great city of Ephesus, and encountered evil spirits. When seven sons of a Jewish priest named Sceva witnessed these exorcisms, they decided to try the same thing. But it didn't work out. "The possessed man went berserk—jumped the exorcists, beat them up, and tore off their clothes. Naked and bloody, they got away as best they could" (Acts 19:16 TM).

Stay away from the enemy. Avoid dealing with situations that you aren't qualified to handle. God's children should not mess with the enemy's power. Whenever someone dabbles with the spirit world, he moves beyond the protection of the Almighty.

If your child wants to dress up for Halloween, make it a learning experience, teaching them about the power of angels in relationship to God's children. Take your Bible and read about demonic power and why there is an enemy of our souls who has been around to give us trouble ever since Eve's encounter in the Garden.

RESOURCE READING: Ephesians 6:10–18

THE DEATH OF GOOD INTENTIONS

One of the illusions we live with is that there is always plenty of time. We procrastinate, full of good intentions, thinking that we'll do something later. If you are given to procrastination, consider the story of the secretary who worked for many years for the Eastman Kodak Company. She never married, but her nieces and nephews were very special to her.

Each year, as part of her salary package, she received stock in the company. "You hang on to that stock," her friends told her. "It will be worth a lot someday." They were right. During the years she owned the stock, Eastman Kodak continued to grow and expand. Because she had no direct dependents, she intended to pass the stock along to her nieces and nephews and other members of the family when she died. She thought she had lots of time to draft a will. But she was wrong. Suddenly felled by illness, she quickly lost strength and life failed her before she could write her will.

How much did the family receive? Nothing. Absolutely nothing. The state stepped in and froze her accounts, and because she had no direct relatives, her estate was claimed by the government.

Good intentions aren't enough. The old woman's nephew, who became the pastor of a large, thriving church, was reminded of that truth a second time. Adjacent to the church property was a large empty lot owned by a businessman who attended the church. "Pastor," he used to say, "I want the church to have that property for future expansion." No one doubted his good intentions. But he never told his attorney, and never signed the deed that would pass that property on to the church. When he suddenly dropped dead of heart failure, his good intentions no longer mattered.

Here's a rule of thumb to follow: "Do your givin' while you're livin', so you're knowin' where it's goin'."

The Bible says it is appointed unto men once to die but after that comes the judgment. May God help us to live with eternity's values in view and consider that we have a gift from God, which eventually must be left behind.

RESOURCE READING: Luke 12

November 2

MAKING PEACE WITH GOD

Making peace with God is the most important thing you will ever do in life, and it isn't something that you can necessarily put off until five minutes before you die. But for many, life gets so full of things that they seldom think about the importance of making peace with God until it's too late.

Making peace with God is not much different than reestablishing any relationship that has been broken by misunderstanding or wrongdoing. Isaiah says, "We all, like sheep, have gone astray, each of us has turned to his own way; and the LORD has laid on him the iniquity of us all" (Isaiah 53:6). Without a shepherd, sheep quickly wander and go astray. That's why the shepherd is so important. Left to their own way, sheep are vulnerable to predators and enemies of all kinds.

Making peace with God begins when you acknowledge that you have gone astray. Down deep in your heart, you know that confession should not be too difficult. The second thing you must do is recognize the voice of the shepherd and acclaim Him as your Lord and Savior. Jesus, using this very analogy, said, "I am the good shepherd." He also said, "I am the way and the truth and the life. . ." (John 14:6).

Now, a word of warning. There are a lot of false shepherds out there—individuals, philosophies, and even religions that claim to take you to God. But there is only one Shepherd who proved that He was the Son of God by dying and rising again the third day. It was this which proved that Jesus was and is the Great Shepherd, the One sent from God.

The final step in making peace with God is to claim His Son as your Shepherd and Savior and begin to follow Him. Too easy? Some think so, but I have learned that when you follow the Shepherd, you will get to know Him, and when you really know Him, you will love Him, and when you love Him, you will obey Him and keep His commandments.

It takes about as long to make peace with God as it does to swallow your pride and ask directions when you are lost.

RESOURCE READING: John 10

November 3

TAKE MY BURDEN

Jesus spoke to a large crowd that had assembled to hear Him. He said, "Come to Me, all you who labor and are heavy laden, and I will give you rest. Take My yoke upon you and learn from Me, for I am gentle and lowly in heart, and you will find rest for your souls. For My yoke is easy and My burden is light" (Matthew 11:28–30 NKJV).

We understand what burdens are. We have family problems, financial woes, and feelings of rejection and insecurity. We understand that Christ is saying, "If you come to Me, I will give you rest." We like that.

But what does it mean that "My yoke is easy and My

burden is light"? With cattle or oxen, a yoke is used to keep the animals under control. It restricts freedom and self-expression. But Jesus emphasizes the word *My.* "My yoke is easy; My burden is light." Compared with what? It remained unsaid, but the people knew. It was the burden of organized religion, which had long before gone beyond the spirit of the law to a strict legalism. As Paul says, the letter kills but the Spirit makes alive.

Lest I be misunderstood, Jesus is not saying that those outside the church who are just plain "good people" are better than those inside. That's not His intent. He is saying very simply that when you follow Him and know Him, your relationship with God becomes meaningful and real—and you find rest for your soul.

Rest for your soul isn't based upon the assurance that you have done all the right things, but rather that Jesus Christ did for you what you could not do for yourself. The spiritual rest that comes to the children of God is the deep assurance that our righteousness has been paid for by the death of Jesus Christ.

Peter puts it graphically: "He himself bore our sins in his body on the tree, so that we might die to sins and live for righteousness; by his wounds you have been healed. For you were like sheep going astray, but now you have returned to the Shepherd and Overseer of your souls" (1 Peter 2:24–25).

"Take My yoke," says Jesus, "and I will give you rest."

RESOURCE READING: Galatians 3:19–29

WISDOM, KNOWLEDGE, AND UNDERSTANDING

A businessman was riding on an airplane when he noticed that the man to his right was wearing his wedding ring on his middle finger and not the "ring finger."

"It's really none of my business," he commented, "but I noticed that your wedding ring is on the wrong finger." "Yep," replied the man. "I married the wrong girl."

Though we chuckle at the humor, the number of people today who end up marrying the wrong person is no laughing matter.

As the writer of Proverbs says, "It takes wisdom to build a house, and understanding to set it on a firm foundation; it takes knowledge to furnish its rooms with fine furniture and beautiful draperies" (Proverbs 24:3–4 TM). Solomon, the likely author, had experience in both kinds of relationships—some good, some not so good. He focuses on three qualities: wisdom, understanding, and knowledge, and suggests that all three are necessary to build a home that will endure.

We need wisdom to choose the right person. Equally as important, we must *be* the right person. The book of James says, "If any of you lacks wisdom, he should ask God, who gives generously to all without finding fault, and it will be given to him" (James 1:5). God gives us wisdom to cope with our relationships.

Solomon also emphasizes understanding. Did you know that the Hebrew word translated "to understand" also means "to listen"? Wise is the parent who picks up nonverbal signals and develops a listening ear. Wise is the husband who understands when a wife needs flowers or a helping hand.

Finally, the writer mentions knowledge. "Through knowledge," he says, the rooms of this house "are filled with rare and beautiful treasures." What are your treasures? Do they include memories, pleasures, experiences together, laughter and joy? Or is your house filled with antiques and exquisite paintings and couches that no one can sit on?

Give me a house any day with a few fingerprints on the walls and dirty dishes in the sink, some toys littering the floor, and the ring of laughter and sounds of joy. Solomon was right: "By wisdom a house is built, and through understanding it is established; through knowledge its rooms are filled with rare and beautiful treasures."

RESOURCE READING: Proverbs 24

November 5

LIVING TOGETHER JUST DOESN'T WORK

Why not live together before you marry? After all, you never buy a pair of shoes without trying them on, right? Is there a better way to find out what a person is really like?

As a starting point, choosing a person to marry isn't the same as choosing a pair of shoes that will be discarded when they get worn or scuffed. Buying a pair of shoes isn't the same as entering into a relationship involving your body, soul, and spirit.

Recently, *U.S. News and World Report* ran a cover story titled "The Trouble with Premarital Sex." The writer, David Whitman, says, "Cohabitation may seem a good 'trial run' for a solid marriage. But in practice, cohabiting couples who marry—many of whom already have children—are about 33 percent more likely to divorce than couples who don't live together before their nuptials. Virgin brides," he says, "are less likely to divorce than women who lost their virginity prior to marriage."[1]

Harvard sociologist Christopher Jencks says that adult premarital sex "may ultimately prove to be a little like smoking dope in the 1960s. In retrospect, maybe it isn't so good for you after all."

Researcher George Barna believes that the kind of a person who will cohabitate is also more likely to disagree with traditional ideas about family and marriage. He or she is more likely to believe that sexual fidelity is unnecessary after marriage, more likely to expect a mom to work full-time, less committed to a marriage, and more likely to be involved in an extramarital affair.

Living together apart from marriage has been proven not to work. Is it possible that God knew something about all of this in the beginning? Might this be the very reason he decreed that a man should leave his father and mother and be joined to his wife in a celebration of joy and commitment, going public with the desire to live together as a husband and a wife, not as lover and companion? I never cease to be amazed how deviations from the norm that societies embrace always end in failure. God's plan produces happiness and joy. No wonder. He's the Divine Architect whose plan still spells success.

RESOURCE READING: Genesis 2:19–25

November 6

WHEN COMMITMENT IS MISSING

S omeone defined a conservative as a liberal whose daughter has become a teenager. Strange, isn't it, that people who sowed their wild oats as teenagers are stronger disciplinarians and more cautious as parents than those who were less carefree in their youth.

In the 1960s, Hugh Hefner launched the playboy revolution, telling us that sex is a personal matter between consenting adults—that it's okay provided two people agree. From that beginning, the fabric of marriage began to unravel. Eventually society came to accept cohabitation as the logical if not inevitable result. But now a generation later, sociologists and family researchers say, "Wait a minute. It just hasn't worked."

Researcher George Barna says that couples who live together apart from marriage show lower levels of overall satisfaction after they marry. "They are also less likely to see their spouse as their best friend. They are less likely to believe that their spouse respects them. They have a greater fear of divorce," and "they are more restless about their marriage and outside relationships."

Missing in all of this is the emotional impact of bonding, the psychological closeness that results when two people give themselves to each other. For women, in particular, this emotional bonding is powerful, and when the commitment of marriage is missing, a woman feels used, cheapened, and angry. Talk of love is meaningless without commitment.

Though we tacitly recognize that morality and premarital abstinence are biblical values, we seldom recognize that what God ordained is the only thing that produces lasting happiness and permanence in relationships.

Today the proportion of adults who believe that sexual expression apart from marriage is "always wrong" has declined to barely one-fourth of the adult population. Nonetheless, the gap between broken homes and lasting commitment continues to climb—something that cannot be lightly ignored.

What society believes isn't the issue. But what God said long ago regarding the commitment of marriage needs to be rediscovered. It still works and it still produces the joy and happiness a bride and groom expect when they stand starry-eyed at the marriage altar. Lowering the standards of society doesn't lower the level of expectation of happiness that we have. God's purpose is to spare us the heartache and loneliness of rejection and abandonment.

RESOURCE READING: Matthew 5:27–32

November 7

IT'S A GLOBAL VILLAGE

We live in a global village. Trends that begin in one part of the world spread quickly, and when it comes to cohabitation—living together as unmarried singles— growing numbers in the former USSR are adopting this practice, says Tatyana Gorka, a sociologist at the Russian Academy of Sciences. Most young Russian couples want to get a handle on finances, make some money, buy furniture for an apartment, and possibly get a small car—not get married and have a family.

Under the Soviet government, there were incentives for couples to marry and have a family—apartments, vouchers admitting them to stores where they could purchase rare imported items, even financial breaks. But all of that is now history. In post-Communist Russia, the desire to make money and to get ahead materially is the driving force. Marriage—as in much of the world—is getting postponed. For Russian males, the average age to marry is twenty-nine. For females, it's twenty-seven—two years older than in 1980.

Though no one can document the changes, the consensus is that the number of couples cohabiting has increased dramatically. Motherhood outside of marriage is on the rise, too, with 21 percent of all Russian births in 1995 out of wedlock compared with 11 percent in 1980.

Today there is a growing desire among Russian youth to experience the sexual freedom which the West has already embraced, but the sad thing is that the moral freedom which was repressed in Russia for so long will no more bring happiness to young Russians than it did to young Americans or any other group or culture anywhere. There is a correlation between the disintegration of families and the undermining of the moral forces upon which families have been built. The issue is far deeper than just morality or values. It includes a relationship with a loving God who has given us guidance for life and living. If God is ignored, then anything is acceptable. But if He exists and has given us a plan for happiness and right living, it is the same for all His children everywhere.

RESOURCE READING: Ephesians 5

November 8

ADOPTED INTO GOD'S FAMILY

I s there a more beautiful expression of love than the adoption of a little child? One adopted child, sensing his importance, chided his new brothers and sisters, saying, "Mommy and Daddy chose me, but they didn't have any say about you." When a child is adopted, the parents not only give love and financial help, they give their name to the child and accept the youngster as their own.

When a child was adopted under Roman law, he was taken before a judge and three times denied any relationship to his natural father. The third time, the judge pronounced him the son of the adopting father. When that happened, he received a new name. If he had committed any felonies or crimes against the state, they were legally wiped out. In a very real sense, when a person was adopted, he became a new person with a new identity and new parents.

That is the very picture used by the New Testament writers to show what happens when a person is born again and becomes an adopted child of God. "Yet to all who received him," writes the apostle John, "to those who believed in his name, he gave the right to become children of God" (John 1:12).

To the Romans, Paul says, "For you did not receive a spirit that makes you a slave again to fear, but you received the Spirit of sonship. And by him we cry, 'Abba, Father.' " (Romans 8:15). To the Galatians Paul writes, "Because you are sons, God sent the Spirit of his Son into our hearts, the Spirit who calls out, 'Abba, Father.' So you are no longer a slave, but a son; and since you are a son, God has made you also an heir" (Galatians 4:6–8).

When you are adopted into God's family, there are new rights and privileges. Taking advantage of those rights and privileges is simply your inheritance as an heir to the estate of the Father. As a believer, you can lift your voice in prayer and cry, "Abba, Father." That is the difference between a son and a servant.

RESOURCE READING: Galatians 4

November 9

KNOWING HIM

When Mark Twain returned from a world cruise, he related his experiences meeting some of the world's great people. His son, then a little boy, listened rapturously and then exclaimed, "You know, Dad, you must know about everybody except God." Unfortunately, the exception makes the rest meaningless. Which is more important, knowing the greats of society, or knowing God? Having a personal relationship with God makes all of life different and meaningful. Saul, who became Paul, had an encounter with God on the road to Damascus. Humbled, he rose from his knees a changed man. From that point on, everything he had considered important was no longer meaningful. "But whatever was to my profit I now consider loss for the sake of Christ," he later wrote to the Philippians (3:7).

Paul says he developed three goals, three great desires: the first was to know Christ, the second was to know the power of His resurrection, and the third was to join the fellowship of His suffering.

Certainly Paul knew Christ. But what he is saying is that he wants to know Him more deeply, more intimately, more completely. He wants to develop an ongoing, deepening relationship.

Can you relate to that? Chances are, what Paul said well expresses the desire of your heart. A person can know a great deal about Christ—about God, for that matter—without knowing Him either personally or intimately.

Don't be content with less than a full, personal knowledge of Christ. He invites you to "come to me, all you who are weary and burdened, and I will give you rest" (Matthew 11:28).

Is the desire of your heart to really know God? Pursue that goal. You don't need to go to a convent or a monastery, but you must come to the Father through His Son, who is revealed through the pages of His Word, and live out the inward love of God as He touches others through you.

The Jesus that you grew up with, the One you heard about in religious education may well be different from the One revealed in the New Testament. Get to know the real Jesus. He'll change your life. Knowing everybody but God falls short of the most important friendship of all.

RESOURCE READING: Philippians 3:1–11

THE POWER OF
HIS RESURRECTION

I f you could make three wishes, what would they be? Fame, fortune, and power? When Paul wrote to friends at Philippi, he told them he had three desires: to know Christ in a meaningful and completely fulfilling relationship, to know the power of His resurrection, and to share the fellowship of His sufferings.

Donald Grey Barnhouse was widowed as a young man, and he had the formidable task of raising a little six-year-old girl who very much missed her mother. Of course he struggled with the loss, but what was far more difficult was trying to explain to his daughter why a loving God would take her mother to be with Him. Nothing Barnhouse said seemed to get through to the little girl.

One day Barnhouse and his daughter were standing on a busy street corner, waiting for the light to change so they could cross the street. Suddenly, a large truck came speeding around the corner, momentarily blocking the sun and casting a shadow over the two standing there. The little girl was frightened. Her daddy picked her up in his arms and began to comfort her. In an instant, a truth crystallized in his thinking.

"When you saw the truck, it scared you," he began, "but let me ask you. Had you rather be struck by the truck or the shadow of the truck?" Of course the little girl replied, "The shadow."

"When your mother died," said the father, "she was hit by the shadow of death because Jesus was hit by the truck [death]." Jesus says, "I am the resurrection and the life. He who believes in me will live, even though he dies" (John 11:25), and "I tell you the truth, he who believes has everlasting life" (John 6:47).

Therein lies the power of the Resurrection, the antidote to the sting of death, the comfort that makes loss bearable. Paul knew what he was asking for when he expressed the desire to know the power of the Resurrection. God will help us to know the power of the Resurrection which dissipates our fuzzy thinking, our misunderstanding, and the fog of our sorrow when we stand before an open grave. Knowing the power of the Resurrection gives strength for living. May God give you that power today.

RESOURCE READING: 1 Thessalonians 4

November 11

THE FELLOWSHIP OF HIS SUFFERINGS

David Jacobs was six years old when he began an uphill battle with cancer which eventually took his life. In the course of his valiant fight, this brave little boy gave us some insights that remind me of the way "a child shall lead them."

One day, as he was about to undergo a chemotherapy treatment, he and his father sat next to a gray-haired man old enough to be David's grandfather.

"Hi," said David, quickly adding, "Have you had this before?"

"Yes," commented the older man, trying to make David feel comfortable.

"Does it hurt much when they put the needle in you?" David asked, getting to the point of the dialogue.

"Yes, it does," said the old man. Then, trying to minimize the issue quickly, he added, "But they try to make it as easy as possible on you."

David sat there for a few moments, trying to come to grips with it all and then turned to the old man and said, "You know something. Jesus knows how this feels because they put a crown of thorns on his head." The old man's eyes filled with tears.

The fellowship of suffering forges bonds that span ages, nationalities, ethnic backgrounds, and a host of other divisive issues. When you are hurting and another person hurts the same way, there is a union of your souls which is very, very strong.

When Paul wrote to the Philippians, he said that one of his desires was to know the fellowship of Christ's suffering. To be honest with you, I know very little personally about the fellowship of suffering, but I have met men and women who know a great deal more.

Paul continues his discussion of suffering, saying that through the fellowship of Christ's suffering we become conformed to His death. It's what Jesus was talking about when He told the disciples, "If anyone would come after me, he must deny himself and take up his cross daily and follow me" (Luke 9:23).

In the fellowship of Christ's suffering we experience the mystical presence of Him who lived, died, and rose again.

RESOURCE READING: Isaiah 53

November 12

THE TRUE MARK OF A PERSON

What is the true mark of an individual? Is it age, net worth, ideas, or accomplishments? To the Eastern mind, a person is often measured by the length of his beard or the whiteness of his hair. To the businessperson, financial net worth is often considered the true mark of an individual. How the money was earned is not as important its accumulation.

A philosopher might suggest that a person's ideas are the true mark of greatness. Who can underestimate the power of an idea? Victor Hugo once said, "Nothing in all the world is as powerful as an idea whose time has come."

The pragmatist would say, "Away with ideas. Away with dreams and visions. Show me what a man has done and I will show you his true mark." Is accomplishment the true mark of an individual?

How do you suppose God determines greatness? In the sight of God, the true mark of an individual is character—not accomplishments, his ideas, or net worth.

"Blessed is the man that walketh not in the counsel of the ungodly, nor standeth in the way of sinners, nor sitteth in the seat of the scornful. But his delight is in the law of the LORD; and in his law doth he meditate day and night" (Psalm 1:1–2 KJV).

God's perspective is certainly different from ours. We fall prey to materialism and pragmatism. We put the emphasis on doing; God puts it on being. We emphasize accomplishment; God looks for character. Here is something to consider: What you *are* is far more important than what you will ever do, whether you are the president of the world's largest bank or push a broom on the streets of the smallest city.

Stop and view life from a different perspective, the perspective of eternity. What are you, anyway? A successful person worth thousands or even hundreds of thousands of dollars but a failure in God's sight, or a humble laborer as the world sees you, yet a success in the eyes of God? God is still seeking men and women of character who will stand and be counted.

RESOURCE READING: Psalm 119:1–11

BUILDING CASTLES IN THE SKY

Ahikar was a very wise man, and his fame spread to all the world. The king, who was jealous of Ahikar's wisdom, devised a test, hoping to embarrass the wise man. The king said, "I will ask Ahikar to build a castle in the sky. If he succeeds, I will not exact tribute; but if not, I will double the tribute that is due to me."

The king agreed to supply the materials if Ahikar would construct the palace in the sky. Ahikar was in a tight spot. For weeks, the wise man was baffled. Just when it seemed that he would be forced to admit defeat, Ahikar got an idea. He took two little boys and trained them to ride on the backs of eagles. On the appointed day, Ahikar came to the palace. "Where, Ahikar, is my castle in the sky?" asked the king.

"Oh, king," said Ahikar, "come outside the palace with me." As the king and the wise man walked outside, the two little boys on the backs of the eagles looked down at the king and shouted, "Send up the materials, O king, and we will build your castle in the sky."

Jesus told the story of a man who, by our standards, lived in chrome-plated luxury. He was extremely wealthy. His was a life of elegance and pleasure, but still he was not satisfied. He vowed, "I will tear down my warehouses and build bigger ones." Was he a wise man? Christ called him a fool. A fool because God had no part in his life.

Faith is more than hoping for castles in the sky. When Christ comes into your life, He gives you the assurance that you will live and abide forever in heaven. Knowing Christ means that the personal presence of Jesus Christ is yours, that He will walk with you and strengthen you day by day. It means that you can walk in fellowship with Him. It means that you will begin to discover what life is all about.

The person who walks with Christ discovers reality and purpose in life. Are you building castles in the sky, or walking with the Lord?

RESOURCE READING: John 14:1–6

November 14

THE SUPERGLUE OF FAITH

Not long ago, I watched a father helping his little boy learn to walk. The little fellow would take a few steps and start to fall. Then his dad would catch him, prop him up again, and encourage him to try again. It occurred to me that by the time this little guy starts school, he will have already begun to lose the simplicity and purity of absolute faith. As he grows, he will learn that the stranger who offers him a ride can't be trusted. He'll learn to guard his wallet, avoid eye contact, and never smile at strangers. I suppose we could blame our culture for this loss of faith, but I wonder whether our children are simply mirroring our own values and lack of trust.

What ever happened to the faith element that Jesus talked about? Is faith completely impractical in our world? Or is there a relationship between the fall of faith and our broken homes and hearts, our meaningless wedding vows, and the fact that many don't seem to know the difference between truth and fantasy?

Paul, who wrote thirteen of the New Testament books, had plenty of street smarts. He wasn't a cleric whose manicured nails were polished and neatly filed. Not only a scholar, he was a tradesman as well—a tentmaker who worked with his hands. He had been in the great cities of Asia. He knew about bribery and how things were done in a corrupt world.

Yet when Paul talked about faith and its importance in relationships, he also talked about hope and love—the three-fold cord that keeps us from drifting into a complete fog of cynicism and distrust.

Faith is totally based on relationships of trust. It can't be reduced to a substance in a laboratory beaker. In fact, it is difficult to find words to describe faith, just as the fragrance of a rose, a breeze of salty air, or the spirit of a relationship are elusive and hard to describe.

Faith is the confident assurance that makes all things possible. Hope is the undying desire for a better tomorrow; love is the healing balm that makes our human relationships vital and enduring. The three go together and form a super-glue of human relations that keep our lives meaningful.

RESOURCE READING: 1 Corinthians 13

November 15

IS THE RED HEIFER REALLY THE SIGN?

They call her Melody, but she has created a lot of discord in the Middle East. Melody is a cow, a red heifer born in Israel in August 1996. What's all the fuss? A red heifer—the same type of animal whose ashes were used in sacrifices on the temple mount before it was destroyed by the Romans in A.D. 70—has not been born in Israel for centuries. Some rabbis see the red heifer as a sign of the imminent coming of the Messiah.

Here's why Melody's birth makes people nervous. Orthodox Jews understand that the temple completed by Solomon, which was destroyed and rebuilt following the return from Babylonian captivity, stood in Jerusalem precisely where the Dome of the Rock and the al-Aksa mosque stand today. Muslims revere this site among the three most holy places in the world, behind Mecca and Medina. When Orthodox Jews talk about dismantling and moving the mosque from Jerusalem to Mecca, Muslims suffer heart palpitations. After all, this is where Mohammed is said to have ascended to heaven.

Back to the red heifer as a sign of the coming of Messiah. Where is that found in either Old or New Testaments? Jesus rebuked the religious leaders of His day because they could not discern the signs of the times. He said, "You are good at reading the weather signs of the skies—red sky tonight means fair weather tomorrow; red sky in the morning means foul weather all day—but you can't read the obvious signs of the times!" (Matthew 16:2 TLB).

When the disciples came to Jesus as He sat on the Mount of Olives and asked, "What are the signs of your coming and of the end of the age?" Jesus says nothing about the birth of a red heifer.

If you want to read some remarkable prophecies, try Ezekiel 36–39 and Isaiah 11:11. Take time to study Daniel 9:24–27.

Sometimes we strain at a gnat and swallow the camel. We ignore the obvious and important and see prophetic significance in the birth of a red cow. When Jesus talked about His return, He told the disciples to look up when they saw these things begin to come to pass. May God help us to see the obvious and important.

RESOURCE READING: Matthew 24:1–36

DO IT NOW

Michael Landon was a regular in the Sala household for many years. Every Sunday night after church, we headed for McDonalds and then raced home in time for *Bonanza*. Landon, who died in his prime, once said, "Whatever you want to do, do it now. There are only so many tomorrows." He was right.

Life is a series of todays that quickly fade into yesterdays. Tomorrow is uncertain. Today is the only day you own. Recognizing the importance of today is not only sound psychologically, but it is biblical as well. The word "tomorrow" is found only fifty-six times in the Bible, but the word "today" appears more than two hundred times.

The Bible stresses the importance of doing things now, of listening to the voice of the Lord today, of making peace with God today. Hebrews 3:7 says, "The Holy Spirit warns us to listen to him, to be careful to hear his voice today" (TLB). "Now is the day of salvation," Paul says in 2 Corinthians 6:2.

When death stares you in the face, it does one of two things: either it causes absolute panic or it helps you reorient your life, your values, and your priorities. People who have stared death in the face and survived have one thing in common: Things that once were important are no longer important. I thought of that fact recently as I saw an interview with a group of individuals who had survived a plane disaster when a gaping hole was torn in the side of a giant 747. Individuals suddenly disappeared, and survivors sat there—a foot away from the jagged edges in the side of the plane—wondering if they too would be sucked out into the darkness of the night.

Those who survived felt guilty that they had lived while others died, but without exception, they said that this near disaster had changed their lives for the better.

Need I remind you that life has an ending as well as a beginning? "The greatest shock in my life," said Billy Graham on a recent birthday, "has been the brevity of life." This from a man who has seen more than seventy birthdays. "Whatever you want to do, do it now. There are only so many tomorrows."

RESOURCE READING: Luke 12:1–20

November 17

IF YOU WANT TO MAKE GOD LAUGH

I f you want to make God laugh, make plans!" Does that mean that we should never try to plan anything? No, but rather, when God is left out of your plan, your game plan may never happen. There is a proverb that says, "The lot is cast into the lap; but the whole disposing thereof is of the LORD" (Proverbs 16:33 KJV).

Whether you climb a mountain, traverse an ocean, build a house or a high-rise building, run in the Olympics, or attempt to plant a garden—or for that matter, do about anything—there are scores of factors over which you have little, if any, control. Like what? Like the economy, the weather, the availability of goods and services, the flow of electrical current that can wipe out machinery, the capriciousness of trade and surpluses, and a host of other things. The fact is, we take for granted a lot of factors over which we have very little control. Does this mean we should sit on our hands, waiting for God to make things happen? Not unless you are expecting a new outpouring of manna from heaven. God honors planning and hard work, but what makes God laugh is the presumption that men and women often have which ignores Him entirely.

Presumption is a sin that God detests. Want to make God laugh? Then make plans and leave Him out of your plans. Apparently this is not simply a problem that those of us who live in the shadow of the twenty-first century struggle with. It's an old one. James, the half brother of Jesus, wrote about this very situation when he penned the letter which bears his name. He wrote to Jewish Christians—probably merchants—and said, "Now listen, you who say, 'Today or tomorrow we will go to this or that city, spend a year there, carry on business and make money.' Why, you do not even know what will happen tomorrow. What is your life? You are a mist that appears for a little while and then vanishes. Instead, you ought to say, 'If it is the Lord's will, we will live and do this or that.' As it is, you boast and brag. All such boasting is evil" (James 4:13–16).

How could it be any plainer?

RESOURCE READING: Proverbs 16

November 18

THE STRENGTH OF
THE MOUNTAIN MOVER

I t's not the size of the mountain but the strength of the mountain mover that counts. When circumstances fog my goals and I'm thinking that I tackled a mountain too high for my ability, I fall back on some truths that help hold me steady. I remind myself that God knew the size of the mountain and the difficulty of the climb before He sent me on my way. He also knew the limitations of my personal strength and the intensity of the difficulty. He also knows that I am not exactly a super climber, but an ordinary plodder with dogged determination not to quit short of reaching my destination.

I'm encouraged by the writings of Jeremiah, a man who was imprisoned more than a few times. He recorded the words of the Almighty, who says, " 'For I know the plans I have for you,' declares the LORD, 'plans to prosper you and not to harm you, plans to give you hope and a future' " (Jeremiah 29:11).

How does God move mountains? Jesus told the disciples, "If you have faith and do not doubt, not only can you do what was done to the fig tree, but also you can say to this mountain, 'Go, throw yourself into the sea,' and it will be done. If you believe, you will receive whatever you ask for in prayer" (Matthew 21:21–22). Wow! What a promise.

Jesus was using a figure of speech, which the disciples clearly understood. He was not actually suggesting that Mt. Tabor, or the Mount of Olives would be cast, literally, into the Mediterranean, but He was saying that God can do the impossible—move the mountain of doubt, fear, suffering, or an otherwise impossible situation. Jesus says that my response to His greatness is believing Him to do what I cannot do. The Bible calls this faith.

If you are climbing a mountain and the weather turns sour, and you can't see your way to the top, waiting is not much fun. But you have no choice. There is spiritual discipline in learning to wait, for then we sense something of the awesome strength of God. It isn't the size of the mountain but the strength of the mountain mover that really counts.

RESOURCE READING: Job 42

WHAT ABOUT
THE CIRCUMSTANCES?

I f you were imprisoned unjustly—not for just a few days but for at least four years—and chances were you would be executed for something politically motivated, would you be happy, even joyful? This was precisely the situation confronting Paul when he wrote to a group of friends in the city of Philippi. In the letter, he mentions joy or joyfulness twelve times.

We harbor the strange illusion that we can control what happens to us, but the fact is most circumstances are beyond our control. Accidents, failures, tragedies—all of these are part of the fabric of circumstances that we cannot control.

We must remember that no set of circumstances can confront God's children without being allowed by our Sovereign God. That's why Paul could maintain the attitude he had.

Facing uninvited or unwarranted circumstances? The following guidelines may serve to encourage you.

Guideline #1: Difficult circumstances will either pro-
    duce bitterness or blessing. Your attitude makes
    the difference. Paul believed that God turned cir-
    cumstances, making them work to his good, not
    his detriment.

Guideline #2: Your response to difficult circumstances
    will be governed by your theology. In other
    words, your ability to accept what the Bible says
    and believe it makes the difference. Paul wrote,
    "Being confident of this very thing, that he which
    hath begun a good work in you will perform it
    until the day of Jesus Christ" (Philippians 1:6
    KJV). God won't leave you in the lurch or forget
    you when the going gets tough.

Guideline #3: Your response to tough times produces a powerful witness in the lives of those who are watching you. You become the gospel to them, the only real example that some may ever see.

Guideline #4: Your unjust suffering and pain forges a mystic bond with the suffering of Jesus Christ. I can't explain that. No one can. It is something that can only be experienced by those who endure. Paul talked about it. He said his goal was "to know Christ and the power of his resurrection and the fellowship of sharing in his sufferings, becoming like him in his death" (Philippians 3:10). If Paul could do it, so can you.

RESOURCE READING: Philippians 1

November 20

FOCUSING ON GOD INSTEAD OF YOUR PROBLEM

John Henry Jowett, the renowned pastor of London's Westminster Chapel, struggled with feelings of unworthiness and inadequacy. In 1920, he wrote to a friend and said, "You seem to imagine that I have no ups and downs, but just a level and lofty stretch of spiritual attainment with unbroken joy and equanimity. By no means! I am often perfectly wretched and everything appears most murky"[1]

Jowett had learned an important lesson: You don't quit when the going gets tough, nor do you spend time moaning about your problems. In times of difficulty and personal distress, Jowett focused on God—His nature, His character, and attributes—and responded in praise and thanksgiving.

He once wrote, "Gratitude is a vaccine, an antitoxin,

and an antiseptic." Talk about therapy for the blues! A vaccine against depression, an antitoxin for the debilitating virus of grumbling, and an antiseptic to cleanse your heart of the disease of self-pity. Praise and thanksgiving are powerful medicine for the soul when it comes to reversing negative and depressing attitudes.

Some, however, find thanksgiving beyond them. They have become so overwhelmed with their problems that their eyes are glued to the earth. Are you one of them? Lift up your eyes, your heart, and your voice and give thanks. Long ago, the psalmist lifted a refrain, "Oh, that men would praise the LORD for his goodness, and for his wonderful works to the children of men!" (Psalm 107:8 KJV).

Ponder the following words: "We have forgotten God. We have forgotten the gracious hand which preserved us in peace and multiplied and enriched and strengthened us, and we have vainly imagined, in the deceitfulness of our hearts, that all these blessings were produced by some superior wisdom and virtue of our own. Intoxicated with unbroken success, we have become too self-sufficient to feel the necessity of redeeming and preserving grace, too proud to pray to the God that made us."

Abraham Lincoln wrote these words in 1863 as the United States was being torn apart by the Civil War. Have you fallen prey to the virus of ingratitude, failing to focus on the goodness of God and the undeserved but rich blessings that come from His hand? Jowett said gratitude is "a vaccine, an antitoxin, and an antiseptic." It's the solution to despair and discouragement.

RESOURCE READING: Psalm 107 (KJV).

BEAT 'EM NOW AND THEN
TO KEEP 'EM IN LINE

W hen I was guest professor at Donetsk Christian University in the Ukraine, I taught a family living section for college students who had come from all over the former USSR. When I asked them to write a family history, a large percentage of the students—if not the majority—told about being beaten or severely punished as children. One young man told me that when he was growing up in Moscow, it was accepted practice for parents to periodically beat their children. He said his parents actually believed that whether or not a child had misbehaved, occasionally thrashing a child was good for him or her.

Does the Bible differentiate between discipline and punishment? Yes, clearly it does. The word *paideuo,* usually translated "to discipline" in the New Testament, is much different from the word *paio,* which means "to strike, hit, or wound." The latter word was used of Jesus Christ when He was scourged by the Roman soldiers. *Paideuo* can also be translated "to instruct, train, correct, or give guidance to," such as a father's guidance of his son, or an instructor's correction of a student.

When a child misbehaves, should he be punished or disciplined? Not simply splitting hairs over semantics, I must point out that there is a vast difference between the two. The emotion generating punishment is anger, while the emotion prompting discipline is love.

The concept of biblical discipline is to get the message across that an individual's behavior is wrong and unacceptable, and in the future this kind of conduct will not be allowed. Some parents, not knowing the difference, do punish their children; but far wiser is the parent who learns that discipline is both necessary and effective.

Discipline balanced with love is a winning combination. It reinforces the learning process that produces well-adjusted individuals. Discipline begins with parents who are in control and who convey the importance of self-control to their kids. The Bible is clear that God disciplines those whom He loves, bringing us back to the path from which we have strayed. The godly parent who loves his child and disciplines him or her in love is modeling this great truth.

May God deliver us from punishment, but may He give parents enough love to learn to discipline. There is a great difference between the two.

RESOURCE READING: Hebrews 12:1–13

November 22

TO DEPART. . .
AND TO BE WITH CHRIST

When Jesus was crucified, one of the thieves put to death with Him cried out, "Lord, remember me when you come into your kingdom!" And Jesus responded, "Today you shall be with me in Paradise" (see Luke 23:42–43). But scores of people are not sure they can apply that to their personal lives. Are they to believe that when God's child draws his last breath here on Earth, his next one is going to be drawn in heaven?

Thirty years after the crucifixion, Paul addressed the same issue in his letter to the church at Philippi. He told them he had a dilemma. He said he wanted to depart and to be with Christ, but remaining in the flesh to help the church was more important or necessary.

What did Paul really mean? Obviously the word *depart* is a euphemism meaning "to die." Understanding how the word was used in the first century gives some insight into Paul's intent. First, the word was used of a boat that was loosed from its moorings in a harbor and gradually began to drift to sea. Then it was used of a door that was flung open with force. Another picture is seen in the following vignette: A person goes to a dinner party at the home of a friend. It's a great evening and no one really wants to leave. The guests stand around and talk, then finally they depart and go home. The same word for *depart* is used in all of these pictures.

The way Paul worded his letter, it is obvious that the action of leaving and arriving take place simultaneously. Leaving the earth means arriving in the presence of Jesus Christ.

That's good news, friend. There's no period of waiting, no purgatory that must first consume your dross. When you are God's child, when your time has come and you leave us here, your next breath is the cleanest, purest air your lungs have ever experienced.

To the Corinthians Paul writes, "We are always confident and know that as long as we are at home in the body we are away from the Lord. . ." Then he adds, "We. . . prefer to be away from the body and at home with the Lord" (2 Corinthians 5:6, 8).

How you die isn't as important as where you are headed after you die. Never forget it.

RESOURCE READING: 2 Corinthians 5:1–10

NEAR-DEATH EXPERIENCE

In 1975, Raymond Moody, a medical doctor, published a book titled *Life After Life.* It chronicled the experiences of 150 people who had died or been near death and then came back. Moody, who was the first to use the expression "near-death experience," tells how these experiences forever changed the lives of the people who had them.[1]

In some cases, as death approached, individuals had flashbacks to childhood. Others saw Jesus standing in the shadows. Some saw light—a brilliant, vivid light that they believed was God—at the end of a long, dark tunnel. But no matter how their experiences differed, their lives changed. They became "more altruistic, less materialistic, and more loving."

Researchers say that a lack of oxygen or the release of enzymes in the brain can trigger flashes of light or duplicate the experiences that some have described. But individuals who have stared death in the face could never be convinced that what they saw was the result of oxygen depletion.

Diane Komp, a pediatric oncologist at Yale, described herself as an atheist until she began working with children who were dying with leukemia and cancer. As she heard dying children tell of choruses of angels and seeing Jesus, she did an about-face. "It changed my view of spiritual matters. Call it a conversion," she said, adding, "I came away convinced that these are real spiritual experiences."

When Paul wrote to the Philippians, he described death and entrance to heaven as departing here and "being with Christ." Had Paul himself had a near-death experience? Was he describing something he had encountered personally? Perhaps! We do know that on several occasions, Paul was knocked about and left more nearly dead than alive.

I'm convinced that some who approach death see what

we who remain on this side cannot see. My mother was one of them. Three days before her death, she spoke of seeing Jesus standing in the shadows saying, "Not yet, Ruby." Three days later, her eyes focused with clarity and I asked, "Mother, what do you see?" The question was never answered, but I'm convinced she was seeing the Savior.

RESOURCE READING: 2 Corinthians 12:1–10

November 24

BUILDING YOUR FAITH

O ver the years, I've learned two important things about my spiritual heroes: They are just as human as I am, and they don't quit when they stumble or get knocked down. Do you want to know how to grow spiritually? Then today's guidelines are just for you.

Guideline #1: Read the fine print. God's Word defines your relationship to Him. Read your Bible with a marking pen or pencil. Underline. Highlight. Put your name on the page and believe what it says.

Guideline #2: Reflect on what you have read. You may need to have a talk with yourself. There's a great deal of difference between knowing your inadequacies and groveling in your failures. Three times in the New Testament we are told that God doesn't play favorites. What God has done for others, He will do for you.

Guideline #3: Rethink your game plan. Ask yourself, "What has God done for me in the past?" Use that as a building block to increase your faith. When David faced Goliath, he reminded himself of several previous encounters with enemies, and then he said, "God will give me this Philistine as well." That's the kind of encounter you need.

Guideline #4: Retrench. One of our greatest failures, I am convinced, based on the letters I've received, is that we quit too soon. We give up on marriages, ourselves, and even on God before we have waited patiently for Him to bring about the very answer we have asked for.

In warfare, when the enemy starts lobbing grenades and the shells start exploding, soldiers dig in. It's amazing how fast foxholes get dug when it's survival that counts. You need to do the same thing when you discover that the enemy knows your position and starts lobbing grenades in your path. May I say it again: Read the fine print, reflect on what God has done in your life, rethink your game plan, and retrench. Those simple guidelines are the keys to building your faith in God and His power.

RESOURCE READING: Ephesians 6

November 25

LOVE—TRUE OR FALSE?

How much do you know about love? Try your wit on the following statements.

1. True or False: "The most important thing, when it comes to love and happiness, is marrying the right person."

False. Sociologists say that choosing the right mate is only one factor; it's even more important to be the right mate yourself. Remember what Jesus says, "In everything, do to others what you would have them do to you, for this sums up the Law and the Prophets" (Matthew 7:12).

2. True or False: "Few people agree on what romantic love is."

False. A study done by one university shows that most men and women agree on the meaning of love. Paul writes, "Love suffers long and is kind. Love envies not; does not make itself proud, is not puffed up. Love doesn't make a fool of anyone. It is not selfish or irritable. . . . Love bears all things. It believes all things, it endures all things" (1 Corinthians 13:4–7, author's paraphrase).

3. True or False: "The strong, silent man has the inside track in matters of love."

False. Communication is paramount if a marriage is to succeed. The wife who talks incessantly and the husband who never talks both handicap their chances of a successful marriage. Communication involves the sharing of two lives—the joys as well as the heartaches.

4. True or False: "If a couple is really in love, the success of their marriage is assured."

False. Sociologist Judson T. Landis concludes from his extensive research that just because two people are in love does not mean that they can live together happily. Love is a strong ingredient in the relationship of a successful marriage, but it takes more than love.

5. Here's an important one. True or False: "The family that prays together stays together."

True. Statistics indicate that the divorce rate is substantially lower among couples who worship and pray together. God has endowed us with a human soul and put love in our hearts to bind us to one another. When two people recognize God and His direction in their lives, their chances of a successful marriage climb substantially. Love—poetry or power? Which is it in your life?

RESOURCE READING: 1 Corinthians 13

November 26

YOU CAN'T OUTGIVE THE LORD. OH YEAH?

Don Phinney was convinced that you can't outgive God. One day he invited me over to see his "books." When I sat down, he went to the kitchen cupboard and brought out a financial ledger—almost four inches thick. Setting the book on the table, Don said, "For forty years, I've kept books with God, and I've proved you can't outgive the Lord." Turning to the front of the book, he pointed out neat columns of figures. "Here," he said, "this was my income, and this is a record of my giving." Pointing to the next set of figures, he said, "When I increased my giving, my income rose."

Then he got to the real reason he had invited me to his home. At the time, I was Don's pastor, and our church was filled with young couples with small children. For most of them, surviving financially was a higher priority than giving to the church. "Tell you what I want you to do," Don continued, "I'd like for you to challenge our people to tithe for one year. At the end of that time, if they can honestly say that God didn't bless them for it, I'll personally give them $1,000."

With an offer like that, how can you lose? I gave the challenge to the church, and a considerable number of couples decided to take it up. What happened? At the end of the year, some said, "We no sooner began giving when we got a salary increase." Others said, "No salary increase for us, but we ended the year with money in the bank—something that has never happened before." Others commented, "Our old car ran great. Never broke down at all, whereas before we were always taking it to the shop for repairs." For three years running, Don extended the offer, and no one ever stepped forward to claim the $1,000.

The church does us a great disservice if it fails to bring us into confrontation with what God says about our resources and our giving. We're the ultimate losers, not the church. Jesus was right. God blesses us with the currency of heaven.

RESOURCE READING: Psalm 1

November 27

THINKING THE THOUGHTS OF JESUS CHRIST

When an actor plays the part of another person, he tries to get inside the person's skin, to saturate himself with the person's thought processes, and to the extent possible become that person. Can that really be done? Yes, say many professional actors.

Charlton Heston says that portraying Moses in the film *The Ten Commandments* greatly influenced his life. "Playing Moses," he said, "marked my life." To prepare for the role, Heston went to the Negev Desert of Israel, walked with the burning winds blowing sand in his face and read what Moses wrote. He tried to think as Moses thought and to feel what he felt.

When Paul wrote to the Philippians, he urged them to strive to do the same thing with Jesus Christ. "Your attitude should be the same as that of Christ Jesus," says Philippians 2:5. Actually, the text can be translated, "Each of you should think the thoughts of Jesus Christ."

How do you think the thoughts of Jesus? Is that really possible? Like an actor preparing for a role, the first step is to learn everything there is to know about the person you seek to emulate. In the case of Jesus, the Bible reveals His life and character to us. Next, you can talk to Him and ask Him to reveal Himself to you. Can you learn to see life from His perspective. Yes, you can.

Thinking the thoughts of Jesus Christ is bound to revolutionize your life, because His thinking is so different. His attitudes and values are different. Even His boundaries are different.

When I peer into the dim, misty future, it seems uncertain and obscure. What I have—what I can put my hands on materially—seems more important in my life. I know that I shouldn't worry, yet bills have to be paid, and I must put bread on the table.

Christ's vision pierces the gloom. He tells me to seek Him first and His righteousness. He knows that heaven is a reality, because He's been there. When He walked this earth, He knew where He was going. May God help me to have the same attitude.

A closing thought: Have you ever noticed how people who have lived together for many years tend to think alike? Apply that insight to thinking the thoughts of Jesus.

RESOURCE READING: Philippians 2:1–11

WHY NOT RIP 'EM OFF?

A bus carrying five passengers was hit by a car, but by the time the police arrived, no fewer than fourteen bystanders had boarded the bus and began complaining of whiplash and moderate to severe back injuries. Amazing, isn't it, what some people will do when there's money involved.

What ever happened to honesty and decency? What one person chooses not to do because of moral conviction, others do with impunity. After all, morality is a personal matter, right?

"As far as I'm concerned, there's nothing wrong with what I've done!" How many times have you heard that line? In other words, I'll decide what's moral and what's acceptable. The problem is that our standards have become fuzzy. Morality no longer has a straight, hard edge to it. It blends from black to white with a hundred shades of gray. "No moral absolutes" is the cry of the free spirit today.

Take, for example, the issue of adultery. In every society known to anthropologists, commitment in marriage has been expected. Though it doesn't always turn out this way, most men and women enter into a marriage contract with the expectation of a committed, monogamous relationship. Men and women vow to keep themselves exclusively for the other until death do them part. From the days of Nathaniel Hawthorne's *Scarlet Letter* to the present, adultery has not been an extracurricular activity that society has embraced with open arms.

Changing the benchmarks of what is decent, proper, and right may make you more comfortable, but if there were ever reasons why God and society agreed that honesty, morality, integrity, and commitment are important, then something is wrong—gravely wrong—when we lower the standards.

May God help us to regain some sanity before another

generation self-destructs. I can't help thinking of the cry of Jeremiah who said, "This is what the LORD says: 'Stand at the crossroads and look; ask for the ancient paths, ask where the good way is, and walk in it, and you will find rest for your souls.' But you said, 'We will not walk in it' " (Jeremiah 6:16). Some things never change.

RESOURCE READING: Jeremiah 6

November 29

CHRIST'S COMING

I recently opened my file marked "Second Coming" and noticed the lead article, written in September, 1994. It begins, "Like many of us, when Harold Camping looks ahead to October, he sees no World Series. Unlike many of us, he also sees no world." The story goes on to tell how Camping predicted the return of Jesus Christ by October 1994. Of course, this did not happen.

The next item was a letter from a *Guidelines* listener, which reads, "God has moved me to write. . .to announce the second coming of Jesus Christ, which will occur on the day of Pentecost in 1986." Of course, he was wrong.

The sad thing about predictions gone wrong is that people tend to scoff and ignore the truth that Christ is returning.

The apostle Peter gives us some wise words of counsel about end times. He writes, "First off, you need to know that in the last days, mockers are going to have a heyday. Reducing everything to the level of their puny feelings, they'll mock, 'So what's happened to the promise of his Coming? Our ancestors are dead and buried, and everything's going on just as it has from the first day of creation. Nothing's changed.' They conveniently forget that long ago all the galaxies and this very planet were brought into existence out of watery chaos by God's word" (2 Peter 3:3–5 TM).

Have you despaired of the return of Jesus Christ? Have you become so busy and so involved in keeping your head above water that you no longer believe this great event may well take place in our generation? You believe it theoretically, but you've filed the truth away in your memory, where it ceases to be very meaningful.

When I went into China for the first time in 1979 and met with brothers and sisters who had been victims of tremendous persecution at the hands of the Communists, I realized they held firmly to the comfort of the fact they would meet Christ—either in death or at His return. "So Christ was once offered to bear the sins of many; and unto them that look for him shall he appear the second time without sin unto salvation" (Hebrews 9:28 KJV). The hope is still as valid as the Word of God. Don't forget it.

RESOURCE READING: 2 Peter 3

November 30

COULD IT BE IN THIS YEAR?

O ur children today are being robbed! A generation ago, the hope of Christ's return was a vital truth that was part of the gospel. But today, it seems that only religious nuts believe that Christ will return.

Check the index of a hymnal and notice how many songs speak of the hope of Christ's return. Whoops! I almost forgot that many churches no longer use hymnals. They have been replaced with contemporary music, overhead transparencies, and celluloids.

For several hundred years, Christians around the world used printed hymnals or hymnbooks containing worship songs and hymns. The two most important books to Christians used to be their Bibles and their hymnals. For many years, little books about the size of a New Testament were printed, containing only the words to hymns—no music. I own several of these, and it is a delight to go back through the old leather-bound volumes and read the words of hymns.

All over the world, the church down through the centuries has sung of the Lord's return and held to that hope in times of difficulty and suffering. It was a great truth based upon the words of Jesus, who said, "I will come again." They believed it, and that truth was a joy and a comfort.

A new millennium is unfolding. Many see prophetic significance in all of this, which may or may not be warranted from a biblical perspective. Yet the fact is that Christ will return, and His return should be a joy that we eagerly anticipate. Scripture says that this certainty should also affect the way we live.

"Our citizenship is in heaven," Paul writes to the Philippians, "and we eagerly await a Savior from there, the Lord Jesus Christ, who, by the power that enables him to bring everything under his control, will transform our lowly bodies so that they will be like his glorious body" (Philippians 3:20–21).

I have no axe to grind with contemporary music, but I see little focus on the reality of Christ's return. If you are a parent, make sure that your children grow up with the great hymns. They are a vital part of our faith.

RESOURCE READING: 1 Corinthians 15

December 1

IT'S THE MONTH OF DECEMBER AGAIN

It's December 1 and Christmas is only twenty-four days away. Suppose this Christmas season, we decide to do things differently. Two simple words can make the difference: Plan ahead! Interested in making this Christmas count? Then consider some of the following ideas:

Idea #1: Get out your calendar and do some strategic planning. Today! Not next week! Include church services and at least one special Christmas concert.

Idea #2: If you have children, make sure they get the facts straight about Christmas. It's amazing how difficult it is for kids to separate myth from reality, Santa Claus from the baby born in a manger. Set up a nativity scene in your home.

Idea #3: Plan a project that expands your horizons. How about adopting a needy family this Christmas? Get everyone involved. Remember, Christmas involves giving—not receiving.

Idea #4: Have your kids make a shoe box gift for a needy child. Include some of the items that your children would like to receive. Let the kids earn some money to pay for this project.

Idea #5: Do something for someone that requires your participation, not simply a bit of charity. Do you know anyone who is elderly and in need of help? Paint the kitchen, clean out the garage, shovel snow. It isn't difficult to find a need.

Idea #6: Evaluate your shopping and spending. An amazing amount of money is spent out of guilt. It's great that your heart is touched by the season, but spending money you don't have doesn't make sense.

January or February will bring a day of reckoning.
Idea #7: Plan a birthday party for Jesus. You would be amazed at the number of people who do not connect the birth of Jesus Christ with December 25. Counter that by hosting a dinner party, or a kid's Christmas party, and at the event take time to read the account of Christ's birth from Scripture and explain what the gift of God's Son means in relation to the season.

Everything I've mentioned requires planning, which is why I'm prompting you to make the days count and to make this Christmas the most meaningful one of your life.

RESOURCE READING: Galatians 4:1–7

December 2

THE COST OF FORGIVENESS

The most striking Christmas card I have received in years came this past season. The headline read: "History Is Crowded With Men Who Would Be Gods." Underneath were the images of nine powerful historical figures: Alexander the Great, Tutankhamen, Julius Caesar, Maharishi Yogi, Adolf Hitler, Vladimir Lenin, Napoleon Bonaparte, Gautama Buddha, and Mao Tse-tung. Who would deny that these individuals aspired to reign as gods with supreme power and authority?

What made the card unique was the message inside, which read: "But Only One God Who Would Be Man." Underneath was a reproduction of a Dutch painting depicting the infant Jesus in the manger with Mary and Joseph looking on.

The record of Scripture is profound and clear. God the Father loved the world so much that He gave His only Son. Think about that for a moment. God, the Son, willingly laid aside His role as God, gave up His seat at the right hand of the Father, to be born of human flesh. God became man, completely human, completely normal.

It is here that the whole issue stretches our understanding, because being completely human and completely God means something marvelous, something supernatural. Paul explains how Jesus laid aside His exercise of deity to become man in Philippians 2.

Was Jesus like us in the sense that He was tempted and torn, at times, between right and wrong? The record says He was in every way tempted as we are, yet without sin. As man He was capable of sinning, but He was also able not to sin—which gives us hope as well.

Many men would be gods, but only one God chose to be man. Amazing, yet true. John adds that "whoever believes in him shall not perish [or be lost] but have eternal life" (John 3:16). That's the bottom line.

RESOURCE READING: John 1:1–12

December 3

AN EYE FOR AN EYE

"An eye for an eye, a tooth for a tooth!" Seems pretty straightforward, doesn't it? If someone hurts you, pay them back in kind, right? You might be surprised to discover that "an eye for an eye" doesn't mean everything you think it means.

In the book of Exodus, Moses gave instruction regarding the compensation that could be demanded when someone injured or killed your animal or servant. He said, "But if there is serious injury, you are to take life for life, eye for eye, tooth for tooth, hand for hand, foot for foot, burn for burn, wound for wound, bruise for bruise" (Exodus 21:23–25). Taken at face value it sounds like Moses is saying, "Sock it to 'em," but the Israelites would have interpreted his words in an entirely different context.

The pagan laws of the day often allowed far greater compensation than the crime actually merited. For example, if someone stole a loaf of bread, the law could exact the dismembering of a hand, or a finger or two, forever maiming the individual. The harshness of the penalty was far greater than the crime. In contrast, Moses was saying, "Look, the price exacted can be no greater than the crime or wrong itself." It was never intended to be an endorsement of vengeance or violence.

Jesus approached the issue from an entirely different perspective. He said, "You have heard that it was said, 'Eye for eye, and tooth for tooth.' But I tell you, Do not resist an evil person. If someone strikes you on the right cheek, turn to him the other also. And if someone wants to sue you and take your tunic, let him have your cloak as well. If someone forces you to go one mile, go with him two miles" (Matthew 5:38–41).

Does Jesus mean that you are to lie down and let everyone walk over you? I don't think so. But I do believe He is saying, "Make peace with your enemy, pay your debts, go the extra mile, and don't live with violence and anger in your heart."

Mao Tse-tung used to say that power comes out of a gun barrel. But Jesus says that real power—the kind that conquers all kinds of evil—comes from a heart of love.

RESOURCE READING: Matthew 5:21–42

December 4

TRUSTING WHEN YOU CANNOT
SEE THE FATHER'S HAND

A short distance from Greenock, Scotland, is the little village where John McNeil grew up. To supplement the family's income, John worked summers for a farmer, whose farm was located in a valley a short distance from their home. John would rise early, walk through a ravine or mountain pass and down into the valley for the day's work.

One evening, as John was returning home, he heard footsteps behind him as he approached the pass. Knowing that robbers sometimes hung out there, he walked faster. The faster he walked, the more rapid became the footsteps behind him. His hands grew clammy from perspiration and his heart beat more rapidly. Finally, a familiar voice pierced the darkness, "John, is that you? I'm your father, and I've come to walk with you!"

What comfort and assurance! "I'm your father; I've come to walk with you!" To help us understand the nature of our relationship with Him, God chose the term "father" to give us an example. Imperfect, yes, because so many have fathers who have disappointed them, yet in that relationship I see qualities, which, when sifted from human weakness, help us understand how much our heavenly Father cares for us as His children. A young woman, who had been often abused by her father, once told me, "If God was anything like my natural father, I would want nothing to do with Him," and understandably so, but God's nature assures us of His love, care, and protection, often when we least see or understand it.

Have you ever had the experience of taking your child to the doctor, and holding the child firmly as the doctor's needle pricked his finger to draw blood? The searching, questioning eyes of the child seem to ask, "Why do you allow me such pain if you love me?" Yet the child clings to his father, even when his understanding is imperfect. In the same manner, we must trust the loving heart of our heavenly Father.

We must never doubt our Father's love and concern when difficulty and hardship come our way. Through these trials we must still hear His voice saying, "It's your Father; I've come to walk with you."

RESOURCE READING: Hebrews 12:1–9

December 5

CREATION BY CHANCE OR CHOICE?

George Gallup, the famous pollster, once remarked, "I could prove God statistically. Take the human body alone. The chance that all the functions of the individual would just happen is a statistical monstrosity."

Just for a moment think of the intricacies of the human body. Let's start with the brain. Ten thousand thoughts pass in and out of your mind every day. Your brain has storage vaults containing bits of information recorded years before, yet the average person uses less than 10 percent of his brain.

Now consider the heart. This muscle the size of a man's fist pumps blood through miles of veins, arteries, and capillaries. Your body is an amazing creation. Your body constantly replaces its cells with new cells on a seven-year cycle. As time goes on and you grow older, the process slows until it eventually stops.

Even more amazing is the fact that every individual—out of the 6.5 billion on Earth—is unique, unduplicated, and without equal. No one on Earth is exactly like you. No one else sees through your eyes or feels what you feel.

Have you ever tried to think through this business of life? How did we get here and where are we headed? Where do we go after death? Were we created by an act of God or by chance?

Suppose we contend that humankind was created by chance. If so, then why death? What lies beyond the grave? What is the purpose of living and life itself? These questions have no answers if man was created by chance. But if God created man, as the Bible simply states, there is an answer to the question, "Where did I come from, why am I here, and what is beyond the grave?"

God tells us in His Word that we were created in His image, physically, mentally, and spiritually. It also tells us that God's creation was marred by the effects of sin, which caused the confusion, the estrangement, the separation from the presence of a loving God. Yet the Bible also tells me how I can be personally related to God through the person of His Son, Jesus Christ. Are you interested in learning what life is all about? Then read the Bible and discover guidelines for living.

RESOURCE READING: Psalm 19

December 6

A THIRST AFTER THE ALMIGHTY

In the Judean wilderness, David cried out, "O God, you are my God, earnestly I seek you; my soul thirsts for you, my body longs for you, in a dry and weary land where there is no water" (Psalm 63:1). Hunted by Saul, David was tired, no doubt wondering if he would ever be able to go home to Bethlehem and sleep without concern for his safety. Yet he did not say that he longed for the comforts of home. No, he cried out that his soul was thirsty for the Lord.

Do you have times in your life when you grow weary of the battle and your soul cries out to God? Do you long to know Him in a deeper and more intimate way?

How does God satisfy that longing? No doubt you have discovered when you are really thirsty, sugary products just don't satisfy. You don't want soft drinks or syrupy juices, you want water—crystal clear, pure, and cool. Nothing satisfies on a hot day like a refreshing drink of water.

If you want to satisfy the deep longing in your heart for God, get rid of the sugary substitutes—the claptrap of religious ceremony and the tinsel of religious experiences. Immerse yourself in the purity of the Word that lets you know and experience God.

To know God intimately, insulate yourself from the noise that keeps you from hearing His voice. When I was in Colorado, I found an outcrop in the Rocky Mountains, just below the timberline, that gave me a majestic view of stunning scenery below. Several afternoons I sat there with an open Bible and thought of God and His working in my life. We need those quiet times, those personal, intimate times without telephones, little children's voices, and the noise of traffic.

Tell God about the deep longing in your heart to know Him and to feel His might and power. In another psalm, David cries, "I reach out for you. I thirst for you as parched land thirsts for rain" (Psalm 143:6 TLB).

"On the last and greatest day of the Feast of tabernacles, Jesus stood and said in a loud voice, 'If anyone is thirsty, let him come to me and drink'" (John 7:37). Only God could say that.

RESOURCE READING: Psalm 63

INFAMOUS DECEMBER 7

Ask a youngster today what's so special about December 7, and he's apt to give you an expressionless stare. But ask your grandfather what happened fifty-nine years ago today and he'll be quick to remember December 7, 1941, when Japanese bombers attacked Pearl Harbor and brought the United States into World War II.

What many people don't know is that simultaneous with the attack on Pearl Harbor, Japanese planes swooped across the island of Luzon in the Philippines and dropped bombs on John Hay Air Base, an American installation, thus bringing the war to the Philippine Islands at the same time.

There's a cemetery in Manila where more than 50,000 Americans and Filipinos who fought gallantly against the Japanese are buried. As I walked along the rows of white crosses and Stars of David with the names of thousands of men on them—mostly young men, I asked myself, "Have we really learned anything from the horrors of war?"

Man's inhumanity to his fellowman seems to be endless. What's the problem? Simply put, the human heart is the center of the problem. "Where do wars and fights come from among you?" asks James, in the New Testament book that bears his name. He then answers his rhetorical question, saying, "Do they not come from your desires for pleasure that war in your members? You lust and do not have. You murder and covet and cannot obtain. You fight and war. Yet you do not have because you do not ask" (James 4:1–2 NKJV).

I'd like to believe that our world leaders have learned something of the tragedy and senselessness of war, but I am unconvinced. I would hope that the United Nations might be a forum where international conflicts can be resolved, but the reality is that until Jesus Christ establishes His kingdom, when men beat swords into plowshares and we no longer lust after the territory and resources belonging to another, there will be wars and rumors of wars.

It is well to pause and remember the tremendous cost—both individually and collectively—that was sustained on December 7, and pray that our world will never see it repeated.

RESOURCE READING: Isaiah 2

December 8

CHRISTMAS AND DEPRESSION

Have you ever wondered why December is a tough month for many people? Suicides, violence, drunk driving, carousing, and depression all increase during December. Why is it a down time for so many? Perhaps it's the pain of loneliness during the holiday season, which should be a time of joy and celebration.

What can you do to turn things around? Try these guidelines for making this month meaningful:

Guideline #1: Get your focus right. You've got to break out of the "poor me" mode and reflect on what Christ's coming means to you. Maybe you're alone. Have you ever pondered the loneliness that Christ faced—the times when the disciples didn't understand, the times when He prayed as others slept, the times He felt very much misunderstood?

Guideline #2: Get out of yourself. Nothing is smaller than the package of your own little world. Drowning grief has never brought happiness to anyone. Alcohol may numb the brain, but it can't overcome loneliness. If you are single, you may be bothered by families going shopping or celebrating. Hey, look around you. There are other singles who may be just as lonely as you. Why not invite someone for dinner?

Guideline #3: Do something for someone else. At Christmas, missions, welfare centers, halfway houses, and churches with outreaches are in need of people to help minister to others. Volunteer at a hospital. Serve Christmas dinner at a mission. Call your pastor and offer to work in the nursery if you can't have your grandchildren in your home because they live somewhere else. Give a gift of love to someone. Find a child, an elderly person, a prisoner, and do something kind.

Guideline #4: Find a friend in Jesus. Instead of sitting home and struggling with loneliness and depression, go to church. Let the music of the season thrill your soul. Take your Bible and read the Christmas story. Study the magnificent Old Testament prophecies that were fulfilled when Jesus was born at Bethlehem. See how God's concern spans the centuries and touches the lonely, the depressed, and the suffering. Instead of this being a down month for you, turn it into an up time. Whatever you do, get beyond the door of your own existence. You'll be glad you did.

RESOURCE READING: John 1:17

December 9

GOING THE SECOND MILE

Brother Rufus was a humble monk. When a misunderstanding developed between him and a friend, he knew he had to confront the individual. When his initial bid to bring harmony was unsuccessful, he knew he needed to bring another person along with him. But who?

If he brought a friend of his, the person with whom he was in conflict would think that the two had ganged up on him. "I know what I will do," he said, "I will take *his* best friend along." Rufus resisted the temptation to tell the friend what the disagreement was about so as not to prejudice the man. What happened? Forgiveness and reconciliation resulted.

The following guidelines will help you go the second mile.

Guideline #1: Get rid of your bitterness. Focus on the value of your friendship and the importance of maintaining the quality of your relationship.

Guideline #2: Realize that God is on your side when you go the second mile. God has been in the business of reconciliation for a long time. After all, He was the One who sent His son to bring reconciliation between Himself and mankind. God always goes the second mile, pursuing our wayward spirits, inviting us back to the conference table of grace.

Guideline #3: Be willing to take the first step. "It was his fault as much as mine." That's not the issue. Someone has to take the first step. Be that person. Chances are that your adversary would also like to resolve this issue.

Guideline #4: Assume responsibility. Leave your shovel at home. Don't dig up the past. Don't focus on who caused the problem; focus on a solution. Simply begin by saying, "Look, I value my friendship with you, and I want us to resolve this problem."

Guideline #5: Pursue peace. That's the advice of

Scripture, which says, "Make every effort to live in peace with all men and to be holy; without holiness no one will see the Lord" (Hebrews 12:14).

Reconciliation is more than just forgetting the past and getting on with your life. It's reconstructing the relationship, rebuilding the household of trust, and letting God help you put the pieces back together with love and forgiveness.

Reconciliation is well worth the cost of humility.

RESOURCE READING: Matthew 18:15–18

December 10

IT'S MINE!

Have you ever seen the Toddler's Creed? It reads, "If I want it, it's mine. If I give it to you and change my mind later, it's mine. If I can take it away from you, it's mine. If I had it a little while ago, it's mine. If we are building something together, all the pieces are mine. If it looks just like mine, it's mine." Any parent who has ever tried to mediate between siblings has to smile.

That same underlying attitude of selfishness—"I want it; it's mine!" is the greatest foe of happiness in life and marriages. Others might say that the greatest problem in marriage is infidelity, lack of communication, finances, or sexual problems, but I think it all boils down to selfishness. No matter what the symptom, the bottom line is the same as in the Toddler's Creed: "I want my needs satisfied first!"

There is only one thing that can change selfishness to generosity. The only chemical strong enough to erode the forces of selfishness is the grace of God. "Therefore, if anyone is in Christ, he is a new creation; the old has gone, the new has come!" wrote Paul (2 Corinthians 5:17). The grace of God changes dispositions, but it isn't always a one-shot, immediate sort of thing. Sanctification is an ongoing work of grace as God keeps chipping off the rough edges, reminding us of our brashness, our rudeness, and our selfishness.

Overcoming the gravitational pull of our old selfish natures isn't accomplished by a single act of generosity. It's a lifestyle that is marked by humility, an understanding of who you really are, and the desire to let God love people through you.

Paul wrote about his young friend Timothy, saying, "I have no one else like him, who takes a genuine interest in your welfare. For everyone looks out for his own interests, not those of Jesus Christ" (Philippians 2:20–21). Thank God for the Timothys, those who serve in love, touching the hearts and lives of others.

There is hope, friend. A bumper sticker reads, "Practice random acts of kindness!" Why not consistent acts of kindness? By extending kindness to you, I receive joy and satisfaction in return. That's a fact.

RESOURCE READING: Matthew 5:43–48

December 11

"I FORGIVE YOU!"

On June 8, 1972, American airman John Plummer was ordered to drop napalm on a Vietnamese village. Plummer was told that there were no civilians in the village, but the next day, he learned otherwise. In a military newspaper, he saw a photo of two children running down the road, screaming and crying. One of them, a nine-year-old-girl, was naked. Her clothing had been burned off her body by the jellied gasoline that had been dropped the day before. Plummer was absolutely devastated.

One picture, they say, is worth a thousand words. In this case, it was worth a thousand nightmares. Though Plummer tried to suppress the image, he couldn't. It devastated his life. Anne Gearan, writing for the Associated Press, said, "For decades, Plummer struggled with his conscience. He drank and divorced. He searched for God." And then God found him. In 1990, John Plummer was converted to Jesus Christ and found God's forgiveness. He said, "I realized I did not have to bear the guilt of my sins—all the hurt I caused other people." He soon gave up his job and became a Methodist pastor.

God had been working on the other side of that photo as well. Pham recovered from the trauma of her experience. Eventually, she, too, became a Christian. The scream that the photo so graphically portrayed became a smile. She married and moved to Canada. In the fall of 1996, Pham spoke at a gathering in Washington, D.C. that John Plummer attended. Following her message, the two met for the first time. When John Plummer stepped forward and said, "I'm so sorry. I'm just so sorry," Pham didn't hesitate. She immediately said, "It's all right. I forgive."

For two hours they talked and cried together, and gradually God began the healing process which only He could perform. The following Sunday, Plummer faced his congregation and told his story. His congregation wept with him.

Today, he still occasionally dreams of that photo, but he says the screams have been silenced. Only the grace of God can bring that kind of healing.

"Father, forgive them," cried Jesus on the cross, "for they know not what they are doing." Can there be a more graphic illustration of the power of forgiveness?

RESOURCE READING: Luke 23:26–43

December 12

THE WAY THAT LEADS TO PEACE

O ne of the early church fathers, Clement of Alexandria, used an interesting expression. He writes of "the path that leads to peace." Though the expression isn't found in the Bible, God tells us hundreds of times that He intends for us to live in peace.

The way that leads to peace. What is it? If peace is your goal, there are four steps, or guidelines, which you must pursue.

Guideline #1: The way that leads to peace is marked by the commitment of two parties who want peace. There are three things you cannot do: Climb a fence that leans toward you. Kiss a girl who leans away from you, and make peace with someone who refuses to negotiate.

When you run up the white flag and indicate that you want peace, it's amazing how often the enemy—not willing to be the first to break ranks—is more than glad to meet you at the peace table.

Guideline #2: The way that leads to peace is marked by the willingness of two individuals to give up their anger and negotiate. Frankly, there are some who enjoy being angry. It allows them to justify their baseness and rottenness. At some point, you must forget who was right and who was wrong. You must consider the benefits of peace to be more worthwhile than the perverse satisfaction of having some justification for your anger.

Guideline #3: The way that leads to peace is marked by the refusal to continue the battle. It's really quite difficult to have a war when nobody wants to fight. There's an old story, well-documented by a variety of sources, which illustrates the point. On Christmas Eve 1914, German and British soldiers were in the trenches facing each other. This was the first Christmas Eve of the war, and neither side was sure if they would fight on Christmas or desist for the day. Finally, British soldiers raised signs in German: "Merry Christmas." Then carols were sung on both sides. Eventually soldiers met in a kind of no-man's-land and exchanged candy and cigarettes. Not until reinforcements were sent in did fighting begin anew.

Guideline #4: The path to peace is marked by goodwill. The path may not be terribly well-worn, but wise are those who travel it.

RESOURCE READING: Hebrews 12

December 13

YOUR PURPOSE IN LIFE

Peter Drucker, a management specialist who works with major corporations, says that you only need to answer two questions to stay on track:

Question #1: What is my business?
Question #2: How is business?

It is amazing how many businesses and individuals start out with focus and purpose and get sidetracked, eventually failing because they lose their direction. In the New

Testament, the Christian life is likened to a race in which the runner fixes his eyes on the Lord and runs patiently, turning neither to the left or the right.

The Old Testament stresses the same thing. Solomon, who knew a lot about human nature, wrote, "Let your eyes look straight ahead, fix your gaze directly before you. Make level paths for your feet and take only ways that are firm. Do not swerve to the right or the left" (Proverbs 4:25–27).

As we approach the end of the year, it's time to take inventory. Remember those resolutions you made at the beginning of the year? What kind of a year has it been for you? Lots of people go through life with no personal goals whatsoever. They take the path of least resistance, making survival their primary objective.

A life of significance means you know what life is about and you go beyond the level of fame, money, or achievement. That's where a spiritual purpose comes into the picture.

Purpose in life must include a relationship with the Creator. Jesus stated the purpose of His life when He said, "The thief's purpose is to steal, kill and destroy. My purpose is to give life in all its fullness" (John 10:10 TLB).

Anyone can see that a lot of the promises of happiness that the world makes are like thieves that take our time, our money, and our joy, but leave us empty and sad. Again Jesus said, "For the Son of Man came to seek and to save what was lost" (Luke 19:10).

What's your level of living, friend? Survival, success, or significance? Do you see a relationship between Christ's coming to Earth and your purpose in life? It's there. It's the Bethlehem connection that can give you a reason for living and make life significant no matter what your income or status.

RESOURCE READING: John 10:1–21

THE INGREDIENTS OF
A PURPOSE-DRIVEN LIFE

W hat drives your life?
"I owe, I owe, so off to work I go," says the message on one bumper sticker. But is debt really the drive shaft of your existence? What are the ingredients of a purpose-driven life? I'm not a philosopher, but when you live long enough and analyze people's mistakes, you form some opinions. You see some who live into their nineties who are bright and cheerful, while others, a third their age, grow bitter and cynical and begin to wither and die. We don't always bury them, but their brains are short-circuited. They are the living dead, who exist, but live for nothing. Theirs is the despair which Solomon talked about when he said, "I declared that the dead, who had already died, are happier than the living who are still alive" (Ecclesiastes 4:2).

The ingredients of a purpose-driven life: 1. Someone to love. 2. Something to do, and 3. Something to hope for. Loving someone helps meet one of your deepest emotional needs. Something to do gives you a sense of purpose, a reason for existing, a cause that goes beyond spending eight or ten hours a day at a job. And something to hope for gives you a connection with tomorrow, which helps you over the rough spots of today.

"OK," you may be thinking, "I agree with those three premises, but how do I get there from here?" For starters, back off from the turmoil of your routine. Sometimes we are so close to things that some space helps us to see things in perspective.

Many people are missing a spiritual dimension in their lives. Acknowledging God brings the desire to reach out in love, even to those who are not very lovable. Serving God gives us a reason for existing and a purpose for doing something well. Our link to God brings the confident assurance that there is more to life than just the immediate. There is a tomorrow, and God is our hope of the future.

The ship drifts when there is no anchor. The traveler without a compass wanders aimlessly, and the pilot who can't find the airport quickly finds himself in distress. That's where the link with the Almighty makes a powerful and stabilizing difference in your life.

RESOURCE READING: Psalm 27

December 15

BUILDING 'EM UP VS.
TEARING 'EM DOWN

Amanda stood with her grandfather, watching the bulldozer dismantle the old Mitton family home. It wasn't that the brick home was falling down from disrepair, or that it had gone hopelessly out of style, but the Mittons were gone, and the neighborhood had changed. A developer had purchased the land and was tearing down the house to build two in its place—hoping to make a tidy sum in the process. Eight-year-old Amanda watched as the powerful machines demolished the structure. "Grandpa," she said, "it takes these guys about ten hours to tear it down, and I bet it took at least ten months to build." Ah, the wisdom of a child.

Amanda was right. Have you ever watched a TV clip of demolition experts bringing down a large building? The technicians plant their dynamite strategically and then with a giant whoosh, the blast goes off and the building is history.

Tearing things down, whether buildings or people, can be done in moments, but the building process takes a long time. Few people ever think through the implication of a one-night stand, a casual fling with someone at the office, or the consequences of saying what immediately comes to your mind. Sure, you can say "I'm sorry" later, or "I really didn't mean what I said," but the damage has been done. Houses and lives can be rebuilt, but never without cost, sometimes great cost.

An unknown author wrote the following: "I stood on the streets of a busy town, watching men tearing a building down. With a 'ho, heave, ho,' and a lusty yell, they swung a beam and a side wall fell. I asked the foreman of the crew, 'Are those men as skilled as those you'd hire if you wanted to build?' 'Ah, no,' he said, 'no, indeed. Just a common laborer is all I need. I can tear down as much in a day or two, as would take skilled men a year to do.' And then I thought as I went on my way, just which of these roles am I trying to play? Have I walked life's road with scriptural care, measuring each deed with rule and square? Or am I of those who roam the town, content with the labor of tearing down?"

RESOURCE READING: Psalm 127

December 16

COMMITMENT

After a revival meeting, a farmer decided to dedicate a section of his farm to the Lord. He chose a piece that was somewhat marshy, but he appeased his conscience.

Shortly thereafter, coal was discovered on the parcel, increasing its value tenfold. The farmer struggled with second thoughts, but said, "God, I gave You the land. I guess You own the coal as well."

The next year he noticed a layer of slime on the Lord's marshy ground. A geologist identified it as oil scum, and an exploratory well brought up black gold. Now the property was worth more than he had ever imagined. Again, he battled his conscience. Surely he was entitled to some of this windfall. Finally he confessed, "Lord, I gave You the land and the coal. I'm giving You the oil as well."

Shortly after oil production began, uranium was discovered near the vein of coal. Now the relatively small plot of land was worth a thousand times more than when the farmer had given it to the Lord. "Lord," he said, "when I gave You the land, I gave You everything on the surface, everything above the surface, and everything beneath the surface. It's Yours, not mine."

Almost every person who says, "I'm Yours, Lord," faces this same issue in one form or another. Two New Testament words—*servant* and *Lord*—define the relationship between a believer and God. Paul called himself a servant of Jesus Christ, and from the moment of his conversion, he considered Jesus Christ to be his Lord.

Under Roman law a servant owned nothing. What he possessed belonged to his master. It was his to use, but never to abuse. When Paul wrote to the Corinthians he said, "Do you not know that your body is a temple of the Holy Spirit. . . ? You are not your own" (1 Corinthians 6:19).

Those last five words, "you are not your own," indicate God's prior claim on those whom He has redeemed. If you have become a Christian, God has a prior claim on your life. When you acknowledge that everything God has given you—your mind, talents, and time—belong to Him, it's amazing what can happen.

RESOURCE READING: 1 Corinthians 6

December 17

THE STEP BEYOND COMMITMENT

William Booth, the founder of the Salvation Army, was once asked, "What's your secret?" Booth thought for a moment and said, "God has had all there was of me!" Few can really say that. One of my spiritual heroes, Dwight L. Moody, could have said the same thing. He wrote, "The world has yet to see a man who is totally dedicated to the cause of Jesus Christ. I will strive to be that man."

"Right," we say to ourselves. More than likely, we can relate to the businessman who approached Moody after a meeting and said, "Mr. Moody, I have turned my business over to God and ever since then, it has gone downhill." Never one to mince words, Moody replied, "Well, if you turned it over to God, what are you worrying about?"

"Yes, but God doesn't pay my bills," you counter, still fearful of what might happen. I'm convinced one of our greatest fears is what might happen if we really turned our lives over to Jesus Christ. You may recognize the force of Paul's words to the Corinthians when he says, "You are not your own, you were bought with a price."

The same word for *bought* was used of slaves who were purchased or redeemed in the marketplace. Paul says we had become slaves to our old nature, to greed, lust, selfishness; but the bondage was broken through the price of Christ's own life on the cross.

What does it mean to commit your life to Jesus? The word *commit* means "to put or place" something. Spiritual commitment, in simple terms, is the recognition that you belong to Jesus Christ and that He is your Lord. It means you are His to use or to put on the shelf; His to touch the lives of thousands or to only bless your family and friends; His to command, whether by sending you through the dark valley or to the heights of the mountains.

When you make this commitment, God's Holy Spirit—God Himself—comes to indwell your body, making it His dwelling place. He gives you guidance and strength, wisdom and direction that you would never have any other way.

Remember what William Booth said: "God has had all

there was of me." Can you say that? If not, what's holding you back?

RESOURCE READING: Proverbs 3

December 18

JUST SIGN ON AND
LET GOD FILL IN THE BLANKS

After his conversion, Paul spent almost ten years of his life in obscurity. Once his sight was restored, he spent three years in the desert, and the next seven years making tents in his hometown of Tarsus. Occupational therapy? Better than that. God was remaking Paul into something He could use. When Paul cried out, "Lord, what will you have me to do?" he wasn't asking for options. He was confirming his commitment.

Everett Howard grew up as a preacher's kid. Still struggling with his life goals after he finished school, he finally decided to commit his life totally to Jesus Christ. He went to the little church his dad pastored, and locked the doors behind him.

Kneeling at the altar, he took a piece of paper and listed everything he was willing to do for God, including being a missionary if God so directed. "When I had finished that well-written page," he said, "I signed my name at the bottom and laid it on the altar. There, alone in the church, I. . . waited for. . .some act of approval from the Lord." But nothing happened. Absolutely nothing.

He prayed again, going over the deal he wanted to make with God. Then it happened. "I felt the voice of God speaking in my heart," he later recounted. "I just felt in my own soul a voice speak so clearly. It said, 'Son, you're going about it wrong. I don't want a consecration like this. Just tear up the paper you've written.'" Everett took his list and wadded it up.

"Then the voice of God seemed to whisper again, 'Son, I want you to take a blank piece of paper and sign your name on the bottom of it, and let Me fill it in.' " And that was exactly what Everett Howard did, and for the next thirty-six years, God filled in that page, one day at a time. When you are committed to God's plan for your life, He'll use you the way He sees best.

RESOURCE READING: Jeremiah 18:1–12

December 19

THE PRINCE OF PEACE

Seven centuries before Jesus was born, Isaiah said that one of His titles would be Prince of Peace; yet Bethlehem has been the scene of strife and bloodshed for years. If you make your way to the Church of the Nativity, the probable site of Jesus' birth, you'll find a fourth-century church, replete with candles, holy water, and centuries of religious trappings including pictures, candles, and other artifacts. A pilgrimage to Israel would be incomplete without a visit to the old church.

Today, Bethlehem is under Palestinian control. Its predominantly non-Jewish population is governed by the Palestinian authority. Outside the ancient church, Palestinian soldiers saunter down through the streets, keeping an eye on the hordes of tourists who disembark from the big buses on Manger Square.

When I was there, I stood in the shadows of the church and tried to soak up the atmosphere. Adjacent to the entrance, loud, raucous music blared from loudspeakers in cafes where local residents drank coffee and some fingered their prayer beads. The walls surrounding the area were covered with graffiti and political messages. Dirty-faced kids who should have been in school were on the streets hawking curios and souvenirs. This was the place where God became flesh and began His thirty-three-year sojourn among us.

This week, we wish each other "peace on Earth." I have no doubt that we are sincere. Yet the strife and pain in our world cries loudly that the message hasn't come through. I can't help wondering how Jesus would respond if he took a taxi from the Tel Aviv airport to Bethlehem, where Mary and Joseph welcomed Him into their hearts and home long ago. What would He say as He walked the streets of His old hometown?

Despite the turmoil in the Middle East, Jesus is still the Prince of Peace! One day He will return and establish His authority, and "of His kingdom there shall be no end."

The world hasn't yet figured it out! Have you? Make Jesus your Lord, and the peace of God which passes understanding shall reign supreme in your heart.

RESOURCE READING: Isaiah 9

December 20

IF YOU HAVEN'T HEARD THE MUSIC

Have you heard the music—the song first sung over the fields of Bethlehem? "Glory to God in the highest, and on earth peace to men on whom his favor rests" (Luke 2:14).

Today, by and large, we've lost the original score. It's

been pushed aside and neglected. But it isn't too late to hear the music.

First, go outside and look up at the starry host of heaven. Out of his experience in a shepherd's field near Bethlehem, David wrote, "The heavens declare the glory of God; the skies proclaim the work of his hands" (Psalm 19:1). You can't gaze upon the stars of heaven without thinking of the hand that put them there.

Now focus your mind on the Bethlehem song—the one the angels sang announcing the birth of Jesus. Here's how Luke recorded this historic event:

"And there were shepherds living out in the fields nearby, keeping watch over their flocks at night. An angel of the Lord appeared to them, and the glory of the Lord shone around them, and they were terrified. But the angel said to them, 'Do not be afraid. I bring you good news of great joy that will be for all the people. Today in the town of David a Savior has been born to you; he is Christ the Lord. This will be a sign to you: You will find a baby wrapped in cloths and lying in a manger.' Suddenly a great company of the heavenly host appeared with the angel, praising God and saying, 'Glory to God in the highest, and on earth peace to men on whom his favor rests'" (Luke 2:8–14).

Sing the tune in your heart. Believe me, it will take you captive and joy will spring up in your soul. "A Savior has been born to you; he is Christ the Lord." Not just another baby, but Christ the Lord, God in the flesh, the joy of heaven who touched our sin-cursed earth to bring the light of heaven into our lives.

If you haven't heard the music, perhaps you haven't been listening. Heads up. Tune in. You can still hear the symphony of joy.

RESOURCE READING: Luke 2:8–20

CHRISTMAS JOY

No emotion is more connected to Christmas than joy—the universal language of an overflowing heart. As we contemplate Christmas, joy should be every person's response to God's great gift.

How do you feel when you give a special gift to your sweetheart, your parents, or the child who wouldn't otherwise receive a Christmas gift? You feel good, right? What you felt was joy. But which was greater? The joy you felt, or the joy in the heart of the person who received the gift?

Though we seldom think about it, there must have been joy in the heart of the Father when He gave heaven's most precious gift: His Son. Angels sang joyfully, and those who heard the song rejoiced with exceeding great joy—the kind that goes to the depth of the soul.

He was a man of sorrows and acquainted with grief, as foretold by Isaiah; but while he lived among us, joy was the strength of Jesus' life. Have you forgotten that Paul tells us the "kingdom of God is. . .joy in the Holy Spirit" (Romans 14:17). The writer of Hebrews says that "for the joy set before him [he] endured the cross" (Hebrews 12:2).

Twice Isaiah says that our response to God's redemption should be to rejoice and even break forth in joyful singing. Here's what he said: "Sing for joy, O heavens, for the LORD has done this; shout aloud, O earth beneath. Burst into song, you mountains, you forests and all your trees, for the LORD has redeemed Jacob, he displays his glory in Israel" (Isaiah 44:23).

By receiving the great gift that brought joy to the heart of the Father, you can begin to catch the joy you have been missing in your life. Joy begins in the person of Jesus Christ. "But to all who received him, he gave the right to become children of God" (John 1:12 TLB). G. K. Chesterton says that "joy. . .is the gigantic secret of the Christian."

Joy in your heart is part of the gift of Christmas. Christmas joy comes from the abiding presence of a living Christ. May it be yours today.

RESOURCE READING: John 1:1–14

December 22

CHRIST'S BIRTH AND PROPHECY

Long about December, magazine articles appear with predictions for the coming year. A few years ago, *Moody* magazine decided to keep track of how many of these "prophecies" came true. They discovered that 97 percent failed to be on target.

God says that the test of a true prophet is quite simple: Do his or her predictions come to pass? Bible scholars count more than 320 amazing Old Testament prophecies, given over hundreds of years, that relate to the birth, life, death, and resurrection of Jesus Christ. Here are several that relate to the nativity:

Amazing prophecy #1: A member of the human race would be the one to deliver the lethal blow to the serpent that led Adam astray. In Genesis 3:15, God tells Eve that her offspring would crush the serpent's head.

Amazing prophecy #2: The deliverer would be a descendant of Jacob, thus bringing the nation of Israel into the picture. Genesis 49:10 says, "The scepter will not depart from Judah, nor the ruler's staff from between his feet, until he comes to whom it belongs and the obedience of the nations is his."

Amazing prophecy #3: The Messiah would be a descendent of David. God promised David: "When your days are over and you rest with your fathers, I will raise up your offspring to succeed you, who will come from your own body, and I will establish his kingdom. He is the one who will build a house for my Name, and I will establish the throne of his kingdom forever" (2 Samuel 7:12–13).

Amazing prophecy #4: The Savior would be born in the city of Bethlehem. Micah 5:2 singles out the little village, and history tells us he was right on. The story of how Mary and Joseph were forced to journey seventy miles from Nazareth to Bethlehem near the end of her pregnancy is amazing in itself.

Amazing prophecy #5: The Savior of the world would be conceived of the Holy Spirit and born of a virgin. Isaiah 7:14 says, "Therefore the Lord himself will give you a sign: The virgin will be with child and will give birth to a son, and will call him Immanuel."

What are the chances that all five events would happen as foretold? Yet they did.

RESOURCE READING: Isaiah 7– 9

December 23

THE LAWS OF
PROBABILITY AND CHRISTMAS

As a parent-to-be, have you ever tried to figure out exactly when your child would arrive? Your doctor may have given you an approximate date, but pinpoint accuracy is pretty rare.

The countdown the original Christmas when Jesus was born to a Jewish maiden, was awesome and amazing. Looking back from our present-day vantage point, we can see how the prophecies that foretold the Messiah's birth begin to narrow down like the concentric circles of a target, with each one getting smaller and more specific, eventually coming together at the precise time of Jesus' birth.

Paul, in his letter to the Galatians, puts these prophecies in perspective. He wrote, "But when the fulness of the time was come, God sent forth his Son, made of a woman, made under the law" (Galatians 4:4 KJV).

In order for Jesus to be born in Bethlehem, Joseph and Mary were forced to take a long and unwanted journey from Nazareth where they resided to Joseph's family hometown of Bethlehem. Here's the story behind the story: "In those days Caesar Augustus issued a decree that a census should be taken of the entire Roman world. (This was the first census that took place while Quirinius was governor of Syria.) And everyone went to his own town to register. So Joseph also went up from the town of Nazareth in Galilee to Judea, to Bethlehem the town of David, because he belonged to the house and line of David. He went there to register with Mary, who was pledged to be married to him and was expecting a child. While they were there, the time came for the baby to be born, and she gave birth to her firstborn, a son. She wrapped him in cloths and placed him in a manger, because there was no room for them in the inn" (Luke 2:1–7).

Finally, the anticipation was over. The child had come. There is rejoicing when a baby is born, and at Jesus' birth, the angels rejoiced, too. They still are rejoicing. It's the song that never ends, the one bringing hope for tomorrow and joy for today. Thank God, the waiting is over.

RESOURCE READING: Luke 2

CHRISTMAS IN
A SHANGHAI PRISON

S omeday they will make the life of Nien Cheng into a
movie. In the meantime, her story has been told in her
book, titled *Life and Death in Shanghai,* which I heartily recommend.

This frail woman, now living in New York, took over
her husband's responsibilities upon his death, but was soon
arrested and sent to prison in 1966. For seven long years, she
was kept in solitary confinement as her captors attempted to
break her indomitable, brave spirit.

In her book, she tells the story of one Christmas, shortly
after the newspaper she had been allowed to receive stopped
coming:

> *"I started to make light scratches on the wall to
> mark the passing days. By the time I had made
> twenty-three strokes, I knew it was Christmas Eve.
> Though the usual bedtime hour had passed, the
> guards were not yet on duty to tell the prisoners to go
> to sleep. While I was waiting in the bitter cold, sud-
> denly, from somewhere upstairs, I heard a young
> soprano voice singing, at first tentative and then
> boldly, the Chinese version of "Silent Night." The
> prison walls resounded with her song as her clear and
> melodious voice floated in and out of the dark corri-
> dors. I was enraptured and deeply moved as I lis-
> tened to her. I knew from the way she rendered the
> song that she was a professional singer who had
> incurred the displeasure of the Maoists. No concert I
> had attended at Christmas in any year meant more
> to me than that moment when I sat in my icy cell
> listening to "Silent Night" sung by another prisoner*

whom I could not see. As soon as she was confident
that guards were not there to stop her, the girl sang
beautifully without any trace of nervousness. The
prison became very quiet. All the inmates listened to
her with bated breath." [1]

Finally the song ended, but the melody had penetrated
the darkness of the prison with the message of hope and
freedom, the same message of hope that came in the form of
a tiny baby on a silent and holy night long ago. Isaiah says,
"The people walking in darkness have seen a great light; on
those living in the land of the shadow of death a light has
dawned" (Isaiah 9:2).

RESOURCE READING: Isaiah 9:1–6

December 25

IT'S CHRISTMAS, FINALLY

Christmas is here, the day when all eternity and all
divinity were compressed into seven or eight pounds
of humanity, with dark hair and chubby hands and beautiful eyes that beheld the choirs of angels and streets of gold.
Christmas is here, the day when the Ancient of Days, the
Alpha and Omega, the One who knows neither beginning
nor ending, laid aside His royal robes of deity and became
fully human, though He was yet fully God. This truth is difficult for us to grasp in our finite humanity.

Christmas involves the full life of Jesus, not just His
birth. You may have seen the following essay, *One Solitary
Life* by an unknown author, before, but I believe it bears
repeating.

"He was born in an obscure village, the child of a

peasant woman. He grew up in still another village, where he worked in a carpenter shop until he was thirty. Then for three years he was an itinerant preacher. He never wrote a book. He never held an office. He never had a family or owned a house. He didn't go to college. He never visited a big city. He never traveled two hundred miles from the place where he was born. He did none of the things one usually associates with greatness.

"He had no credentials but himself. He was only thirty-three when the tide of public opinion turned against him. His friends ran away. He was turned over to his enemies and went through the mockery of a trial. He was nailed to a cross between two thieves. While he was dying, his executioners gambled for his clothing, the only property he had on earth. When he was dead, he was laid in a borrowed grave through the pity of a friend.

"Nineteen centuries have come and gone, and today he is the central figure of the human race and the leader of mankind's progress. All the armies that ever marched, all the navies that ever sailed, all the parliaments that ever sat, all the kings that ever reigned, put together, have not affected the life of man on this earth as much as that one solitary life."

RESOURCE READING: Matthew 1

December 26

NOW THAT'S IT'S OVER,
LET'S GET ON WITH THE BUSINESS

It's the day after Christmas and all through the house, there are piles of junk, cast-off toys, and piles of unwanted gifts to be returned. Already the kids have found that the cardboard boxes their toys came in are more interesting to play with than the items themselves, and maybe you're asking yourself, "Is this all the thanks I get for busting my britches to buy this stuff?"

You've already made the decision to trash the tree by tomorrow and you're ready to get on with the business—whatever that is.

I feel compelled to ask: What's the business, anyway? What is the main thing in your life? Is there any correlation between the focus of yesterday—Christmas—and what drives and motivates your life after the Christmas decorations are gone and the poinsettias have wilted?

Maybe you're not in such a hurry to get Christmas out of the way. Maybe you like to bask in the reality of the Incarnation. For you, Jesus is not a babe whose manger is getting pretty old and dusty. He is a living person, a known factor, a living presence in your life. For you, Christmas is not a festivity but a birthday. Enriched, you begin to ponder the coming year.

The real Jesus—the One who became flesh at Bethlehem, the One who wants to touch the lives of people through you today—isn't pushed aside so easily as packing up the Christmas decorations and forgetting the whole season.

I love the way Eugene Peterson puts it in his paraphrase of John 1: "The Word became flesh and blood, and moved into the neighborhood. We saw the glory with our own eyes, the one-of-a-kind glory, like Father, like Son, generous inside and out, true from start to finish" (John 1:14 TM).

Did you catch it? Jesus moved into our neighborhood. Life can never go back to what it was before He came. "Getting on with the business" after Christmas must include the risen Lord who will someday return from heaven. As you "get on with the business," make sure that dispensing His love and grace is your business.

RESOURCE READING: Psalm 110

BINDING THE STRONG MAN

When Jesus is accused by the Pharisees of casting out demons by the power of the devil, He counters with a question: "If Satan drives out Satan, he is divided against himself. How then can his kingdom stand?" (Matthew 12:26). Jesus then follows with another hard-to-answer question: "How can anyone enter a strong man's house and carry off his possessions unless he first ties up the strong man? Then he can rob his house" (Matthew 12:29).

One of the reasons that Jesus made people uncomfortable is that He cut to the core of issues. He never glossed over things or sugarcoated His message. He drew the line, putting God on one side and Satan on the other, and then He tells us to "bind the strong man." In other words, "Don't let Satan have an inch of your life."

Is there an area of your life or your thinking where you are spiritually bound, and you know it isn't good? Is there something in your life that you desperately wish you could break out of, but you feel powerless in your own strength to master?

If your answer is yes, whatever thought just came to your mind is an area that you need to deal with, whether it is a bad temper, sexual addiction, pornography, drugs, or disbelief. "Bind the strong man," was Jesus' advice. Can you do that? Certainly, by saying, "Yes, Lord" to God's purpose in your life. Jesus also says, "I tell you the truth, whatever you bind on earth will be bound in heaven, and whatever you loose on earth will be loosed in heaven" (Matthew 18:18).

As He began His ministry at Nazareth, Jesus proclaimed that He had come to fulfill what the prophet Isaiah had written: "The Spirit of the Sovereign LORD is on me, because the LORD has anointed me to preach good news to the poor. He has sent me to bind up the brokenhearted, to proclaim freedom for the captives and release from darkness for the prisoners" (Isaiah 61:1). Jesus came to release us from the territory which Satan has held.

Don't settle for less than God's best in your life. Bind the strong man and let God's power and presence invade that part of you which rightfully belongs to Him. You'll be glad you did.

RESOURCE READING: 1 John 4

December 28

MAKE IT A HABIT

Habit is the flywheel of society. It keeps the fisherman at sea in the winter and it sends the farmer to his field no matter what the weather. Habit keeps the prostitute on the street and the alcoholic and the addict looking for a bottle or a fix. Habits, of course, work both ways—good ones and bad ones.

Years ago, Harvard University psychology professor William James wrote, "If we realized the extent to which we are mere walking bundles of habits, we would give more heed to their formation. We are spinning our own fates," he wrote, "good or evil—and never to be undone."

Are you a victim of your habits? Or can you change your habits and lifestyle? Habits can be broken, but it takes strong motivation, something stronger than the force of habit, to create change.

Second Corinthians 5:17 says, "Therefore, if anyone is in Christ, he is a new creation; the old has gone, the new has come!" Being a new person, a new creation means new habits. The following guidelines can make a difference in your life.

Guideline #1: Break the old habit decisively. Don't cut a dog's tail off an inch at a time. The Ephesians burned their magic books in one great fire. Draw a line, cross it—and by the grace of God, never return.

Guideline #2: Establish a new habit immediately. "In the main," wrote Henry James, "all experts agree that abrupt acquisition of the new habit is the best way."

Guideline #3: Go public with your commitment. Tell your friends. Sign a pledge. Paint a sign, or fly a banner, but don't go back. Make a clean break with past habits and friends who drag you down.

Guideline #4: Reach out for God's strength. The Bible is full of promises of help. The Holy Spirit within you supplies the strength you need to be the person He wants you to be. He makes the difference.

RESOURCE READING: Colossians 3

December 29

THE OLD TREE AT VINNITSA

If you are into religious relics, there's a new stop on the tourist circuit. Next to a Russian Orthodox Church about 150 miles from Kiev in the Ukraine, people stand in long lines to get a chance to view the image of a cross in the trunk of an old maple tree.

Here's the story: Ilya Borobchuk was the caretaker of the Russian Orthodox Church in Vinnitsa, where an old maple tree threatened to fall on the roof of the church. Believing the roof was more important than preserving the old tree, the caretaker asked to remove it. Permission denied. Then the caretaker began stripping the tree of its bark, hoping it would die so it could be removed. The tree didn't die, but Borobchuk finally got his way and the old tree was removed.

"When the old maple was cut down," according to Associated Press reports, "Borobchuk and others saw a dark shape in the center of the yellowish stump: a cross. When the trunk was cut up, they were surprised to find the cross running the length of the tree." Thus far, thousands of pilgrims have come and, according to the local bishop, more than twenty people have been miraculously healed by a visit to the tree.

Locals say that the old maple tree was an execution spot for hundreds of people under Communism and that their blood cries out to God, who graciously has touched the lives of hurting, suffering people.

How central is the Cross? Not the one imbedded in the old maple tree in Vinnitsa, or the one found in jewelry stores, adorned with precious stones and a hefty price tag, but the old bloodstained cross where Jesus was crucified.

Paul reminds us that nothing is more central to our salvation than the cross upon which Christ gave His life. He wrote, "In him we have redemption through his blood, the forgiveness of sins, in accordance with the riches of God's grace" (Ephesians 1:7).

Don't wait until Holy Week to ponder the importance of the Cross. Remember, it was part of the gift which was first bestowed at Bethlehem, the gift of life which brings salvation and forgiveness. Thank God for the Cross.

RESOURCE READING: Luke 23

December 30

THE CHALLENGE OF THE NEW YEAR

Then Jesus took his disciples up the mountain and gathered them around him. He taught them saying:

"Blessed are the poor in spirit, for theirs is the kingdom of heaven. Blessed are the meek. Blessed are they that mourn. Blessed are the merciful. Blessed are they that thirst for justice. Blessed are you when you suffer. Be glad and rejoice for your reward is in heaven."

Simon Peter said, "Are we supposed to remember this?"

Andrew, his brother, asked, "Do we have to write this down?"

James said, "Are we going to have a test on this?"

Philip said, "I haven't got anything to write on."

Bartholomew said, "Are we going to have to turn this in?"

John said, "The other disciples didn't have to learn this."

Matthew said, "I have to go to the bathroom!"

And Jesus wept.

No doubt every teacher can relate to those responses. Of course, I took a few liberties with the text of the Beatitudes in Matthew 5, but the humor points out that appropriating what we know is tough at best.

Today we stand on the threshold of a new year. What have you learned from this past year? What can you do to ensure that you make the most of this coming year?

Guideline #1: Take inventory of your life. Include family, your relationship with God, your personal goals, finances, and your purpose in life. Are you on target, sidetracked, or dead in the water?

Guideline #2: Rethink your purpose in life. Get out a pencil and make three columns:
1. "Life as it was last year"
2. "Life as I want it in the New Year"
3. "How shall I get there?"

Guideline #3: Make God your senior partner in life. Jesus says, "Seek first his kingdom and his righteousness, and all these things will be given to you as well" (Matthew 6:33). I am convinced that most of our failures are because we missed God's voice. Stop and hear Him say, "Hey, this is the path you need to walk."

When a person is in Christ, he or she becomes a new person. The old passes away. The new changes your life and destiny. That's what the grace of God is all about.

Resource reading:: 2 Corinthians 5

December 31

WHO'S AFRAID OF THE NEW YEAR?

Facing a new year can be somewhat scary. Who knows what the year will hold: bane or blessing? Have you ever asked yourself, "Why fear the unknown?"

"Fear is not limited to people who are in such a serious state of mental illness as to require hospital care," says Dr. G. Ernest Thompson. "It often casts its evil influence on the happiness of people of average and normal environment. Indeed, few of us are entirely free of some of the common anxieties that put a blight on life. Not one of us ever carries on a normal existence for any period of time without encountering the reality of fear."

Is there an answer to this age-old problem of fear? When Paul writes to Timothy, he says, "God has not given to us the spirit of fear; but of power, and of love, and of a sound mind" (2 Timothy 1:7 KJV). Paul's statement tells us that unhealthy, debilitating fear is not from God.

Paul knew what he was talking about. He had battled all kinds of fear. Read the book of 2 Corinthians. He admits that when he came into northern Greece, he faced conflicts on the outside and fears within (see 2 Corinthians 7:5). In fact, he was surrounded by fear.

How did Paul fight this monster called fear? The first key is knowing that God's power is greater than your fear. The realization that God is with you and that He is greater and more powerful by far than anything that will ever confront you quickly destroys fear.

The second antidote to fear is what Paul calls love. His words are reminiscent of Christ's comments about fearing none who could hurt the body. Love is a power greater than fear.

The third element that defeats fear is a sound mind, the result of a conscience that is free of guilt. Nothing torments our minds more than feelings of guilt. You do not have to be tormented by fear. Look to Christ and commit your life to Him. Remember, God has not given us the spirit of fear. He gives the spirit of love, of power, and of a sound mind.

RESOURCE READING: 2 Corinthians 7

If you would like to get in touch with the author, you can write to him at the following address:

DR. HAROLD SALA
Box G
Laguna Hills, CA 92654
Phone: 949-582-5001/Fax: 949-582-5026
Web: http://www.guidelines.org
E-mail: glines@ibm.net

NOTES

January 3rd

1. "Chromosome Study Stuns Evolutionists," Hugh Ross, *Facts and Faith,* volume 9, number 3, 3.

February 4th

1. Mike Fabarez, *Connection,* (San Clemente, CA: Pacific Coast Church Newsletter), Vol. 3, No. 8, August, 1995, 1–2.

March 3rd

1. Joyce Brothers, "Men and Women—the Differences," *Women's Day,* February 9, 1982, 140.

March 5th

1. Joyce Brothers.
2. Ibid.

April 13th

1. Diane M. Komp, M.D., *Images of Grace* (Grand Rapids, MI: Zondervan Publishing House, 1996), 18.

April 15th

1. Wade Horn, "Why There Is No Substitute for Parents," *Imprimis,* Vol. 26, No. 6, June 1997, 3.

April 19th

1. A.W. Tozer, "The Old Cross And The New," a pamphlet published by Christian Publications, Harrisburg, PA.

June 1st

1. James Hewett, *Illustrations Unlimited,* (Wheaton, IL: Tyndale House Publishers, 1989).

July 9th

1. Paul Tournier as quoted by H. Norman Wright in *Christian Marriage and Family Relationships,* (Glendale: Church Press, 1972), 32.

July 29th

1. "Are the Bible's Stories True?" *Time,* Vol. 146, No. 25, December 18, 1995, (cover story).

August 3rd
1. Guy P. Duffield, "The Sovereignty of God,"
   monograph distributed by Guidelines Inc.,
   Laguna Hills, CA, 2.

August 7th
1. A. W. Tozer, *The Knowledge of the Holy* (Lincoln,
   Neb: Back to the Bible, 1971), 60.

August 10th
1. A. W. Tozer, *The Pursuit of God* (Harrisburg:
   Christian Publications, 1858), 7.

August 11th
1. A. W. Tozer.

August 12th
1. Ron Mehl, *God Works the Night Shift* (Sisters, Ore:
   Multnomah Books, 1994), 60.

August 29th
1. *Orange County Register,* August 12, 1997, Metro,
   8.

August 30th
1. "Most Married, but Little Missed," *Los Angeles
   Times,* July 19, 1997, pp. A-1, 19.

September 27th
1. Catherine Booth as quoted by Vernon Grounds,
   Christmas newsletter, December, 1996.

October 3rd
1. Dan Coats, "Points to Ponder," *Reader's Digest,*
   June 1996, 252.

November 5th
1. David Whitman, "The Problem With Adult
   Pre-Marital Sex" *U.S. News and World Report,*
   May 19, 1997, (cover story).

November 20th
1. John Henry Howett as quoted by Warren
   Wiersbe, *Walking With the Giants* (Grand Rapids:
   Baker Book House, 1978), 263–264.

November 23rd

  1. Ray Moody in "Life After Life" as quoted by
     Brendan Koerner, *U.S. News and World Report*,
     March 31, 1997, 61.

December 24th

  1. Nien Cheng, *Life and Death in Shanghai* (London:
     Grafton Books, 1986), 215.

ABOUT THE AUTHOR

DR. HAROLD SALA is the founder and president of Guidelines International, a ministry with a worldwide outreach through radio, television and video programs. His radio commentary, "Guidelines—A Five Minute Commentary on Living" is heard on an international network of more than six hundred stations and is broadcast in seventeen languages, reaching into more than one hundred countries.

Dr. Sala, who holds a Ph.D. in English Bible, is an international speaker and lecturer, and his books (*Tomorrow Starts Today* is his twenty-fourth) have been published in Russian, Chinese, Burmese, Thai, Spanish, Korean, Japanese, Tagalog, and Pidgin.